THE JOHN MACARTHUR
Pastor's Library

PREACHING

HOW *to* PREACH BIBLICALLY

JOHN MACARTHUR

and THE MASTER'S SEMINARY FACULTY

NELSON REFERENCE & ELECTRONIC
A Division of Thomas Nelson Publishers
Since 1798

www.thomasnelson.com

Published in association with the literary agency of Wolgemuth & Associates, Inc.

Library of Congress Cataloging-in-Publication Data

MacArthur, John 1939–
    Preaching: how to preach biblically / Adapted from Rediscovering expository preaching / John MacArthur, general editor, and The Master's Seminary Faculty : Richard L. Mayhue, associate editor; Robert L. Thomas, associate editor.
      p. cm.
    Includes bibliographical references and index.
    ISBN-10: 1-4185-0004-6
    ISBN-13: 978-1-4185-0004-7
    1. Preaching 2. Bible—Homiletical use. I. Mayhue, Richard L., 1944– II. Thomas, Robert L., 1928– III. Title.
BV4211.2.M16 1992
251—dc20   92–10804
                                                 CIP

Printed in the United States of America

3 4 5 6 7 — 11 10 09 08 07 06

Dedicated to
Expositors-in-Training
at
The Master's Seminary,
past, present, and future.

Contents

Part V. PREACHING THE EXPOSITION

Preface

In keeping with the purposes of The Master's Seminary, this volume aims to motivate and equip this and the next generation of Christian leaders in providing wholesome spiritual nourishment for God's people from His Word. These materials combine, in a highly condensed form, all aspects of The Master's Seminary program, which is designed to shape men of God to proclaim the Word of God effectively, so that nonbelievers can be evangelized and believers can be equipped to do the work of ministry.

The writers have targeted both the seasoned preacher and the student of preaching/teaching. It has also been written to help serious laymen in their ministry of the Word. We envision the book as a potential textbook in homiletics at the Bible college and seminary levels. Pastors without seminary training can profit from this volume too, as can veteran pastors who, like us, are continually seeking a higher level of expository excellence.

This is *not* intended as an unabridged treatment of biblical exposition. No single chapter exhausts its subject. Rather, the comprehensive scope of the work, dealing as it does with theological, exegetical, and homiletical aspects of preaching, is its intended strength. The flow of the book moves from biblical foundations for preaching through a detailed process of developing an exposition and then to the actual delivery of an expository message. The discussions build a bridge from the study disciplines a pastor learned in seminary to the sermon he preaches in a local church. This volume suggests how to progress purposefully from one phase to the next in readying oneself to minister to God's people.

More specifically, the fourfold aim is

1. To *clarify* the need for and meaning of expository preaching, that is, to answer the question, "*What* is expository preaching?"
2. To *verify* the theological and historical demand for expository preaching, that is, to answer the question, "*Why* insist on expository preaching?"
3. To *specify* the essential elements and steps involved in preparation for and participation in expository preaching, that is, to answer the question, "*How* does one go about expository preaching?"
4. To *exemplify* the reality of expository preaching, that is, to answer the question, "*Who* have been or who are promoters and practitioners of expository preaching?"

Our president, John MacArthur, known worldwide as a gifted expositor, has contributed a significant portion of this book. His colleagues on

The Master's Seminary faculty, with an average of more than thirty years' experience in preaching and in the seminary training of preachers, also have contributed from the treasury of their areas of expertise. The reader will quickly appreciate their united affirmations on exposition that emerge amidst a variety of individual expressions and methodological preferences.

Their unanimity regarding Bible exposition centers in the priority of faithfully, accurately, and effectively imparting the content of the authoritative and inerrant biblical text. Yet the reader will see differences in their emphases on how this is done best. One prefers preaching without notes, while another advocates the use of notes or even a full manuscript. One sees the need for almost all sermon outlines to match the sequence of the text, with another allowing more flexibility for use of nonsequential outlines. One emphasizes the importance of presenting a solution to each difficult interpretive problem; another leans toward telling an audience frankly when sermon preparation has not yielded a conclusive answer. One stresses the importance of not neglecting the overriding message of Old Testament narrative sections, but another features the cautious use of Old Testament narrative characters as illustrations in sermonizing. These are samples of the methodological variety that the careful reader will detect. This volume does not insist on a single, mechanical approach to preaching but rather focuses attention on *essential* dynamic elements of Bible exposition for any age; in other words, primary concentration is on the Scriptures and the central place of Christ in declaring their meaning.

The reader will also note a diversity in the "levels" of treatment of the different topics. At one extreme are the chapters whose documentation is copious, and at the other are those in which documentation is minimal. This diversity is, to some extent, a consequence of the nature of the subject and, to a lesser degree, the choice of each contributor. Each has handled his phase of exposition in the manner he deemed wisest.

The book outlines four broad phases that follow the actual progression of the preaching experience. They include: (1) the godliness of the man who comes to study the Word of God, (2) the ability of the godly man in studying Scripture exegetically, (3) the skill of the godly man in merging all his study materials into a message form that is true to the text and relevantly applies Scripture to his own generation, and (4) the dynamics of the godly man in proclaiming his exposition in a spiritually convincing and compelling way.

An Appendix contains an example of John MacArthur's notes from his exegetical study and his subsequent preaching manuscript. To maximize the benefit of this unique feature, readers may write: Word of Grace Ministries, P.O. Box 4000, Panorama City, CA 91412, or call 1-800-55-GRACE to order a CD of the message Dr. MacArthur delivered from these preaching notes. Then, in addition to comparing his exegetical notes with his preaching notes, readers can hear the way he actually preached the message. Ask for tape GC 54–47, "The Man of God." In chapter 5, "The Man of God and Expository Preaching," readers can also see how the same material has become a published essay. For further help, request the four-message album, "Insight into a Pastor's Heart: Convictions and Observations about Preachers and Preaching," taken from chapel services at The Master's Seminary.

In the Additional Reading section at the end of the volume, we avoided listing scores of books on preaching that are no longer in print or do not make a significant contribution; instead, we selected several of the best available and affordable volumes on preaching. The inclusion of a work in this list is not intended as an endorsement of everything in that work but reflects the faculty's favorable impressions of its general thrust. Conversely, the exclusion of a title does not necessarily reflect negatively on that work. We encourage the reader to make the listed works his first acquisitions to supplement the material presented here.

Extensive literature related to sermon preparation and preaching is documented in endnotes. For the reader who chooses to pursue these sources, they can be a gold mine for further study. Those who prefer may, of course, read just the body of the text. The Index of Authors will be useful in locating all the references to a particular writer.

John MacArthur and The Master's Seminary faculty pray that the Lord Jesus Christ will be pleased to use *Preaching: How to Preach Biblically* to encourage fellow expositors and to groom a new generation of expositors who will preach with the same passion the apostles had for God and His Word.

Richard L. Mayhue
Robert L. Thomas

Introduction

I am continually overwhelmed by the responsibility and liability that possess the preacher of God's Word. We all look with indignation at the lawyer or judge who, for the motive of personal wealth, distorts the truth in attacking the reputation and personal possessions of people, while reducing them to poverty. We respond with similar indignation to the quack doctor who, by incompetence, hazards the health and life of someone for the purpose of financial gain. Such people deserve to be considered criminals; the pain and loss of their victims should rightly be laid to their account.

Offering oneself this way as the counselor or healer to care for someone in the time of crisis and then, through negligence, lack of skill, or selfish greed, making havoc of their lives is unconscionable. Medical and legal associations have set standards in an attempt to prevent such malpractice.

But what about me as the purveyor of God's truth, the physician of the soul? Shall I not be held responsible to God for any perversion of truth, however witless, and for my negligence and lack of skill? What earthly regulatory association validates me? Do not I, who preach God's Word, face a higher court than the legal bar or any medical tribunal? James wrote, "Let not many of you become teachers, my brethren, knowing that as such we shall incur a stricter judgment" (James 3:1).

No profession has as high a liability potential as that of one who preaches God's Word. God will judge every preacher on the truthfulness and accuracy of his preaching. Any failure as a spokesman for God brings not only shame (2 Tim. 2:15) but judgment. The Holy Spirit has promised that all who pastor God's flock must "give an account" (Heb. 13:17). There will be a day of reckoning for the preacher. Only a tested and qualified kind of person has the right to be considered a lawyer, a judge, or a physician. The standard is significantly higher for the preacher!

What is it that equips a man to be qualified for preaching responsibility? Certainly I could argue for the following elements: reverence for God, respect for the dignity of pastoral duty, good sense, sound judgment, clear and deep thinking, love of reading, commitment to diligent study, and meditation. A good memory, graceful command of words, knowledge of society's thinking are also essential traits. Uncommon talent and effort are needed to explain obscure passages of Scripture, to resolve intricate applications of the Word to lives, and to defend the truth against opposers. All these are duties at the heart of the preacher's life and ministry.

A small amount of skill and ability alone will never enable a preacher to teach doctrine, expound on the deep things of God, convince the stubborn mind, capture the affections and will, or spread light over dark realities so as to eliminate the shadows of confusion, ignorance, objections, prejudice, temptation, and deceit. Above all, if the preacher is to detect the errors of his hearers and if he is to free men from their strongholds of ignorance, convince their consciences, stop their mouths, and fulfill his responsibility to proclaim all the counsel of God, he must be skilled in the Word. This is the preacher's only weapon, the most powerful, two-edged sword of the Word, which alone cuts to the depths of the soul and spirit.

Assuming God has designed a preacher with the mental skill, the personal discipline with diligence, and the gift of the Spirit for preaching, success still calls for a profound knowledge and faithful proclamation of the Word. The preacher must, above all, become like Ezra, who had "set his heart to study the law of the LORD, and to practice it, and to teach His statutes and ordinances" (Ezra 7:10) or like Apollos, who was "mighty in the Scriptures" (Acts 18:24).

No text of Scripture is as powerful in affirming this calling to use all our skills to exposit the Word as the potent mandate of 2 Timothy 4:1–4:

> I solemnly charge you in the presence of God and of Christ Jesus, who is to judge the living and the dead, and by His appearing and His kingdom: preach the word; be ready in season and out of season; reprove, rebuke, exhort, with great patience and instruction. For the time will come when they will not endure sound doctrine; but wanting to have their ears tickled, they will accumulate for themselves teachers in accordance to their own desires; and will turn away their ears from the truth, and will turn aside to myths.

The *seriousness* of the preacher's commission is expressed in verse 1: "I solemnly charge you in the presence of God and of Christ Jesus." The preacher is under the scrutiny of God and Jesus Christ, who will judge everyone someday.

The aged warrior Paul sought to confront his younger son in the faith with a sense of his weighty responsibility. Such a weight must have been felt by John Knox when he was compelled to preach and, in anticipation of it, locked himself in a room and wept for days because he feared the seriousness of that duty.

The perfect judge will render perfect judgment on the quality, accuracy, zeal, and effort of the preacher. Pleasing God and Jesus Christ is the issue, not pleasing men. The judgment of men is flawed and eternally inconsequential. The judgment of God, perfect and eternally consequential, is the only verdict that matters.

The *subject* of the preacher's commission is expressed in verse 2: "preach the word." Preaching God's Word is the mandate. We are not only to retain the sound Word (2 Tim. 1:13), to accurately handle the Word (2:15), and to guard the Word (1:14), but we are to proclaim it.

Paul said it succinctly in Colossians 1:25: "Of this church I was made a minister according to the stewardship from God bestowed on me for your benefit, that I might fully carry out the preaching of the word of God." This kind of expository preaching achieves six great ends.

Expository preaching expresses exactly the will of the glorious Sovereign and allows God to speak, not man.

Expository preaching retains the thoughts of the Spirit and brings the preacher into direct and continual contact with the mind of the Holy Spirit who authored Scripture.

Expository preaching frees the preacher to proclaim all the revelation of God, producing a ministry of wholeness and integrity.

Expository preaching promotes biblical literacy, yielding rich knowledge of redemptive truths.

Expository preaching carries ultimate divine authority, rendering the very voice of God.

Expository preaching transforms the preacher, leading to transformed congregations.

Like the *stimulus* of the preacher's commission, the *scope* is also stated in 2 Timothy 4:2: "Be ready in season and out of season; reprove, rebuke, exhort, with great patience and instruction." The preacher is always ready to preach, whether or not it is convenient to do so. He is eager to expose sin and encourage righteous behavior. He does it with patience and not with irritation, bitterness, or despair. His preaching always contains sound doctrine that shows people God's true standard.

The *stimulus* of the preacher's commission is expressed in verses 3 and 4: "For the time will come when they will not endure sound doctrine; but wanting to have their ears tickled, they will accumulate for themselves teachers in accordance to their own desires; and will turn away their ears from the truth, and will turn aside to myths."

Sinners will be intolerant of the uncomfortable truths. That is to be expected. On the other hand, they will want to hear comfortable lies. They may seek what is sensational, entertaining, ego-building, nonthreatening, and popular. But what we preach is dictated by God, not by the crowds we face. Psychiatrist and Christian writer John White has penned some compelling words that deserve to be heard:

Until about fifteen years ago psychology was seen by most Christians as hostile to the gospel.

Let someone who professes the name of Jesus baptize secular psychology and present it as something compatible with Scripture truth, and most Christians are happy to swallow theological hemlock in the form of "psychological insights."

> Over the past fifteen years there has been a tendency for churches to place increasing reliance on trained pastoral counselors. . . . To me it seems to suggest weaknesses in or indifference to expository preaching within evangelical churches. . . . Why do we have to turn to the human sciences at all? Why? Because for years we have failed to expound the whole of Scripture. Because from our weakened exposition and our superficial topical talks we have produced a generation of Christian sheep having no shepherd. And now we are damning ourselves more deeply than ever by our recourse to the wisdom of the world.
>
> What I do as a psychiatrist and what my psychologist colleagues do in their research or their counselling is of infinitely less value to distressed Christians than what God says in his Word. But pastoral shepherds, like the sheep they guide, are following (if I may change my metaphor for a moment) a new Pied Piper of Hamelin who is leading them into the dark caves of humanistic hedonism.
>
> A few of us who are deeply involved in the human sciences feel like voices crying in a godless wilderness of humanism, while the churches turn to humanistic psychology as a substitute for the gospel of God's grace.[1]

I recently hosted a discussion at the Expositors' Institute, a small-group colloquium on preaching hosted by the Shepherds' Fellowship. In preparation for that seminar, I took a yellow legal pad and began listing the negative effects of the superficial brand of preaching that is so rife in modern evangelicalism.

I initially thought I might be able to name about ten, but quickly my list had sixty-one entries. I have distilled them to fifteen by combining and eliminating all but the most crucial ones. Here they are, roughly in the order they occurred to me. This is what is wrong with superficial, marginally biblical preaching:

1. It usurps the authority of God over the soul. Whether a preacher boldly proclaims the Word of God or not is ultimately a question of authority. Who has the right to speak to the church? The preacher, or God? Whenever *anything* is substituted for the preaching of the Word, God's authority is usurped. What a prideful thing to do! In fact, it is hard to conceive of anything more insolent that could be done by a man who is called by God to preach.

2. It removes the lordship of Christ from His church. Who is the Head of the church? Is Christ really the dominant teaching authority in the church? If so, why are there so many churches where His Word is not being faithfully proclaimed? When we look at contemporary ministry, we see programs and methods that are the fruit of human invention, the offspring of opinion polls and neighborhood surveys, and other pragmatic artifices. Church-growth experts have in essence wrested control of the church's agenda from her true Head, the Lord Jesus Christ. Our Puritan forefathers resisted the imposition of government-imposed liturgies for precisely this reason: they saw it as a direct attack on the headship of Christ over His own church. Modern preachers who neglect the Word of God have yielded the ground those men fought and sometimes died for. When Jesus Christ is exalted among His people, His power is manifest in the church. When the church is commandeered by compromisers who want to appease the culture, the gospel is minimized, true power is lost, artificial energy must be manufactured, and superficiality takes the place of truth.

3. It hinders the work of the Holy Spirit. What is the instrument the Spirit uses to do His work? The Word of God. He uses the Word as the instrument of regeneration (James 1:18; 1 Pet. 1:23). He also uses it as the means of sanctification (John 17:17). In fact, it is the *only* tool He uses (Eph. 6:17). So when preachers neglect God's Word, they undermine the work of the Holy Spirit, producing shallow conversions and spiritually lame Christians, if not utterly spurious ones.

4. It demonstrates appalling pride and a lack of submission. In the modern approach to "ministry," the Word of God is deliberately downplayed, the reproach of Christ is quietly repudiated, the offense of the gospel is carefully eliminated, and "worship" is purposely tailored to fit the preferences of unbelievers. That is nothing but a *refusal* to submit to the biblical mandate for the church. The effrontery of ministers who pursue such a course is frightening to me.

5. It severs the preacher personally from the regular sanctifying grace of Scripture. The greatest personal benefit that I get from preaching is the work that the Spirit of God does on my own soul as I study and prepare for two expository messages each Lord's day. Week by week the duty of careful exposition keeps my own heart focused and fixed on the Scriptures, and the Word of God nourishes me while I prepare to feed my flock. So I am personally blessed and spiritually strengthened through the enterprise. If for no other reason, I would never abandon biblical preaching. The enemy of our souls is after preachers in particular, and the sanctifying grace of the Word of God is critical to our protection.

6. It clouds the true depth and transcendence of our message and therefore cripples both corporate and personal worship. What passes for preaching in some churches today is literally no more profound than what preachers in our fathers' generation were teaching in the five-minute children's sermon they gave before dismissing the kids. That is no exaggeration. It is *often* that simplistic, if not utterly inane. There is nothing deep about it. Such an approach makes it impossible for true worship to take place, because worship is a transcendent experience. Worship should take us above the mundane and simplistic. So the only way true worship can occur is if we first come to grips with the depth of spiritual truth. Our people can only rise to heights in worship proportional to the depths to which we have taken them into the profound truths of the Word. There is no way they can have lofty thoughts of God unless we have plunged them into the depths of God's self-revelation. But preaching today is neither profound nor transcendent. It does not go down and it does not go up. It merely aims to entertain.

By the way, true worship is not something that can be stimulated artificially. A bigger, louder band and more sentimental music might do more to stir people's emotions, but that is not genuine worship. True worship is a response from the heart to God's *truth* (John 4:23). You can actually worship *without* music if you have seen the glories and the depth of what the Bible teaches.

7. *It prevents the preacher from fully developing the mind of Christ.* Pastors are supposed to be undershepherds of Christ. Too many modern preachers are so bent on understanding the culture that they develop the mind of the culture and not the mind of Christ. They start to think like the world and not like the Savior. Frankly the nuances of worldly culture are virtually irrelevant to me. I want to know the mind of Christ and bring that to bear on the culture, no matter what culture I may be ministering to. If I am going to stand up in a pulpit and be a representative of Jesus Christ, I want to know how *He* thinks, and that must be my message to His people too. The only way to know and proclaim the mind of Christ is by being faithful to study and preach His Word. What happens to preachers who obsess about cultural "relevancy" is that they become worldly, not godly.

8. *It depreciates by example the spiritual duty and priority of personal Bible study.* Is personal Bible study important? Of course. But what example does the preacher set when he neglects the Bible in his own preaching? Why would people think they need to study the Bible if the preacher does not do serious study himself in the preparation of his sermons? There is now a movement among some of the gurus of "seeker-sensitive" ministry to trim, as much as possible, all explicit references to the Bible from the sermon. Above all, do not ever ask your people to turn to a specific Bible passage, because that kind of thing makes "seekers" uncomfortable. (Some "seeker-sensitive" churches actively discourage their people from bringing Bibles to church lest the sight of so many Bibles intimidate the "seekers.") This suggests it is dangerous to give your people the impression that the Bible might be important!

9. *It prevents the preacher from being the voice of God on every issue of his time.* Jeremiah 8:9 (NKJV) says, "The wise men are ashamed, / They are dismayed and taken. / Behold, they have rejected the word of the LORD; / So what wisdom do they have?" When I speak, I want to be *God's* messenger. I am not interested in exegeting what some psychologist or business guru or college professor has to say about an issue. My people do not need my opinion; they need to hear what *God* has to say. If we preach

as Scripture commands us, there should be no ambiguity about whose message is coming from the pulpit.

10. *It breeds a congregation that is as weak and indifferent to the glory of God as their pastor is.* "Seeker-sensitive" preaching fosters people who are consumed with their own well-being. When you tell people that the church's primary ministry is to fix for them whatever is wrong in this life—to meet their needs, to help them cope with their worldly disappointments, and so on—the message you are sending is that their mundane problems are more important than the glory of God and the majesty of Christ. Again, that sabotages true worship.

11. *It robs people of their only true source of help.* People who sit under superficial preaching become dependent on the cleverness and the creativity of the speaker. When preachers punctuate their sermons with laser lights and smoke, video clips and live drama, the message they send is that there is not a prayer the people in the pew could ever extract such profound material on their own. Such gimmicks create a kind of dispensing mechanism that people cannot use to serve themselves. So they become spiritual couch potatoes who just come in to be entertained. Whatever superficial spiritual content they get from the preacher's weekly performance is *all* they will get. They have no particular interest in the Bible, because the sermons they hear do not cultivate that. They are wowed by the preacher's creativity and manipulated by the music, and that becomes their whole perspective on spirituality.

12. *It encourages people to become indifferent to the Word of God and divine authority.* Predictably, in a church where the preaching of Scripture is neglected, it becomes impossible to get people to submit to the authority of Scripture. The preacher who always aims at meeting "felt needs" and strokes the conceit of worldly people has no platform from which to confront the man who wants to divorce his wife without cause. The man will say, "You don't understand what I *feel.* I came here because you promised to meet my felt needs. And I'm telling you, I don't feel like I want to live with this woman any more." You cannot inject biblical authority into that. You certainly would not have an easy time pursuing church discipline. That is the monster superficial preaching creates. But if you are going to try to deal with sin and apply any kind of authoritative principle to keep the church pure, you *must* be preaching the Word.

13. *It lies to people about what they really need.* In Jeremiah 8:11, God condemned the prophets who treated people's wounds superficially. That verse applies powerfully to the plastic preachers who populate so many prominent evangelical pulpits today. They omit the hard truths about sin and judgment. They tone down the offensive parts of Christ's message. They lie to people about what they really need, promising them "fulfillment" and

earthly well-being, when what people really need is an exalted vision of Christ and a true understanding of the splendor of God's holiness.

14. It strips the pulpit of power. "The word of God is living and power-ful, and sharper than any two-edged sword" (Heb. 4:12 NKJV). Everything else is impotent, giving merely an illusion of power. Human strategy is not more important than Scripture. The showman's ability to lure people in should not impress us more than the Bible's ability to transform lives.

15. It puts the responsibility on the preacher to change people with his cleverness. Preachers who pursue the modern approach to ministry must think they have the power to change people. That too is a frightening expression of pride. We preachers cannot save people, and we cannot sanctify them. We cannot change people with our insights and cleverness, by entertaining them, or by appealing to their human whims, wishes, and ambitions. There is only One who can change sinners. That is God, and He does it by His Spirit through the Word.

So preach the Word, even though it is currently out of fashion to do so (2 Tim. 4:2). That is the only way your ministry can ever truly be fruitful. Moreover, it assures that you *will* be fruitful in ministry, because God's Word never returns to Him void; it always accomplishes that for which He sends it, and prospers in what He sends it to do (Is. 55:11 NKJV).

The preacher who brings the message people most *need* to hear will often be the preacher they least *like* to hear. But anything less than a commitment to expository preaching by the preacher will reduce his sheep to a weak, vulnerable, and shepherdless flock.

For those of you who want to preach the Word accurately and power-fully because you understand the liability of doing anything less; for those of you who want to face the Judge on the day of reckoning and experience the Lord's pleasure with your effort; for those of you who are eager to let God speak His Word through you as directly, convictingly, and powerfully as He gave it; and for those of you who want to see people transformed radically and living godly lives, there is only expository preaching.

I have long sought a book for my students that would pull together all the component instructions regarding expository preaching. I believe this is it, and I am indebted to the vision of Dr. Richard L. Mayhue, the wisdom of Dr. Robert L. Thomas, and the rich instruction of the faculty of The Master's Seminary. The very fact that an entire faculty could share this common effort reflects their shared passion to produce a skilled generation of expositors.

If you desire to be one of those shepherds after God's own heart, who will feed His sheep on divine knowledge of spiritual understanding through biblical exposition (Jer. 3:15), this book is a *must* for you. My prayer is that this volume will help equip you to the level that will satisfy God's desire for your calling.

John MacArthur

Part I

Proving the Priority of Expository Preaching

1

Rediscovering Expository Preaching

Richard L. Mayhue

Biblical preaching's authenticity is significantly tarnished by contemporary communicators who are more concerned with personal relevance than with God's revelation. Scripture unmistakably requires a proclamation focused on God's will and mankind's obligation to obey. With men wholly committed to God's Word, the expository pattern commends itself as preaching that is true to the Bible. Exposition presupposes an exegetical process to extract the God-intended meaning of Scripture and an explanation of that meaning in a contemporary way. The biblical essence and apostolic spirit of expository preaching need to be recaptured in the training and preaching of men who are freshly committed to "preaching the Word."

The Master's Seminary joins with others[1] in accepting the urgent responsibility for transmitting the Pauline legacy to "preach the word" (2 Tim. 4:2). This volume signals an effort to instill in twenty-first-century preachers a pattern of biblical preaching inherited from their predecessors.[2]

Every generation shares the kind of dire circumstances that Amos prophesied for Israel: "'Behold, days are coming,' declares the Lord GOD, / 'When I will send a famine on the land, / Not a famine for bread or a thirst for water, / But rather for hearing the words of the LORD'" (Amos 8:11). The last several centuries have proved this need again.

REVIEWING RECENT TRENDS

In an explanation of Hebrews 8:10, the Puritan commentator William Gouge (1575–1653) remarked,

> Ministers are herein to imitate God, and, to their best endeavour, to instruct people in the mysteries of godliness, and to teach them what to believe and practice, and then to stir them up in act and deed, to do what they are instructed to do. Their labour otherwise is likely to be in

vain. Neglect of this course is a main cause that men fall into as many errors as they do in these days.[3]

To this editorial by Gouge, Charles Spurgeon (1834–1892) added a word about nineteenth-century England:

> I may add that this last remark has gained more force in our times; it is among uninstructed flocks that the wolves of popery make havoc; sound teaching is the best protection from the heresies which ravage right and left among us.[4]

John Broadus (1827–1895) decried the death of good preaching in America too,[5] and G. Campbell Morgan (1863–1945) noted,

> The supreme work of the Christian minister is the work of preaching. This is a day in which one of our great perils is that of doing a thousand little things to the neglect of the one thing, which is preaching.[6]

The following typical laments evidence that little improvement had been made by the mid-twentieth century:

> Except for the growing worldliness of its members, the pulpit is the church's weak spot.[7]
> But the glory of the Christian pulpit is a borrowed glow. . . . To an alarming extent the glory is departing from the pulpit of the twentieth century. . . . The Word of God has been denied the throne and given a subordinate place.[8]
> Yet it remains true that "whatever be the marks of the contemporary pulpit, the centrality of Biblical preaching is not one of them."[9]
> In a tradition that focuses on the centrality of the written Word, few subjects are more important than the interpretation and proclamation of that Word. Everyone stresses the necessity of a solid exegesis of the text, but few are adept at providing such an exegesis and preaching effectively from it.[10]

By the mid-1980s a national Congress on Biblical Exposition (COBE) convened to urge a return to true biblical exposition.[11] COBE's recurring theme demanded that the American church must return to true biblical preaching or else the Western world would continue its descent toward a valueless culture. Commenting on the uniqueness of America in contemporary culture, Os Guiness noted with concern that "in all my studies I have yet to see a Western society where the church pews are so full and the sermons so empty."[12]

John MacArthur's review of preaching patterns in the late eighties led him to observe,

Specifically, evangelical preaching ought to reflect our conviction that God's Word is infallible and inerrant. Too often it does not. In fact, there is a discernible trend in contemporary evangelicalism *away* from biblical preaching and a drift *toward* an experience-centered, pragmatic, topical approach in the pulpit.[13]

In the nineties an irresistible urge for a focus in the pulpit on the *relevant* seemingly existed, with a resultant inattention to God's *revelation*. Siegfried Meuer alerted Christians in the 1960s to the same "contemporary danger."[14] He likened the direction of his day to the earlier trends of Harry Emerson Fosdick, who wrote in the twenties, "The sermon is uninteresting because it has no connection with the real interests of the people. . . . The sermon must tackle a real problem."[15] Meuer noted that Fosdick opened the floodgate for philosophy and psychology to inundate the modern pulpit with unbelief.

Fosdick's philosophy sounds alarmingly similar to the advice given in a recent publication on relevant contemporary preaching:

> Unchurched people today are the ultimate consumers. We may not like it, but for every sermon we preach, they're asking, "Am I interested in that subject or not?" If they aren't, it doesn't matter how effective our delivery is; their minds will check out.[16]

The implied conclusion is that pastors must preach what people want to hear rather than what God wants proclaimed. Such counsel sounds the alarm of 2 Timothy 4:3, which warns: "For the time will come when they will not endure sound doctrine; but wanting to have their ears tickled, they will accumulate for themselves teachers in accordance to their own desires." What is the necessary response? The generation of preachers facing all the spiritual opportunities and satanic obstacles of this new millennium must rediscover and reaffirm expository preaching. We agree with Walter Kaiser's appraisal:

> Regardless of what new directives and emphases are periodically offered, that which is needed above everything else to make the Church more viable, authentic, and effective, is a new declaration of the Scriptures with a new purpose, passion, and power.[17]

REVISITING SCRIPTURE

When warnings about a drift away from biblical preaching sound, the only reasonable response is to return to the scriptural roots of preaching and reaffirm its essential nature. A reexamination of the heritage of proclamation in the Bible should focus on two elements: the mandates to preach and the manner of preaching.

Mandates to Preach

The Gospels, Acts, the Epistles, and Revelation provide many examples and exhortations to preach the truth in fulfillment of God's will. As a reminder of the apostolic legacy and as a reaffirmation of the scriptural authority for Bible-based preaching, five significant mandates are representative of the larger number of passages.

Matthew 28:19-20—"Go therefore and make disciples of all the nations, baptizing them in the name of the Father and the Son and the Holy Spirit, teaching them to observe all that I commanded you; and lo, I am with you always, even to the end of the age."

1 Timothy 4:13—"Until I come, give attention to the public reading of Scripture, to exhortation and teaching."

2 Timothy 2:2—"And the things which you have heard from me in the presence of many witnesses, these entrust to faithful men, who will be able to teach others also."

2 Timothy 4:2—"Preach the word; be ready in season and out of season; reprove, rebuke, exhort, with great patience and instruction."

Titus 2:1—"But as for you, speak the things which are fitting for sound doctrine."

Manner of Preaching

In his discussion of κηρύσσω (*kēryssō*, meaning "I preach," or "I proclaim"), Friedrich notes at least thirty-three different verbs employed by New Testament writers to portray the richness of biblical preaching.[18] In the following discussion, the four most prominent of these are examined briefly.

Κηρύσσω (*kēryssō*) sees general use throughout the Gospels, Acts, and the Epistles. John the Baptist (Matt. 3:1), Jesus (Matt. 4:17), and Paul (Acts 28:31) all engaged in the action of preaching as indicated by this verb. To Timothy, Paul commended this same activity, telling him to preach the Word (2 Tim. 4:2).

Εὐαγγελίζω (*euaggelizō*, meaning "I preach the gospel") is practically interchangeable with *kēryssō* (Luke 8:1; Acts 8:4–5). Paul and Barnabas preached the good news of the Word of the Lord (Acts 15:35).

Μαρτυρέω (*martyreō*, meaning "I testify," or "I bear witness") is a legal term picturing the communication of truth from one who has a first-hand knowledge. John the Baptist bore witness to the Light (John 1:7–8), and John the apostle testified to the Word of God (Rev. 1:2).[19]

Διδάσκω (*didaskō*, meaning "I teach") focuses on the purpose and content of the message transmitted, without excluding elements of the three previous verbs. As part of the Great Commission, Jesus commanded His disciples to teach (Matt. 28:20). Paul recommended teaching to Timothy (1 Tim. 6:2 and 2 Tim. 2:2). Teaching is sometimes associated with *kērysso* (Matt. 11:1) and *euaggelizō* (Acts 5:42). The content of what is taught focuses on the way of God (Matt. 22:16) and the Word of God (Acts 18:11).[20]

In addition to these four prominent words, there are many others that significantly enhance the biblical manner of communicating God's Word. For example, in Acts 8:31 the Ethiopian eunuch invited Philip to "guide" or "lead" (ὁδηγέω [*hodēgeō*]) him through Isaiah 53. Paul "explained" or "laid out" (ἐκτίθημι [*ektithēmi*]) the kingdom of God (Acts 28:23; see 18:26). Paul told Timothy that he was to "entrust" or "commit" (παρατίθημι [*paratithēmi*]) what he had heard from the apostle to faithful men that they might teach others also (2 Tim. 2:2).

Jesus' interaction with the two disciples on the road to Emmaus adds further dimensions to biblical preaching. He "explained," or "interpreted" (διερμηνεύω [*dicrmēneuō*]) the things about Himself in the Old Testament from Moses to the prophets (Luke 24:27). They, in turn, marveled at the way He had "opened," or "explained" (διανοίγω [*dianoigō*]) the Scriptures (v. 32; see v. 45).

It would be profitable to study additional words such as ἀναγγέλλω (*anaggellō*, meaning "I announce" or "I declare") in Acts 20:27; ἀναγινώσκω (*anaginōskō*, meaning "I read") in 1 Timothy 4:13; παρακαλέω (*parakaleō*, meaning "I exhort, comfort") in 1 Timothy 4:13; ἐξηγέομαι (*exēgeomai*, "I declare") in Acts 15:12; λαλέω (*laleō*, "I speak") in John 3:34; διαλέγομαι (*dialegomai*, "I discuss, argue") in Acts 17:17; and φθέγγομαι (*phtheggomai*, "I utter") in Acts 4:18. Yet, this brief survey is enough to conclude that the one common link in all the biblical terms in their contexts is a focus on the things of God and Scripture as exclusively central in the preacher's message. Without question, this feature alone marks the uniqueness of scriptural preaching. A biblical and theological content is the *sine qua non,* or indispensable quality, of New Testament proclamation.

With this biblical foundation, the contemporary mode of New Testament preaching can be identified.

DEFINING EXPOSITORY PREACHING

Discussions about preaching divide it into three types: topical, textual, and expository. Topical messages usually combine a series of Bible verses that loosely connect with a theme. Textual preaching uses a short text or passage that generally serves as a gateway into whatever subject the preacher chooses to address. Neither the topical nor the textual method represents a serious effort to interpret, understand, explain, or apply God's truth in the context of the Scripture(s) used.

By contrast, expository preaching focuses predominantly on the text(s) under consideration along with its (their) context(s).[21] Exposition normally concentrates on a single text of Scripture, but it is sometimes possible for a thematic/theological message or a historical/biographical discourse to be expository in nature. An exposition may treat any length of passage.

One way to clarify expository preaching is to identify what it is *not*.[22]

1. It is not a commentary running from word to word and verse to verse without unity, outline, and pervasive drive.
2. It is not rambling comments and offhand remarks about a passage without a background of thorough exegesis and logical order.
3. It is not a mass of disconnected suggestions and inferences based on the surface meaning of a passage but not sustained by a depth-and-breadth study of the text.
4. It is not pure exegesis, no matter how scholarly, if it lacks a theme, thesis, outline, and development.
5. It is not a mere structural outline of a passage with a few supporting comments but without other rhetorical and sermonic elements.
6. It is not a topical homily using scattered parts of the passage but omitting discussion of other equally important parts.
7. It is not a chopped-up collection of grammatical findings and quotations from commentaries without a fusing of these elements into a smooth, flowing, interesting, and compelling message.
8. It is not a Sunday-school-lesson type of discussion that has an outline of the contents, informality, and fervency but lacks sermonic structure and rhetorical ingredients.
9. It is not a Bible reading that links a number of scattered passages treating a common theme but fails to handle any of them in a thorough, grammatical, and contextual manner.
10. It is not the ordinary devotional or prayer-meeting talk that combines running commentary, rambling remarks, disconnected suggestions, and personal reactions into a semi-inspirational discussion but lacks the benefit of the basic exegetical-contextual study and persuasive elements.

Before proceeding farther, consider the English word group "expose, exposition, expositor, expository." According to Webster, an exposition is a discourse to convey information or explain what is difficult to understand.[23] Applying this idea to preaching requires that an expositor be one who explains Scripture by laying open the text to public view in order to set forth its meaning, explain what is difficult to understand, and make appropriate application.

John Calvin's centuries-old understanding of exposition is very similar:

First of all, Calvin understood preaching to be the explication of Scripture. The words of Scripture are the source and content of preaching. As an expositor, Calvin brought to the task of preaching all the skills of a humanist scholar. As an interpreter, Calvin explicated the text, seeking its natural, its true, its scriptural meaning. . . . Preaching is not only the explication of Scripture, it is also the application of Scripture. Just as Calvin explicated Scripture word by word, so he applied the Scripture sentence by sentence to the life and experience of his congregation.[24]

Exposition is not so much defined by the form of the message as it is by the source and process through which the message was formed. Unger poignantly captures this sense:

No matter what the length of the portion explained may be, if it is handled in such a way that its real and essential meaning as it existed in the mind of the particular Biblical writer and as it exists in the light of the overall context of Scripture is made plain and applied to the present-day needs of the hearers, it may properly be said to be *expository preaching*. . . . It is emphatically not preaching about the Bible, but preaching the Bible. "What saith the Lord" is the alpha and the omega of expository preaching. It begins in the Bible and ends in the Bible and all that intervenes springs from the Bible. In other words, expository preaching is Bible-centered preaching.[25]

Two other definitions of exposition help clarify what it is:

At its best, expository preaching is "the presentation of biblical truth, derived from and transmitted through a historical, grammatical, Spirit-guided study of a passage in its context, which the Holy Spirit applies first to the life of the preacher and then through him to his congregation."[26]

In the 1950's ML-J [D. Martyn Lloyd-Jones] was virtually alone in England in engaging in what he meant by 'expository preaching'. For preaching to qualify for that designation it was not enough, in his view, that its content be biblical; addresses which concentrated upon word-studies, or which gave running commentary and analyses of whole chapters, might be termed 'biblical', but that is not the same as exposition. To expound is not simply to give the correct grammatical sense of a verse or passage, it is rather to set out principles or doctrines which the words are intended to convey. True expository preaching is, therefore, *doctrinal* preaching, it is preaching which addresses specific truths from God to man. The expository preacher is not one who 'shares his studies' with others, he is an ambassador and a messenger, authoritatively delivering the Word of God to men. Such preaching presents a text, then, with that text in sight throughout, there is deduction, argument and appeal, the whole making up a message which bears the authority of

Scripture itself. Given such a conception, a faithful discharge of the teaching office necessitates the preacher being able to say, with Paul, 'We are not as many, which corrupt the word of God: but as of sincerity, but as of God, in the sight of God speak we in Christ' (2 Cor. 2:17). If this involves a staggeringly high view of preaching, it was nothing more, Dr. Lloyd-Jones believed, than is required of the ministerial office.[27]

In summary, the following minimal defining elements identify expository preaching:

1. The message finds its sole source in Scripture.[28]
2. The message is extracted from Scripture through careful exegesis.
3. The message preparation correctly interprets Scripture in its normal sense and its context.
4. The message clearly explains the original God-intended meaning of Scripture.
5. The message applies the Scriptural meaning for today.

The spirit of expository preaching is exemplified in two biblical texts:

And they read from the book, from the law of God, translating to give the sense so that they understood the reading (Neh. 8:8).

Therefore I testify to you this day, that I am innocent of the blood of all men. For I did not shrink from declaring to you the whole purpose of God (Acts 20:26–27).

A particular example is Jesus' expounding of Isaiah 61:1–2 in the synagogue (Luke 4:16–22). He later gave a thematic exposition of Himself to the disciples on the road to Emmaus (Luke 24:27, 32, 44–47). In Acts 8:27–35 Phillip expounded Isaiah 53:7–8 for the Ethiopian eunuch. Stephen preached a historical/biographical expository sermon to the Jews before they stoned him (Acts 7:2–53).

Greer Boyce has aptly described expository preaching as follows:

In short, expository preaching demands that, by careful analysis of each text within its immediate context and the setting of the book to which it belongs, the full power of modern exegetical and theological scholarship be brought to bear upon our treatment of the Bible. The objective is not that the preacher may parade all this scholarship in the pulpit. Rather, it is that the preacher may speak faithfully out of solid knowledge of his text, and mount the pulpit steps as, at least, "a workman who has no need to be ashamed, rightly handling the word of truth."

The preacher's final step is the most crucial and most perilous of all. It is to relate the biblical message both faithfully and relevantly to modern life. At this point all his skill as a craftsman must come into play. We must be warned that faithful exposition of a text does not of itself produce an effective sermon. We need also to be warned, however, that faithfulness to the text is not to be sacrificed for the sake of what we presume to be relevancy. This sacrifice too many modern preachers seem willing to make, producing, as a result, sermons that are a compound of moralistic advice, their own unauthoritative and sometimes unwise opinions, and the latest psychology. Expository preaching, by insisting that the message of the sermon coincide with the theme of the text, calls the preacher back to his true task: the proclamation of the Word of God in and through the Bible.[29]

UNDERSTANDING THE EXPOSITORY PROCESS

Discussing the biblical foundations and the definition of expository preaching, while essential, is relatively easy. The real challenge comes when one has to move from the classroom to the weekly pulpit. Unless the preacher clearly understands the expository process, he will never achieve his potential in the craft of expository preaching.

As a frame of reference for this discussion, we propose that the expository process include four standard elements: preparing the expositor, processing and principlizing the biblical text(s), pulling the expository message together, and preaching the exposition. These four phases need equal emphasis if the exposition is to be fully effective in the sight of both God and the congregation.

Preparing the Expositor[30]

Since God should be the source of expository messages, one who delivers such a message should enjoy intimate communion with God. This is the only way the message can be given with greatest accuracy, clarity, and passion.

At least seven areas of preparation qualify a man to stand in the pulpit and declare, "Thus saith the Lord!":

1. The preacher must be a truly regenerated believer in Jesus Christ. He must be a part of God's redeemed family (John 1:12–13). If a man is to deliver a personal message from the heavenly Father effectively, he must be a legitimate spiritual son or the message will inevitably be distorted.
2. The preacher must be appointed and gifted by God to the teaching/preaching ministry (Eph. 4:11–16 and 1 Tim. 3:2). Unless a man is divinely enabled to proclaim, he will be inadequate, possessing only human ability.[31]

3. The preacher must be inclined and trained to be a student of God's Word. Otherwise, he cannot carry out the mandate of 2 Timothy 2:15 to "cut straight" the Word of God's truth.
4. The preacher must be a mature believer who demonstrates a consistent godly character (1 Tim. 3:2–3).[32]
5. The preacher must be dependent upon God the Holy Spirit for divine insight and understanding of God's Word (1 Cor. 2:14–15). Without the Spirit's illumination and power, the message will be relatively impotent.[33]
6. The preacher must be in constant prayerful communion with God to receive the full impact of the Word (Ps. 119:18). The obvious one to consult for clarification is the original author.[34]
7. The preacher must first let the developing message sift through his own thinking and life before he can preach it. Ezra provides the perfect model: "For Ezra had set his heart to study the law of the LORD, and to practice it, and to teach His statutes and ordinances in Israel" (Ezra 7:10).

Processing and Principlizing the Biblical Text

A man in tune with God's Spirit and Word is ready to begin a process to discover not only what God originally meant by what He said but also appropriate principles and applications for today.[35]

1. *Processing the biblical text*[36]—A man cannot hope to preach effectively without first having worked diligently and thoroughly through the biblical text. This is the only way the expositor can acquire God's message. Two preachers from different eras comment on this essential feature:

> A man cannot hope to preach the Word of God accurately until he has first engaged in a careful, exhaustive exegesis of his text. Herein lies the problem, for competent exegesis requires time, brain power, "blood, sweat, and tears," all saturated with enormous doses of prayer.[37]

> You will soon reveal your ignorance as an expositor if you do not study; therefore diligent reading will be forced upon you. Anything which compels the preacher to search the grand old Book is of immense service to him. If any are jealous lest the labor should injure their constitutions, let them remember that mental work up to a certain point is most refreshing, and where the Bible is the theme toil is delight. It is only when mental labor passes beyond the bounds of common sense that the mind becomes enfeebled by it, and this is not usually reached except by injudicious persons, or men engaged on topics which are unrefreshing and disagreeable; but our subject

is a recreative one, and to young men like ourselves the vigorous use of our faculties is a most healthy exercise.[38]

2. *Principlizing the biblical text*—Preaching does not stop with understanding ancient languages, history, culture, and customs. Unless the centuries can be bridged and the message made contemporary and relevant, the preaching experience differs little from a classroom encounter. One must first process the text for original meaning and then principlize the text for current applicability.[39] One's study falls short of the goal if this step is omitted or slighted.

Pulling the Expository Message Together

At the third stage the expositor has finished his deep study and asks himself, "How can I blend my findings in such a way that my flock will understand the Bible and its requirements for their lives today?" In a sense, the art of exposition commences here.[40]

Nolan Howington uses a graphic description to relate exegesis and exposition: "Thus an exegete is like a diver bringing up pearls from the ocean bed; an expositor is like the jeweler who arrays them in orderly fashion and in proper relation to each other."[41]

Titles, outlines, introductions, illustrations, and conclusions enter the process at this stage. The message moves from the raw materials mined by exegesis to the finished product of exposition, which the hearers, it is hoped, will find interesting, convicting, and compelling. The key to this step is remembering what distinguishes exposition: explaining the text, especially parts that are hard to understand or apply. It is equally important to remember not only the text, but the audience as well.

F. B. Meyer offers this advice when thinking of the listeners and what sermonic form the message will take:

> There are five considerations that must be met in every successful sermon. There should be an appeal to the Reason, to the Conscience, to the Imagination, to the Emotions, and to the Will; and for each of these there is no method so serviceable as systematic exposition.[42]

Preaching the Exposition

The final decision to be made by the expositor relates to his preaching mode, whether from memory or from notes. This step is perhaps the most neglected in preparation by those committed to true exposition. Too often expositors assume that proper work done in the study will ensure that the pulpit will care for itself. It is true that there is no substitute for hard work in the study, but equally hard work in the pulpit will reward both the preacher and the flock to a much greater degree. James Stalker effectively draws attention to this challenge:

Ministers do not get enough of result in the attention, satisfaction and delight of their hearers for the work they do; and the failure is in the vehicle of communication between the study and the congregation— that is to say, in the delivery of the sermon. What I am pleading for is, that there should be more work to show for the coal consumed.[43]

At the point of delivery, it is essential for the expositor to be clear in his purpose. Otherwise, the message preached may be far afield from the message studied and the message of Scripture. J. I. Packer makes this point by contrasting what preaching is not with what it is:

The purpose of preaching is not to stir people to action while bypassing their minds, so that they never see what reason God gives them for doing what the preacher requires of them (that is manipulation); nor is the purpose to stock people's minds with truth, no matter how vital and clear, which then lies fallow and does not become the seedbed and source of changed lives (that is academicism). . . . The purpose of preaching is to inform, persuade, and call forth an appropriate response to the God whose message and instruction are being delivered.[44]

Also of importance is the language used in communicating the message. It should be clear, understandable, picturesque, and most of all, biblical. The following strong warning issued decades ago is still applicable:

I urge adherence to Biblical terminology. Much modern preaching has taken a psychological and sociological turn. It is mysterious and mystical. It sets forth psychiatric ideas, often using the terms of the psychiatrist rather than those of the Christian evangelist. It speaks of repression, fixations, traumas, neuroses, and syndromes, world without end. I claim that in the main these are not terms that the Holy Spirit can use effectively.[45]

Another crucial matter is the dynamics of speech, that is, audience relationship and communicative effectiveness. Vines and Allen outline three basic principles for every expositor:

In short, effective communication from the pulpit must be informed by Aristotle's rhetorical triad of logos, ethos, and pathos. This involves a thorough knowledge of the subject matter and here is where there is no substitute for thorough exegesis. It involves a thorough knowledge of the speaker-audience dynamic such that the preacher must speak from integrity and his audience must know of his sincerity and genuineness. Finally, it involves a knowledge of people and how they respond to the spoken word.[46]

Above all, the expositor must expound the Word as Paul did in Corinth (1 Cor. 2:1–5).[47] He did not come as a clever orator or scholarly genius; he did not arrive with his own message; he did not preach with personal confidence in his own strength. Rather, Paul preached the testimony of God and Christ's death, and this with well-placed confidence in God's power to make the message life-changing. Unless this kind of wholesale dependence on God marks the modern expositor's preaching, his exposition will lack the divine dimension that only God can provide.

In summary, of the four steps in the complete expository experience—preparing the expositor, processing and principlizing the biblical text, pulling the expository message together, and preaching the exposition—no phase can be omitted without seriously jeopardizing the truthfulness or usefulness of God's Word mediated through the expositor.

CONSIDERING EXPOSITIONAL ADVANTAGES[48]

Expository preaching best emulates biblical preaching both in content and style. This is the chief benefit. Besides this, other advantages listed in random order include the following:

1. Expositional preaching best achieves the biblical intent of preaching: delivering God's message.
2. Expositional preaching promotes scripturally authoritative proclamation.
3. Expositional preaching magnifies God's Word.
4. Expositional preaching provides a storehouse of preaching material.
5. Expositional preaching develops the pastor as a man of God's Word.
6. Expositional preaching ensures the highest level of Bible knowledge for the flock.
7. Expositional preaching leads to thinking and living biblically.
8. Expositional preaching encourages both depth and comprehensiveness.
9. Expositional preaching forces the treatment of hard-to-interpret texts.
10. Expositional preaching allows for handling broad theological themes.
11. Expositional preaching keeps preachers away from ruts and hobby horses.
12. Expositional preaching prevents the insertion of human ideas.
13. Expositional preaching guards against misinterpretation of the biblical text.
14. Expositional preaching imitates the preaching of Christ and the apostles.
15. Expositional preaching brings out the best in the expositor.

Reclaiming Expository Preaching

In the dawn of a new millennium, we must reclaim the science and art of expository preaching for the coming generation. No one said it would be easy. It is quite the opposite. No other method of preaching requires so much work. At the same time, no other method rewards so richly.

> If the suggestions which have been offered are well founded, it will be obvious that expository preaching is a difficult task. It requires much close study of Scripture in general, and much special study of the particular passage to be treated. To make a discourse which shall be explanatory and yet truly oratorical, bearing a rich mass of details but not burdened with them, full of Scripture and abounding in practical applications, to bring even dull, uninformed, and unspiritual minds into interested and profitable contact with an extended portion of the Bible—of course, this must be difficult.[49]

While a dominant trend among today's preachers is toward consumer satisfaction and contemporary relevancy, we reaffirm that biblical preaching must be first directed toward divine satisfaction and kingdom relevance. Reflect carefully on Mark Steege's clarion call to expositional preaching and its note of biblical authority:

> Through our preaching the Lord seeks to change men's lives. We are to be evangelists, to awaken men to their high calling in Christ. We are to be heralds, proclaiming the messages of God to men. We are to be ambassadors, calling men to be reconciled to God. We are to be shepherds, nourishing and caring for men day by day. We are to be stewards of the mysteries of God, giving men the proper Word for their every need. We are to be witnesses, telling men of all that God has done for them. We are to be overseers, urging men to live their lives to God. We are to be ministers, preparing men to minister with us to others. As we reflect on each of these phases of our work, what emphasis each gives to the importance of preaching! What a task the Lord has given us![50]

Although R. L. Dabney wrote over a century ago, we join him today in urging

> that the expository method . . . be restored to that equal place which it held in the primitive and Reformed Churches; for, first, this is obviously the only natural and efficient way to do that which is the sole legitimate end of preaching, convey the whole message of God to the people.[51]

2

The Mandate of Biblical Inerrancy: Expository Preaching[1]

John MacArthur

The special attention evangelicalism has given to the inerrancy of Scripture in recent years carries with it a mandate to emphasize expository preaching of the Scriptures. The existence of God and His nature requires the conclusion that He has communicated accurately and that an adequate exegetical process to determine His meaning is required. The Christian commission to preach God's Word involves accurately transmitting that meaning to an audience, a weighty responsibility. A belief in inerrancy thus requires, most important of all, expositional preaching that does not have to do primarily with the homiletical form of the message. In this regard, expository preaching differs from what is practiced by non-inerrantists.

The theological highlight of recent decades has without question been evangelicalism's intense focus on biblical inerrancy.[2] Much of what has been written defending inerrancy[3] represents the most acute theological reasoning our generation has produced.

Yet it seems our commitment to inerrancy is somewhat lacking in the way it fleshes out in practical ministry. Specifically, evangelical preaching ought to reflect our conviction that God's Word is infallible and inerrant. Too often it does not. In fact, there is a discernible trend in contemporary evangelicalism away from biblical preaching and a drift *toward* an experience-centered, pragmatic, topical approach in the pulpit.

Should not our preaching be biblical exposition, reflecting our conviction that the Bible is the inspired, inerrant Word of God? If we believe that "all Scripture is inspired by God" and inerrant, must we not be equally committed to the reality that it is "profitable for teaching, for reproof, for correction, for training in righteousness; that the man of God may be adequate, equipped for every good work" (2 Tim. 3:16–17)? Should not that magnificent truth determine how we preach?

Paul gave this mandate to Timothy: "I solemnly charge you in the presence of God and of Christ Jesus, who is to judge the living and the dead, and by His appearing and His kingdom: *preach the word;* be ready in season and out of season; reprove, rebuke, exhort, with great patience and instruction" (2 Tim. 4:1–2, emphasis added). Any form of preaching that ignores that intended purpose and design of God falls short of the divine plan. J. I. Packer eloquently captured the pursuit of preaching:

> Preaching appears in the Bible as a relaying of what God has said about Himself and His doings, and about men in relation to Him, plus a pressing of His commands, promises, warnings, and assurances, with a view to winning the hearer or hearers . . . to a positive response.[4]

The only logical response to inerrant Scripture is to preach it *expositionally.* By expositionally, I mean preaching in such a way that the meaning of the Bible passage is presented *entirely* and *exactly* as it was intended by God. Expository preaching is the proclamation of the truth of God as mediated through the preacher.[5]

Admittedly, not all expositors have an inerrant view. See William Barclay's treatment of Mark 5 or John 6 in *The Daily Study Bible Series.* It is also true that not all with an inerrant view practice expository preaching. These are, however, inconsistencies because an inerrantist perspective demands expository preaching, and a non-inerrantist perspective makes it unnecessary.

Putting it another way, what does it matter that we have an inerrant text if we do not deal with the basic phenomena of communication: words, sentences, grammar, morphology, syntax, etc.? And if we do not, why bother preaching it?

In his much-needed volume on exegetical theology, Walter Kaiser pointedly analyzed the current anemic state of the church due to flock-feeding that is rendered inadequate because of the absence of expository preaching:

> It is no secret that Christ's Church is not at all in good health in many places of the world. She has been languishing because she has been fed, as the current line has it, "junk food"; all kinds of artificial preservatives and all sorts of unnatural substitutes have been served up to her. As a result, theological and Biblical malnutrition has afflicted the very generation that has taken such giant steps to make sure its physical health is not damaged by using foods or products that are carcinogenic or otherwise harmful to their physical bodies. Simultaneously a worldwide spiritual famine resulting from the absence of any genuine publication of the Word of God (Amos 8:11) continues to run wild and almost unabated in most quarters of the Church.[6]

The cure is expository preaching.

The mandate, then, is clear. Expository preaching is the declarative genre in which inerrancy finds its logical expression and the church has its life and power. Stated simply, inerrancy demands exposition as the only method of preaching that preserves the purity of Scripture and accomplishes the purpose for which God gave us His Word.

R. B. Kuiper reinforced this mandate when he wrote, "The principle that Christian preaching is proclamation of the Word must obviously be determinative of the content of the sermon."[7]

INERRANCY, EXEGESIS, AND EXPOSITION

Postulates and Propositions

I would like to begin the main discussion with these logically sequential postulates that introduce and undergird my propositions (as well as form a true basis for inerrancy).[8]

1. God is (Gen. 1:1; Ps. 14; 53; Heb. 11:6).
2. God is true (Ex. 34:6; Num. 23:19; Deut. 32:4; Ps. 25:10; 31:6; Is. 65:16; Jer. 10:8, 10–11; John 14:6; 17:3; Titus 1:2; Heb. 6:18; 1 John 5:20).
3. God speaks in harmony with His nature (Num. 23:19; 1 Sam. 15:29; Rom. 3:4; 2 Tim. 2:13; Titus 1:2; Heb. 6:18).
4. God speaks only truth (Ps. 31:5; 119:43, 142, 151, 160; Prov. 30:5; Is. 65:16; John 17:17; James 1:18).
5. God spoke His true Word as consistent with His true Nature to be communicated to people (a self-evident truth that is illustrated at 2 Tim. 3:16–17 and Heb. 1:1).

Therefore, we must consider the following propositions.

1. God gave His true Word to be communicated *entirely* as He gave it, that is, the whole counsel of God is to be preached (Matt. 28:20; Acts 5:20; 20:27). Correspondingly, every portion of the Word of God needs to be considered in the light of its whole.
2. God gave His true Word to be communicated *exactly* as He gave it. It is to be dispensed precisely as it was delivered, without altering the message.
3. Only the exegetical process that yields expository proclamation will accomplish propositions 1 and 2.

Inerrancy's Link to Expository Preaching

Now, let me substantiate these propositions with answers to a series of questions. They will channel our thinking from the headwaters of God's revelation to its intended destination.

1. Why preach?

Very simply, God so commanded (2 Tim. 4:2), and the apostles so responded (Acts 6:4).

2. What should we preach?

The Word of God, that is, *Scriptura sola* and *Scriptura tota* (1 Tim. 4:13; 2 Tim. 4:2).

3. Who preaches?

Holy men of God (Luke 1:70; Acts 3:21; Eph. 3:5; 2 Pet. 1:21; Rev. 18:20; 22:6). Only after God had purified Isaiah's lips was he ordained to preach (Is. 6:6–13).

4. What is the preacher's responsibility?

First, the preacher needs to realize that God's Word is not the preacher's word. But rather,

He is a messenger, not an originator (εὐαγγελίζω [euaggelizō]).
He is a sower, not the source (Matt. 13:3, 19).
He is a herald, not the authority (κηρύσσω [kēryssō]).
He is a steward, not the owner (Col. 1:25).
He is the guide, not the author (Acts 8:31).
He is the server of spiritual food, not the chef (John 21:15, 17).

Second, the preacher needs to reckon that Scripture is ὁ λόγος τοῦ θεοῦ (*ho logos tou theou,* "the Word of God"). When he is committed to this awesome truth and responsibility,

> His aim, rather, will be to stand under Scripture, not over it, and to allow it, so to speak, to talk through him, delivering what is not so much his message as its. In our preaching, that is what should always be happening. In his obituary of the great German conductor, Otto Klemperer, Neville Cardus spoke of the way in which Klemperer "set the music in motion," maintaining throughout a deliberately anonymous, self-effacing style in order that the musical notes might articulate themselves in their own integrity through him. So it must be in preaching; Scripture itself must do all the talking, and the preacher's task is simply to "set the Bible in motion."[9]

A careful study of the phrase λόγος θεοῦ (*logos theou,* "the Word of God") finds over forty uses in the New Testament. It is equated with the Old Testament (Mark 7:13). It is what Jesus preached (Luke 5:1). It was the message the apostles taught (Acts 4:31; 6:2). It was the word the Samaritans received (8:14) as given by the apostles (v. 25). It was the message the Gentiles received as preached by Peter (Acts 11:1). It was the word Paul preached on his first missionary journey (Acts 13:5, 7, 44, 48, 49; 15:35–36). It was the message preached on Paul's second missionary journey (Acts 16:32; 17:13; 18:11). It was the message Paul preached on his third missionary journey (Acts 19:10). It was the focus of Luke in the Book of Acts in that it spread rapidly and widely (6:7; 12:24; 19:20). Paul was careful to tell the Corinthians that he spoke the Word as it was given from God, that it had not been adulterated and that it was a manifestation of truth (2 Cor. 2:17; 4:2). Paul acknowledged that it was the source of his preaching (Col. 1:25; 1 Thess. 2:13).

As it was with Christ and the apostles, so Scripture is also to be delivered by preachers today in such a way that they can say, "Thus saith the Lord." Their responsibility is to deliver it as it was originally given and intended.

5. How did the preacher's message begin?

The message began as a true word from God and was given as truth because God's purpose was to transmit truth. It was ordered by God as truth and was delivered by God's Spirit in cooperation with holy men who received it with exactly the pure quality that God intended (2 Pet. 1:20–21). It was received as *Scriptura inerrantis* by the prophets and apostles, that is, without wandering from Scripture's original formulation in the mind of God.

Inerrancy, then, expresses the quality with which the writers of our canon received the text we call Scripture.

6. How is God's message to continue in its original true state?

If God's message began true and if it is to be delivered as received, what interpretive processes necessitated by changes of language, culture, and time will ensure its purity when currently preached? The answer is that only an exegetical approach is acceptable for accurate exposition.

Having established the essential need for exegesis, the next logical question is, "How is interpretation/exegesis linked with preaching?"

Packer answered best:

> The Bible being what it is, all true interpretation of it must take the form of preaching. With this goes an equally important converse: that, preaching being what it is, all true preaching must take the form of biblical interpretation.[10]

7. Now, pulling our thinking all together in a practical way, "What is the final step that links inerrancy to preaching?"

First, the true text must be used. We are indebted to those select scholars who labor tediously in the field of textual criticism. Their studies recover the original text of Scripture from the large volume of extant manuscript copies that are flawed by textual variants. This is the starting point.

Without the text as God gave it, the preacher would be helpless to deliver it as God intended.

Second, having begun with a true text, we need to interpret the text accurately. The science of hermeneutics is in view.

> As a theological discipline hermeneutics is the science of the correct interpretation of the Bible. It is a special application of the general science of linguistics and meaning. It seeks to formulate those particular rules which pertain to the special factors connected with the Bible. . . . Hermeneutics is a science in that it can determine certain principles for discovering the meaning of a document, and in that these principles are not a mere list of rules but bear organic connection to each other. It is also an art as we previously indicated because principles or rules can never be applied mechanically but involve the skill (*technē*) of the interpreter.[11]

Third, our exegesis must flow from a proper hermeneutic. Of this relationship, Bernard Ramm observed that hermeneutics

> stands in the same relationship to exegesis that a rule-book stands to a game. The rule-book is written in terms of reflection, analysis, and experience. The game is played by concrete actualization of the rules. The rules are not the game, and the game is meaningless without the rules. Hermeneutics proper is not exegesis, but exegesis is applied hermeneutics.[12]

Exegesis can now be defined as the skillful application of sound hermeneutical principles to the biblical text in the original language with a view to understanding and declaring the author's intended meaning both to the immediate and subsequent audiences. In tandem, hermeneutics and exegesis focus on the biblical text to determine what it said and what it meant originally.[13] Thus, exegesis in its broadest sense will include the various disciplines of literary criticism, historical studies, grammatical exegesis, historical theology, biblical theology, and systematic theology. Proper exegesis will tell the student what the text says and what the text means, guiding him to make a proper personal application of it.

> Interpretation of Scripture is the cornerstone not only of the entire sermon preparation process, but also of the preacher's life. A faithful student of Scripture will seek to be as certain as possible that the interpretation is biblically accurate.[14]

Fourth, we are now ready for a true exposition. Based on the flow of thinking that we have just come through, I assert that expository preaching is really exegetical preaching and not so much the homiletical form of the message. Merrill Unger appropriately noted,

It is not the length of the portion treated, whether a single verse or a larger unit, but the manner of treatment. No matter what the length of the portion explained may be, if it is handled in such a way that its real and essential meaning as it existed in the light of the overall context of Scripture is made plain and applied to the present-day needs of the hearers, it may properly be said to be expository preaching.[15]

As a result of this exegetical process that began with a commitment to inerrancy, the expositor is equipped with a true message, with true intent, and with true application. It gives his preaching perspective historically, theologically, contextually, literarily, synoptically, and culturally. His message is God's intended message.

Now because this all seems so patently obvious, we might ask, "How did the church ever lose sight of inerrancy's relationship to preaching?" Let me suggest that in the main it was through the "legacy of liberalism."

THE LEGACY OF LIBERALISM

An Example

Robert Bratcher, a former research assistant with the American Bible Society, is the translator of ABS's *Good News For Modern Man* and also an ordained Southern Baptist pastor. As one of the invited speakers to a seminar of the Christian Life Commission of the Southern Baptist Convention, he addressed the topic "Biblical Authority for the Church Today." Bratcher was quoted as saying,

Only willful ignorance or intellectual dishonesty can account for the claim that the Bible is inerrant and infallible. No truth-loving, God-respecting, Christ-honoring believer should be guilty of such heresy. To invest the Bible with the qualities of inerrancy and infallibility is to idolatrize [sic] it, to transform it into a false god.[16]

This thinking is typical of the legacy of liberalism that has robbed preachers of true preaching dynamics. I ask, "Why be careful with content which does not reflect the nature of God, or with content whose truthfulness is uncertain?"

False Notions

Bratcher and others who would subscribe to "limited" or "partial" inerrancy are guilty of error along several lines of reasoning.[17] *First*, they have not really come to grips with that which Scripture teaches about itself.

Benjamin Warfield focused on the heart of the issue with this inquiry: "The really decisive question among Christian scholars . . . is thus seen to be, 'What does an exact and scientific exegesis determine to be the Biblical doctrine of inspiration?' "[18]

The answer is that nowhere do the Scriptures teach that there is a dichotomy of truth and error, nor do the writers ever give the slightest hint that they were aware of this alleged phenomenon as they wrote. The human writers of Scripture unanimously concur that it is God's Word; therefore it must be true.

Second, limited or partial inerrancy assumes that there is a higher authority to establish the reliability of Scripture than God's revelation in the Scriptures. They err by *a priori* giving the critic a place of authority over the Scriptures. This assumes the critic himself is inerrant.

Third, if limited inerrancy is true, then its promoters err in assuming that any part of the Scriptures is a trustworthy communicator of God's truth. An errant Scripture would definitely disqualify the Bible as a reliable source of truth.

Presuppositions are involved either way. Will men place their faith in the Scriptures or the critics? They cannot have their cake (trustworthy Scripture) and eat it too (limited inerrancy).

If the Bible is unable to produce a sound doctrine of Scripture, then it is thus incapable of producing, with any degree of believability or credibility, a doctrine about any other matter. If the human writers of Scripture have erred in their understanding of Holy Writ's purity, then they have disqualified themselves as writers for any other area of God's revealed truth. If they are so disqualified in all areas, then every preacher is thoroughly robbed of any confidence and conviction concerning the alleged true message he would be relaying for God.

The Bottom Line

G. Campbell Morgan, hailed as the twentieth century's "prince of expositors," was a messenger widely used by God. There was a time in his life, however, when he wrestled with the very issue we discuss. He concluded that if there were errors in the biblical message, it could not be honestly proclaimed in public.

Here is the account of young Campbell Morgan's struggle to know if the Bible was surely God's Word:

> For three years this young man, seriously contemplating a future of teaching and ultimately of preaching, felt the troubled waters of the stream of religious controversy carrying him beyond his depth. He read the new books which debated such questions as, "Is God Knowable?" and found that the authors' concerted decision was, "He is not knowable." He became confused and perplexed. No longer was he sure of that which his father proclaimed in public, and had taught him in the home.

Other books appeared, seeking to defend the Bible from the attacks which were being made upon it. The more he read, the more unanswerable became the questions which filled his mind. One who has never suffered it cannot appreciate the anguish of spirit young Campbell Morgan endured during this crucial period of his life. Through all the after years it gave him the greatest sympathy with young people passing through similar experiences at college—experiences which he likened to "passing through a trackless desert." At last the crisis came when he admitted to himself his total lack of assurance that the Bible was the authoritative Word of God to man. He immediately cancelled all preaching engagements. Then, taking all his books, both those attacking and those defending the Bible, he put them all in a corner cupboard. Relating this afterwards, as he did many times in preaching, he told of turning the key in the lock of the door. "I can hear the click of that lock now," he used to say. He went out of the house, and down the street to a bookshop. He bought a new Bible and, returning to his room with it, he said to himself: "I am no longer sure that this is what my father claims it to be—the Word of God. But of this I am sure. If it be the Word of God, and if I come to it with an unprejudiced and open mind, it will bring assurance to my soul of itself." "That Bible found me," he said, "I began to read and study it then, in 1883. I have been a student ever since, and I still am (in 1938)."

At the end of two years Campbell Morgan emerged from that eclipse of faith absolutely sure that the Bible was, in very deed and truth, none other than the Word of the living God. Quoting again from his account of the incident: " This experience is what, at last, took me back into the work of preaching, and into the work of the ministry. I soon found foothold enough to begin to preach, and from that time I went on."

With this crisis behind him and this new certainty thrilling his soul, there came a compelling conviction. This Book, being what it was, merited all that a man could give to its study, not merely for the sake of the personal joy of delving deeply into the heart and mind and will of God, but also in order that those truths discovered by such searching of the Scriptures should be made known to a world of men groping for light, and perishing in the darkness with no clear knowledge of that Will.[19]

May God be pleased to multiply the tribe of men called "preachers" who, being convinced of the Bible's inerrant nature, will diligently apply themselves to understand and to proclaim its message as those commissioned of God to deliver it in His stead.

Our Challenge

One of the most godly preachers ever to live was Scotland's Robert Murray McCheyne. In the memoirs of McCheyne's life, Andrew Bonar wrote,

It was his wish to arrive nearer at the primitive mode of expounding Scripture in his sermons. Hence when one asked him if he was ever afraid of running short of sermons some day, he replied—"No; I am just an interpreter of Scripture in my sermons; and when the Bible runs dry, then I shall." And in the same spirit he carefully avoided the too common mode of accommodating texts—fastening a doctrine on the words, not drawing it from the obvious connection of the passage. He endeavoured at all times to preach the mind of the Spirit in a passage; for he feared that to do otherwise would be to grieve the Spirit who had written it. Interpretation was thus a solemn matter to him. And yet, adhering scrupulously to this sure principle, he felt himself in no way restrained from using, for every day's necessities, all parts of the Old Testament as much as the New. His manner was first to ascertain the primary sense and application, and so proceed to handle it for present use.[20]

The expositor's task is to preach the mind of God as he finds it in the inerrant Word of God. He understands it through the disciplines of hermeneutics and exegesis. He declares it expositorily then as the message which God spoke and commissioned him to deliver.

John Stott deftly sketched the relationship of the exegetical process to expository preaching:

Expository preaching is a most exacting discipline. Perhaps that is why it is so rare. Only those will undertake it who are prepared to follow the example of the apostles and say, "It is not right that we should give up preaching the Word of God to serve tables. . . . We will devote ourselves to prayer and to the ministry of the Word" (Acts 6:2, 4). The systematic preaching of the Word is impossible without the systematic study of it. It will not be enough to skim through a few verses in daily Bible reading, nor to study a passage only when we have to preach from it. No. We must daily soak ourselves in the Scriptures. We must not just study, as through a microscope, the linguistic minutiae of a few verses, but take our telescope and scan the wide expanses of God's Word, assimilating its grand theme of divine sovereignty in the redemption of mankind. "It is blessed," wrote C. H. Spurgeon, "to eat into the very soul of the Bible until, at last, you come to talk in Scriptural language, and your spirit is flavoured with the words of the Lord, so that your blood is Bibline and the very essence of the Bible flows from you."[21]

Inerrancy demands an exegetical process and an expository proclamation. Only the exegetical process preserves God's Word entirely, guarding the treasure of revelation and declaring its meaning exactly as He intended it to be proclaimed.[22] Expository preaching is the result of the exegetical process. Thus, it is the essential link between inerrancy and proclamation. It is mandated to preserve the purity of God's originally given inerrant Word and to proclaim the whole counsel of God's redemptive truth.[23]

3

The History of Expository Preaching

James F. Stitzinger

The history of expository preaching begins with an understanding of the revelatory and explanatory preaching recorded in Scripture. Legitimate preaching in the Church Age continues the expository preaching begun in the Bible. History unveils a limited but rich ongoing legacy of biblical expositors up to the present day. These men who poured their lives into expounding God's Word command careful attention from today's biblical expositors.

The rich heritage of expository preaching in church history centers in a relatively small number of men who have committed themselves to this type of preaching.[1] These men who were devoted to expounding the Scriptures are an encouragement and a challenge because of the profound results of their ministries. Dargan noted that "preaching is an essential part and a distinguishing feature of Christianity, and accordingly the larger history of general religious movements includes that of preaching."[2] He further observed that "a reciprocal influence must be reckoned with: the movement has sometimes produced the preaching, the preaching sometimes the movement, but most commonly they have each helped the other."[3] This profound influence of preaching in general applies especially to expository preaching. It has been a significant factor in the history of the church, earning a role as a worthy topic of study.

The apostle Paul spoke of his preaching as "not in persuasive words of wisdom, but in demonstration of the Spirit and of power" (1 Cor. 2:4). In establishing the pattern for the church, he instructed Timothy to "preach the word" (2 Tim. 4:2). God has used the faithful efforts of expository preachers of His Word to bring honor to His name and to increase the faith of His saints (1 Cor. 2:5) throughout history.

The *history* of expository preaching is a principal division of the overall science and art of homiletics.[4] In emphasizing the importance of such a study, Garvie wrote the following over seventy years ago:

The best approach to any subject is by its history; if a science, we must learn all we can about previous discoveries; if an art, about previous methods. The Christian preacher will be better equipped for his task today, if he has some knowledge of how men have preached in former days. . . . While in preaching even, as in human activities of less moment, there are fashions of the hour which it would be folly to reproduce when they have fallen out of date, yet there are abiding aims and rules of preaching, which must be taken account of in each age, and which can be learned by the study of the preaching of the past. Admiration of the great and the good, even without imitation, makes a man wiser and better; the Christian preacher will enrich his own manhood by intimacy with those in whose worthy succession he stands. . . . He will be least in bondage to the past, who is least ignorant of it, and he will be most master of the present whose knowledge is least confined to it.[5]

Indeed, great value results from understanding those who have given themselves to a life of biblical exposition. The current generation, whose history has yet to be written, can learn much from those whose history is now complete. Time yet remains to change, refocus, improve, and be moved to greater accomplishment. An exposure to the history of expository preaching furnishes a context, a reference point, and a basis for distinguishing the transient from the eternal. It will motivate a person toward and increase his confidence in faithful Bible exposition. In the words of Stott, he will glimpse "the glory of preaching through the eyes of its champions in every century."[6] The history of expository preaching has an abundance of principles and lessons to teach those who study it.

THE BIBLICAL PERIOD

Historical study of expository preaching must begin with a proper understanding of the record of preaching in Scripture. Preaching in the Bible is in two basic forms: revelatory preaching and explanatory preaching. All post-biblical preaching has the backdrop of the preaching recorded in Scripture and must trace its roots to this source.

Those originally charged with the task of proclaiming God's Word revealed God to man as they spoke. This Word from God came through different instruments, including the prophet who spoke a divine word from the Lord, the priest who spoke the law, and the sage who offered wise counsel (Jer. 18:18). The Old Testament is replete with the utterances of these revelatory preachers who accurately conveyed God's message to men.

One of the earliest examples of revelatory preaching is the final charge of Moses to Israel (Deuteronomy 31—33). This address was delivered with tremendous ability and clarity by one who once described himself as "slow of speech and slow of tongue" (Ex. 4:10). In his two farewell addresses

Joshua offered profound words of revelation and explanation to his people (Josh. 23:2–16 and 24:2–27). Broadus points to the "finely rhetorical use of historical narrative, animated dialogue, and imaginative and passionate appeal"[7] in these messages from the Lord.

David and Solomon gave profound examples of revelatory and explanatory preaching of the Word in poetic form. David devoted many psalms to revealing the nature and character of God (Ps. 8, 9, 16, 22, 24, 34, 68, 110, 145). An equal number explained God to the people (Ps. 23, 32, 37, 40, see especially 32:8). The Psalms provide an extraordinary wealth of instruction about the nature and content of preaching.[8]

Solomon used proverbs to provide instruction (Prov. 1:2, 3) and taught through an address at the dedication of the temple (2 Chr. 6:1–42). "The Preacher" of Ecclesiastes 12:9, 10 also gave an explanatory discourse on the philosophy of life in which he sought by wisdom (Eccl. 1:12, 13) to deliver "words of truth correctly" (Eccl. 12:10) and was eminently successful.

Perhaps the greatest examples of Old Testament preaching are found among the prophets.[9] An examination of their messages reveals both revelation and explanation. Broadus points to this fact and its relevance for today's preachers:

> Alas! that the great majority of the Christian world so early lost sight of the fact, and that many are still so slow, even among Protestants, to perceive it clearly. The NT minister is not a priest, a *cleric*—except in so far as all Christians are a priesthood—he is a *teacher* in God's name, even as the OT prophet was a teacher, with the peculiar advantage of being inspired. You also know that it was by no means the main business of the prophets to predict the future . . . but that they spoke of the past and the present, often much more than of the future.[10]

Prophetic messages were not only predictions of the future (e.g., Is. 9; 53), but often called the people to repentance and obedience (1:2–31) or offered the people an explanation of the Word of the Lord (ch. 6). "The prophets were preachers."[11] A number of passages in which explanation was the focus and purpose of the messages include Josiah's command to repair and reform the house of the Lord (2 Kin. 22; 23); Ezra's study and teaching of the law (Ezra 7:10), Nehemiah's comments about the law (Neh. 8:1–8), and Daniel's explanation of his vision of seventy weeks (Dan. 9). Prophets who spoke of their work as instruction are Samuel (1 Sam. 12:23), Isaiah (Is. 30:9), and Jeremiah (Jer. 32:33). John the Baptist has a special place because he blended fearless determination with deep humility (John 1; 3:22–30) as he "bore witness" to Christ and called men to repentance and faith (Mark 1:4; John 1:15, 29).

What is clear in the Old Testament is that after a body of revelation had been given, the people would return to it with a need to have it expounded or explained. This was particularly true of the hard-to-understand portions. Old Testament preaching provided necessary clarification.

A history of Bible expositors must include Christ, who is both the model of preaching and the message of what is preached. Jesus came preaching (Mark 1:14) and teaching (Matt. 9:35). He was quite young when He began to display His understanding of Scripture (Luke 2:42, 46–50). As with earlier spokesmen, His preaching included both revelation and explanation. The sermons of Christ, such as in the Sermon on the Mount (Matthew 5—7) and the one at Nazareth (Luke 4:16–30), are models of explanation and exposition for all time. In Matthew 5 Jesus said, "You have heard that it was said . . . but I say to you. . . ." In so doing, He instructed and enlightened His listeners and amplified the text, much to the people's amazement. He stands head and shoulders above all who share the title "preacher" with him.[12] Many qualities of Christ's teaching and preaching can be quickly identified. Among them are the following: (1) He spoke with authority (Matt. 7:29); (2) He made careful use of other Scriptures in His explanations (Luke 24:27, 44); (3) He lived out what He taught (Luke 2:40, 52); (4) He taught simply to adapt to the common man (Mark 12:37); and (5) His teaching was often controversial (Matt. 10:35–37). To be understood properly, Christ must be seen "not as a scientific lecturer but as a *preacher*, a preacher for the most part to the common people, an open-air preacher, addressing restless and mainly unsympathizing crowds."[13] He taught His listeners the truth and explained it to them in simple but profound words. Some were confounded (Luke 4:28) while others rejoiced (Matt. 7:28). To-day's expository preacher should model his ministry after the expositional work of Christ. He should study Christ's method carefully, "not as an example to be slavishly imitated, but as an ideal to be freely realized."[14] The teaching of Christ shows that exposition can take various forms, as long as it is faithful to the distinct purpose of explication of Scripture.

The preaching of the apostles and other early church leaders contributes significantly to the history of expository preaching. The messages of Peter (Acts 2:14–36), Stephen (7:2–53), James (15:13–21), and Paul (17:16–31) have elements of both revelatory and explanatory preaching. The Epistles are, for the most part, written expositions designed to teach various lessons. As Barclay points out,

> Paul's letters are sermons far more than they are theological treatises. It is with immediate situations that they deal. They are sermons even in the sense that they were spoken rather than written. They were not carefully written out by someone sitting at a desk; they were poured out by someone striding up and down a room as he dictated, seeing all the time in his mind's eye the people to whom they were to be sent.

Their torrential style, their cataract of thought, their involved sentences all bear the mark of the spoken rather than of the written word.[15]

Paul, in particular, gave his life to preaching Christ (1 Cor. 1:23; 2:2; 2 Cor. 4:5) to reveal who He was and to explain Him to people (1 Thess. 4:1; 1 Tim. 1:5). A careful study of this apostle as a teacher and expository preacher of Christ yields deep insights regarding that preaching.[16] As Broadus said of Paul, "Thousands have unconsciously learned from him how to preach. And how much richer and more complete the lesson may be if we will apply ourselves to it consciously and thoughtfully."[17]

Paul told Timothy to "preach the word" (2 Tim. 4:2), to "teach and preach these principles" (1 Tim. 6:2), and to "instruct" (1 Tim. 6:17; see also 1 Thess. 5:14). Revelatory preaching was not involved here. While earlier preachers of Scripture gave both revelatory and explanatory messages, the Timothys sent out by them were to concentrate on explanations, expositing the Word to people who needed to understand the truth (1 Tim. 4:13; 2 Tim. 2:15; 4:2–5). As the New Testament era drew to a close, the work of biblical preachers became that of explanation only, rather than of revelation and explanation.

The preaching in the Bible mandates *only one biblical response* for the post-biblical age: Continue to explain and exposit the message now fully revealed (Heb. 1:1–3). *All preaching must be expository preaching* if it is to conform to the pattern of Scripture. It is an extension of the explanatory or expositional dimension of preaching by Old Testament and New Testament preachers.

Since exposition is rooted in Scripture, a study of its history in the church must occur against this background. A commitment to expository preaching as well as to the quest to identify the thread of expositors throughout church history, is possible only in light of preaching as seen in the Bible.

The Early Christian Church, 100–476

The rapid deterioration of primitive Christianity has been well documented.[18] A lack of expository preaching in the post-apostolic period is evidence of this, but it is not the only problem. The ordinance of believers' baptism rapidly turned to the doctrine of baptismal regeneration. The Lord's Supper shifted from being a memorial for believers to being viewed widely as a sacrament conveying saving grace. Christian leadership rapidly changed from the biblical offices of elder and deacon to the human hierarchy of priests with the authoritarian excesses of the "bishop," along with his unbiblical concept of "apostolic succession." One of the major causes of deterioration was the importation of Greek philosophy into Christian thinking by the church fathers. This attempted "integration" resulted in a complete erosion of biblical theology in the perspectives of many of the fathers. Concerning this shift, Hatch writes,

> It is impossible for any one, whether he be a student of history or no, to fail to notice a difference of both form and content between the Sermon on the Mount and the Nicene Creed. The Sermon on the Mount is the promulgation of a new law of conduct; it assumes beliefs rather than formulates them; the theological conceptions which underlie it belong to the ethical rather than the speculative side of theology; metaphysics are wholly absent. The Nicene Creed is a statement partly of historical facts and partly of dogmatic inferences; the metaphysical terms which it contains would probably have been unintelligible to the first disciples; ethics have no place in it. The one belongs to a world of Syrian peasants, the other to a world of Greek philosophers.[19]

The three products of the Greek mind were abstract metaphysics (philosophy), logic (the principles of reasoning), and rhetoric (the study of literature and literary expression). The addition of Greek rhetoric to Christianity brought great emphasis on the cultivation of literary expression and quasi-forensic argument.[20] "Its preachers preached not because they were bursting with truths which could not help finding expression but because they were masters of fine phrases and lived in an age in which fine phrases had a value."[21]

A significant indication of this adaptation is the turning away from preaching, teaching, and the ministry of the Word. Into its place moved the "art of the sermon" that was more involved with rhetoric than with truth.[22] The Greek "sermon" concept fast became a significant tradition. In his well-written article, Craig concludes that the "'sermon' was the result of Syncretism—the fusion of the Biblical necessity of teaching with the unbiblical Greek notion of rhetoric."[23] He continues,

> These sermons were not just a setting forth of Greek-influenced theology. They were in fact external copies of the rhetorical manner of the most popular Greek philosophers of the day. *It is not just what was said in the sermon, it is that the entire presentation and format was carried over from paganism.*[24]

The same secularization of Christian preaching has dominated the church until the present day. The committed biblical expositor has often been the exception rather than the rule. Thus, expositors mentioned here deserve special attention as representatives of a rare and noble group.

The first four hundred years of the church produced many preachers, but few true expositors. The apostolic fathers (ca. 96–125) followed a typological method of interpretation in their works. Second-century fathers (ca.

125–190) such as Justin Martyr and Tertullian composed apologies in defense of Christianity. Third-century fathers (ca. 190–250) such as Cyprian and Origen were polemicists, arguing against false doctrine. Origen's utilization of an allegorical method of interpretation stimulated an increased interest in exposition of the text. Unfortunately, his allegorizing was detrimental to true biblical exegesis and reduced interest in exposition among his followers in the Alexandrian School.

In the fourth century (ca. 325–460), a significant group engaged in serious Bible study. Six notable preachers in this period were Basil, Gregory of Nazianzen, Gregory of Nyssa, Augustine, John Chrysostom, and Ambrose. In addition to his theological writings Augustine (354–430) produced over six hundred sermons. Among his works were expositions of the Psalms and homilies on John's Gospel, 1 John, and the synoptic Gospels. Some of his sermons could be described as exegetical,[25] but his interpretations were usually allegorical and imaginative, as was true of others of his day.

The most significant exception in the early period was John Chrysostom (347–407). Along with Theodore of Mopsuestia, he headed the Antiochene school of interpretation, which rejected the allegorical approach. In sharp contrast to his contemporaries, Chrysostom preached verse-by-verse and word-by-word expositions on many books of the Bible. Included were homilies on Genesis, Psalms, Matthew, John, Acts, Romans, 1 and 2 Corinthians, and the other Pauline epistles.[26] He has been called "golden-mouthed" because of his great ability to attract an audience and hold them spellbound throughout a sermon. Schaff remarked, "He is generally and justly regarded as the greatest pulpit orator of the Greek church. Nor has he any superior or equal among the Latin Fathers. He remains to this day a model for the preacher."[27]

Chrysostom's preaching was characterized by simple Bible exposition,[28] fearless proclamation of morality rather than dogma, deep earnestness, and application directed to the common man. This powerful expositor once said, "You praise what I have said, and receive my exhortation with tumults of applause; but show your approbation by obedience; that is the only praise I seek."[29]

THE MEDIEVAL PERIOD, 476–1500

The medieval period was perhaps the sparsest for expository preaching. James Philip describes the period as follows:

> The influence of the scholastic theology of the universities, which from the beginning were clerical institutions, took over, and the combination of theology and philosophy, and the application of Aristotelian logic to the interpretation of Scripture, with its speculation, analysis and ratiocination imposed an intolerable incubus upon preaching which virtually

destroyed it as an effective means for communicating the gospel. It is not surprising, therefore, that hardly any counterparts to the comprehensive patristic expositions of complete books of the Bible are to be found in medieval ecclesiastical literature.[30]

Late medieval sermons were characterized by allegorical interpretation with its faulty exegetical method, just as it was employed by the interpreters of Homer and introduced into the church by the second- and third-century fathers.[31] While the period produced some famous preachers, such as Peter the Hermit, Bernard of Clairvaux, and Thomas Aquinas, none handled the text in an expository fashion. Faint hints of Bible exposition have been detected among independent groups such as the Paulicians, Waldenses, and Albigenses, despite the fact that these groups are commonly dismissed as "heretics."[32]

As the medieval period drew to a close, several pre-Reformation leaders rekindled the fire of expository preaching. Among these was John Wycliffe (1330–1384), who was deeply concerned about proclaiming the Word. He denounced the preaching of his day, stating that all sermons that did not treat the Scripture should be rejected.[33] William Tyndale (1494–1536) held a similar opinion. A glimpse of his preaching is reflected in this comment on methods of interpretation in his day:

> They divide scripture into four senses, the literal, typological, allegorical, and analogical. The literal sense is become nothing at all: for the pope hath taken it clean away, and hath made it his possession. He hath partly locked it up with the false and counterfeited keys of his traditions, ceremonies, and feigned lies; and driveth men from it with violence of sword: for no man dare abide by the literal sense of the text, but under a protestation, 'If it shall please the pope.' . . . Thou shalt understand, therefore, that the scriptures hath but one sense, which is the literal sense. And that literal sense is the root and ground of all, and the anchor that never faileth, whereunto if thou cleave, thou canst never err or go out of the way.[34]

Others, including John Huss (1373–1415) and Girolamo Savonarola (1452–98), became students and preachers of Scripture.[35] Unwittingly, humanists like Erasmus (1469–1536) and John Colet (1466–1519) helped lay the groundwork for the expositional preaching to come.[36] Their emphasis upon the publishing and study of original documents such as the Greek New Testament had this effect. Erasmus's Greek New Testament published as *Novum Instrumentum* (1516) and *Novum Testamentum* (1518) led to an intense study of Scripture. Despite their contributions, however, none of the humanists became faithful expositors. Instead, they provided a basis for the revival of expository preaching during the Reformation.

THE REFORMATION PERIOD, 1500–1648

The Reformation was built on the foundation of the centrality of the Bible. Principles such as *Sola Deo Gloria* ("glory to God alone"), *Sola Gratia* ("by grace alone"), and especially *Sola Scriptura* ("the Scriptures alone") resulted from the study and teaching of the Word. *Sola Scriptura* meant "the freedom of Scripture to rule as God's word in the church, disentangled from papal and ecclesiastical magisterium and tradition."[37] It viewed the Word as supreme over tradition and the sacraments. Several important Reformation leaders are noteworthy.

Martin Luther (1483–1546) spoke of the supreme importance of the Word when he wrote, "The Word comes first, and with the Word the Spirit breathes upon my heart so that I believe."[38] He also noted,

> Let us then consider it certain and conclusively established that the soul can do without all things except the Word of God, and that where this is not there is no help for the soul in anything else whatever. But if it has the Word it is rich and lacks nothing, since this Word is the Word of life, of truth, of light, of peace, of righteousness, of salvation, of joy, of liberty, of wisdom, of power, of grace, of glory, and of every blessing beyond our power to estimate.[39]

Luther became a believer through his efforts to learn and expound the Scriptures.[40] His words were, "I greatly longed to understand Paul's Epistle to the Romans and nothing stood in the way but one expression, 'the justice of God.'" After his conversion he added, "The whole of Scripture took on a new meaning, and whereas before the 'Justice of God' had filled me with hate, now it became to me inexpressibly sweet in greater love."[41]

Luther proved himself an expositor by producing commentaries on Genesis, Psalms, Romans, Galatians, Hebrews, and 2 Peter and Jude as well as sermons on the Gospels and the Epistles. Luther stressed the importance of preaching to the simple, not the learned,[42] the importance of humility in the study of the Bible,[43] and that preaching should be simple, not erudite.[44] He also spoke of how to preach in three brief steps: "First, you must learn to go up to the pulpit. Second, you must know that you should stay there for a time. Third, you must learn to get down again."[45] In his famous reply before the Diet of Worms, he said, "My conscience is captive to the Word of God."[46] He later said, "I simply taught, preached, wrote God's Word: otherwise I did nothing. . . . The Word did it all."[47]

Ulrich Zwingli (1484–1531) also studied the Bible carefully in its original languages and applied to the text his "considerable linguistic and exegetical abilities."[48] He set about to preach

> simple didactic Bible lessons, moving to more difficult subjects only after his hearers . . . had adequate instruction. His chief objective in

preaching was to repeat the Word of God unabbreviated and unadulterated, clearly setting out the Law and the Prophets, vehemently calling his hearers to repentance and, with the gentleness of a shepherd, guiding the community to salvation. The actions of the preacher should correspond to his words, and he must be prepared, if necessary, to accept a martyr's fate.[49]

Influenced by Zwingli was the Anabaptist, Balthasar Hubmaier (1485–1528), who, despite heavy persecution, produced writings filled with the exposition of Scripture.[50]

The most significant expositor of the Reformation era was John Calvin (1509–1564). "Sunday after Sunday, day after day, Calvin climbed up the steps into the pulpit. There he patiently led his congregation verse by verse through book after book of the Bible."[51] In the first edition of his *Institutes* (1536) Calvin wrote, concerning ministers, "Their whole task is limited to the ministry of God's Word, their whole wisdom to the knowledge of his Word: their whole eloquence, to its proclamation."[52] Twenty-three years later (1559), he added these other relevant comments: "Wherever we see the Word of God purely preached and heard . . . it is not to be doubted, a church of God exists."[53] Calvin also emphasized "the ministry of the Word and sacraments, and how far our reverence for it should go, that it may be to us a perpetual token by which to distinguish the church."[54]

In the preface to his *Romans Commentary,* Calvin stated "that lucid brevity constituted the particular virtue of an interpreter."[55] Parker summarizes Calvin's method as follows: "The important thing is that the Scripture should be understood and explained, how it is explained is secondary."[56] Calvin showed his concern for clarity and brevity by declaring, "The chief virtue of the interpreter lies in clear brevity."[57] He described the paramount duty of the expositor: "Since it is almost his only task to unfold the mind of the writer whom he has undertaken to expound, he misses his mark, or at least strays outside his limits, by the extent to which he leads his readers away from the meaning of his author."[58] He delineated the preacher's task of speaking for God in his comment on Isaiah 55:11: "The Word goeth out of the mouth of God in such a manner that it likewise 'goeth out of the mouth' of men; for God does not speak openly from heaven, but employs men as his instruments, that by their agency he may make known his will."[59]

The evidence of his sincerity was a life spent expounding God's Word. As senior minister of Geneva, Calvin preached twice each Sunday and every weekday on alternating weeks from 1549 until his death in 1564. He preached more than two thousand sermons from the Old Testament alone. He spent a year expositing Job and three years in Isaiah.[60] In addition to his preaching were the lectures on the Bible that led to his biblical commentaries.[61] Said Calvin, "Let us not take it into our heads either to seek out God anywhere else than in his Sacred Word, or to think anything about him that is not prompted by his Word, or to speak anything that is not taken from that Word."[62]

Calvin influenced many of his contemporaries, including Henry Bullinger (1504–1575)[63] and John Knox (1513–1572).[64] Knox argued that he was called to "instruct . . . by tongue and lively voice in these most corrupt days [rather] than compose books for the age to come."[65] Several Anglican preachers, including John Jewel (1522–1571),[66] Hugh Latimer (1485–1555),[67] and Thomas Cartwright (1535–1603),[68] also practiced expositional preaching.

THE MODERN PERIOD, 1649–PRESENT

The post-Reformation era produced a number of important expositors, including several Puritans. More than anything else, the Puritans were preachers. Preaching was so central that many of the Puritans emphasized it by moving their pulpit, with its open Bible, to the center of the church to make the pulpit the focus of the church instead of the altar.[69] To the Puritans, "true preaching is the exposition of the Word of God. It is not a mere exposition of the dogma or the teaching of the church. . . . Preaching, they said, is the exposition of the Word of God; and therefore it must control everything."[70] Lloyd-Jones also suggested that the Puritans saw preaching as the distinguishing mark of true Christianity as compared with religion. While religion (Islam, etc.) puts its emphasis on what man does in his attempt to please and placate his God, Christianity is primarily a listening to God as "God is Speaking": "Religion is man searching for God: Christianity is God seeking man, manifesting Himself to him, drawing Himself unto him. This, I believe is at the back of the Puritan idea of placing in the central position the exposition on the Word in preaching."[71]

William Perkins (1558–1602), an early Puritan expositor, had a profound influence on the entire Puritan movement.[72] He viewed preaching of the Word as the giving of the testimony of God Himself. Perkins developed these thoughts in *The Art of Prophesying,* the first manual of its kind for preachers in the Church of England. Perkins identified four principles to guide the preacher:

1. To read the text distinctly out of the canonical Scriptures.
2. To give the sense and understanding of it, being interpreted by the Scripture itself.
3. To collect a few and profitable points of doctrine out of the natural sense.
4. To apply the doctrines, rightly collected, to the life and manner of men in a simple and plain speech.[73]

Perkins also taught that the insight to expound Scripture belongs only to Christ. Man receives the capacity of interpreting one Scripture passage by another, but only as a gift from Christ.[74]

Many followed this humble but noble tradition. They sometimes preached for several hours at a time, believing that "no great Scriptural truth can be presented in less than an hour or two."[75] Concerning the Puritans, Webber observes,

> Some of the preachers of those days derived their divisions and subdivisions from the text, but more often than not, the divisions and subdivisions were based partly upon the thoughts of the text and partly upon ideas suggested by the general nature of the subject. This rage for minute analysis was often at the expense of literary style and clearness.[76]

Nevertheless, the Puritans as a whole were dominated by a sense of the presence of God. They sought to be faithful to the Word and to the plain practical preaching of the Word.[77] Some major Puritan preachers who demonstrated great ability as expositors were Joseph Hall (1574–1656),[78] Thomas Goodwin (1600–1680),[79] Richard Baxter (1615–1691),[80] and John Owen (1616–1683).[81] Speaking of Goodwin, Brown comments,

> Comparing him with eminent contemporaries like John Owen and Richard Baxter, it has been said that Owen preached earnestly to the understanding, reasoning from his critical and devout knowledge of Scripture; Baxter preached forcibly to the conscience, reasoning from the fitness of things; while Goodwin appealed to the spiritual affections, reasoning from his own religious experience and interpreting Scripture by the insight of a renewed heart.[82]

The diversity of style among the Puritans is remarkable in light of the thread of commitment to a faithful explanation of the text common to them all. Each had his own emphasis, as exemplified in the famous phrase of Baxter, who said, "I preach as never like to preach again, and as a dying man to dying men."[83]

Other significant Puritan expositors were Thomas Manton (1620–1677),[84] John Bunyan (1628–1688),[85] and Stephen Charnock (1628–1680).[86] Also William Greenhill (1581–1677), a Puritan expositor, preached a major series of lectures on Ezekiel.[87] All these men were diligent students of the Word, seeking to clearly explain the truths of Scripture to others.

As the Puritan era gave way to the Evangelical Awakening, preaching that was generally topical, such as that of John Wesley and George Whitefield, replaced expository preaching. Nevertheless, several nonconformists during this period were Bible expositors. The most notable were John Gill (1697–1771)[88] who published nine volumes of biblical exposition between 1746 and 1763, and Matthew Henry (1662–1714).[89] Both were heavily influenced by the Puritans. In the next fifty years other notable exceptions to the topical preachers were Andrew Fuller (1754–1815),[90] Robert Hall (1764–1831),[91] John Brown (1784–1858),[92] John Eadie (1810–1876), and Alexander Carson (1776–1844). Eadie is well known for his commentaries that resulted from his remarkable preaching ministry. Carson was often regarded as a master of expository preaching on a level with Alexander Maclaren.[93]

The later nineteenth century produced several important biblical expositors in Britain and America, including James H. Thornwell (1812–1862)[94] and John A. Broadus (1827–1895). Broadus has been termed "The Prince of Expositors."[95] He described his principles of expository preaching in *On the Preparation and Delivery of Sermons* in 1870. Subsequent revisions of this book have reduced its original thrust and value.[96] Broadus's view of preaching was to preach "the definite doctrines of the Bible, and . . . [an] abundant exposition of the Bible text."[97]

Others in this period were John C. Ryle (1816–1900),[98] Charles J. Vaughan (1816–1897), Alexander Maclaren (1826–1910), Joseph Parker (1830–1902),[99] and Charles Haddon Spurgeon (1834–1892). The period ends with the founding of the *Expository Times* in 1889 by James Hastings.[100] Hastings was the editor of several dictionaries, encyclopedias, and commentary sets, which, along with the *Times,* promoted expository preaching. William Robertson Nicoll (1851–1923) was a biblical expositor and also edited a journal called *The Expositor.* Published from 1886 to 1923, it also promoted the exposition of Scripture.

Several expositors of this period are notable. Alexander Maclaren achieved international fame as an expositor. After 1869 he preached to more than two thousand people each week at Manchester. Beginning in obscurity, he preached for sixty-three years. He read one chapter of the Hebrew Bible and one of the Greek each day throughout his life.[101] In 1896 he penned these words:

> I believe that the secret of success for all our ministries lies very largely in the simple charm of concentrating their intellectual force on the one work of preaching. I have tried to make my ministry a ministry of exposition of Scripture. I know that it has failed in many respects, but I will say that I have endeavored from the beginning to the end to make that the characteristic of all my public work. I have tried to preach Jesus Christ, and the Jesus Christ not of the Gospels only, but the Christ of the Gospels and Epistles: He is the same Christ.[102]

Maclaren's thirty-two volumes of sermons, as well as his contributions to *The Expositor's Bible,* are highly regarded even to this day.[103]

Charles Haddon Spurgeon is highly regarded as a preacher and expositor.[104]

He preached over 3,560 sermons, which comprise the sixty-three volumes of the *Metropolitan Tabernacle Pulpit* published between 1855 and 1917. Though insisting he was a faithful expositor of the text,[105] his exegesis is at times difficult. Webber makes the following comparison:

> In his preaching, he differed from F. W. Robertson. Robertson made a painstaking study of his text, probing it, and drawing out of it the truths that were in it. Spurgeon reversed the process. He selected his text, and then strove to group about the text closely related Bible truths . . . [at times stressing teachings] even though his text made no mention of [them].[106]

Spurgeon viewed Whitefield as a hero and a preaching model,[107] though the latter was more topical and theological than expositional. Spurgeon's genuinely expositional work was his *Treasury of David,*[108] in which he provides a careful verse-by-verse exposition along with "hints to preachers."

The twentieth century has produced a few significant biblical expositors, some of whom have been outstanding: Harry Allan Ironside (1876–1951),[109] Donald Grey Barnhouse (1895–1960), James M. Gray (1881–1935), William Bell Riley (1861–1947), Wallie Amos Criswell (1909–2002), James Denny (1856–1917), George Campbell Morgan (1863–1945), William Graham Scroggie (1877–1958), D. Martyn Lloyd-Jones (1899–1981), John Robert Walmsley Stott (1921–), James Montgomery Boice (1938–2000), Eric J. Alexander, Stephen F. Olford (1918–2004),[110] and R. Albert Mohler, Jr.[111]

G. Campbell Morgan was a powerful expositor of the Word whose works are rich in explanation and textual illustration. Morgan read and studied the entire Bible and his exposition was based on a careful exegesis, viewed in light of the whole Bible.[112] Morgan expressed this thought:

> It will be granted that preachers are to preach the Word. You say that means the Bible. Does it? Yes. Is that all? No. Yes, it is all there. But you want more than that, more than all. The Word is truth as expressed or revealed. The Word is not something that I have found out by the activity of my own intellectual life. The Word is something which my intellectual life apprehends, because it has been expressed. . . . And that is what we have to preach. God's revelation, the truth, as it has been expressed. We must enter upon the Christian ministry on the assumption that God has expressed Himself in His Son, and the Bible is the literature of that self-expression. The minute we lose our Bible in that regard, we have lost Christ as the final revelation. . . . Every sermon that fails to have some interpretation of that holy truth is a failure. . . . Preaching is not the proclamation of a theory, or the discussion of a doubt. . . . Speculation is not preaching. Neither is the declaration of negations preaching. Preaching is the proclamation of the Word, the truth as the truth has been revealed.[113]

Morgan believed that the Bible was absolutely true[114] and spent his life in careful exposition, as evidenced in his numerous published expositions.[115]

D. Martyn Lloyd-Jones was a gifted expositor who saw preaching not as "preaching a sermon for each service, but simply [as] continuing where he was in the ongoing exposition of a book of the Bible."[116] His preaching stemmed from careful exegesis and featured a careful setting forth of the meaning and application of his texts. This continued the rich tradition of Joseph Parker and Alexander Maclaren.[117] Lloyd-Jones produced a significant book on expository preaching in which he wrote the following in the chapter entitled "The Primacy of Preaching":

> To me, the work of preaching is the highest and the greatest and the most glorious calling to which anyone can ever be called. If you want something in addition to that I would say without any hesitation that the most urgent need in the Christian Church today is true preaching, it is obviously the greatest need of the world also.[118]

Lloyd-Jones knew of no substitute for the task of expounding the Word in the church.[119] He identified three types of preaching (evangelistic, instructional teaching, and purely instructional), but he held that all preaching must be expository, both in its preparation and in its presentation to the people.[120] For Lloyd-Jones the highest priority was biblical exposition, an evident fact to anyone investigating his life.[121]

Greatest caution is necessary in a survey of this nature when it arrives at the point of commenting on contemporary expositors. The history book on them cannot be closed because additional ministry remains for them to fulfill. A historical survey would not be complete without a tentative word regarding the apparent contribution of several representative preachers of the present to expository preaching, with due recognition that much may yet transpire before the "history book" on their ministries is closed.

John R. W. Stott, one such example,[122] has followed in the same expository tradition as Lloyd-Jones. Concerning preaching, he said:

> True Christian preaching (by which I mean "biblical" or "expository" preaching, as I shall argue later) is extremely rare in today's Church. Thoughtful young people in many countries are asking for it, but cannot find it. Why is this? The major reason must be a lack of conviction about its importance.[123]

Stott dwelt on importance of expository preaching as follows:

> I cannot myself acquiesce in this relegation (sometimes even grudging) of expository preaching to one alternative among many. It is my contention that all true Christian preaching is expository preaching. Of course,

if by an "expository" sermon is meant a verse-by-verse exposition of a lengthy passage of Scripture, then indeed it is only one possible way of preaching, but this would be a misuse of the word. Properly speaking, "exposition" has a much broader meaning. It refers to the content of the sermon (biblical truth) rather than its style (a running commentary). To expound Scripture is to bring out of the text what is there and expose it to view. The expositor prys open what appears to be closed, makes plain what is obscure, unravels what is knotted and unfolds what is tightly packed. The opposite of exposition is "imposition," which is to impose on the text what is not there. But the "text" in question could be a verse, or a sentence, or even a single word. It could be a verse, or a paragraph, or a chapter, or a whole book. The size of the text is immaterial, so long as it is biblical. What matters is what we do with it.[124]

Stott offers the contemporary student of expository preaching a cogent argument as to the nature and content of true biblical preaching. He is worthy of careful attention.

Another current example of Bible expositors is John MacArthur. For some he has emerged as a notable American expositor at the end of the twentieth century and the beginning of the twenty-first century, continuing in the heritage of Lloyd-Jones. He is currently publishing a commentary of expositions on the entire New Testament.[125] He has described this commentary in the following way:

My goal is always to have deep fellowship with the Lord in the understanding of His Word, and out of that experience to explain to His people what a passage means. . . . The dominant thrust of my ministry, therefore, is to help make God's living Word alive to His people. It is a refreshing adventure. This NT commentary series reflects the objective of explaining and applying Scripture. Some commentaries are primarily linguistic, others are mostly theological, and some are mainly homiletical. This one is basically explanatory, or expository. It is not linguistically technical, but deals with linguistics when this seems helpful to proper interpretation. It is not theologically expansive, but focuses on the major doctrines in each text and on how they relate to the whole of Scripture. It is not primarily homiletical, though each unit of thought is generally treated as one chapter, with a clear outline and logical flow of thought.[126]

MacArthur sees expository preaching as concerned primarily with the content of the Bible.[127] He notes,

The Bible is the Word of God. It emanates from the holiness of God. It reflects the mind and the heart and the will of God, and as such, it must be treated with a tremendous amount of respect. The Bible is not to be dealt with flippantly, it is not to be approached with lack of diligence, it is not to be dealt with in a cursory manner, it is to be dealt with tremendous commitment.[128]

This emphasis upon precision in handling the Scriptures has characterized MacArthur's ministry.[129]

Other contemporary preachers could be identified by name as expositors, but enough characteristics of Bible exposition have been mentioned in this survey and are elaborated upon in other parts of this volume to facilitate recognition of who they are. It is hoped the number of such individuals will increase dramatically.

AN INESCAPABLE CONCLUSION

A study of the history of expository preaching makes it clear that such preaching is deeply rooted in the soil of Scripture. Thus, it is the only kind of preaching that perpetuates biblical proclamation in the church. Throughout history, a few well-known men in each generation, representative of a larger body of faithful expositors, have committed themselves to this ministry of biblical exposition.

Their voices from the past should both encourage the contemporary expositor and challenge him to align his preaching with the biblical standard. Scripture demands nothing less than God-enabled exposition as demonstrated by those worthy saints who have dedicated their lives to this noble task.

Part II

Preparing the Expositor

4

The Priority of Prayer and Expository Preaching

James E. Rosscup

Prayer is not an elective but the principal element in the kaleidoscope of spiritual characteristics that should mark a preacher. These traits unite into a powerful spiritual force; they build a spokesman for God. Jesus, the finest model, and other effective spokesmen for God have been mighty in prayer, while also exhibiting the virtues of godliness and dependence on the Lord. The composite of spiritual qualities whose center is prayer marks out God's long line of proclaimers in the Old Testament, the New Testament, and in church history to the present day. Some books on essentials for preaching slight prayer, but others acknowledge its invaluable role. Preachers who follow the biblical model take prayer very seriously. In sermon preparation, they steep themselves in prayer.

The preacher who follows the biblical way finds prayer to be a superb spiritual asset. Throughout church history great preachers have been men of prayer. Contemporary preachers who desire God to display His power in their ministries will bathe their preaching in prayer.

THE NECESSITY OF PRAYER FOR SPIRITUALITY

If the preacher is to deliver God's message with power, prayer must permeate his life and furnish a lifelong environment for the fruit of the Spirit (Gal. 5:22, 23). His spiritual example causes others to take his message seriously. As a follower of God, his spiritual credibility forcefully attracts others to follow him because, as a trailblazer, he practices single-minded devotion to God. He humbly renders all glory to God and submits to His Word. He demonstrates honesty and discipline of the tongue, time, mind, and body, along with fervent resourcefulness. As he calls others to obedience, God uses his trailblazing leadership to mark the way. All desirable spiritual qualities, particularly godliness and dependence on God, are basic ingredients in the experience of a praying preacher.

Godliness

A praying man of God is passionate in pursuing God and His values (Ps. 42:1, 2). He runs hard after God in a life shaped by the godliness he recommends for others. He is deeply serious about God's principle of following righteousness and wants God to show him His salvation (Ps. 50:23). God's light shines ever more brightly in him, compelling his hearers to seek the beauties of God.

The Preacher's Greatest Example Was Jesus. From boyhood, the heart of the Savior was fixed on "the things of My Father" (Luke 2:49, author's translation). His passion as He entered public ministry was "to fulfill all righteousness" (Matt. 3:15). Taking His resolute stand for God against the devil, He experienced severe testing and made godly value choices based on the Word of God (Matt. 4:1–11). Near the end of His life, He celebrated it as having been godly: "I glorified Thee on the earth, having accomplished the work which Thou hast given Me to do" (John 17:4).

A Further Example Was Paul. Paul had been "crucified with Christ" (Gal. 2:20). In light of this, he lived in godliness that consistently reflected his death with Christ. His empowering secret was "Christ lives in me." Paul was an imitator of Christ in godly values and service (1 Cor. 11:1). He did not take the easy way but faced the hardships entailed in a godly pursuit (1 Cor. 4:9–13; 2 Cor. 6:3–10).

A Modern Example Was Phillips Brooks. Phillips Brooks (1835–1893) had power in heralding God's Word at the Church of the Holy Trinity in Philadelphia and at Trinity Church in Boston. Piety was of utmost importance in his sermon preparation.

> Nothing but fire kindles fire. To know in one's whole nature what it is to live by Christ; to be His, not our own; to be so occupied with gratitude for what He did for us and for what He continually is to us that His will and His glory shall be the sole desires of our life . . . that is the first necessity of the preacher.[1]

Godliness does not stand alone. It includes dependence, its inseparable companion.

Dependence on the Power of God

Jesus covered His territory like a flame, preaching God's Word in the Spirit's power (Luke 4:14). He said, "'The Spirit of the Lord is upon Me, Because He anointed Me to preach the gospel'" (Luke 4:18). Through the Spirit's enablement, He proclaimed release to the captives and recovery of sight to the blind. "The Father abiding in Me does His works," He acknowledged (John 14:10). If Jesus, the man, depended on divine power, how much more do other preachers need to do the same!

Paul relied on the Spirit (Rom. 15:19). He thus counseled other believers (Gal. 5:16–18) to follow his example. He preached to the Corinthians "in demonstration of the Spirit and of power" (1 Cor. 2:4). God was his sufficiency (2 Cor. 3:5, 6; 4:7). In preaching, he took to heart the Christ's principle of the vine and its branches: "apart from Me, you can do nothing" (John 15:5).[2]

Prayer, with its companion spiritual virtues, is indispensable to biblical preaching. It saturates the preacher and godly preaching, indicates the preacher's dependence on God, and is authentically biblical.

The Necessity of Prayer in Sermons of the Bible

In ministries during Bible times, prayer perpetually played a major role. Since biblical days, prayer has remained a top priority for biblical preachers.

Books That Slight Prayer's Importance

It is puzzling that books on essentials of sermon preparation frequently do *not* discuss prayer. This is even more perplexing when these authors claim to teach the *biblical* pattern. Prayer is not prominent among their essentials, as though prayer has no vital part.[3] Neglect of prayer unbiblically casts it in a minor role. A sense of fairness would give these writers the benefit of the doubt and question whether they intended to leave such an impression. Yet when little or nothing is said about prayer and much is made of human craft and polish, only one conclusion is possible.[4] Some books require a long search to find even a brief idea of private prayer's importance. The reader does not see it in chapter titles, subheadings, or topical indices.[5] Instead, it may appear at the end or in a short discussion as an afterthought. Happily, some authors, who at times write little about prayer, grant it a crucial place in other books.[6] How can a writer ever give prayer so little attention, if Scripture makes it of such urgent consequence in preparation to preach?

Books That Emphasize Prayer's Importance

Other books on preaching, or biographies of preachers, assign much space to prayer. They refer to it often,[7] or put it first,[8] or state strong convictions about its critical importance in preparing messages.[9] Even entire books are devoted to prayer's significance in preaching.[10]

The truth is that many things are important in preaching. No conscientious herald of God fully chooses to neglect any of them. He will labor hard on the exegesis of his text, use reliable sources, stimulate his mind from a breadth of reading, take pains to be accurate, and get a clear outline. He will search for vivid analogy, memorize Scripture, nourish an evangelistic and edifying purpose, and be always looking to God. He may write out his message entirely or preach it from notes. He will integrate details and form clear transitions. He will know the people to whom he speaks. He will pay attention to earnestness, enthusiasm, artistic touches, forcefulness, grace, and tasteful humor. He will be concerned about enunciation, gestures, courage, posture, timing, eye contact, and will guard against hurtful remarks.

The emphasis on prayer need not undercut any of these aspects, but *these others should not remove the spotlight from the necessity of prayer.* Unfortunately, preachers become unbalanced in several ways:

1. They emphasize prayer alone and shirk the responsibility to be God's workmen through faithful study.
2. They put all their emphasis on human aspects of sermon preparation and have no pervasive dependence on God in prayer. God can bless, in spite of this, but the preacher serves up only a product of human craft. This kind of sermon's fine technique is impressive, but it lacks vital spiritual forcefulness.
3. They emphasize homiletical ingenuity, but offer only a shallow exposure to God's Word through neglect of diligent labor in study and prayer. They have little to feed the spiritually hungry and reflect little dependence on God.

But there is good news! Preachers can and should be balanced. They can emphasize a prayerful choice of a text and prayerful diligence in studying the passage and books that clarify its meaning. They should search diligently for relevant illustrations, labor earnestly to organize their material well, and build good transitions. They pray the whole time. Then they deliver their message, fortified by a godly life and a reliance on God. This is the preferred way. Prayer is a major force, while the other essentials are not taken lightly.

Proclamation in Old Testament Times

What role has prayer played during Bible times and since? An examination of prayerful preaching by men with a great impact for God is very informative.

Moses. The lawgiver Moses had a ministry similar to that of today's preacher. He spoke God's Word and demonstrated its relevance to needs of his day. Prayer figured heavily in his ministry.[11]

For example, Moses pleaded with God to spare Israel after their idolatrous worship of a golden calf. He interceded with God to retain His purpose in *redemption* of Israel from Egypt. He was zealous that God preserve His *reputation* from all taint of dishonor before the ungodly. He also implored God to furnish a *remembrance* of His own covenant pledge (Ex. 32:11–13). He begged God to forgive His people (v. 32).

Samuel. To encourage his people, Samuel, a priest and a prophet, used God's loyalty to His covenant aim for Israel's good (1 Sam. 12:22). He saw the Lord's steadfastness as consistent with His reputation. For God to renege on His promise would make Him unfaithful to His Word and character, sacrificing His very honor. Samuel knew God's covenant purpose to possess Israel, and he submitted his will to God's purpose. Walking in step with God, he told his hearers, "Far be it from me that I should sin against the LORD by ceasing to pray for you" (v. 23).

The link between *preaching* God's Word to people and *praying* for them is evident. Prayer harmonizes with God's will. Rather than sinning by failing to pray, the preacher Samuel took the God-honoring way: "I will instruct you in the good and right way" (v. 23). He set an example for every preacher in three ways: his *perception* of God's will found in God's Word, his *prayer* for the people to embrace God's will, and his *proclamation* of God's will. All three elements, bathed in prayer, were crucial.

Daniel. Daniel was the human channel God used to record His prophetic plan for centuries to come. Daniel's preparation for this task revolved around prayer. He prayed for God's *information* about Nebuchadnezzar's dream. He prayed for the *interpretation* of the dream (Daniel 2). Later, he meditated on Jeremiah 25 and 29 in regard to the seventy years God had set for Israel to be in Babylonian exile (Dan. 9), and he made three requests for his people: the restoration of Jerusalem (Dan. 9:16), the rebuilding of the temple (v. 17), and the return of the people (vv. 18, 19). God answered that He would grant all three in His time (vv. 24–27). In Daniel 10, the aged prophet humbled himself for three weeks of fasting and prayer (vv. 2–3). He prayed (v. 12) and received God's Word about developments in Persia, Greece, and later powers (chs. 10—12).

Proclamation in New Testament Times

Jesus. The Savior used prayer to prepare Himself for ministry.[12] Luke referred more often to Jesus' prayer than the other Gospel writers. This fits Luke's emphasis on Jesus' humanity. Jesus is king (Matthew), servant (Mark), and God (John), but He is also man and prays as a man.

Prayer was of overwhelming importance in the preaching of Jesus. The Son of Man commenced and consummated His ministry on earth in prayer (Luke 3:21, 22; 24:49–51). He saw prayer as vital when people were thronging to hear Him preach. Differing from some of today's preachers, Jesus took the awesome demand on His time as a call to keep prayer as a top priority. He "would often slip away to the wilderness and pray" (Luke 5:16). The desert solitude with God was an essential before serving a multitude that gathered to hear. For preachers sensitive to His heartbeat, bent knees are as crucial to the kingdom as opened study tools. Christ's vigil before

God reflected His value system. Jesus depended on God, even though He was Himself God in the flesh!

Back from such a rendezvous in prayer, Jesus was ready to preach and to confound antagonistic religious experts (Luke 5:17). One wonders what the lips of the preacher had prayed. Was it for wisdom to meet trials or for the crowds to have their blinders removed in order to see their desperate spiritual need (Luke 5:15, 26)? One thing is certain; whatever He prayed, the Jesus who preached was the Jesus who prayed.

Before appointing the twelve disciples, Jesus "went off to the mountain to pray" (Luke 6:12). Exhibiting His dependence on and submission to God by an all-night session in prayer, Jesus later preached the Sermon on the Plain (Luke 6:20–49). Still later, one of the Twelve requested, "Lord, teach us to pray" (Luke 11:1). In response, the praying preacher taught the "Disciples' Prayer" (Luke 11:2–4) and other matters related to prayer (Luke 11:5–13).

Prayer preceded Jesus' announcements about the church and the keys of the kingdom (Matt. 16:18–19, preceded by Luke 9:18), about His death and resurrection, about a man losing his soul, men being ashamed of Him, and His future coming (Luke 9:18–28). It also prefaced His transfiguration (Luke 9:18, 29–35).

Jesus urged His disciples to pray as He was molding them into preachers. "Beseech the Lord of the harvest to send out workers into His harvest" (Matt. 9:38). Observing that priority would keep the preachers praying all their lives.

Early Christians. An urgency to pray gripped early Christians. In Acts they prayed in the midst of many circumstances.[13] Luke continued his emphasis on prayer in this, his second volume. The prayers of these early saints are a great stimulant to others who want to please God. They prayed, awaiting the Spirit's coming with power at Pentecost (Acts 1:14; see 1:5–7; 2:33), an important preparation for Peter's potent message recorded in Acts 2. Their prayers also sought God's choice in replacing Judas among the Twelve (Acts 1:15–26).

Prayer was one of four Christian essentials of the primitive church (Acts 2:42). If it was that important then, how crucial it must be for preachers today! Believers prayed on a regular schedule (Acts 3:1; 10:9) as well as at any moment of urgency. Peter and John furnish an example. They were God's channels for His miraculous healing of the lame man (Acts 3:7–10). Later, they prayed with others for boldness in witnessing (Acts 4:29–31), a prayer that God answered in enabling them to face enemies. They were empowered, unified, and selfless. Later, the apostles declared the importance of prayer in preaching: "We will devote ourselves to prayer, and to the ministry of the word" (Acts 6:4). The order of their words is interesting.[14] Even if mentioning prayer first is not significant, it is self-evident that prayer is just as primary for preachers as is the Word.

Paul. Paul prayed that God would help new converts grow (Acts 14:23). Apparently, he viewed prayer as inseparable from preaching (see Eph. 6:18–20), as did his predecessors (see Eph. 6:4). Behind the prayer of Acts 14:23 and the appointment of elders lies the reminder of God's concern for new believers. Their spiritual growth depended on the appointment of elders who could exhort them and feed them from the Word of God (see Eph. 6:22). Prayer was needed to undergird this process.

Paul and his associates prayed when they preached God's Word in Europe (Acts 16:13). They penetrated the heavenly curtain before they penetrated the human curtain (Acts 16:14). God used prayer to prosper their ministry, which was also *His* ministry.

Paul's dependence on prayer in preaching is synonymous with his dependence on God rather than human ability (see 1 Cor. 2:1–5). This did not rule out his skillful use of effective techniques of communication, however. Just as Jesus adopted good methods, such as parables, so did Paul.[15] Paul, however, depended ultimately on the Cross-centered content of God's Word and the power of God's Spirit for effectiveness in preaching, a dependence exhibited in prayer.

Paul's dependence on God also surfaces in his appeals for others to pray for him (Eph. 6:18–20). As a part of his call for Christians to don God's armor, he detailed that armor and bade them pray "all-out" for him. Note the fourfold use of "all":

1. *All situations.* Pray "by means of ($\delta\iota\acute{\alpha}$ [*dia*]) all prayer and petition." Engage in every form of prayer. The word $\pi\rho o\sigma\epsilon\upsilon\chi\hat{\eta}s$ (*proseuchēs*) can mean prayer in general, in all its expressions,[16] such as praise/thanks, confession, petition, and intercession. "Petition" ($\delta\epsilon\acute{\eta}\sigma\epsilon\omega s$ [*deēseōs*]) specifies each request.[17]
2. *All seasons.* "At all times" takes in all prayer opportunities. Pray "in the Spirit" for the success of the preacher and the preached Word. Ask in submission to the Spirit's will and wisdom, with reliance on His power and motives aligned with His values.
3. *All steadfastness.* Paul wanted them "alert with all perseverance and petition." "Keep alert" ($\dot{\alpha}\gamma\rho\upsilon\pi\nu\acute{\epsilon}\omega$ [*agrupneō*]) refers to staying awake to carry out a task. Alert prayer is with "all perseverance" ($\pi\rho o\sigma\kappa\alpha\rho\tau\acute{\epsilon}\rho\eta\sigma\iota s$ [*proskarterēsis*]). The related verb means "to hold fast to."[18] The same word is used for the early Christians who *clung* to the Word (Acts 2:42). Paul wanted alert, tenacious people praying for him in every specific request ($\delta\acute{\epsilon}\eta\sigma\iota s$ [*deēsis*]).
4. *All subjects.* Paul wants prayer warriors to intercede for "all the saints," including himself: "pray on my behalf" (Eph. 6:19). Pray for what? Paul mentions "boldness" twice. He wants to fearlessly wield the sword of the Spirit, preaching "as I ought to speak" (Eph. 6:20).

Speaking with boldness suits the fact that, if filled with the Spirit (Eph. 5:18), Paul would speak "in the strength of His might" (Eph. 6:10). Boldness is necessary if the preacher is to triumph over fear and the forces pitted against his success (Eph. 6:12). It also matches a message that provides every spiritual blessing (Eph. 1:3) and an inheritance with God (Eph. 1:11, 14). The preacher should not voice such truths in a vague, weak, compromising, or confusing way.

The kind of prayer that drenched Paul's sermons is also suggested in Philippians 4:6. "In everything" includes *more* than sermons as objects of prayer, but it certainly entails every aspect of sermon preparation, too. "By prayer" again uses the word προσευχή (*proseuchē*), a general word for prayer.[19] Paul continued "and supplication" (δέησις [*deēsis*]), meaning a "special petition [request] for the supply of wants."[20] Paul exhorted, "Let your requests be made known." These requests (αἰτήματα [*aitēmata*]), as J. B. Lightfoot supposes, are "the several objects of δέησι."[21]

Such praying is "with thanksgiving." Why? The praying person wants to show gratitude for past answers that sweetened life. Thanks is also apropos for God's present bounty in granting anwers to His audience. Thanksgiving is due the Spirit for His help (Rom. 8:26, 27; Eph. 6:18–20; Phil. 1:19). These illustrate the many reasons for gratitude.

Prayer has continued through the centuries of church history since the New Testament era.

THE NECESSITY OF PRAYER FOR POWER IN PREACHING TODAY

The clarion call for prayer as preparation for preaching also resounds in preachers of relatively modern times up to the present. Preachers pray and solicit others to pray for their messages. God's power in preaching results.

Power Through Preachers' Prayers

R. Kent Hughes, current senior pastor of the College Church of Wheaton, Illinois, assessed scores of books on preaching, and was frequently disappointed that authors said little or nothing about prayer. This led him to comment,

> This, and what experience God so far has given me in preaching and prayer, has brought a conviction. Should I ever write a book on essentials for preaching, I know now that I would devote at least a *third* of it to spiritual preparation in matters such as prayer. This would be the *first* third.[22]

E. M. Bounds (1835–1913) served as a Civil War chaplain for the Confederacy. He later pastored several churches and became a man driven by prayer. His morning habit was to pray from four to seven o'clock. His listeners commented on his powerful public prayers and his messages. At least eight of his manuscripts on prayer[23] and a biography[24] have been published. Bounds' books have aroused many to greater fervor in prayer. He wrote,

> The young preacher has been taught to lay out all his strength on the form, taste, and beauty of his sermon as a mechanical and intellectual product. We have thereby cultivated a vicious taste among the people and raised the clamor for talent instead of grace, eloquence instead of piety, rhetoric instead of revelation, reputation and brilliancy instead of holiness.[25]

Much in this is true, but it is not an either/or situation. The combination of homiletical skill *and* much prayer is the answer. Bounds also wrote, "Light praying will make light preaching. Prayer makes preaching strong [the God who answers prayer does this] . . . and makes it stick."[26]

David Larsen, professor of homiletics at Trinity Evangelical Divinity School, also has emphasized prayer:

> Strange it is that any discussion of preaching should take place outside the context of believing prayer. We have not prepared until we have prayed. . . .
> We cannot represent God if we have not stood before God. It is more important for me therefore to teach a student to pray than to preach.[27]

After a powerful message by Alexander Whyte (1836–1921), pastor of Free Saint George's West in Edinburgh, Scotland, a listener exulted, "Dr. Whyte, you preached today like you had just emerged from the throne chamber of the Almighty." The preacher replied, "In point of fact, I have."[28]

At an ordination of a man preparing to preach, Whyte advised, "Be up earlier than usual to meditate and pray over it. Steep every sentence of it in the Spirit. . . . And pray after it."[29]

A biographer says that as much as Whyte valued public worship and prepared diligently for it, secret prayer was more important to him. The "master notes of his preaching"[30] were discipline, prayer, inner motive, humility before God and men, and purity acquired through suffering. The same writer notes that Whyte's secret prayer led to public prayer that had a powerful impact on people. One of Whyte's students spoke of the days when "every sermon in Free St. George's was a volcano, and every opening prayer a revelation."[31] Whyte "never grew weary of emphasizing the need of prayer and of discipline in the Christian life—the need of humility and of 'ever-new beginnings.' "[32]

A "morning watch" was almost as regular as the sunrise for H. A. Ironside (1876–1951). This expositor meditated in his Bible and prayed for an hour,[33] and afterward gave himself to more intensive study and further prayer. Rivers of living water overflowed from his times with God to crowds who heard him. He insisted, "If we would prevail with men in public, we must prevail with God in secret."[34]

Those at Trinity Chapel in Brighton, England, heard searching messages by Frederick W. Robertson (1816–1853). Some have called him the greatest of the English preachers. In early years, he concentrated on reading about David Brainerd and Henry Martyn.[35] He bathed his life in communion with God, longing to be conformed to the image of Christ and adjusting his values to His ideals.[36] He prayed without ceasing, different concerns drawing his attention each day: Sunday, parish and outpouring of the Spirit; Monday, special devotion; Tuesday, spread of the gospel; Wednesday, kingdom of Christ; Thursday, self-denial; Friday, special examination and confession; Saturday, intercession.[37]

Charles Finney (1792–1875), evangelistic in focus, followed Jesus' example, slipping away to engage in special vigils of prayer. Speaking after much prayer, he saw God bring great blessing on his ministry.[38] He was convinced about the importance of prayer:

> Without this you are as weak as weakness itself. If you lose your spirit of prayer, you will do nothing, or next to nothing, though you had the intellectual endowment of an angel. . . . The blessed Lord deliver, and preserve His dead church from the guidance and influence of men who know not what it is to pray.[39]

Finney said, "I would say that unless I had the spirit of prayer I could do nothing."[40] If even for a moment he lost the sense of the spirit of grace and prayer, he could not preach with power and was impotent in personal witness.

A famous Methodist preacher of England, William Sangster (1900–1960), felt closeness to God to be of utmost importance in preparing a message, because after prayerful study,

> the preacher seems to fade out and leave the hearers face to face with God. . . . If we are driven to make comparisons, we must insist that grace-gifts are more important than natural gifts. It is true that the Holy Spirit can work on very little, and if *effectiveness* is borne in mind rather than popularity, the unction of the Spirit is the greatest gift of all.[41]

For more than forty-six years George W. Truett (1867–1944) pastored the First Baptist Church in Dallas, Texas. After time with his family each evening, he went to his library to study and pray from 7 P.M. until midnight.[42]

He also prepared at other hours. Once he was aboard a ship tossed by heavy winds and waves. The distress prompted a request for Truett to preach. He went alone with God, seeking a fitting message. After prayer, he found the message in Hebrews, "Ye have need of patience." When he announced his subject, the storm-weary people smiled their approval.[43]

Truett had a passion that people be saved. He said that the person who would win others to Christ must pray much for himself and for them.[44] Requests came from all over the world for Truett to pray. On a Dallas street, he met a noted elderly criminal lawyer. "Dr. Truett," the man said, "I was at your church Sunday, and heard what you said about prayer. I don't suppose you ever pray for a sinner like me."

Truett responded, "I have prayed for you, by name, daily, for years," and produced a notebook with the lawyer's name in it to prove it.

The lawyer's lips trembled and his eyes grew moist. "Thank you, Doctor, thank you for remembering a hardened old sinner."[45]

Thomas Armitage painted this picture of prayer:

A sermon steeped in prayer on the study floor, like Gideon's fleece saturated with dew, will not lose its moisture between that and the pulpit. The first step towards doing anything in the pulpit as a thorough workman must be to kiss the feet of the Crucified, as a worshipper, in the study.[46]

Whitesell, a teacher of preaching, bore down on prayer:

The preacher must be a man of prayer. . . . He should pray for his messages . . . soak them in prayer, . . . pray as he goes into the pulpit, pray as he preaches insofar as that is possible, and follow up his sermons with prayer.[47]

Also writing in support of this point was Sinclair Ferguson, Scottish pastor who in 1982 became professor of systematic theology at Westminster Theological Seminary:

For me, it is of primary importance that all my preparation be done in the context of a praying spirit . . . looking to the Lord and depending on the grace of His illuminating and enlivening Spirit. This is punctuated by specific ejaculations and periods of petition for both exposition and application. . . .

  To use a picture from John Owen, I think of the Spirit moving among the people, giving to each a parcel of identical shape, size, and wrapping (the sermon); but . . . the gift inside is specially appropriate to each. My prayer, therefore, is that my material may be in harmony with His purpose and my spirit sensitive to His gracious character, so that I may not distort Him in my words or by my spirit.[48]

An expositor at many Plymouth Brethren conferences, Henry Holloman, professor of systematic theology at Talbot School of Theology, has said,

> Behind every good biblical preacher is much hard labor in preparation (1 Tim. 5:17; 2 Tim. 2:15). However, only prayer can assure that his work is not wasted and that his message will spiritually impact the hearers. As the biblical preacher interweaves prayer with his preparation, he should focus on certain petitions: (1) that he will receive God's message . . . in spiritual as well as mental *comprehension,* 1 Cor. 2:9–16; (2) that God's message will first grip his own heart in strong *conviction,* 1 Thess. 1:5; (3) that he will clearly and correctly convey God's message in the power of the Spirit in effective *communication,* . . . 1 Thess. 1:5; (4) that the Spirit will use the message to produce proper response and change, . . . spiritual *transformation,* 2 Cor. 3:18 . . . and (5) that the whole process and finished product will accomplish God's purpose in *glorification* of God through Christ, 1 Cor. 10:31; 1 Pet. 4:11.[49]

Holloman clarified that "knowledge and organization is what we must do, but prayer gives us what only God can do."

John MacArthur, pastor-teacher of Grace Community Church, Sun Valley, California, sees prayer as inseparable from preparing and preaching.

> During the week . . . locked up with my books, . . . study and . . . communion mingle as I apply the tools of exegesis and exposition in . . . open communion with the Lord. I seek His direction, thank Him for what I discover, plead for wisdom and insight, and desire that He enable me to live what I learn and preach.
>
> A special burden for prayer begins to grip my heart on Saturday evening. Before I go to sleep, I . . . spend one final time going over my notes. That involves an open line of communication with God as I meditatively and consciously offer my notes up to the Lord for approval, refinement and clarity.
>
> I awake Sunday morning in the same spirit of prayer. Arriving at the church early, I spend time . . . in prayer, then join elders who pray with me for the messages. On Sunday afternoon, I go through a similar time of reviewing my evening message prayerfully.[50]

John Stott said a preacher, like a father (1 Thess. 2:11), should pray for his church family. Preachers will only make time for this hard and secret work if they love people enough. "Because it is secret and therefore unrewarded by men, we shall only undertake it if we long for their spiritual welfare more than for their thanks."[51]

Andrew Blackwood, longtime professor of homiletics at Princeton Theological Seminary, counsels the preacher to lay down one rule and never make an exception: start, continue, and end with prayer.[52] A biblical sermon, he says, will likely be worth whatever the preacher invests in it, the time he devotes, the thought he gives, and the prayer. For

> in his study the prophet can build his altar and on it lay the wood. There he can lovingly place his sacrifice . . . sermon . . . but still he knows that the fire must come down from God. Come it will, if he prays before he works, and if he works in the spirit of prayer.[53]

Edward Payson (1783–1827) exemplified sermon preparation by diligent study infused with hours of prayer. He pastored the Second Congregational Church of Portland, Maine. His reading rapidity, sharpness in assimilating details, and good scholarship were notable.[54] He studied the writings of Jonathan Edwards and others,[55] but his greatest zeal was in studying the Bible and praying for God's help in interpreting and applying it.[56] Prayer was "the most noticeable fact in his history."[57] He "studied theology on his knees. Much of his time he spent literally prostrated with the Bible open before him, pleading the promises."[58]

Payson's discipline led him to guard his time. His usual schedule was twelve hours a day for study, two for devotion, two for relaxing, two for meals and family devotions, and six for sleep.[59] In his diary and letters, comments like the following recur: "Was much assisted in my studies . . . enabled to write twelve pages of my sermon. It was the more precious, because it seemed to be in answer to prayer."[60] He wrote on March 17, 1806, that since beginning to plead God's blessing on his preparation, "I have done more in one week than in the whole year before."[61]

Even in cases when Payson felt he had been weak in preaching, his people were refreshed. When lifeless in devotions, he often prayed on to victory.[62] God greatly enlivened this preacher much as He quickened the psalmist.[63] Payson prayed for hours for the lost and often witnessed to them. He saw many saved and added to the church.

A brother told Payson he felt discouraged about preaching because of inexperience and ignorance. Payson wrote to him, admitting that he himself always felt inadequate:

> This led me to pray almost incessantly. . . . He who has thus guided me, and thousands of others equally foolish will, I trust, guide you. . . . If we would do much for God, we must ask much of God; . . . I cannot insist on this too much. Prayer is the first thing, the second thing, and the third thing necessary for a minister, especially in seasons of revival. . . . Pray, then, my dear brother, pray, pray, pray.[64]

The greatly used preacher Charles Spurgeon (1834–1892) put heavy emphasis on prayer. He felt that ministers ought to pray without ceasing (1 Thess. 5:17). "All our libraries and studies are mere emptiness compared with our closets. We grow, we wax mighty, we prevail in private prayer,"[65] he wrote. He prayed in choosing a topic, getting into the spirit of a text, seeing God's deep truths, lifting those truths out, receiving fresh streams of thought, and for delivery. For

> nothing can so gloriously fit you to preach as descending fresh from the mount of communion with God to speak with men. None are so able to plead with men as those who have been wrestling with God on their behalf.[66]

Spurgeon studied hard, but he got some of his best thoughts while praying.[67] Or, feeling fettered, he secretly groaned to God and received unusual liberty. "But how dare we pray in the battle if we have never cried to the Lord while buckling on the harness!"[68]

After preaching, Spurgeon found prayer strategic. "If we cannot prevail with men for God, we will, at least, endeavor to prevail with God for men."[69]

So the preacher who does his work God's way prays, but he also enlists others to pray for the success of the Word.

Power Through Others' Prayers

Early in this century, John Hyde prayed for speakers at conferences in India. He and R. M'Cheyne Paterson prayed for a month for a conference in 1904. George Turner joined them for three of those weeks.[70] God saved hundreds of people and renewed believers. Hyde knelt for hours in his room or was prostrate on the floor, or he sat in on a message while interceding for the speaker and the hearers.

Dwight L. Moody (1837–1899), founder of the Moody Bible Institute, often saw God work in power when others prayed for his meetings in America and abroad. He often wired R. A. Torrey at the school, urging prayer. Faculty and students prayed all evening or into the early morning or all night.[71]

After Moody's death, Torrey (1856–1928) preached in many countries. He, too, had prayer backing. In Australia, twenty-one hundred home prayer groups met for two weeks before he arrived. God turned many lives around.[72] After Torrey died, Mrs. Torrey said, "My husband was a man of much prayer and Bible study. He denied himself social intercourse with even his best friends, in order that he might have time for prayer, study, and the preparation for his work."[73]

Torrey said, "Pray for great things, expect great things, work for great things, but above all pray."[74] He told church members, "Do you want a new minister? I can tell you how to get one. Pray for the one you have till God makes him over."[75] He believed, "Prayer is the key that unlocks all the storehouses of God's infinite grace and power."[76] He was for many years pastor of the Chicago Avenue Church in Chicago, Illinois, later called Moody Memorial Church. Much of the growth there resulted from prayer by Torrey and his praying people who met on Saturday nights and Sunday mornings.[77]

Payson, already mentioned, rallied people to meet for prayer in "Aaron and Hur Societies" in fours and fives for an hour. They prayed before Payson preached.[78] A preacher needs to lead in prayer and also to get the church

> excited to pray for the influences of the divine Spirit; and that they should frequently meet for this purpose. . . . In that duty we explicitly acknowledge, not only to Him, but to our fellow creatures, that nothing but the influences of His Spirit can render any means effectual, and that we are entirely dependent . . . on His sovereign will.[79]

Payson depended on others' prayers. His speaking schedule was often heavy. He prepared four sermons a week and sometimes sermons for the press. Within a two-month period he also had three ordination messages, two messages for missions societies, and one for a women's asylum.[80] No matter how busy, he kept his own prayer vigils. His biographer says that "prayer . . . was eminently the business of his life . . . through which he derived inexhaustible supplies."[81] He adds that "his conversation was in heaven."

Spurgeon said much about others praying. The preacher, no matter how brilliant, godly, or eloquent, has no power without the Spirit's help:

> The bell in the steeple may be well hung, fairly fashioned, and of soundest metal, but it is dumb until the ringer makes it speak. And . . . the preacher has no voice of quickening for the dead in sin, or of comfort for living saints unless the divine spirit [Spirit] gives him a gracious pull, and begs him speak with power. Hence the need of prayer for both preacher and hearers.[82]

Spurgeon said he would plead even with tears for others' prayers.[83] Only by abundant intercession could the church prosper or even continue. He saw the Monday-night prayer meeting at London's Metropolitan Tabernacle as "the thermometer of the church."[84] For years a large part of the main auditorium and first gallery were filled at these meetings.[85] In Spurgeon's mind, the prayer meeting was "the most important meeting of the week."[86]

THE PRIMACY OF PRAYER

Prayer reigns supreme, along with the Word of God, in ministries of the Old Testament, New Testament, and since then. The preacher today, as always, needs a wise balance between different aspects of sermon preparation that depend on human skill and the facets that call on God for His almighty power. The man who represents God in the pulpit should cultivate an ever-growing passion to be the most prayerful and diligent channel he can be for broadcasting the greatest message of all time.

5

The Man of God and Expository Preaching

John MacArthur

Behind the content of his message is the character of the expositor. He must be set apart from mundane matters, lifted above worldly aims and ambitions, and devoted singularly to God's service. In 1 Timothy 6:11–14, Paul lists four characteristics of such a man of God: He is marked by what he flees from, follows after, fights for, and is faithful to.

In Scripture, God's spokesmen are often referred to by different titles such as prophet, elder, evangelist, and pastor.[1] Generally these titles refer to the task the man executes. One title, however, refers to the *character* of the man holding an office. That title is "man of God." It is used frequently in the Old Testament. Moses (Deut. 33:1; 1 Chr. 23:14; Ezra 3:2), the anonymous prophet who pronounced divine judgment on Eli's family (1 Sam. 2:27), Samuel (1 Sam. 9:6), David (Neh. 12:24, 36), Elijah (1 Kin. 17:18), and Elisha (2 Kin. 4:8, 9) are among those designated "men of God." In each case, the term "man of God" refers to someone who represented God by speaking His Word.

Although the title is quite common in the Old Testament, appearing approximately seventy times, it is used only three times in the New Testament. In 2 Peter 1:21, the plural form refers to the Old Testament prophets. In 2 Timothy 3:16, 17 Paul used the title to refer to those like Timothy who preached the Word, though the principle of Scripture's perfecting power in that text extends its range of reference to all believers (see Ps. 19:7–9). The third use, the topic of the present discussion, is in 1 Timothy 6:11, where Paul addressed Timothy as "you man of God."

By calling Timothy a man of God, Paul identified him with a long line of spokesmen for God extending back into the Old Testament. Paul no doubt intended a reminder of this noble lineage to strengthen Timothy's resolve to stand firm in the face of the pressures of ministry. Timothy's ministry in Ephesus certainly did not lack for pressures, of course: false doctrine, sinful and unqualified leaders, ungodliness, and tolerance of sin, to name a few. Paul reminds Timothy that he was "God's man," thereby adding a tremendous weight of responsibility to his ministry. He represented God.

In 1 Timothy 6:11–14, Paul listed four marks of a man of God: A man of God must be identified by what he flees from, what he follows after, what he fights for, and what he is faithful to.

A Man of God Is Marked by What He Flees From

In verse 11, Paul commanded Timothy to "flee from these things." "Flee" translates the Greek word φεύγω (*pheugō*), from which the English word *fugitive* is derived. It is used in extrabiblical Greek literature to speak of running from a wild animal, a poisonous snake, a deadly plague, or an attacking enemy. It is an imperative in the present tense and could be translated "keep on continually fleeing." A man of God is a lifelong fugitive, fleeing those things that would destroy him and his ministry. In other places Paul listed some of the threats: immorality (1 Cor. 6:18), idolatry (10:14), false teaching (1 Tim. 6:20; 2 Tim. 2:16), and false teachers (3:5), as well as youthful lusts (2:22).

From what does Paul advise Timothy to flee in this passage? The immediate context indicates it is a love for money. In 1 Timothy 6:9–10, Paul warned:

> But those who want to get rich fall into temptation and a snare and many foolish and harmful desires which plunge men into ruin and destruction. For the love of money is a root of all sorts of evil, and some by longing for it have wandered away from the faith, and pierced themselves with many a pang.

A man of God must flee the evils associated with the love of money: various temptations, snares, harmful desires which lead to destruction, apostasy, and sorrow. Greed is the enemy. It will destroy the man of God, so he must run from it.

Love of money and material possessions is a characteristic sin of false teachers. From Balaam, that greedy prophet for hire (Deut. 23:4; 2 Pet. 2:15), to Judas, who betrayed our Lord for thirty pieces of silver (Matt. 27:3); from the false prophets characterized by Isaiah as greedy dogs (Is. 56:11) to the covetous prophets of Jeremiah's day (Jer. 6:13; 8:10) and the prophets who prophesied for money, of whom Micah speaks (Mic. 3:11); from those slaves of their own appetites who deceived the Romans (Rom. 16:18) and the empty talkers and deceivers of Crete, who upset whole families for the sake of sordid gain (Titus 1:11), all the way to the money-hungry televangelists and prosperity gospel preachers of our own day, false teachers have been characterized by greed.

But that is not true of a man of God. A man of God is not like those who, in Paul's words, were "peddling the word of God" (2 Cor. 2:17). He is not a spiritual con artist. He has to proclaim God's message, not what he thinks will sell. He is in the business of piercing men's hearts with God's truth, not tickling their ears. He does nothing for personal gain.

This is precisely why a pastor, overseer, or elder must be "free from the love of money" (1 Tim. 3:3). This virtue guards against two real dangers: first, the temptation to pervert the ministry by using God's Word to make oneself rich, and second, by contrast, the danger of neglecting the ministry in order to become rich through outside enterprises.

Paul went out of his way to avoid being charged with greed in his ministry. He told the Ephesian elders,

> "I have coveted no one's silver or gold or clothes. You yourselves know that these hands ministered to my own needs and to the men who were with me. In everything I showed you that by working hard in this manner you must help the weak and remember the words of the Lord Jesus, that He Himself said, 'It is more blessed to give than to receive.'" (Acts 20:33–35)

Paul was so sensitive about being accused of preaching for profit that, although he had every right to be supported financially in his ministry (1 Cor. 9:3–15), he waived that right so the gospel would not be hindered (1 Cor. 9:12). To the Thessalonians he wrote, "For you recall, brethren, our labor and hardship, how working night and day so as not to be a burden to any of you, we proclaimed to you the gospel of God" (1 Thess. 2:9). He defended the right of every preacher to be paid by those who received his ministry (see Gal. 6:6) but forbade the sin of greed and discontent (1 Tim. 6:6–8).

A man may call himself a preacher, but if he is in the ministry for the money, he is not a man of God. He has prostituted the call of God for personal gain. Our Lord warned, "You cannot serve God and mammon" (Matt. 6:24). A man of God should never put a price on his ministry, never charge an appearance fee for proclaiming the Word. He should be content with the support that the Lord provides through the giving of His people. Anyone who puts a price on his ministry devalues it.

A Man of God Is Marked by What He Follows After

A man of God is known not only by what he runs from, but also by what he runs toward. Behind are the sins which could destroy him; ahead lie the virtues that make his ministry powerful. As long as we live on this earth, the man of God can never stop running. If he stops fleeing evil, it will catch him; and if he stops pursuing righteousness, it will elude him. His entire life and ministry is one of flight from what is wrong and pursuit of what is right. The Greek verb translated "pursue" διώκω [diōkō]) is another present imperative, indicating the continuous nature of his pursuit.

In the second part of 1 Timothy 6:11, Paul listed six virtues to be pursued by every man of God: righteousness, godliness, faith, love, perseverance, and gentleness. The first two are overarching general principles, while the last four are more specific.

Righteousness

The first of the general principles, "righteousness" δικαιοσύνη [dikaiosynē]), refers to right behavior toward both God and man. The reference here is not to imputed righteousness received at salvation but to the practical righteousness to be exhibited in our lives.

Since the practice of righteousness is a mark of God's people, obviously it must be modeled by the man of God who is an example to all believers. In Psalm 15:1 David asked, "O LORD, who may abide in Thy tent? / Who may dwell on Thy holy hill?" In the next verse he gave the answer: "He who walks with integrity, and works righteousness."

Throughout the book of Proverbs, God's redeemed people are called "the righteous" (see 11:9, 10; 12:5; 18:10; 21:18). Those whom the Lord loves are those who pursue righteousness (15:9). Isaiah referred to the faithful remnant of Israel as "you who pursue righteousness" (Is. 51:1).

Righteousness as the mark of a true believer is also the lesson of the New Testament. In the Sermon on the Mount, Jesus described true believers as "those who hunger and thirst for righteousness" (Matt. 5:6), and He warned His hearers that "unless your righteousness surpasses that of the scribes and Pharisees, you shall not enter the kingdom of heaven" (Matt. 5:20). First John 3:10 sums it up: "By this the children of God and the children of the devil are obvious: anyone who does not practice righteousness is not of God."

If righteousness is the mark of a true Christian, how much more must it characterize the man of God! He must be like Timothy, whom Paul exhorted, "In speech, conduct, love, faith and purity, show yourself an example of those who believe" (1 Tim. 4:12). The psalmist said it specifically: "He who walks in a blameless way is the one who will minister to me" (Ps. 101:6). The man of God does no less.

Seventeenth-century England knew no greater model of a godly, righteous pastor than Puritan Richard Baxter. In his masterful work *The Reformed Pastor* (which should be read by every pastor), he exhorted his fellow ministers to

Take heed to yourselves, lest your example contradict your doctrine, and lest you lay such stumbling-blocks before the blind, as may be the occasion of their ruin; lest you unsay with your lives, what you say with your tongues; and be the greatest hinderers of the success of your own labours. . . . It will much more hinder your work, if you contradict yourselves, and if your actions give your tongue the lie, and if you build up an hour or two with your mouths, and all the week after pull down with your hands! This is the way to make men think that the Word of God is but an idle tale, and to make preaching seem no better than prating. He that means as he speaks, will surely do as he speaks. One proud, surly, lordly word, one needless contention, one covetous action, may cut the throat of many a sermon, and blast the fruit of all you have been doing. . . .

Certainly, brethren, we have very great cause to take heed what we do, as well as what we say: if we will be the servants of Christ indeed, we must not be tongue servants only, but must serve him with our deeds, and be "doers of the work, that we may be blessed in our deed." As our people must be "doers of the word, and not hearers only"; so we must be doers and not speakers only, lest we "deceive our own selves. . . ." We must study as hard how to live well, as how to preach well.[2]

How tragic when a pastor's life undercuts his message. The best and most powerful expository sermons will be of no effect if the preacher's life lacks righteousness. The man of God must live a life of obedience to God's Word. He, of all people, must practice what he preaches, or no one else will. The Lord allows only a righteous man of God legitimately to preach the message of God's righteousness in Christ. Paul's fear was that he might fall to sin and be disqualified from preaching (1 Cor. 9:27). The man of God must be morally above reproach (1 Tim. 3:2; Titus 1:6).

Godliness

"Godliness" ($\epsilon \grave{\upsilon} \sigma \acute{\epsilon} \beta \epsilon \iota \alpha$ [eusebeia]) is closely connected with righteousness. Righteousness may speak of outward conduct, godliness of the inward attitude. Godliness is the spirit of holiness, reverence, and piety that directs righteous behavior. Right behavior flows from a right attitude; correct conduct flows from proper motive. The basic meaning of eusebeia is reverence for God. The man characterized by godliness has a worshiping heart. He knows what it means to "live in the fear of the LORD always" (Prov. 23:17). He not only does right but also thinks right; he not only behaves properly but also is properly motivated. He is a man who serves God with reverence and awe (Heb. 12:28). Though he lives his life in the conscious presence of the holiness of God, paradoxically he may feel very unholy, like Isaiah (see Is. 6).

Righteousness and godliness are together the two indispensable qualities of a man of God, and yet they are his lifelong pursuit. They are central to his usefulness; they are at the core of his power. He possesses them and yet pursues them (see Phil. 3:7–16). An unsanctified preacher is useless to God and a danger to himself and people. Richard Baxter wrote,

> Many a tailor goes in rags, that maketh costly clothes for others; and many a cook scarcely licks his fingers, when he hath dressed for others the most costly dishes. . . . It is a fearful thing to be an unsanctified professor, but much more to be an unsanctified preacher.[3]

God takes a dim view of such men. Psalm 50:16–17 read, "But to the wicked God says, / 'What right have you to tell of My statutes, / And to take My covenant in your mouth? / For you hate discipline, / And you cast My words behind you.'" Jeremiah's words to unholy shepherds are frightening. "Woe to the shepherds . . . who are tending My people: 'You have scattered My flock and driven them away, and have not attended to them; behold, I am about to attend to you for the evil of your deeds'" (Jer. 23:1–2). He accused them of being "polluted" (Jer. 23:11).

A man of God must constantly guard his heart, his motives, his desires, and his conduct, knowing that nothing good dwells in his flesh (Rom. 7:18). He must "cleanse [himself] from all defilement of flesh and spirit, perfecting holiness in the fear of God" (2 Cor. 7:1). No less a man of God than the apostle Paul said, "I *am* the foremost of sinners" (1 Tim. 1:15) not "I *was* the foremost of sinners." He knew his sinful tendencies and his need to use all the means of grace to allow the Spirit to conquer them.

A friend once told the great nineteenth-century Scottish preacher Alexander Whyte that a visiting evangelist had said that another preacher, Dr. Wilson, was not a converted man.

Leaping from his chair, Whyte exclaimed, "The rascal! Dr. Wilson not a converted man!"

His friend then told him that the evangelist had also said that Whyte, himself, was not converted. Whyte sat down, buried his face in his hands, and was silent for a long time. Then he told his friend, "Leave me, friend, leave me! I must examine my heart!"[4]

Seldom has the need for a man of God to guard his heart been as forcefully stated as by Richard Baxter:

> Take heed to yourselves, lest you live in those sins which you preach against in others, and lest you be guilty of that which daily you condemn. Will you make it your work to magnify God, and, when you have done, dishonor him as much as others? Will you proclaim Christ's governing power, and yet condemn it, and rebel yourselves? Will you preach his laws, and wilfully break them? If sin be evil, why do you live in it? If it

be not, why do you dissuade men from it? If it be dangerous, how dare you venture on it? If it be not, why do you tell men so? If God's threatenings be true, why do you not fear them? If they be false, why do you needlessly trouble men with them, and put them into such frights without a cause? Do you 'know the judgment of God, that they who commit such things are worthy of death;' and yet will you do them? 'Thou that teachest another, teachest thou not thyself? Thou that sayest a man should not commit adultery,' or be drunk, or covetous, art thou such thyself? 'Thou that makest thy boast of the law, through breaking the law dishonourest thou God?' What! shall the same tongue speak evil that speakest against evil? Shall those lips censure, slander, and backbite your neighbour, that cry down these and the like things in others? Take heed to yourselves, lest you cry down sin, and yet do not overcome it; lest, while you seek to bring it down in others, you bow to it, and become its slaves yourselves: 'For of whom a man is overcome, of the same he is brought into bondage.' 'To whom ye yield yourselves servants to obey, his servants are ye to whom ye obey, whether of sin unto death, or of obedience unto righteousness.' Oh brethren! it is easier to chide at sin, than to overcome it.[5]

John Flavel, another Puritan, agreed with Baxter: "Brethren, it is easier to declaim against a thousand sins of others, than to mortify one sin in ourselves."[6]

A man of God must take great pains to rid himself of a dichotomy between the man he *seems to be* in the pulpit and the man he *is* out of it. Spurgeon wrote,

Let the minister take care that his personal character agrees in all respects with his ministry.

We have all heard the story of the man who preached so well and lived so badly, that when he was in the pulpit everybody said he ought never to come out again, and when he was out of it they all declared he never ought to enter it again. From the imitation of such a Janus may the Lord deliver us. May we never be priests of God at the altar, and sons of Belial outside the tabernacle door; but on the contrary, may we, as Nazianzen says of Basil, "thunder in our doctrine, and lightning in our conversation." We do not trust those persons who have two faces, nor will men believe in those whose verbal and practical testimonies are contradictory. . . . True ministers are always ministers.[7]

Only those who practice righteousness and godliness are fit for the Master's service. In 2 Timothy 2:21, Paul wrote to Timothy, "Therefore, if a man cleanses himself from these things, he will be a vessel for honor, sanctified, useful to the Master, prepared for every good work." The noble Scottish man of God Robert Murray McCheyne echoed Paul's sentiments when he spoke the following words of advice to a young pastor being ordained:

> Do not forget the culture of the inner man—I mean of the heart. How diligently the cavalry officer keeps his sabre clean and sharp; every stain he rubs off with the greatest care. Remember you are God's sword, His instrument—I trust a chosen vessel unto Him to bear His name. In great measure, according to the purity and perfections of the instrument, will be the success. It is not great talents God blesses so much as great likeness to Jesus. A holy minister is an awful weapon in the hand of God.[8]

Pursuing righteousness and godliness requires self-denial. Paul, in 1 Corinthians 9:27, not only articulated his fear of disqualification, but his defense against it: "I buffet my body and make it my slave, lest possibly, after I have preached to others, I myself should be disqualified." He feared that after preaching to others, he might be ($\dot{\alpha}\delta\acute{o}\kappa\iota\mu o\varsigma$ [adokimos])—tested and found unqualified for service. To avoid that, Paul practiced self-discipline, especially of his bodily appetites. Everyone is quite familiar with the tragedy of those who have been disqualified from the ministry because of failure to exercise this discipline.

A man of God obviously will lean on the Lord for his strength and, in so doing, become a man of prayer. John Owen warned, "A minister may fill his pews, his communion roll, the mouths of the public, but what that minister is on his knees in secret before God Almighty, that he is and no more."[9] Spurgeon added, "If there be any man under heaven, who is compelled to carry out the precept—'Pray without ceasing,' surely it is the Christian minister. . . . The fact is, the secret of all ministerial success lies in prevalence at the mercy-seat."[10] The leaders of the early church were men who devoted themselves to prayer (Acts 6:4).

The man of God must also avoid the danger of what Spurgeon called "ministerialism—the tendency to read our Bibles as ministers, to pray as ministers, to get into doing the whole of our religion as not ourselves personally, but only relatively, concerned in it."[11] In his book *The Christian Ministry*, Charles Bridges warned against this danger:

> For if we should study the Bible more as Ministers than as Christians— more to find matter for the instruction of our people, than food for the nourishment of our own souls, we neglect then to place ourselves at the feet of our Divine Teacher, our communion with Him is cut off, and we become mere formalists in our sacred profession. . . . We cannot live by feeding others; or heal ourselves by the mere employment of healing our people; and therefore by this course of official service, our familiarity with the awful realities of death and eternity may be rather like that of the grave-digger, the physician, and the soldier, than the man of God,

viewing eternity with deep seriousness and concern and bringing to his people the profitable fruit of his contemplations. It has well been remarked—that, 'when once a man begins to view religion not as of personal, but merely of professional importance, he has an obstacle in his course, with which a private Christian is unacquainted.' It is indeed difficult to determine, whether our familiar intercourse with the things of God is more our temptation or our advantage.[12]

We must never study a passage to find a sermon. We must study a passage to see completely the truth the Lord is teaching in it, and prepare the sermon out of the overflow of that comprehensive grasp and personal application of the passage. Second Timothy 3:16–17 indicates that the Scripture is first to teach, reprove, correct, and train the man of God into righteous maturity, equipping him for every good deed. Then through him it does the same for the people who hear him.

Two Internal Virtues

The specific virtues Paul mentions in 1 Timothy 6:11 correspond to the two general virtues of righteousness and godliness. Two are internal and two are external.

"Faith" ($\pi\iota\sigma\tau\iota\varsigma$ [pistis]), means confident trust in God for everything, an absolute loyalty to the Lord. It is unwavering confidence in God's power, plan, provision, and promise. The man of God lives by faith. He trusts in the sovereign God to keep His word, to meet all his needs, and provide the resources he needs to pursue his ministry. He can say with Paul,

> I have learned to be content in whatever circumstances I am. I know how to get along with humble means, and I also know how to live in prosperity; in any and every circumstance I have learned the secret of being filled and going hungry, both of having abundance and suffering need. I can do all things through Him who strengthens me (Phil. 4:11–13)

because "my God shall supply all your needs according to His riches in glory in Christ Jesus" (Phil. 4:19).

To live a life of faith is to live a life free of frustration, free from a compulsion to force things to happen or to manipulate people. It is to live in a state of relaxed desperation. The man of God is desperate, because of the tremendous weight of responsibility his ministry entails, yet he is relaxed because of his confidence in the sovereignty of God.

The frenzied activities, programs, plans, and gimmicks indulged in by some pastors are evidence of their lack of faith in God's sovereignty. By trying to build their churches themselves, they find themselves in competition with the One who alone can build His church (Matt. 16:18). The man of God must demonstrate faith in God for his personal sanctification and ministry, being confident that if he follows the biblically prescribed pattern of prayer and ministry of the Word (see Acts 6:4), his ministry will glorify God and be fruitful.

"Love" (ἀγάπη [agapē]) refers to a volitional love, not an emotional feeling. It is a love that is unrestricted, unrestrained, and unconditional. It should be interpreted in this passage in its broadest sense. It means love to everybody—love to God, men, believers, and non-believers. As our Lord said in Matthew 22:37–39, " 'You shall love the Lord your God with all your heart, and with all your soul, and with all your mind.' This is the great and foremost commandment. The second is like it, 'You shall love your neighbor as yourself.' "

The man of God is especially a lover of God. He longs for God, like the psalmist who wrote, "As the deer pants for the water brooks, / So my soul pants for Thee, O God. / My soul thirsts for God, for the living God; / When shall I come and appear before God?" (Ps. 42:1, 2). From the indwelling Holy Spirit comes love for God welling up within a believer (Rom. 5:5). He understands the cry of Paul's heart, "O, that I may know Him" (see Phil. 3:10). His desire is to be one of the spiritual fathers of whom John wrote, "You know Him who has been from the beginning" (1 John 2:13). Because he loves God, he loves the people God loves (see 1 John 5:1, 2).

As he loves God enough to turn from sin, he also loves others enough to confront their sin. True love "does not rejoice in unrighteousness, but rejoices with the truth" (1 Cor. 13:6). He understands the principle that "Better is open rebuke / Than love that is concealed. Faithful are the wounds of a friend" (Prov. 27:5, 6). He loves the world of the unredeemed enough to feel compulsion to preach the truth to them (2 Cor. 5:11–14, 20).

Two External Virtues

"Perseverance" (ὑπομονή [hupomonē]) translates a word that means literally "to remain under." It is not passive resignation, but victorious, triumphant endurance, an unswerving loyalty to the Lord in the midst of trials. Paul expressed such loyalty in Acts 20:22–24:

> And now, behold, bound in spirit, I am on my way to Jerusalem, not knowing what will happen to me there, except that the Holy Spirit solemnly testifies to me in every city, saying that bonds and afflictions await me. But I do not consider my life of any account as dear to myself, in order that I may finish my course, and the ministry which I received from the Lord Jesus, to testify solemnly of the gospel of the grace of God.

Although the man of God may undergo severe trials, severe anguish, and severe difficulty, he neither wavers nor compromises. He continually trusts

God, no matter what the circumstances. As Peter put it, "Therefore, let those also who suffer according to the will of God entrust their souls to a faithful Creator in doing what is right" (1 Pet. 4:19). This is the endurance of the martyr willing to die before betraying his Lord, of the shepherd prepared to lay down his life for his flock, just as his Master did. It characterizes the person who, under the worst circumstances, refuses to magnify his own rights and needs.

Perseverance is an essential quality of a man of God because he can expect more trials than the average Christian. Richard Baxter warned his fellow pastors to

> take heed to yourselves, because the tempter will more ply you with his temptations than other men. If you will be the leaders against the prince of darkness, he will spare you no further than God restraineth him. He beareth the greatest malice to those that are engaged to do him the greatest mischief. . . . Take heed, therefore, brethren, for the enemy hath a special eye upon you. You shall have his most subtle insinuations, and incessant solicitations, and violent assaults.[13]

Paul endured constant trials, as a reading of 2 Corinthians 11:23–28 indicates. And apparently only one of the apostles died of old age.

"Gentleness" ($\pi\rho\alpha\ddot{\upsilon}\pi\acute{\alpha}\theta\iota\alpha$ [praupathia]) is the second external virtue. It can also be translated "meekness" or "humility." The man of God has nothing to boast about. With Paul he recognizes that though he labors, it is God's power working through him to bring effectiveness in ministry (see Col. 1:29). He remembers the words of the Lord in Luke 17:10: "When you do all the things which are commanded you, say, 'We are unworthy slaves; we have done only that which we ought to have done.'" No place for ugly pride exists in Christian ministry. The man of God has the mind of Christ, which is the mind of humility (Phil. 2:18).

A true man of God seeks to exalt his Master, not himself. Righteousness, godliness, faith, love, perseverance, and gentleness are the goal of a man of God. They are his lifelong objectives. If those virtues are not a preacher's constant aim, he is not a man of God, but a self-appointed preacher.

A MAN OF GOD IS KNOWN BY WHAT HE FIGHTS FOR

In 1 Timothy 6:12, Paul commanded Timothy to "fight the good fight of faith; take hold of the eternal life to which you were called, and you made the good confession in the presence of many witnesses." The man of God is a fighter. He is a polemicist, a contender, a battler, a soldier. He must understand that ministry is war and he is fighting on the side of truth against error. To perceive ministry as anything less is to lose. He battles the world, he battles the flesh, and he battles the devil and his kingdom of darkness. He battles sin, heresy, apathy, and lethargy in the church.

That the ministry is warfare was brought home forcefully to me when, as a young pastor, I confronted a demon-possessed woman. She had a supernatural strength, overturning office furniture and kicking my shins until they bled. In a voice not her own she said to me, "Not him . . . not him . . . get him out." I realized then that those demons knew a war was in progress, and they also knew which side I was on.

Paul very clearly saw the ministry as a battle. In 2 Timothy 2:3, 4 he told Timothy, "Suffer hardship with me, as a good soldier of Christ Jesus. No soldier in active service entangles himself in the affairs of everyday life, so that he may please the one who enlisted him as a soldier." He chose to minister in Ephesus despite the many adversaries he encountered there (1 Cor. 16:8, 9). And at the end of his life he was able to exclaim triumphantly, "I have fought the good fight" (2 Tim. 4:7).

Sadly, many pastors are so entangled in the affairs of everyday life that they do not realize fully the intensity of the battle. Others are fighting the wrong battle. Martin Luther once said,

> If I profess with the loudest voice and clearest exposition every portion of the truth of God except precisely that little point which the world and the devil are at that moment attacking, I am not confessing Christ, however boldly I may be professing Christ. Where the battle rages, there the loyalty of the soldier is proved, and to be steady on all the battlefield besides, is mere flight and disgrace if he flinches at that point.[14]

Still others go AWOL from the battle, fleeing to another church or ministry at the first sign of trouble. A young man once said to me, "I'm going into the pastorate, but I'm being careful about the church I accept. I want one that has no problems." I replied that the only churches I knew of that had no problems were those that had no people! We must accept the fact that we are in a battle. Paul's words in 2 Timothy 3:12, "all who desire to live godly in Christ Jesus will be persecuted," are doubly true of pastors, since they are the special targets of the enemy. The man of God must be willing to follow his Master even to death (Luke 9:23, 24).

Both occurrences of the word "fight" in 1 Timothy 6:12 are from the same root word, from which the English word *agony* is derived. It is used in military contexts and of athletic events, including wrestling and boxing. It speaks of the concentration, effort, and discipline required to win a contest. In Paul's day, boxing was a far more serious affair than it is today. In contrast to the well-padded boxing gloves used by modern boxers, boxers in the Greek and Roman games wore gloves lined with lead and iron. And the loser of the match had his eyes put out. Thus, Paul's imagery of the ministry as a fight had very serious undertones. Like the verbs in 1 Timothy 6:11, ἀγωνίζομαι (*agōnízomai*) is a present imperative, indicating the continuous nature of our struggle. "Good" (καλός [*kalos*]) is best translated "excellent" or "noble." Paul told Timothy (and us) to experience the role of a man of God with a noble commitment to the contest for the truth.

The man of God is thrilled to be a soldier. It is not that he goes out of his way to antagonize people and make enemies, but he is willing to fight the battle for truth. It is greatly disturbing to live in a time when battling for truth is looked upon as divisive and unloving. Far too many in the church today are willing to compromise theologically to avoid conflict, forgetting Jude's exhortation to "contend earnestly for the faith" (Jude 3).

As in Jude 3, the Greek text of 1 Timothy 6:12 has the definite article before "faith." Paul said, "Fight for *the* faith," that is, the contents of the Word of God, the sum total of Christian doctrine. That is the highest cause in the world, and we must fight for it without compromise.

In the second part of verse 12, Paul offered encouragement for the fight: "Take hold of the eternal life to which you were called, and you made the good confession in the presence of many witnesses." What did Paul mean by that? He did not tell Timothy to get saved, because he was already saved. What he said was, in effect, Get a grip on eternal life. Live in the light of eternity. "Set your mind on the things above, not on the things that are on earth" (Col. 3:2), because "our citizenship is in heaven" (Phil. 3:20). As the old hymn put it, the man of God is to live "with eternity's values in view." If he does that, he will not mind making sacrifices in this life. The man of God has an eternal perspective; he is not in the ministry merely for what he can gain in this life. As Jim Elliot, missionary and martyr to the Auca Indians, wrote, "He is no fool who gives what he cannot keep to gain what he cannot lose."[15] Living and ministering in the light of eternity keep the focus of the man of God on the importance of the battle.

Paul further encouraged Timothy by reminding him that he was "called," a reference to God's effectual call to salvation. In response to that call, Timothy had publicly confessed Jesus as Lord. Paul may have referred to the occasion of Timothy's baptism or ordination, but more likely to every confession Timothy had made, beginning with his conversion.

The man of God rises above the struggles for perishable, useless things. He fights for what is eternal—the truth of God. It is only by divorcing himself from the things of this world and living in light of eternity that he can hope to succeed.

A MAN OF GOD IS KNOWN BY WHAT HE IS FAITHFUL TO

In 1 Timothy 6:13–14, Paul stressed the importance of being faithful: "I charge you in the presence of God, who gives life to all things, and of

Christ Jesus, who testified the good confession before Pontius Pilate, that you keep the commandment without stain or reproach until the appearing of our Lord Jesus Christ."

The main emphasis of Paul's exhortation is upon the phrase "the commandment" in verse 14. Some argue that it is the gospel, others say it is the contents of this epistle, and still others say it is the entire new covenant. I believe it is best interpreted in the broadest sense of the complete, revealed Word of God. Being nourished in the Word, the man of God is first and foremost a guardian of the treasure of the truth he is to proclaim. He must preserve it from any error or misrepresentation. Paul warned Timothy to guard it and handle it accurately (1 Tim. 4:6, 7; 6:2–4; 6:20; 2 Tim. 1:13; 2:15) as well as to work hard at preaching and teaching it (1 Tim. 5:17; 2 Tim. 4:2). Paul commanded Timothy to keep or guard the Word. How is this done? It is done not only by preaching the Word, but by living it. As noted earlier in this discussion, nothing is so tragic as a pastor who undercuts his message with his poor behavior. God forbid that our lives should ever bring a stain or reproach on the Word.

To provide further motivation for Timothy to be faithful, Paul reminded him that he ministered in the sight of God the Father and Jesus Christ (1 Tim. 6:13). The Father is the one who "gives life to all things," or, in other words, who raises the dead. That is a powerful motivation for a man of God. Even if faithfulness costs him his life, the God who raises the dead is watching over him.

Not only is the Father watching over His men, but they also have the example of the Lord Jesus "who testified the good confession before Pontius Pilate." Christ held fast His confession, even in the face of death. He is the perfect illustration of one who courageously remained faithful to the Word, no matter what the cost. Jesus told Pilate the truth about who He was, even though it cost Him His life. The man of God can do no less.

A SOBERING RESPONSIBILITY

There is no greater privilege than to be a man of God and preach His Word. But along with that privilege comes a fearful responsibility. James warned that teachers face a stricter judgment (James 3:1). Throughout Scripture are examples of that. For instance, Moses and Aaron were denied entrance into the Promised Land because of one act of disobedience. A most graphic example occurs in 1 Kings 13. Verse 1 introduces an unnamed man of God from Judah, who came north to deliver a prophecy to Jeroboam, the king of Israel. God had strictly charged him not to eat bread or drink water while he was there. But when another prophet deceived him, he disobeyed God and ate and drank with him (1 Kin. 13:19). God's reaction was swift:

> Now it came about, as they were sitting down at the table, that the word of the LORD came to the prophet who had brought him back; and he cried to the man of God who came from Judah, saying, "Thus says the LORD, 'Because you have disobeyed the command of the LORD, and have not observed the commandment which the LORD your God commanded you, but have returned and eaten bread and drunk water in the place of which He said to you, "Eat no bread and drink no water"; your body shall not come to the grave of your fathers.'" (1 Kin. 13:20–22)

Shortly after leaving, he was attacked and killed by a lion (1 Kin. 13:24).

Being a man of God includes a tremendous responsibility. May God help each of us by His grace to remain faithful to Him and to be that true man of God who is blessed and not punished.

6

The Spirit of God and Expository Preaching

John MacArthur

It is impossible to properly understand God's objective revelation in Scripture apart from the illuminating work of the Holy Spirit. Illumination is not equated with either revelation or inspiration. It communicates no new divine truth, but rather enables us to *comprehend* God's truth in the final and complete revelation of it in Scripture. No clear understanding of Scripture leading to powerful preaching is possible without the Spirit's work of illumination.

Charles Haddon Spurgeon, the noblest of all nineteenth-century preachers, gave the following warning to students at his Pastor's College:

> If there is to be a Divine result from God's Word, the Holy Ghost must go forth with it. As surely as God went before the children of Israel when He divided the Red Sea, as surely as He led them through the wilderness by the pillar of cloud and fire, so surely must the Lord's powerful presence go with His Word if there is to be any blessing from it.[1]

Spurgeon's warning is just as compelling today as when he first gave it. Powerful preaching is not manipulative preaching designed to play on the emotions. It is not shallow, devotionally oriented "sermonettes for Christianettes." It is neither benign storytelling, sociological commentary on current events, nor pop psychology designed to make everyone feel good. Powerful preaching occurs only when a Spirit-illumined man of God expounds clearly and compellingly God's Spirit-inspired revelation in Scripture to a Spirit-illumined congregation.

ILLUMINATION[2]

Illumination is the work of the Holy Spirit that opens one's spiritual eyes to comprehend the meaning of the Word of God. It involves the preacher of Scripture and his audience. God's objective and historically past revelation in Scripture cannot be understood accurately apart from the present, personal, and subjective work of the Holy Spirit. "Illumination," which applies only to believers,[3] is simply the continued work of the Spirit by which He causes enlightened understanding of doctrine and how it should be applied to life. Believers walking in disobedience cannot understand the spiritual truths of Scripture any better than unbelievers. That is precisely why Peter exhorted those who would grow in the Word first to "[put] aside all malice and all guile and hypocrisy and envy and all slander" (1 Pet. 2:1, 2). James wrote, "Therefore putting aside all filthiness and all that remains of wickedness, in humility receive the word implanted" (James 1:21).

Though the Bible has no specific technical term for illumination, it nevertheless has much to say about it. Psalm 119 is essentially the commitment of a believer to the authority of the Word interspersed with cries for illumination. Here are examples of the pleas for illumination: "Open my eyes, that I may behold / Wonderful things from Thy law" (Ps. 119:18); "Teach me, O LORD, the way of Thy statutes, / And I shall observe it to the end. / Give me understanding, that I may observe Thy Law, / And keep it with all my heart" (Ps. 119:33–34).[4]

In Luke 24:45, the disciples grasped the meaning of the Old Testament only after Jesus "opened their minds to understand the Scriptures." For believers today it is the Spirit of Christ who provides comparable understanding.

In Ephesians 1:17, 18, Paul prayed "that the God of our Lord Jesus Christ, the Father of glory, may give to you a spirit of wisdom and of revelation in the knowledge of Him. I pray that the eyes of your heart may be enlightened, so that you may know what is the hope of His calling, what are the riches of the glory of His inheritance in the saints."

Paul recognized the need for illumination if Christians were to progress in sanctification, and often prayed for them to have it (see Phil. 1:9–11 and Col. 1:9–11). The indwelling Holy Spirit provides the answer to that prayer as the apostle John explained in 1 John 2:20, 27: "But you have an anointing from the Holy One, and you all know. . . . And as for you, the anointing which you received from Him abides in you, and you have no need for anyone to teach you; but as His anointing teaches you about all things, and is true and is not a lie, and just as it has taught you, you abide in Him."

ILLUMINATION DISTINGUISHED FROM REVELATION AND INSPIRATION

Illumination is best defined by distinguishing it from two related theological terms: revelation and inspiration.

"Revelation" refers to the act by which God makes known what is otherwise unknowable. Theologians sometimes call it "special revelation." "Natural revelation," that which may be observed in nature and experience regarding the existence and power of God (Rom. 1:20), is not specific or full enough to bring redemption, so God gave clear, unmistakable "special revelation" in Scripture. That gift was a free act motivated by love and grace through which God disclosed the fullness of His truth to man. The Holy Spirit was the agent of that revelation. In 1 Corinthians 2:10, Paul affirmed that "God revealed [His Word] through the Spirit; for the Spirit searches all things, even the depths of God." The Holy Spirit alone is competent to reveal God's truth, for only He can search the "depths" of God. Since He Himself is God, He is omniscient and knows the mind of God perfectly (see Rom. 8:26).

Were it not for God's sovereign choice to reveal Himself, we could not know enough of His truth to be saved. Since we live in the natural world, locked into the space-time box, we cannot break out of that box into the supernatural world. The only knowledge we have of that realm is what God adds to our confining situation. We can know nothing of His redemptive plan or His will for our lives except by revelation.

"Inspiration" is the vehicle by which God's special revelation came to man. It was the process by which "men moved by the Holy Spirit spoke from God" (2 Pet. 1:21). It was the means by which God's revelation was inscripturated.

Inspiration is *verbal*. The very words of Scripture are inspired, not merely the thoughts or concepts of the writers. In 1 Corinthians 2:12 and 13, Paul wrote,

> Now we have received, not the spirit of the world, but the Spirit who is from God, that we might know the things freely given to us by God, which things we also speak, not in words taught by human wisdom, but in those taught by the Spirit, combining spiritual thoughts with spiritual words.

"We" in this passage does not include all Christians, but is limited to inspired speakers and writers. Paul and the other writers of Scripture received God's revelation. They were the instruments God used to transmit this revelation to man. In the next verse, Paul added a description of how the Spirit illumines all Christians to receive that inspired revelation.

Inspiration is also *plenary*. All the Bible is inspired, not merely the parts of it dealing with matters of faith and practice. Paul emphatically stated in 2 Timothy 3:16 that "*all* Scripture is inspired by God" (emphasis added). *Inspired* translates the Greek word *theopneustos,* which literally means "God-breathed." Scripture is not a human product into which God breathed spiritual life. On the contrary, it originated by being breathed out by God. And since it is ridiculous to charge the God of truth with inspiring error, the Bible's plenary inspiration guarantees its inerrancy.

Contrary to the teaching of many, neither special revelation nor inspiration are occurring today. The Bible contains God's final and complete written revelation to man (see Jude 3 and Rev. 22:18, 19). Currently, the Holy Spirit instructs and guides a believer, not by revealing newly inspired data, but by bringing illumination to God's already revealed Word.

To argue that God must, through the Spirit, continue giving oral or written revelation today is to treat lightly the Spirit's revelation in the Scripture and to deny the sufficiency of God's Word. It is, in fact, a total disregard of the value of illumination by an attempted substitution of alleged revelation. These three ministries of the Spirit must not be confused. Biblical writers received *revelation* when God *inspired* Scripture. We receive *illumination* when the Spirit makes the words of Scripture live for us. Confusing illumination with revelation or inspiration will inevitably lead to error. Illumination is not the reception of new revelations from the Spirit. Rather it is the Spirit's application of the truths of God's complete revelation in Scripture to spiritual life.

Despite the fact that illumination is always connected to the revealed Word, throughout church history some people have claimed illumination apart from the Scripture. Calvin described these people as "giddy men" who were "not so much under the influence of error as madness."[5] He went on to chide them for not realizing that the writers of Scripture, who received revelation, had the highest regard for parts of the Word written before their time.[6] He strongly warned,

> What an infatuation of the devil, therefore, to fancy that Scripture, which conducts the sons of God to the final goal, is of transient and temporary use? Again, I should like those people to tell me whether they have imbibed any other Spirit than that which Christ promised to his disciples. . . . But what kind of Spirit did our Saviour promise to send? One who should not speak of himself (John xvi. 13), but suggest and instil the truths which he himself had delivered through the word. Hence the office of the Spirit promised to us, is not to form new and unheard-of revelations, or to coin a new form of doctrine, by which we may be led away from the received doctrine of the gospel, but to seal on our minds the very doctrine which the gospel recommends.[7]

Luther took a dim view of those who claimed extrabiblical illumination. He often referred to them as "swarmers," likening them to bees swarming around with no place to land. "The swarmers, he said, were aimlessly flying around in the cloudland of their own dreams and refused to base their faith on the Bible."[8]

While Luther was in exile at the Wartburg Castle, Andreas Carlstadt, a friend and fellow reformer at Wittenberg, nearly wrecked Luther's work there by initiating radical social and religious reforms based on an alleged inner leading of the Spirit and not on Scripture. Only Luther's timely return from exile and courageous action saved the situation.

OTHER MISCONCEPTIONS ABOUT ILLUMINATION

Certain further misconceptions about illumination must be recognized and avoided. First, *illumination does not mean that everything about God can be known and understood.* Deuteronomy 29:29 says, "The secret things belong to the LORD our God, but the things revealed belong to us." Paul, in his great doxology at the end of Romans 11, exclaimed, "Oh, the depth of the riches both of the wisdom and knowledge of God! How unsearchable are His judgments and unfathomable His ways!" (Deut 29:33). God has given a true, but not an exhaustive revelation of Himself. For example, illumination does not mean all the apparent paradoxes of Scripture can be resolved. Man in his finiteness does not have all the answers.

Second, *illumination does not eliminate the need for human teachers.* Some have wrongly understood 1 John 2:27 to teach such. This misinterpretation does violence to the intent of that text and contradicts Ephesians 4:11–13, which states that God uses the teaching of gifted men to bring the church to maturity. The Holy Spirit uses leaders to assist the church in understanding the riches of Scripture. John actually said in 1 John 2:27 that the resident Holy Spirit teaches the believer to distinguish the truth of the gospel from heresy so that he is not deceived by false teachers.

Third, *illumination does not extend beyond God's Word.* Illumination does not mean a Christian will have better insights as a businessman or a lawyer than an unbeliever would have. It does not guarantee that Christians will sail through school without studying because the Holy Spirit helps them understand biology and history. Its scope is limited to God's Word.

Fourth, *illumination does not eliminate the need for diligent Bible study.* "The illumination of the Spirit is no prayer-meeting substitute for the hard work of learning Hebrew and Greek and using the standard lexicons, commentaries, and other research materials."[9] On one hand, Paul encouraged Timothy that "the Lord will give you understanding in everything" (2 Tim. 2:7). He then exhorted Timothy to "Be diligent to present yourself approved to God as a workman who does not need to be ashamed, handling accurately the word of truth" (2 Tim. 2:15).

This should be noted especially by preachers. "The biblical interpreter cannot wait for lightning bolts to hit him. He must study, read, and struggle to be in a position to receive the Spirit's illumination. It is not enough to open one's mouth and expect God to fill it at 11:00 o'clock on Sunday morning."[10] Paul taught that elders who worked hard at preaching and teaching were worthy of double honor (1 Tim. 5:17). Far too many preachers enter the pulpit without adequate preparation to rightly divide the Word. They have good reason to be ashamed.[11]

The same tension between the divine and human elements in inspiration is also present in illumination. The Holy Spirit's inspiration did not preclude effort on the part of the writers. Luke, for example, even though he received divine revelation to write, "investigated everything carefully from the beginning" (Luke 1:3) before writing his Gospel. If human exertion was a component in inspiration, how much more is the need for diligent study in conjunction with illumination.

Finally, *illumination does not guarantee doctrinal unity*. People often ask why so many doctrinal differences exist between Spirit-illumined men. Three main answers respond to that question. First, some passages are very difficult to interpret and data are not conclusive enough for a dogmatic conclusion that all will accept.

Apart from the difficult texts, another reason for disagreement is the practice of interpreting a text in light of theological presuppositions rather than letting it speak for itself. For many, doctrinal and ecclesiastical traditions tend to control exegesis. But theology must be based on exegesis, rather than exegesis on theology.

The third reason for doctrinal differences is a lack of comprehensive work in Bible study. The more diligent and careful Bible study is, the less likely men are to disagree with other diligent and careful students of the Word. And where disagreement remains, the greater likelihood is that a difference of opinion can be resolved when differing parties have studied an issue thoroughly.

THE NECESSITY OF ILLUMINATION

Illumination, though often considered secondary to revelation and in-spiration, is equally important. Without revelation and inspiration, we would have no Bible. Without illumination, we can have no accurate understanding of the Bible. It would be of little use to have a special revelation from God that no one could understand. So illumination is the culmination of the revelatory process.

The necessity for illumination begins at the time of initial salvation. Unbelievers cannot properly understand Scripture because the gospel is veiled to them and they are blinded by Satan (2 Cor. 4:3, 4). That veil must be supernaturally lifted (2 Cor. 3:16). Since fallen man is dead to the things of God (Eph. 2:1), the Spirit must remove his limitation and impart an understanding of saving spiritual truth.

Commenting on the significance of this need, Woolley wrote,

> There is a difference of viewpoint between the Christian and the non-Christian, between the man who has been renewed by the Spirit of God and the man who has not. That difference in viewpoint has a vital bearing upon the question of the clarity of the Scriptures. The spiritual man has, through his regeneration, a basis for comprehension which the

natural man lacks. Given equal mental gifts and powers, therefore, the spiritual man has a key, as it were, which the other lacks to unlock the meaning of Biblical statements.[12]

The importance of illumination was included in the Reformers' teaching on *sola scriptura*. In *The Bondage of the Will,* Luther wrote,

> Nobody who has not the Spirit of God sees a jot of what is in the Scriptures. All men have their hearts darkened, so that, even when they can discuss and quote all that is in Scripture, they do not understand or really know any of it. . . . The Spirit is needed for the understanding of all Scripture and every part of Scripture.[13]

Calvin also advocated illumination as necessary for a proper understanding of the Scripture:

> The testimony of the Spirit is superior to reason. For as God alone can properly bear witness to his own words, so these words will not obtain full credit in the hearts of men, until they are sealed by the inward testimony of the Spirit. . . . For though [Scripture] in its own majesty has enough to command reverence, nevertheless, it then begins truly to touch us when it is sealed in our hearts by the Holy Spirit.[14]

The definitive passage on the necessity of illumination is 1 Corinthians 2:6–11. In that passage, the apostle Paul explained why illumination is essential.

The Corinthian Background

It is proverbial to say that the Corinthian church was riddled with problems. Paul devoted most of his first letter to correcting the practical and doctrinal errors that marred the church. The first issue was human philosophy (1 Corinthians 1—2). The Corinthians had become enamored with the pagan philosophies that dominated their day, viewing them as a necessary supplement to God's wisdom. In no uncertain terms Paul warned them of the incompatibility of human wisdom and divine wisdom. Man does not accept God's wisdom (1 Cor. 1:18), as God does not accept man's wisdom (1 Cor. 1:19–24). And of the two, God's wisdom is incomparably and infinitely superior (1 Cor. 1:25).

A situation comparable to the one at Corinth exists in the church today. Human philosophies have enamored and captured believers. Many uncritically accept evolution as a fact and try vainly to harmonize it with the first two chapters of Genesis. Psychology has made massive inroads into the church, redefining spiritual problems into nonbiblical categories, thereby convincing many that the Bible is insufficient to deal with those problems.[15] In every era, the church constantly has faced the challenge of guarding against the encroachment of human wisdom. Successful resistance to this encroachment comes only to those who have a thorough understanding of the Word of God. Those without that knowledge of Scripture fall prey to human wisdom's deceptions.

The Folly of Human Wisdom (1 Cor. 1:20)

"The folly of human wisdom" does not imply human inability to understand the natural world, nor does it mean that unbelievers are devoid of information and intelligence about physical things. Men can and do have wisdom in such fields as science, technology, medicine, and finance. In fact, Jesus said in Luke 16:8 that unbelievers are often wiser in financial matters than believers. In fact, they have enough power of observation and reason to be aware of the existence of a sovereign powerful God (Rom. 1:20).

What human wisdom fails to understand is the reality of the divine/spiritual dimension. Unbelievers can grasp, to a certain extent, the external clarity of Scripture, but they cannot see the inner reality of Scripture. That requires the Spirit's illumination. Human wisdom is useless, even harmful, when it addresses the moral character of man and his spiritual self. The truth is that our day is witnessing an aggressive effort to reclassify all man's problems from a moral model to a medical model: Sin is now sickness. Human wisdom is withdrawing more and more from theology and thus showing its utter lack of spiritual comprehension. And human wisdom is not redemptive. Its diagnosis is wrong and its cure is spiritually useless. It does not give true knowledge of God and cannot transform the soul.

Luther distinguished between internal and external clarity, a perspective explained by Ramm:

> To Luther there was an outer and an inner clarity of Scripture. By the usual laws or rules of language, a Christian could understand the Scripture as a written document. This is the external clarity of Scripture. Due to man's sinfulness he needs an inward assist so that he might grasp the spiritual Word of God as the Word of God. The Word of God is a spiritual entity and can only be understood in faith with the help of the Holy Spirit. This is the internal clarity of Scripture.[16]

Ramm further illustrated the point with two examples from Søren Kierkegaard, the Danish philosopher and father of modern existentialism:

> Kierkegaard poses the question how a lover reads a love letter from his lover when they happen to speak two different languages. The first thing the lover must do with the letter is to translate it. He gets out his dictionary of the foreign language—perhaps even a grammar—and goes

to work. He translates it word by word, line by line, paragraph by paragraph, until the entire translated letter is on the desk before him.

But doing all that hard work of translating that letter into his language is not to read the letter as a love letter. Now that he has the complete translation he relaxes, leans back in his chair, and reads the translated letter as a love letter.

So it is with Holy Scripture. We cannot avoid all the hard work of looking up Hebrew and Greek words, puzzling over constructions, consulting commentaries, and other such helps. But doing this careful academic job of translating and interpreting Scripture is not to read the Word of God as the Word of God. Unfortunately that is where the professor stops. But to read Scripture as the Word of God he must read it the second time. Now it is no longer an academic task but it is a case of letting God's Word get through to man's soul *as God's Word*. It is in the second reading of the letter that the Holy Spirit, the Hermes from heaven, enters into the process of understanding Holy Scripture.

Kierkegaard gives us a second illustration. A little boy is to be spanked by his father. While the father goes for the rod, the boy stuffs the bottom of his pants with several table napkins. When the father returns and administers the whipping the boy feels no pain as the napkins absorb the whack of the rod. The little boy represents the biblical scholars. They pad their britches with their lexicons, commentaries, and concordances. As a result the Scripture never reaches them as the Word of God. Having nullified its power by shielding themselves with their academic paraphernalia, they thus never hear the Scriptures as the Word of God. If they would unpack their books from their britches (which are necessary rightfully used, as illustrated in the story of the love letter) then the Scriptures could get through to them as the Word of God. Allowing Holy Scripture to get through to us as the Word of God is the special work of the Holy Spirit.[17]

Natural ability, intellect, acumen, education, insight, experience, and wisdom make no contribution to the transforming spiritual comprehension of divine truth in Scripture. Secular universities usually have courses on the Bible as literature or as a component in the study of comparative religions. To them, it is nothing more than religious literature, valued for its historic, cultural, prosaic, and poetic contribution. To God and those whom God's Spirit illumines, it contains the only true message of eternal life in Christ Jesus.

The True Wisdom (1 Cor. 2:6–9)

Even though unbelievers are prone to write off Christianity as foolish nonsense because it rejects human wisdom about spiritual matters, Paul insisted that it is the true wisdom. He wrote, "Yet we do speak wisdom among those who are mature" (1 Cor. 2:6). "Mature" ($\tau \acute{\epsilon} \lambda \epsilon \iota o \varsigma$ [teleios]) does not refer to a special group of elite Christians. Paul was not teaching some sort of gnosticism. Rather, it is a reference to all Christians (see the use of *teleios* to refer to all believers in Heb. 10:14). Christians know God's revelation, and thus are mature enough to grasp true spiritual wisdom. They understand the profound wisdom of the cross, that God in Christ became man and died for the sins of the world. That very wisdom is foolishness to the unsaved (1 Cor. 1:18). Christians understand that God's wisdom is infinitely greater than man's (see Rom. 11:33).

Since human wisdom does not extend to the spiritual realm, Paul said in 1 Corinthians 2:6 that he spoke true wisdom only among those who are saved. In verses 6–9, he advanced the general point by giving specific reasons why man cannot discover true spiritual wisdom.

The first reason is in the second half of verse 6. True wisdom, wrote Paul, is a wisdom, "not of this age, nor of the rulers of this age, who are passing away." It is outside man's frame of reference, not being found in the world system. It is not of this age (*aἰών* [*aiōn*]), that is, of this time or era.

Nor does true wisdom come from the "rulers of this age." *Rulers* could be better translated "leaders." It refers to the world's leading lights, both religious and philosophical. The two are closely allied, for when philosophy speaks of ultimate concerns, it becomes religious in nature. Despite the intelligence and education of these leaders, Paul said they are "passing away." The Greek word *καταργέω* (*katargeō*) could also be translated "rendered ineffective." Human wisdom is limited in extent and power, and ultimately useless. That the human leaders of Paul's day did not understand true wisdom is clear because they "crucified the Lord of glory" (1 Cor. 2:8). And the leaders in our day prove their lack of understanding of true wisdom by rejecting Jesus Christ and His claims. They stand with His crucifiers. Even the noblest and highest of men have no natural access to true wisdom. It is eternal and ever living, but they are temporal and always die.

A further reason for man's inability to understand true spiritual wisdom is expressed in 1 Corinthians 2:7. Paul wrote, "But we speak God's wisdom in a mystery, the hidden wisdom, which God predestined before the ages to our glory." *But* is a strong adversative conjunction. Paul stressed the sharp contrast between God's wisdom and man's wisdom. In the Greek text "God's" is in an emphatic position, stressing the supernatural character of spiritual wisdom. Paul reinforced this point by referring to God's wisdom as a "mystery." The term does not refer to complicated, secret, or occult knowledge, but to something having been hidden that is now revealed, namely, New Testament revelation (see Eph. 3:4–10). Christians know this mystery, but it is still hidden to unbelievers.

In contrast to earthly human wisdom, God's wisdom is transcendently heavenly. The latter part of verse 7 describes God's wisdom as having been "predestined before the ages to our glory." From all eternity, God planned to reveal His wisdom to unworthy sinners, that they might spend eternity with Him. Such wisdom is as high above mere human wisdom as the heavens are above the earth.

Paul closes this section in verse 9 by stressing once again man's total inability to discover true wisdom: "Things which eye has not seen and ear has not heard, / And which have not entered the heart of man, / All that God has prepared for those who love Him." Between them, those three avenues account for man's ways of gathering knowledge. Men discover knowledge by sight, hearing, or reasoning (as represented by the "heart of man"). Sight and hearing refer to an empirical, objective method for discovering truth, and reasoning to the rationalistic subjective means. But God's wisdom is not discoverable by either empiricism or rationalism. It is taught by the Holy Spirit to those who love Him.

THE RESULTS OF ILLUMINATION

At least four benefits accrue from the spiritual dynamic of illumination:

1. *The Christian is not enslaved to tradition or dogma.* The Holy Spirit is a personal resident truth-teacher who illumines and instructs believers. No longer are they stuck with whatever the church in the past decided to make authoritative. They can examine everything in the light of Scripture.
2. *Every Christian can understand Scripture.* One of the monumental accomplishments of the Reformers was the giving of the Bible back to the man in the pew. Through the preceding centuries, it was in the exclusive domain of the Roman Catholic Church and its priesthood. The story is told of a horrified Roman Catholic priest who said to Luther, "Martin, don't you realize what would happen if every plough boy and shoemaker were permitted to read the Bible?" To which Luther replied, "Yes; we'd have more Christians!" Scripture is not a closed book to be understood only by the spiritually elite. Every believer can understand Scripture.
3. *Through illumination, Bible study becomes personal communion with God.* Scripture *is* God's propositional revelation to man. It does not *become* revelation through illumination. The Spirit does, however, make the Word come alive through illumination.
4. *Illumination produces joy.* The hearts of the two disciples on the road to Emmaus burned with joy when Jesus explained the Scriptures to them (Luke 24:32). The Spirit's enlightening work has the same effect.

A FINAL WORD

As noted earlier in this discussion, illumination is not something that operates apart from a believer's effort. What is our responsibility? The answer is in Psalm 119:130: "The unfolding of Thy words gives light." God's words are unfolded to us first by discovery. Through diligent Bible study, we unfold or unwrap God's truth. We discover that meditation with a view to applying the truth deepens its impact. Discovery and meditation combined bring the brightest light of illumination to our hearts.

We dare not neglect the illuminating work of the Spirit in our own lives as we study the Scriptures in preparation for our messages. And we must realize that our sermons will accomplish nothing apart from the Spirit's work of illuminating our congregations.

Part III

Processing and Principlizing the Biblical Text

7

Hermeneutics and Expository Preaching

James E. Rosscup

The expositor who represents God fills roles comparable to those of explorers, detectives, historians, trackers, and prospectors. He needs the perspective of one who wants to do his best possible work in meeting a variety of challenges in analyzing his text before preaching. He must utilize sound principles of hermeneutics such as scrutinizing the relevant context, watching for significant grammatical constructions, studying broader usages of the words in his text, learning to distinguish literal and figurative language, making allowance for progressive revelation, incorporating insights gained from other pertinent passages, and wisely using information on the customs of biblical times. Implementation of these and other important principles will ensure that the expositor accurately represents the truth of God's Word.

In a sense, God's expositor is all at once an explorer, a detective, a historian, a tracker, and a prospector. In searching out God's message, he is a Columbus navigating the expansive seas of Scripture to bring news of a fairer world. He is a Sherlock Holmes poking for clues that will cause God's truth, justice, and mercy to prevail. He is akin to Catton, who, in his famous Civil War trilogy,[1] delved into history and cast events in their original light. Again, he is comparable to Tom Tobin, scout and expert in Colorado trail signs, who could find clues most men had missed.[2] A Bible expositor is a pathfinder of trails[3] that people *need* to follow but sometimes miss. For the sake of others, he serves as a prospector who pans for gold in the streams of living water, the Word.[4]

This chapter aims to review how expository preachers fulfill their charge to preach the Word. To achieve their best, that *God* enables them to be as spiritual explorers, detectives, historians, trackers, and prospectors, they must focus on time-honored principles of biblical interpretation to assure that the preached message is God's Word and not some counterfeit.

First, the relation between using hermeneutics (rules of interpretation) and doing exegesis and exposition needs to be kept in mind. John MacArthur articulates the steps:[5]

1. Use the true text, God's Word, as closely as you can responsibly determine it by consulting specialists on textual criticism.
2. Employ the science of hermeneutics, with its interpretive principles.
3. Let these principles expose the meaning of a passage (that is, do an exegetical study of the text) as a person follows prescribed rules in playing a game. Exegesis, then, is the application of hermeneutical principles to decide what a text says and means in its own historical, theological, contextual, literary, and cultural setting. The meaning thus obtained will be in agreement with other related Scriptures.
4. Preach the exposition that flows from this process. Make conspicuous the true and essential original meaning and apply this meaning to present needs of hearers in their own cultural situation.

This is the historically recognized way to interpret and proclaim God's Word.

SPECIFIC PRINCIPLES THAT GUIDE THE INTERPRETER[6]

Four decades of teaching principles for interpreting the Bible has been very rewarding personally. One dividend has been in hearing former students who are now preachers tell how the principles have helped them prepare messages. Comments have run something like this: "After I learned how to use the principles, I could do in an hour what it used to take me many hours to do, so I could get much more done in my allotted study time. I now see how to get to the crux of an issue and can use many lines of evidence to verify that what I am preaching is God's Word, not some ill-formed opinion I formerly assumed to be right."

Key interpretive principles, used with skill developed through practice, provide reliable aid in determining what God's Word says and means. The expositor can mature in competence as an interpreter if he employs these important guidelines diligently and sanely. Furthermore, he can use these as a foundation for enhancing his hermeneutical skill.

Skillful Use of Good Tools[7]

It is obvious that a preacher should use *good* tools. However, many preachers habitually rely on inferior sources. Just as a surgeon, dentist, and carpenter need to have and know how to use the right tools, so does the expositor. He cannot afford to be careless about his choice of tools or how he uses them any more than his listeners who may specialize in one of these other professions or trades.

Laziness, an alleged busy life, and/or lack of Spirit-controlled discipline (see Gal. 5:23) are some of the excuses for poor tool choice or use. It is easy to slough off biblical languages in seminary, but the one who does will lack the indispensable study tools of a skilled workman. Without them, a preacher can fall prey to writers who are scintillating but unreliable in many of their assertions and much of their logic. Such clever writers push their Scripture-twisting ideas and the preacher who feeds on their mistakes provides them with even further exposure. Preachers too often snatch up misleading information printed in shallow, easy-to-zip-through sources. These featherweights in the pulpit usually foster featherweights in the pew.

On one occasion, a speaker was teaching about the devil before a group of Christians. He was right when he said the English tranlsation "devil" is from the Greek word *diabolos*. It is from *dia* and *ballos;* the latter is the noun related to the verb *ballō,* "to throw," he correctly concluded. "Now," he went on, "I found out that *dia* means 'under.' The devil is strong, but God has thrown him down under His power, and we can live in God's victory over him." "Amens" from the audience endorsed this profound promise. But part of it was not true. The speaker would have been dismayed to look up *diabolos* in a reputable Greek source. *Dia* is derived from the root *duo,* meaning "two," and in composition it can mean "two, between, through."[8] *Dia* in usage comes to mean "through" and various other things, but never "under." Another word that often means "under" is *hupo*.[9] The speaker allowed himself to be deceived, with the result that he misled others, too. *Diabolos* as discussed in knowledgable sources is limited to the meanings "accuser, slanderer, one who maligns."[10]

This is an important commitment for the preacher. Let him make sure that he is serious about dispensing truth instead of shoddy error. He must employ good tools in his work if he is to do so. A man disciplined by this perspective will labor to employ sound principles to interpret the Word of God.

What the Bible Says in Context

What a preacher claims a passage says can be very different from what it actually says. Some have contended that Jonah had to die in the sea monster's belly. The supposed necessity is not, however, exclusively derived from what Jonah *says*. It arises from a preacher's logic based on his own surmisings about Jonah and on what Jesus said in Matthew 12:40: "For just as Jonah was three days and three nights in the belly of the sea monster, so shall the Son of Man be three days and three nights in the heart of the earth." Jesus did die; so the reasoning is that Jonah had to die. Only then, the theory concludes, can Jonah's experience be a full analogy and a true "type" of Jesus.

However, neither of the two contexts supports such a necessity. Nowhere does Jonah 2 say the prophet died. The context is full of expressions to indicate he was alive—in distress, to be sure, but not dead. In Matthew 12:39, the "sign of Jonah the prophet" prepares us for the analogy of *how* Jonah was a sign (v. 40). The point of verse 40 is to make the *time element* prominent, that is, three days and three nights. The same period is also specified for Jonah's submarine-like ride (Jon. 1:17). Jesus said Jonah was *in* the sea creature, but does not speak of his death. That fits well with the Jonah 2 context where Jonah is always conscious. It is better not to insist on Jonah's death as a requirement in Jesus' analogy. The analogy that the interpreter can insist on is the aspect of the corresponding time periods. He then needs to find out what "three days and three nights" meant in that culture.[11]

The expositor needs to observe every clue regarding what a context allows explicitly and also what it does not permit. He should seek proof in the biblical context just as the TV detective Columbo probed for clues in his context. From properly handled clues the preacher will get his points, not from jumping to conclusions originating with his own imagination.

What does God's servant look for in context? Many things! Everything! Does he see connecting words such as "and," "therefore," and "for"? What do these words show? What is the significance of verb tenses?

Can he spot series or patterns in a context? For example, a string of five participles in Ephesians 5:19–21 follows Paul's command not to be getting drunk with wine but to be filled with (by) the Spirit (Eph. 5:18). What does the series suggest, and what view most probably fits the contextual flow based on the many factors in the passage? How does the string of participles fit best with the command idea in verse 18?

Is some word repeated in a way to draw attention to the point? The preacher will find "believe" three times in a verse at the end of the parable about two sons (Matt. 21:32). Is this significant, and how does it relate to the parable?

The preacher can lead in being "all eyes" to see and "all ears" to hear and obey. He examines contexts for contrasts, such as, not getting drunk with wine *but* being filled with (by) the Spirit. He looks to see if other contrasts are arranged in a pattern into which this contrast fits. He studies to learn how this contrast relates to other verses, sections, and the whole epistle.

Adjectives ought not elude the expositor's relentless investigation. Does a verse indicate "the *Holy* Spirit" or just say "the spirit"? The expositor will profit from determining which phrases can refer to the Spirit of God and contextual reasons that indicate such a reference. He will find several ways to designate the Spirit of God by probing the immediate context, the context of an entire Bible book (such as Ephesians), the context of a given writer's collection of books (such as Paul's epistles), the context of a whole testament, and the context of the whole Bible.

Turning over every stone and often discovering "golden nuggets," the preacher should seek principally the overall point that governs details of a context. For example, Spirit filling (Eph. 5:18) fits with the broader theme of believers' conduct (Ephesians 4—6) stemming from their spiritual wealth (Ephesians 1—3). Repetition of the word *walk* in the context (Eph. 4:1, 17; 5:1, 8, 15) indicates this. Being filled is part of a description of what Christian behavior should be. The Christian walk is a composite of related themes. It is in *unity* with other Christians (Eph. 4:1–16), *holiness* (Eph. 4:17–32), *love* (Eph. 5:1–6), *light* (Eph. 5:7–17), and *the Spirit* (Eph. 5:18—6:20). A search of other parts of Paul's writings, the New Testament, and the Bible discloses that the Spirit of God promotes such a life of unity, holiness, etc. Penetrating deeper into the Ephesians context, the expositor discovers something else: a walk in the Spirit is a life of *fullness* (Eph. 5:18), one that *flows* into church, family, and business life (Eph. 5:19—6:9), a *fight* for which Christians must put on God's armor (Eph. 6:10–17), and *fellowship* with God and saints in prayer (Eph. 6:18–20).

These aspects of context are only glimpses of more extensive treasures. The motivated servant will keep on scrutinizing a context. Such industry helps him expose pockets of biblical gold and even open up mother lodes. He will often cry out over his joy of discovery. He has his own version of "Eureka!" He exults, "I found it! Oh, praise God for helping me to see!"

The Glamor of Grammar

A Bible expositor will find grammar to be a true friend in helping him grasp God's intended meaning in a passage. He can profit much here if he avoids being sidetracked by a preoccupation with grammar as an end in itself.

Grammar involves the relationship of words and phrases to each other. Details of grammar clarify the ideas which the human writer (and God) intended the original readers (and subsequent readers) to grasp. A preacher should be proficient in the elements of grammar. If he does not know grammar, he is at the mercy of commentators who at times clash in their views on constructions of a text. By knowing grammar, the expositor can apply it with growing skill to learn God's message.

Commitment to the best he can be for the Lord can keep a preacher from lazy excuses and a lack of strong motivation. Such enemies lurk in ambush and have damaged many a preacher who could have been more useful.

How important it is to perceive the right construction of a text and to outline it for a message! One can be accurate in representing details as the Word relates them and avoiding artificiality and falsification. An accurate appreciation of the layout of clauses in Paul's prayers of Ephesians 1:15–23 and 3:14–21 is possible. Or, to note Paul's main verbs in 5:18, "do not be getting drunk but be being filled" (author's translation from the Greek) and the five Greek participles (Eph. 5:19–21) that carry on the force of the command to be filled is also a possibility for the expositor. The people who obey and are filled with (or by) the Spirit will have the accompanying virtues expressed by these participles: that is speaking to others in worshipful reality, singing, making melody, thanking God, and submitting to other Christians. When a preacher understands the relationships of words, he can recount these details about Ephesians 5:18 and capture the basic thought flow.

Whether a preacher has learned biblical grammar well in school or not (and he should have), faithful study in good study sources pays off. In either case, he can improve if he dedicates himself to learning grammar and using good tools. He can be enriched by the writings of experts in grammars,[12] exegetical commentaries, and journal articles. He is not forced to rely on books written for popular appeal at the shallow level of a light, generalized Sunday school quarterly or lower. Why should he be limited to drinking from the poisoned wells of writers who have a knack for teaching error with a colorful flair? Why not zealously assure sound results in dependable works and then correlate what is learned with all the interpretive principles, including grammar? Praying for God's guidance all along the way is necessary, because God, whose servant the expositor is, has the most concern that he get His message straight.

Word Meaning—an El Dorado

Dedicated study of key Bible words in top sources will supply the speaker with great treasures. Eternal truths have far greater worth than the fabulous Jackson and Gregory mines in the Colorado gold rush of 1859 and the years following.

It is important to deal with every word, yet to devote more inquiry to key terms. A concordance lists all the passages where a word occurs. The sermon-maker can find in his original language and English Bibles the settings of a word in a given book, all the books of a biblical writer, or in the Old or New Testament. In a lexicon, he locates possible meanings the word can have in differing situations. His task is to find the right idea in the setting of his present text.

For example, *lion* has several meanings in Scripture: an animal frightening in power, Babylon as a terrifying invader (Jer. 4:7), the nation Israel or a leader (Ezek. 19:2),[13] an analogy for Satan (1 Pet. 5:8), and Christ (Rev. 5:5), to name several. Behind each are the ideas of awesome power, authority, and ability to overcome.

Many words have distinct meanings in different passages. The words for "world," "baptism," "spirit," "fire," "star," and "crown" are typical of these. The expositor, as a useful steward of God's Word, must study and acquire a deepening perception of valid distinctions between word usages. He also must guard against appropriating unchecked statements by other preachers. Some may sound impressive, but they delude the carelessly gullible who do not take time to check them. Absolute-type pronouncements can thunder as if from Sinai's heights: "Darkness is always evil in Scripture,"[14] or "birds are invariably evil in the Bible."[15] Or a speaker may insist without qualification, "God never hears the prayer of an unsaved man."[16] These kinds of statements need to be qualified by further stipulations before being granted hermeneutical validity. In some contexts each of the statements may be true, but it is too much to make them universal guidelines for the whole Bible.

It is wise for the expositor to trace a word in all its contexts. This gives him a "feel" for the word and the aspect of the message it covers in each context. He can present only a summary for his audience, but his carefully studied conclusion can stand before God and men. A word study can sharpen an expositor's mind and heart toward a greater sensitivity for a biblical writer's goals and attitude.

One can add colorful details by consulting a lexicon. Barber lists a number of lexicons in *The Minister's Library*.[17] The more helpful Old Testament works are by Brown/Driver/Briggs, Holladay, and Koehler and Baumgartner.[18] Valuable New Testament aid is available in Abbott-Smith and Arndt and Gingrich.[19] Other profitable lexical works are the two-volume *Theological Wordbook of the Old Testament* by R. Laird Harris, et al. (Chicago: Moody, 1980) and Vine's *Expository Dictionary* (see notes 8 and 10 in this chapter). The latter lists each word in English, then (in the edition cited, note 10) keys the Hebrew or Greek for each word to the numbering system in Strong's *Concordance* and the *New American Standard Concordance*.

Two sources guide users to the very quarter of a page and the exact sub-point that defines almost every word in every verse of the Bible. These useful tools are by Bruce Einspahr (*An Index to Brown, Driver and Briggs' Hebrew-English Lexicon* [Chicago: Moody, 1980]) and John Alsop (*An Index to the Revised Bauer-Arndt-Gingrich Greek Lexicon,* 2d ed. [Grand Rapids: Zondervan, 1981]). Even a preacher who knows no Hebrew or Greek can go immediately to the lexicon's classification and definition of a word in English.

Another source is the three-volume *New International Dictionary of New Testament Theology,* edited by Colin Brown (Grand Rapids: Zondervan, 1975–78). It handles significant New Testament words in English, and David Townsley and Russell Bjork's *Scripture Index to the NIDNTT* (Grand Rapids: Zondervan, 1985) provides convenient help in its use. The preacher is able to look up the word on which he needs information without a prolonged search.

A monumental work edited by Gerhard Kittel and Gerhard Friedrich is the ten-volume *Theological Dictionary of the New Testament* (Grand Rapids: Eerdmans, 1964–76). Volume 10 has handy indices for English keywords, Greek keywords, Hebrew and Aramaic words, and Scripture references. Eerdmans has also published a one-volume abridgement by Geoffrey Bromiley (1985), giving the essence of the larger work and costing much less.

Other resources that convey the riches of biblical words include *The New Bible Dictionary,* edited by J. D. Douglas (Grand Rapids: Eerdmans, 1970), *The Zondervan Bible Pictoral Dictionary,* edited by M. C. Tenney (Grand Rapids: Zondervan, 1963), *The International Standard Bible Encyclopedia,* 4 volumes, edited by Geoffrey Bromiley (Grand Rapids: Eerdmans, 1979–86), and *The Zondervan Pictorial Encyclopedia of the Bible,* 5 volumes, edited by M. C. Tenney (Grand Rapids: Zondervan, 1975).

Exegetical commentaries also include, among other information, good material about words. Barber (*The Minister's Library*) has good listings for the Old Testament (pp. 129–31) and New Testament (pp. 167–69) in conjunction with each book. Journal articles often help with word meanings.

Preachers must handle God's Word with integrity. This is much better than a half-baked, trumped-up supposition. Even in word study, a ministry can be one of truth, good for now as well as for the future judgment seat of Christ.

Distinguishing the Literal and the Figurative

Much of the time classifying the literal and the figurative is not difficult. It is often obvious if a word is used in its literal sense. This is the basic foundational connotation and the starting point of a word's usage in a language. A figurative usage analogous to the word's basic connotation is frequently apparent.

Even in Bible days a lion was first a four-legged animal. This basic idea made it natural to liken a person or thing to a lion, that is, someone or something lion-like in power and authority. Scripture has its sword of the Spirit (Eph. 6:17), the milk of the Word (1 Pet. 2:2, 3), and Jesus as the door (John 10:9). Jesus is the door into salvation corresponding in the *spiritual* realm to a doorway as an entrance into the sheepfold in the *physical* sphere (John 10:1–3, 9).

Sometimes the expositor faces a problem when the distinction between literal and figurative is not so obvious. Yet even here by diligent investigation with the use of various interpretive principles and good authorities on words, such as lexicons, exegetical commentaries, etc., he can determine the main possibilities with their supporting arguments.[20] He can sort these out to arrive at a carefully weighed decision.

Other problems are more difficult. For instance, in predictions of future battles, will horses, spears, swords, and arrows be the same type of weapons as they were in the biblical day when the prophecy was uttered? Will there be a return to the use of these? Or does the preacher see them as culturally conditioned terms to help the immediate audience grasp the idea, as starting-points analogous to some other form of weapons when the battle occurs much later, weaponry of a future time? Weaponry does change through the centuries.

If the expositor opted for the latter view on *weaponry,* does consistency require that he apply the same principle to everything in the Old Testament? No. He need not take the *land* God promised Abraham and his descendants (see Gen. 12:7) to be a different future form, such as a spiritual "land of the church" or all the present spiritual blessings in Christ (see Eph. 1:3). If this were true, the church would be spiritual Israel and, for some interpreters, Israel as a nation would have no distinctive destiny after Christ's Second Advent. However, a particular land mass (such as Palestine) remains the same as time passes, at least within the present earthly system. Besides, Scripture says much that suggests a future return of repentant Israelite people to Palestine. All this is the same, despite changes in military weaponry.

Writers with the sharpest interpretive skills will continue to differ in their view of weaponry. This is true even where they concur that literal battles will occur in a return of Israel to Palestine. Whether spears remain as comparable spear-like weapons hurled by footmen and cavalrymen or turn out to be weapons launched from future machines, they are still real physical weapons, though different in form. Charity stimulates tolerance and seeks a spirit of unity in exalting Christ even when God's servants hold different interpretations. This is possible here because no fundamental truth of Scripture is at stake.

When should the preacher be literal? He should always use the literal idea of a term as his starting point. It is a base from which to assess the possibility of a sensible figure. He ought to be literal when this yields the best sense, that is , when context and word usage point this way. A context of straightforward history will probably not use a term figuratively, though this may occur. If it does, factors of that text or a comparable one must demonstrate it to be so. But books with many figures, such as the Psalms, Isaiah, Zechariah, and Revelation, often have their own built-in justifications for symbolic ideas to fit with other details.

Sometimes even where figurative terms are frequent, other expressions may be literal. For example, it is debatable whether to view the New Jerusalem as literal or not. Contextually, the new heaven and new earth are as literal as the old heaven and old Earth that they succeed (Rev. 21:1—22:5). Also, precise measurements are given for the city as if it too were literal.

Further, the tree of life (Rev. 22:2) can be just as literal/physical as the tree of life and other trees in the Garden of Eden (Genesis 2—3). Such evidence persuades many to understand a literal city and tree, even in a context where the "book of life" (Rev. 20:15) can be a figure for a record of which God is aware.

Obviously the lion that Samson defeated was four-legged. Just as reasonably, the lion that stalks from its thicket in Jeremiah 4 is emblematic of lion-like Babylon, because Jeremiah identifies Babylon as the invader of Judah (Jer. 20:4) and many details in chapter 4 portray the lion as a human army.

The point is to bring all the interpretive principles to bear on a text, diligently sifting evidence and watching for indicators that point to a literal or a figurative idea.[21] Occasionally, even after painstaking study, the preacher may not be able to reach a conclusion before preaching. He should depend on the Lord for an understanding of how to explain the passage, but at times frankly admitting a need for more light will reflect humility and integrity to his audience.[22] The Spirit can use even this to beget confidence that the people can rely on this man of truth.

Progressive Revelation: God's Gradual Unveiling

The whole divine program was not revealed to man all at once. God has revealed aspects of His plan in stages as the drama of the Bible has unfolded. Gradual revelation is evident, even in direct prophecy and the predictive element in typology.[23] People need faith and patience to await the fulfillment of stages God has projected ahead of time.

A preacher sensitive to progressive revelation should be careful to make clear distinctions. For example, from a contemporary perspective he has a broad grasp of the long-range ramifications of Genesis 3:15. He stands at the peak of advanced revelation and can draw illuminating details from both testaments. Yet, he also sees that Adam and Eve were at an early point in the progressive unfolding of the redemptive plan. They had no access to later implications that provide a contemporary preacher with a composite picture. They surely could not say to God, "Oh, we get it; You will send the Christ to defeat Satan and pay the penalty for sins such as ours." We have no scriptural indication that God revealed that much to them.

Later passages help us integrate many details into the stream of progressive revelation. We see particulars of Jesus' birth, person, ministry, death, resurrection, and ascension. But later knowledge of these does not warrant reading them back into early Old Testament days as though God's people knew them from the time of their first prediction.[24]

To illustrate further, a post-crucifixion perspective cannot point to the supposed cross-shaped arrangement of the tabernacle furniture as an evidence that such a layout in itself pointed to Christ's cross. This perception is too advanced to attribute to the Old Testament saint. God's Word has enough clear language referring to the cross, so that a preacher need not make claims that have the tone of the "hocus pocus" or at best are arbitrary. Why not dwell on the well-stocked larder of truth that is preachable, without contrivance? God has not called us to a display of ingenuity to add to His already unequalled progressive revelation!

Scriptural Help in Interpreting Scripture[25]

The Bible throws much light on itself through cross-references. God has mightily used preachers who steep themselves in the Word and obey it through His power. Living in it day and night (Ps. 1:1–3), they grasp valid connections between various passages and fill out the picture regarding the many aspects of truth. This principle of Scripture interpreting Scripture supplements the use of context, word study, grammar, and other hermeneutical rules.

The sense of "life" (ζωή; *zōē*) in the Gospel of John—eternal, spiritual life as God's gift received when a person believes in Christ—prepares the preacher for the same word in 1 John. Based on reasonable evidence that the apostle John wrote both books, it makes sense that he would use the same word with the same connections to convey the same concept, unless evidence to the contrary surfaces. The two books use the word in a variety of ways that have the same sense. A person who believes in Christ passes from death to life (John 5:24; 1 John 3:14). Also, "life" occurs often in the Gospel and recurs in 1 John with the adjective *aiōnios* ("eternal"). Further, the "life" is a gift related to Christ (John 3:16; 1 John 5:11, 12). The books refer to "life" in other similar semantic relationships. This type of observation builds the preacher's confidence so that, when he speaks on 1 John, he can properly cross-reference the "life" there with the "life" similarly used in John's Gospel.

These relationships lead to affirmations such as the following. In his Gospel, John's overall purpose is to describe the signs (miracles) of Jesus that men might believe and have eternal life (John 20:30, 31). In 1 John he adds the ways in which people can test their profession of faith to have life and be properly assured that they have genuinely believed and do have the life (1 John 5:13; see 2:3–5, etc.).

Cross-referencing, implemented with competent sensitivity to clues in each context, avoids making invalid connections and adds insights for preaching.[26] It is best not to strain a cross-reference if evidence for a relationship is not solid. The passion of the man who follows hard after God prizes a certainty that he communicates God's Word alone and not dross of his own invention.

Color from Bible Customs

God gave His word to people in differing cultures, so the preacher must see a text in its own culture. Once he has done this, he can proceed to help his hearers see how truths apply where their customs differ from the original setting. God's servants today have much to learn about the idea of a Bible passage in a setting of long ago.[27]

Preparing to preach through the parables of Jesus by using good sources can provide a "newsreel" of enlightenment. Many commentaries and books specialize in parables; and works on customs in Jesus' time help explain historical circumstances. The preacher who uses his time wisely has opportunity to sift and fit data into a full picture and compare and evaluate views. He can visualize human predicaments both when Jesus taught and today, and apply truth with gripping relevance.

A verse may mean something different from what one first supposes. Romans 12:20 is an example. A Christian who does good to an enemy heaps "burning coals upon his head." Dealing good to an enemy has much in common with Proverbs 25:21, 22, "If your enemy is hungry, give him food . . . ; / And if . . . thirsty, give him water. . . ." That refers to kindness, but hot coals can cause excruciating pain. So, some teach that Romans 12:20 means that kindness increases a person's guilt as he resists God. This leads to his suffering a greater degree of fiery punishment in rejecting God and such kindness. However, Romans 12 highlights kind intentions toward enemies, not vengeful motives (vv. 14, 15, 17, 18, 20, 21). In a cross-fertilization of cultures in the Bible world, Klassen describes an Egyptian custom that fits a loving view, not a harsh one.[28] According to the custom, a person who became penitent submissively carried coals of fire on his head in a bowl. The coals symbolized his change to a tender mind. That custom agrees with the Romans 12 focus on a love deed that could melt a person to repentance.

The view is quite possible. Whether it is correct or not is not the main point, however. The importance of the principle is the main issue. Seek to see the custom a biblical writer pictures as it occurred in his day. The preacher who disciplines his mind to this often finds added light on what the Word means.

Another example of interpreting a custom has to do with the "white stone" which Christ promises as a reward to the Christian overcomer (Rev. 2:17).[29] One will not find what that phrase meant in first-century culture by guesswork based on white stones in today's culture.

References to geography must be pursued in trustworthy sources on biblical geography.[30] Accuracy and vivid descriptions of location, distance, terrain, climate, vegetation, and such things enhance an exposition. Often it is wise to verify information by checking several sources, especially if a carefully attested idea influences a choice of views.

We are all limited. Only Jesus Christ knows the things of the Word perfectly, and He is the perfect exegete of truth. A keen interpreter is diligent in his own study, but is also eager to learn from others. After all, other interpreters have been taught by the Spirit, too.[31]

A POSTSCRIPT

Space allows only a brief mention of other hermeneutical axioms.

1. *The checking principle*. Check a view and all its details in reliable sources by specialists. On historical details, consult dependable sources on history.[32] For geography, look to experts in geography.[33] On word meaning, go to better lexicons and thoroughly researched commentaries. Above all, avoid leaning on weak sources, that is, nonspecialists who themselves should have depended on reliable sources, but for one reason or another may not have done so. Checking with genuine rather than pseudo experts applies in every area: such as parables, prophecy, typology. It can even be fruitful for blocks of Scripture. Works specializing on a shorter portion may provide help that commentaries on the whole Bible do not cover as thoroughly. Concentrated studies deal with such examples as creation, the flood, Abraham, the tabernacle, Psalm 25, the trial and death of Jesus, His resurrection, Romans 6—8, 1 Corinthians 13, Hebrews 11, Revelation 2; 3, 20, and 21; 22. Topical works discuss marriage, divorce, angels, spiritual warfare, the New Age Movement, and more.

Some resources provide annotated bibliographies on Bible matters. Such helps are very valuable.[34] On any matter, consult the better sources. It does not make sense to be second rate in preparing to preach the unsearchable riches of Christ.

2. *The verification principle*. Probe for biblical validation that a duty is obligatory for all times and not just for a particular biblical character or for a specific time. Use other principles to view a matter from every possible angle. To illustrate, God's command to Jacob to "leave this land" (Gen. 31:15), that is, leave Haran to return to Canaan, is not applicable to a Christian today who is his own person in his own situation. The general principle may be gleaned that God willingly directs a believer, a truth verifiable in other Scriptures. But Genesis 31 does not give marching orders to do something like go AWOL from military service or leave California for another state. Discerning God's will regarding each believer's exact movements depends on a variety of considerations.

3. *The regulation principle*. Scripture, not experience, regulates doctrine. Pastoral expositors should direct God's sheep to concentrate on what the Great Shepherd says in His Word properly interpreted. Any claim that the Bible plus an experience provide a norm to depend on should be evaluated using God's Bureau of Standards, His Word.

This discussion has not treated every important hermeneutical rule, but it has touched on the ones usually most crucial to a faithful ministry in the Word. When skillfully employed, these will assist biblical heralds of God in extracting the truth from the Word that God would have them proclaim to others.

8

Exegesis and Expository Preaching

Robert L. Thomas

A distinctive characteristic purpose of expository preaching is its instructional function. An explanation of the details in a given text imparts information that is otherwise unavailable to the average untrained parishioner and provides him with a foundation for Christian growth and service. The importance and centrality of thorough exegesis in preparing the expositor for this service cannot be overstated. Exegesis must itself be on a solid footing and must lead to development in supplementary fields, which in turn provide important data for expository preaching too. With the raw material of sermon preparation thus obtained, common-sense principles must be applied in putting the material into a form that the congregation can receive with ease and learn from.

The distinguishing mark of expository preaching, also called Bible exposition, is the biblical interpretation communicated through the sermon. The expositor must teach his audience the meaning of the text intended by its author and understood by its original recipients. Because the original languages of the Old and New Testaments are inaccessible to almost all congregations, precise and detailed interpretations of Scripture will be also. So a Bible expositor's central responsibility is to acquaint the hearers with these interpretations that were previously unknown to them. The final test of the effectiveness of Bible exposition is how well individuals who hear the sermon can read the passage with greater comprehension of its exact meaning than they could before they heard the message and demonstrate a willingness to obey what they have learned.

The point that differentiates expository sermons from other types is not the cleverness of their outlines or their catchy clichés. Neither is it the relevance of the message to everyday life. These are helpful and necessary as communicative tools and devotional helps, but they do not distinguish expository preaching from other kinds of sermons. A sermon could still be expository without them, but if the explanation of what the author meant is missing, so is the heart of Bible exposition.

The unique contribution of Bible exposition is its substantial enhancement of the listeners' comprehension of Scripture's intent. Those who listen to expository preaching have opportunity to submit to the Holy Spirit who first inspired the text as He now illumines that text to them. This is the best avenue for building up the saints. The New Testament puts heavy emphasis on using the mind as the principal avenue to Christian growth (for example, Rom. 12:2; 1 Pet. 1:13), so the preacher should do the same.[1]

BUILDING TOWARD BIBLE EXPOSITION

The Critical Role of Exegesis

The responsibility on the shoulders of one who preaches this kind of message is heavy. He must have a *thorough* understanding of the passage to be preached before devising the mechanics for conveying his understanding to the congregation. If at all possible, he must be a *trained* exegete with a working knowledge of the biblical languages and a systematic method for using them to analyze the text.[2]

A chapter such as this cannot provide a program of exegetical training. Theological seminaries exist for this purpose. It is also beyond the present scope to formulate a system of exegesis for the Greek New Testament (or the Hebrew Old Testament). A few suggestions regarding exegesis are in order, however, so as to identify what this foundational process entails.

Accurate exegesis is ultimately dependent on the leading of the Holy Spirit in the exegete's research. Apart from His guidance, not only does the meaning of the text evade him, but also valid applications of the text will prove elusive (1 Cor. 2:14). Since God is a God of order (14:33, 40) and rational creatures created in His image and regenerated by His Spirit are capable of grasping divine logic, the leading of the Spirit in exegetical study will be in accord with divine reason accessible to the exegete.

Exegesis deals with the original languages of Scripture: Greek in the New Testament and Hebrew and Aramaic in the Old Testament. It does not satisfy itself with the uncertainties of working from a translation or translations, when study in the original languagues is possible. Translations can never cover all the nuances of the original text. This is the key area in which an expositor can add to his listeners' knowledge of the text because they usually will be limited to what they can glean from a translation in their native tongue.

Exegesis also builds upon sound hermeneutical principles. Probably the greatest breakdown in biblical studies at the beginning of the twenty-first century is in this field. Challenges galore have been launched against time-honored guidelines for interpreting the Bible. These challenges come from a wide variety of sources. The average pulpiteer may easily be "blown away" if he is not alert to detect the widespread aberrations that are in circulation. The importance of vigilance in this regard merits the inclusion of several illustrations of the contemporary problem among evangelicals.

Old Testament scholar William LaSor asserts that New Testament writers did not follow a grammatico-historical method in their use of the Old Testament, so Bible interpreters today should not be limited by that method.[3] What he fails to observe, however, is that New Testament writers received direct, divine revelation, whereas contemporary interpreters do not. Therefore, they cannot take the liberties with the text that the New Testament writers took with the Old Testament text.[4]

Theologian Paul Jewett understands Paul to be inconsistent with himself regarding the role of women in the church, concluding that Paul advocates sexual equality in one of his books (Gal. 3:28) and inequality in another (1 Cor. 11:3).[5] This opinion, in essence, dispenses with the well-known "analogy of faith" principle in the biblical interpretation. It sees the Bible as inconsistent with itself.

Philosopher Anthony Thiselton informs us that hermeneutics is a circular process and human prejudgments make objective interpretation impossible.[6] Such a pronouncement discourages attempts to learn the original meaning of the text and opens the floodgate for uncontrolled interpretive subjectivism. At best, it has the effect of destroying the goal of objectivity that traditional Protestant interpretation has always pursued and, at worst, it signals an end of rationality in studying the Bible.

Missiologist Krikor Haleblian advocates the principle of contextualization, whereby each culture is allowed to form its own system of hermeneutics based on the praxis of ministry in meeting its own peculiar needs.[7] Yet if each culture formulated its own principles of interpretation to make the Bible mean something conceived as necessary for its own isolated situation, objective control of what the Bible means is terminated. The connotations for the original recipients of the writings have become completely irrelevant.

Redaction critic I. Howard Marshall cites as nonhistorical a number of sayings attributed to Christ in the Gospels, viewing them to be later additions added by the church for clarifying purposes.[8] Traditional interpretation, on the other hand, views the Gospels as containing accurate historical data about Jesus.[9]

The circulation of such subtle hermeneutical variations has contributed heavily to the interpretive confusion prevalent in evangelicalism in the last several decades.[10] These can become a serious hindrance to accurate exegesis and ultimately to expository preaching if they are not shunned.

Exegesis also presupposes a text that is determined through following valid text-critical principles. The canons of the Old Testament and New Testament are also in place and are the object of the expositor's interpretive efforts. Regarding each book under scrutiny, a thorough background knowledge of authorship, date of writing, destination, and the like, the field called biblical introduction, is also a necessary foundation for exegesis.

Exegesis itself incorporates a study of individual words, their backgrounds, their derivation, their usage, their synonyms, their antonyms, their figurative usages, and other lexical aspects. Elaboration on Greek and Hebrew words in pulpit exposition is by far the most frequently encountered homiletical use of exegesis, but it is only a small beginning. Of at least equal, and probably greater, importance is the way the words are joined in sentences, paragraphs, sections, etc. This area of syntax is too frequently overlooked. Yet only a full appreciation of syntactical relationships can provide a specific understanding of the flow of thought that the Spirit intended in His revelation through the human writers of the Scripture.

A thorough familiarity with the historical background of each book is also imperative. Without this, the meaning to readers in the original setting is beyond reach of the expositor and, hence, of his audience, too.

The church at the beginning of the twenty-first century is the beneficiary of a rich treasure of Bible teaching published throughout the centuries of the Christian era. Gifted teachers whom Christ has placed in the church have preserved their interpretations on the printed page. It behooves the exegete to take full advantage of these God-given sources of enrichment in acquiring a keener mastery of the meaning he must teach.

It is naive to assume that these gifted writers never disagree in their interpretations. It is the challenge of the Bible expositor under the guidance of the Spirit to evaluate each of the conflicting opinions in light of sound hermeneutical principles and exegetical procedures and to settle on the one that he feels to be correct. This is what he will preach to his congregation as the true interpretation.

After the tedious process of exegetical analysis, the expositor will have amassed an immense amount of data, much of it technical, but he should also have arrived at a detailed comprehension of the Scripture's interpretation.[11] He must now select from this massive accumulation of material the parts that are most significant to transmit to his listeners.

A major precaution to observe is not to preach exegetical data from the pulpit. Because the expositor has been enlightened so much by what he has discovered, his initial impulse may be to pass on to his people the excitement of his discovery in the same terminology as he received it. This is a major mistake. Very few in the pew have a background sufficient to enable them to comprehend the kind of technical data derived from exegesis. So the minister of the Word must adapt his explanations to suit the vocabulary and interest level of those to whom he speaks. He must develop a technique of conveying in the language of a nonspecialist what he has learned from his specialized analysis. How he does so may vary. It may be through paraphrase, description, analogy, illustration, or in a multitude of other ways. Yet, he must explain the text in a way that is interesting and understandable to his people. This lucid explanation is at the core of Bible exposition.

Auxiliary Fields of Study

Bible exposition includes much more than exegesis. In a logical development of theological and ministerial disciplines, it is built upon other fields of investigation as well. These other fields of study are based on exegesis, too, but they amplify exegesis by stipulating different ways of applying it. The other disciplines include the following:

1. *Biblical and Systematic Theology.* One cannot reach an accurate perception of God and His works without basing it on a correct interpretation of the Bible. It is vital that these theological perspectives be incorporated into expository preaching at appropriate times.

2. *Church History.* The doctrinal and ethical development of the Christian church from century to century can be evaluated properly only through the eyes of a correctly understood Bible. Lessons learned by earlier generations of believers, both good and bad, make excellent sermon illustrations. They also encourage imitation of exemplary behavior of saints of the past and guard Christians from repeating the mistakes of those who have gone before.

3. *Apologetics.* The New Testament is clear in its instruction to Christians about defending the faith against attack (Phil. 1:7; 1 Pet. 3:15, 16). Philosophies of religion vary widely because the nature of philosophy lends itself so readily to mere human reasoning. Logic is not necessarily purely secular, however. Under the control of conclusions reached in biblical exegesis, apologetic methodologies can apply sound logic in responding to those who attack the integrity of the Bible and the Christian faith. Well-rounded expository preaching will incorporate these biblically oriented answers whenever necessary.

4. *Applicational Ministries.* Also based on exegesis is a wide assortment of services in which the principles of Scripture rightly interpreted are applied to human experience. Practical uses of the Bible are multiple and varied, but they must be controlled. Correct interpretation is the *only* suitable control. If the meaning of the text in its original setting does not regulate application, applications become extremely subjective and essentially invalid. Applicational ministries include the following:

a. *Homiletics.* The field of sermon preparation and delivery is broad, but the structure of the sermon and the motivation for its delivery must be rooted in the text. All too often secular methodologies and ideas that are only human have determined the shape of a sermon. If thorough exegesis is the foundation of a message, this will not happen.

b. *Counseling.* The counsel that the Bible prescribes is administered most effectively through members of Christ's body who possess the gift of exhortation. This gift, along with the gift of teaching, forms an effective combination that makes up what is called preaching (Rom. 12:7, 8). Exhortation (or "encouragement," as the Greek term can also be rendered) includes rebuke to the wayward Christian and comfort to the one beset by grief. It covers the broad spectrum of advice on how to live the Christian life. Unfortunately, much of what passes itself off as Christian counseling is more secular than it is biblical.[12] This is because it is not on a solid exegetical footing. Expository preaching does well to include the right kinds of application to the assembled group, just as it should be done on an individual or small-group basis, that is, a counseling situation.

c. *Christian Education.* Education that is really Christian will derive from exegesis. What is true of secular educational methodologies will not necessarily apply in efforts to impart biblical truth. For example, the secular assumption that something must be experienced before it can be learned is the reverse sequence of what the Bible prescribes. Doctrine precedes and determines practical experience in the biblical pattern. Utilization of biblical principles of education in messages whose purpose is to teach the meaning of Scripture is another supporting element of Bible exposition.

d. *Administration.* Unfortunately, many have attempted to incorporate secular administrative philosophies into local-church operations. Pragmatism has often been given as a reason for this: "If it works in the business world, use it." Such reasoning is ethically inferior, however. The biblical dimension in administration gives first attention to principle: "Is it right according to Scripture?" The Bible has much to say about how to rule or govern. In fact, it designates a special gift of the Spirit for carrying out this function (see Rom. 12:8; 1 Cor. 12:28). Since, under normal circumstances, the Bible expositor will serve his church in an administrative capacity, it can be expected that exegetically based principles of leadership sometimes will be reflected in his preaching.

e. *Missions and Evangelism.* Missions and evangelism are proper goals in Christian service, but the means used to reach these goals are not always so proper. Even here man-made schemes have replaced scripturally prescribed methods of winning lost people to Christ. When missionary methods and evangelistic techniques are based on what the Bible teaches, however, both the means and the end are God-honoring. Hence, exegesis must also be the footing on which Christian outreach is built. Expository preaching will, in turn, build on missions and evangelism rightly construed in those aspects of the sermon devoted to bringing an offer of salvation.

f. *Social Issues*. How Christians should involve themselves in combating the ills of society and helping meet the multiplied needs of the world as a whole must stem from an accurate understanding of the Word too. Scripture clarifies certain causes that are very worthy and supplies outlines of how God's people can help alleviate suffering and rectify injustice. Christians have responsibilities as citizens in the world. The preacher who features Bible exposition should amplify these responsibilities when they are appropriate to the passage he is developing.

The breadth of Bible exposition is enormous; yet its central core is always biblical exegesis. In review, the relationships of various disciplines and their climax in an exposition of the Word may be shown in Figure 8–1, which pictures the relationships between fields of theological study.

The diagram reflects the building blocks that lead eventually to Bible exposition, beginning at the first level and progressing to the fourth. It also shows the crucial role of biblical exegesis in the process. If there is a breakdown in exegesis, the whole structure, of which expository preaching is the climax, collapses. Based on thorough exegesis, Bible exposition can fruitfully draw upon the full spectrum of theological disciplines.

PRACTICAL SUGGESTIONS FOR EXPOSITORY PREACHERS

The previous remarks reflect that exegesis and Bible exposition are not the same. Exegesis has been defined as "the critical or technical application of hermeneutical principles to a biblical text in the original languages with a view to the exposition or declaration of its meaning."[13] Since exegesis leads to exposition but is not identical with it, a few suggestions about how to make the transition from one to the other are in order.

As in the process of exegesis, it is also true of the transition from that point to sermon preparation and delivery that the leading of the Spirit of God is indispensable. This is the only way of accomplishing the work of God in the lives of people through preaching (see 1 Thess. 1:5). The preacher must be a man in whom the Spirit has been and is at work before he can be an instrument through whom the Spirit will work in the lives of others as he preaches.

A previously issued warning is worth repeating here: A transition from exegesis to Bible exposition is mandatory. Pulpiteers who are fluent enough to expound the technical data of exegesis and still hold the attention of an average congregation have been and are extremely rare. The information gleaned from exegesis must be put into a format that fits the understanding of the person in the pew and is applicable to his or her situation.

As Figure 8–1 directs, exegesis must also be expanded to embody other fields of doctrinal and ethical relevance. A preacher need not include every

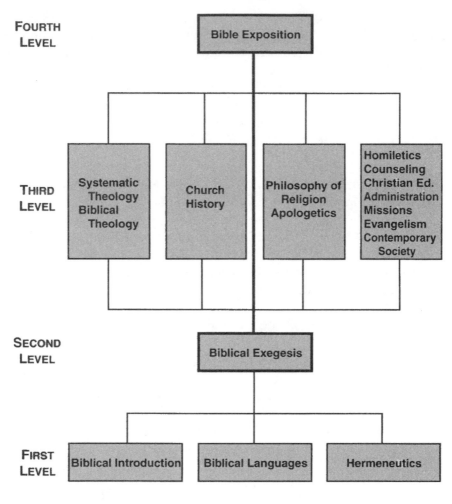

FOURTH LEVEL — Bible Exposition

THIRD LEVEL — Systematic Theology, Biblical Theology | Church History | Philosophy of Religion, Apologetics | Homiletics, Counseling, Christian Ed., Administration, Missions, Evangelism, Contemporary Society

SECOND LEVEL — Biblical Exegesis

FIRST LEVEL — Biblical Introduction | Biblical Languages | Hermeneutics

Figure 8–1
Relationships Between Fields of Theological Study

field in every sermon he preaches. These are areas that may be introduced as the nature of the passage and the occasion of the sermon require.

Beyond these general suggestions, some specific pointers may be beneficial. These miscellaneous guidelines are the ones that have seemed most apropos to this writer in personal preaching, listening to other preachers, and preparing would-be expositors during forty-five years of teaching biblical exegesis:

1. The preacher should review the results of the exegetical study and select parts that will most typically represent his detailed interpretation of the passage. Time will not allow him to include everything he has learned, so he must select what is most important for his congregation to hear. What

is not used immediately can be filed and employed later in an appropriate message. Thus, all of one's labors have value sooner or later.

2. In his sparing use of technical terminology that may be unintelligible to his audience, the expositor should not shy away from referring occasionally to Greek words that lie behind the English translation. When doing so, he can help his cause by comparing the Greek term to an English word derived from it. For example, δύναμις (*dynamis*), the Greek word for "power," could be compared to the English word *dynamic*.[14] This gives the listeners a point of reference to facilitate recollection of the Greek term. To repeat another precaution, however, this type of sermon material must be used only *occasionally*. The expositor must be careful not to overuse Greek terminology.

3. The Bible expositor should describe as best he can the thoughts of the human writer of Scripture that resulted in his writing what he did. These subjective impressions were products of the Holy Spirit's inspiration and are key elements in a precise understanding of accurate interpretation. A writer's logical developments are best captured through close attention to features of syntactical exegesis referred to above. The use of conjunctions in the New Testament is particularly strategic in cultivating a sensitivity to movement of thought in the text. This type of information is most effectively passed on to the audience in the form of descriptions or paraphrases of the text.

4. Public presentation is not the proper forum to resolve in detail difficult interpretive problems, but an expositor's awareness of the problems should be reflected in his presentation. After surveying the possible viewpoints, he should include one or two good reasons why he has selected a solution as the correct one. If he were to skim past a problem in the text without noticing it, he would shake the confidence of those listeners who may be aware of the problem. Tough issues should not be left unsolved, no matter how hard they are. If the preacher is indecisive, his indecision will be multiplied into outright confusion among his hearers who have nowhere else to turn for an answer. They have nothing comparable to the tools of a trained exegete to grapple with obscure passages. With particularly difficult matters, the expositor does well to admit publicly his personal struggle in reaching a decision, but he should nevertheless not shy away from expressing his own preferred answer in each problem passage.

5. A careful personal translation of the passage to be preached based on thorough exegesis is a primary prerequisite in sermon preparation. In producing it, the preacher should read the text repeatedly in the original language and then turn to English translations for further enlightenment on how others have rendered the words. As opportunity arises, the expositor's personal translation may be made available to the congregation in a published form.

6. The sermon's proposition and outline should have an interpretational rather than an applicational orientation. This reinforces the central purpose of the sermon as a teaching device. It is primary that listeners should carry away an understanding of the text's *meaning*. Suggestions of practical effects on Christian living are quite appropriate in the message, but without being founded on the original intention of the author, they will be short-lived. Besides, long after the sermon is over, the Holy Spirit will add to these suggested practical lessons others of an individual nature as people reflect on what the text means. Preaching is first and foremost a service to the mind as groundwork for a service to the heart. The will and emotions are influenced in a lasting way only in proportion to the degree that the mind has learned correct biblical teaching and the level of behavior consonant with that teaching.

7. In an ideal situation, the sequence within the sermon structure should follow the sequence of the passage of Scripture being treated, but sometimes the nature of the passage and/or the occasion of the sermon may require a sermon outline that draws upon emphases within the passage in a nonsequential order. The latter approach may sometimes be the best pedagogical tool for helping the audience grasp the fundamental thrust of the passage. Whenever the out-of-sequence outline is used, a tracing of the passage's sequential flow should be included in the introduction or elsewhere in the sermon. A combined emphasis from the sequential summary and the text's underlying principles tendered nonsequentially will greatly benefit the hearers when they are reviewing the passage privately after the sermon.

8. An expositor should make every effort not to preach preconceived notions of what a given text may say. His sacred trust is to let the text speak for itself and not impose on it what he thinks or wishes it said. Much too frequently, a preacher conceives of what his congregation's needs are and rushes naively to a text to support his conception. The interpretive results are tragic and, beyond this, the preacher's prime reason for standing before people has suffered abuse.

9. The proper choice of an English translation on which to base a sermon is the subject of chapter 17 in this book, but whatever version is chosen, the preacher will have to correct or clarify the translation during the message. During a message, he must be careful to limit these corrections, perhaps to only two or three, for fear of shaking the confidence of his listeners in the Bible they hold in their hands. After all, part of his goal is to cultivate a hunger among his people to study the Bible privately. Too many criticisms of that Bible will undermine their dependence on a given translation and fuel a "what's-the-use?" attitude on their side.

10. Contemporary preaching is best done by people who possess the spiritual gifts of teaching and exhortation (Rom. 12:7, 8; 1 Cor. 12:28, 29;

Eph. 4:11). It combines a ministry primarily to the human intellect with one addressed primarily to the will. Teaching provides instruction in doctrine, which is the basis for exhortations on how to live more consistently for Christ. No two people have these combined gifts in equal strengths, nor do they have the gifts in the same proportions. So each person is completely unique and should not try to produce an exact imitation of someone else's preaching. Among prospective preachers in particular, the tendency is to observe a preacher with a strong "charisma"—an indescribable appeal and attractiveness with listeners—and to try to imitate him. This is a mistake because no two members of the body of Christ have identical functions or were meant to be clones of one another.

11. The speaker should have a general idea of the average level of comprehension of those addressed. He should gear most of his remarks just below that level, but periodically he should rise above that level a bit.[15] This will challenge his people and keep them from getting bored with hearing so much that they already know. If he stays above that level too much, they will become frustrated and lose interest because they are in the dark about what is being preached. Balance is the key.

12. Every expository message should teach something that the recipients did not already know before hearing the sermon.[16] To some congregations unaccustomed to an expository ministry this may be uncomfortable at first. They have not come to the church service to be instructed because sermons they have heard in the past have consisted of a series of personal experiences or a string of platitudes without a firm biblical basis and not of instruction about the meaning of the text. Their orientation has been reflected in the oft-repeated philosophy, "Our problem isn't that we don't know enough, but that we don't put what we do know into practice." This ill-conceived philosophy assumes that knowing and doing are antithetical—that is, that they form an "either/or" pair—when in reality they are not. The real situation is better stated, "Our problem is that we don't know enough *and* that we don't put what we do know into practice." Instruction must be the prime objective if long-lasting, spiritually improved behavior is to result. Meeting the challenge of Bible exposition to teach the previously unknown is facilitated by the expositor's familiarity with the original text. Usually he will have more than he can teach in his allotted time. As the saying goes, "His sermon barrel will never run dry."

13. The preacher of God's Word should take care not to overload his congregation. The average Christian can digest only so much at one sitting, particularly when he is being taught unfamiliar material. The messenger must be very sensitive to the capacity of those who sit under his ministry and govern his teaching accordingly.

14. How much a Bible expositor can teach effectively in one sermon is the function of a wide variety of factors. It will depend upon his combination

of giftedness in teaching and exhortation, the nature of the sermon text, his method of preparation, the attention-span of his hearers, and other factors. As a general rule with most congregations in the American culture, the first fifteen to twenty minutes is the best time to emphasize teaching in a message.[17] After this, listeners tend to become mentally fatigued, so to speak, and added effort is necessary to hold their attention. More applications of the text and illustrations of its principles are good ways to spark attentiveness. This does not mean that the first half of the sermon must be devoid of applications and illustrations, nor that the last half must completely ignore teaching. It is rather a matter of the proportional emphasis to be given to each in successive parts of the sermon.

15. In expository preaching, teaching of the "not already known" should be mingled with what listeners do already know or what they can glean for themselves from reading an English translation. This familiar material furnishes them with a point of reference to which they can relate the new instruction received. Without this anchor, they have no way to assimilate the message with their already formulated Christian beliefs. With this reference point their broad comprehension of Christian doctrine as a whole can be expanded.

16. The expositor should avoid the pitfall of sensationalism. The temptation is strong to gear one's message for novelty. Forcing upon the original text a spectacular connotation that it was never intended to convey is all too common. A preacher may do this sort of thing for the shock-effect and the consequent popularity it produces. If he opts for this route to gain applause or acceptance by his listeners, he has abused his responsibility and privilege as a proclaimer of God's Word. The line separating the selfish motives of a sensation-seeker and the unselfish motives of a humble attempt to maintain audience attention is sometimes very fine. God's servant must be careful not to cross that line in the wrong direction.[18]

OUR CHALLENGE

In summary, the preacher's God-given responsibility is to deliver accurately and effectively to his listeners what the Holy Spirit meant when He inspired the writers to pen the Scriptures. Anything short of this is not expository preaching and falls short of fulfilling the divine mandate to "preach the Word" (2 Tim. 4:2). To communicate accurately and effectively through the power of the Holy Spirit what has been written in Scripture is the most fulfilling service that a person can render to others.

In any book about the "how to's" of preaching, goals so high that they are unattainable are usually upheld. This criticism is applicable to the above remarks. One offering this kind of advice lays himself open to the charge of being so idealistic that he is not realistic. Yet to lower the standards, just because human imperfections prohibit perfect achievement, is to sacrifice the high ideals that befit the calling to preach the whole counsel of God. The man of God engaged in preaching must continue his efforts to improve his role in this eternal service for the benefit of other human beings and the glory of God. When the final tally is in, he recognizes, of course, the Holy Spirit as ultimately responsible for giving the increase through the proclamation of the Word of God. In the process, however, he will have done his best to be a vessel fit for the Master's use (2 Tim. 2:21).

9

Grammatical Analysis and Expository Preaching

George J. Zemek

The expositor is challenged to preach *the Word,* not merely to ser-
monize *from* or *about* it. If people are to be graciously and wonderfully changed, preachers must offer them sermons that expound the
words from the Word. The man of God must not get in the way, but
rather allow the texts to "preach" themselves. The methodology that
is discussed and exemplified here provides a means of maximizing
the text's sovereignty and efficacy. What comes forth in a sermon is
what the Spirit has powerfully breathed into that text of Scripture.
The result is that God is pleased not only with one's theological
orthodoxy, but also with the methodological orthopraxy.

Preparing for genuine expository preaching involves far more than
just engaging in legitimate word studies.[1] Not only are the Bible's words
God-breathed (2 Tim. 3:16), but so also are the relationships of those words
to one another. Therefore, the preacher committed to handling the Word of
Truth accurately (2 Tim. 2:15) must be willing to expend considerable effort
studying syntactical (that is, pertaining to the interrelationships of words,
phrases, clauses, etc.) as well as semantical (that is, pertaining to words and
their contextual meanings) dimensions of the biblical text.

This not only sounds like hard work, it is! However, it is an absolutely
essential labor, since biblical theology informs us that the Holy Spirit uses
those very words, phrases, clauses, etc. from His Word to produce and
sustain life changes in people. Shortcuts are not an option for the preacher
seriously committed to aligning his exegetical and homiletical methodology
with the theology (especially his bibliology, hamartiology, and soteriology)
he professes to uphold.[2]

The implications of 2 Timothy 4:2 are obvious as John Stott has noted,
"Timothy is to 'preach' this word, himself to speak what God has spoken."[3]
The content of his proclamation is carefully delineated: It is "the word" that
he is to herald. In practice, this implies "the exclusive validity of expository
preaching," and "expository preaching at its best" is "textual preaching."[4]

Consequently, if we faithfully herald the words from the Word (that is, genuine textual exposition), "the sermon is nothing less than a representation of the Word of God."[5]

No wonder Peter urged that "if anyone speaks, he should do it as one speaking the very words of God" (1 Pet. 4:11a, NIV). It is therefore possible, if total faithfulness to the biblical text is our goal, to approach what Paul wrote about in 1 Thessalonians 1:5 and 2:13. As Runia concludes, "If today's preacher brings the same message [that is, the now inscripturated prophetic-apostolic Word] . . . God also speaks through him. Then his [that is, the preacher's] word too is not just a human word, but the Word of God Himself."[6]

Therefore, significant blame comes to the spiritual chefs who, though adequately trained in the culinary arts to create gourmet meals, have become short-order cooks noted for their limited fast-food menus. A consistent diet of greasy spiritual burgers and fries will never nourish a strong and healthy body of Christ. Men of God know this to be true and must respond with more than lip service confessions of shortcomings in this vital area of ministry.[7] Now is the time to bring forth fruit commensurate with "repentance."

THE ESSENTIALS OF TEXTUAL EXPOSITION

Two general essentials characterize textual exposition. The first relates to the sermon's objectivity, and the second to its applicability.

The Controlling Essential

Authentic textual exposition, above all, must be *inductive,* that is, the biblical passage itself should provide all the components of a message. "We do wrong when we take a text and read our message into it."[8] Kaiser aptly stresses the centrality of the biblical text along with attendant prerequisites for handling and organizing it in an inductive fashion:

> What is so lacking . . . is exactly what needs to be kept in mind with respect to every sermon which aspires to be at once both Biblical and practical: it must be derived from an honest exegesis of the text and it must constantly be kept close to the text. . . . Let it be stated as a sort of first principle that preparation for preaching is always a movement which must begin with the text of Scripture and have as its goal the proclamation of that Word in such a way that it can be heard with all its poignancy and relevancy to the modern situation without dismissing one iota of its original normativeness. . . . If the text of Scripture is the central concern, then a mastery of [more realistically, a *growing proficiency* in] Hebrew, Aramaic, and Greek is a basic requirement. . . . The exegetical route is not easy; it requires a lot of work, but in the end it is just as rewarding as it is awesome in its initial demands. . . . Background studies . . . are exceedingly helpful and necessary as a proper

preparation for approaching a Biblical text. But finally we must come to the *text itself.*[9]

And when we do come to that text, we must never violate its Spirit-given sovereignty. The preacher must allow it to control his theological conceptions and homiletical creativity, not vice versa.

Of special significance are the stylistic, structural, and especially the grammatical and syntactical features of a given text:

> We contend that the original languages serve best when we become aware of the syntax and grammar involved in phrases, clauses, and sentences. . . . The serious exegete should learn to master the basic principles of Greek and Hebrew grammar and syntax. . . . At the heart of exegesis there should be a detailed syntactical analysis which involves identification of (1) the theme proposition; (2) the relationship . . . of all other sentences, clauses, and phrases in the paragraph to that theme proposition; and (3) the connection of the paragraph with other paragraphs. Without such analysis the results of exegesis fall stillborn on the ears of the congregation. . . . Time and again the exegete may be saved from would-be disaster and the perils of subjectivism by relying on the text's own pattern of emphasis as it is often indicated by some stylistic, grammatical, or rhetorical device that supplies the authoritative basis for principlizing that text. . . . The whole objective . . . is to let the Scriptures have the major, if not the only, role in determining the shape, logic, and development of our message. It is to be hoped that God's men and women will be challenged to reread that very same Biblical text on their own soon after they have heard the message. Even if they cannot recall the outline (they probably will not—sorry!), that Word of Scripture will still speak to them because they have thought through its structure and shape in such a way as to have decisively met God in that text.[10]

Based upon the God-breathed phenomena of a passage,[11] every effort must be made to protect *the text's* freedom of speech. From the sermon title, to the introduction, proposition, body, and conclusion, the text's voice must never be muffled.

Most importantly, objective data from a biblical text must determine the body of a sermon. Based on its grammatical and syntactical phenomena, the text must be allowed to surface and evidence itself in the sermon outline.[12] Inductive methodology is particularly indispensable at this point, since the outline should progressively communicate the development of a unit of Scripture.

The Dynamic Essential

Without violating the original intention(s) of the author of a text, it should be handled in a fashion conducive to contemporary application in life. In general, "state the author's proposition, arguments, narrations, and illustrations in timeless abiding truths with special focus on the application of those truths to the current needs of the Church."[13] This is not easily taught, but it may be "caught" (that is, perceived and developed) with increasing experience and practice. This "skill" should mature as the preacher's theological understanding broadens and as his scriptural insight into life's situation deepens.

A METHODOLOGY FOR TEXTUAL EXPOSITION

The following methodology is compatible with most portions of Scripture that are syntactical-homiletical (that is, major units of thought bound together by language connectors such as conjunctions) or conceptual-homiletical (that is, major units bound together by logical ties only) entities. Homiletical entities or units act as major facets in the development of an author's overall message. As a major facet, each unit contributes distinctively to the total message of its book, epistle, etc. Therefore, each exhibits a unique thrust and meaning. It is this thrust or meaning that must control the formulation of a sermon's overall thesis or proposition.[14]

A unit's main theme is normally developed in distinct stages. These stages or "points" form smaller units, which are usually discernible from grammatical and syntactical features in the text. Larger units are usually marked by stylistic, logical, and conceptual features. This latter phenomenon almost always dictates that a proposition have a plural noun, but that proposition must emerge through inductive study of the data of the text. The text itself should control the number of outline points, their substance, and their integration into the over-arching meaning of the whole unit.[15] Exegetical considerations, not homiletical niceties, should shape the ultimate exposition.

General Suggestions for Outlining

Before this procedure is illustrated, some general suggestions regarding the production of outlines that are both exegetical and homiletical will clarify the technique. Almost always, analysis should begin with a schematic of the passage to be preached. Segments of larger homiletical units may be sketched in various ways such as concept mapping.[16] Informed "doodling" on photocopies of the original text and various translations is frequently helpful. Interrelationships and the progressive advancement of various paragraphs and/or conceptual clusters should receive special attention. Shorter texts, however, lend themselves more readily to well-rounded textual exposition since that method normally entails substantive communication of the depth, not merely the breadth, of a text.

Within these parameters of volume control, most texts contain a variety of internal indicators that lend themselves to various forms of graphic representation. For example, line,[17] indentational (block),[18] or a combination of indentational and line diagrams provides an invaluable method to picture a text's grammar and syntax. The flesh of an expository message should hang on its inductively exposed, grammatical skeleton.

At the clause level, the grammatical interrelationships of various parts of speech, depicted more concretely through a diagram, are visible. This provides inductive control and input for properly outlining and expounding the smallest units of a text. The syntactical relations of clauses should be shown on the diagram by dotted lines and levels of indentation. This forces the preacher in his preparations to make the necessary decisions to bring an understanding of the logical advancement of coordinate and subordinate clauses in his text. Since clause identifications (that is, the types of clauses) and their relationships within a context constitute major factors in the analysis of a larger exegetical-homiletical entity,[19] this stage is vital if a message is to be inductive at the macro level.[20] It should also be kept in mind that in addition to the grammatical and syntactical hinges of a text, certain stylistic phenomena may convey a framework for the argument and/or other interpretive keys.[21]

As a preface to a few examples of outlining, two suggestions to help construct accurately inductive and dynamically applicational outlines are in order: (1) be descriptive, and (2) maintain parallelism in phraseology. The phrasing of points and subpoints should be graphic. If a statement is built on a semantical observation, it should be semantically descriptive.[22] Similarly, if it comes from grammatical, syntactical, or stylistic sources, it should bear descriptive imprints of those sources.[23] Parallelism is essential at all levels of an outline so as to avoid mixing apples and oranges. As Kaiser strongly urges,

> It is . . . important to make sure that the main points are in a parallel structure—if one is a phrase, then all should be phrases instead of a single word or a sentence. If one is in the imperative form or an interrogative, then it is best that the others also follow suit. Likewise, nouns should correspond with nouns, verbs with verbs, and prepositions with prepositions. Thus, if the first point begins with a preposition, so should each of the other main points. . . . Like the main points, the subpoints must also be in parallel structure.[24]

Selected Examples for Outlining

A variety of representative preaching texts appear in the following examples. Length of the passages will vary, as will their inductive determinants for organization. Commencing with a few one-verse models, the discussion then moves to longer and more complex examples.

Ezra 7:10. After a careful examination of the explanatory statement of Ezra 7:10 in its argumentative and historical contexts, its affirmations can be properly understood.[25] Then its inherent semantical and grammatical features surface. From these inductive phenomena, one may produce an outline that is true to the text.

The place to begin is on the grammatical base line as depicted in figure 9–1. The subject, of course, is Ezra; however, it is the combination of the causative verb הֵכִין (*hēkin*) plus the object לְבָבוֹ (*lĕbabô*) that is of special interest. This clause's object, a word normally rendered "heart" (here "his heart"), is an extremely significant anthropological term. It expresses the center of man's personal being with special emphases upon his rational and volitional capacities. Here, when combined with a causative form of כּוּן (*kûn*), meaning "to make firm, prepare, ready, direct, set, etc.," it conveys an emphasis upon the rational and volitional inclinations of Ezra's mind and/or will. Therefore, the verse focuses on his characteristic *mindset.*[26]

Now it is time to move from the horizontal level to the vertical substructure. Three subordinate adverbial phrases not only provide grammatical evidence of the passage's emphasis on the mindset,[27] but the infinitives of purpose involved also point that mindset in three particular directions. These phrases of intentionality thus both complement and complete the major message. Note in the diagram and outline below how all these exegetical observations converge in the plural noun proposition and the major points that issue from it.

John 3:6. The maxim in John 3:6 constitutes the nucleus of a familiar discussion about the spiritual necessity of new birth. The truth of the verse is expressed in poetic parallelism.[28] This literary vehicle provides the basis for a twofold division, that is, the two affirmations conceptually related in an antithetical fashion. The symmetry of the verse goes beyond a *general* contrasting relationship of the first clause to the second and vice versa. For example, both participles come from the same verb, both are neuter gender,[29] both are passive voice,[30] both are articular,[31] both have prepositional phrases with ἐκ (*ek*),[32] both objects of ἐκ (*ek*) are articular, the identical verbs in both clauses are equative, and both predicates are anarthrous.[33] Amidst all this, the stark contrast between "flesh" and "spirit" emerges at the semantical and theological level.

With the parallelism of the major clauses and the internal grammar and syntax of each member, the major points, along with the subpoints, are conspicuous. Also, the correspondences of the "jot and tittle" form, the significance of the equatives, and an emphasis on the impact of the semantical-theological contrast contribute to forming a descriptive outline that interrelates with a properly contextualized plural-noun proposition (see fig. 9–2).

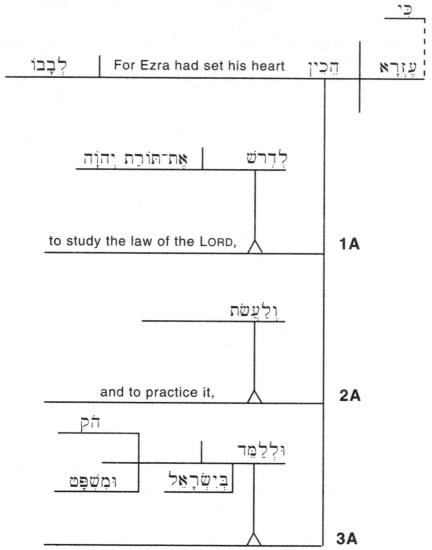

and to teach His statues and ordinances in Israel.

Outline of Ezra 7:10:

The three primary INTENTIONS of Ezra's mind-set towards the Word give preachers an example worth emulating:

1A. To Study the Word Diligently
2A. To Practice the Word Diligently
3A. To Communicate the Word Diligently

Figure 9–1
Diagram of Ezra 7:10

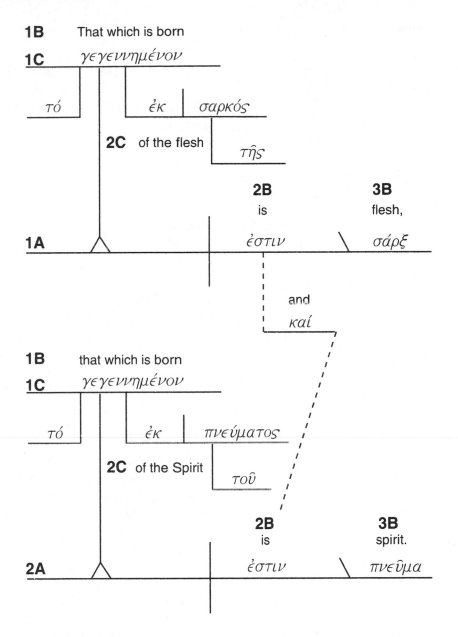

Outline of John 3:6:

The two most important EQUATIONS in the world point out the way of salvation by showing that life can only be generated after its kind:

1A. The Equation of the Generation of *Temporal Life* After Its Kind
  1B. The History (that is, Human) of This Equation
    1C. The Reality of It

Figure 9–2
Diagram of John 3:6

          2C. The Roots of It
      2B. The Harmony of This Equation
      3B. The Heredity of This Equation
   2A. The Equation of the Generation of *Eternal Life* After Its Kind
      1B. The History (that is, Heavenly) of this Equation
          1C. The Reality of It
          2C. The Roots of It
      2B. The Harmony of This Equation
      3B. The Heredity of This Equation

Figure 9–2 (*continued*)
Outline of John 3:6

Proverbs 28:13. The poetic structure of Proverbs 28:13 is quite similar to John 3:6 in using antithetical couplets to convey important spiritual truths. So the verse also lends itself to a two-point outline. The focal point of the proverb is two radically different ways of handling transgression (that is, acts of spiritual rebellion).[34] The first way points to one who characteristically covers over his sins.[35] In contrast, the second points to one who not only confesses his transgressions but also abandons them.

Predictably, the Lord responds differently to these two ways of handling transgression, so the leading verbs represent the antithetical verdicts or "rewards" of the Lord. One subject experiences negative providence, but the other would enjoy personal comfort. The outline below flows from the diagram and integrates these subtle double-antitheses in a way which maintains the form, reflects the critical terms, and carries the total impact of the proverb (see fig. 9–3).

Psalm 119:97–100. The first half of the *mem* stanza of Psalms 119 (vv. 97–100) exemplifies conceptual and grammatical bonding. The theme of youthfulness brings back one of the psalm's recurrent issues (such as, v. 9). However, it is the nearly identical pattern of syntax and grammar in verses 98, 99, and 100 that supplies cohesion. Each verse has an affirmation followed by a substantiation (note the כִּי [*kî*] clauses). Furthermore, the preposition מִן (*min*) functioning comparatively occurs within each primary affirmation or "assertion" (see fig. 9–4). This phenomenon, though seemingly minor, gives the verses their special import to the effect that the Word of God powerfully compensates for a young man's circumstances (see the phrasing of the preposition in the outline in fig. 9–4).

Verse 97 is an introduction, but it is not unrelated. Implicitly, it alludes to the underlying bases of the forthcoming assertions by characterizing the psalmist's attitude toward the Word of God (see similar expressions and intimations of attitude throughout the psalm's 176 verses). Before comparing

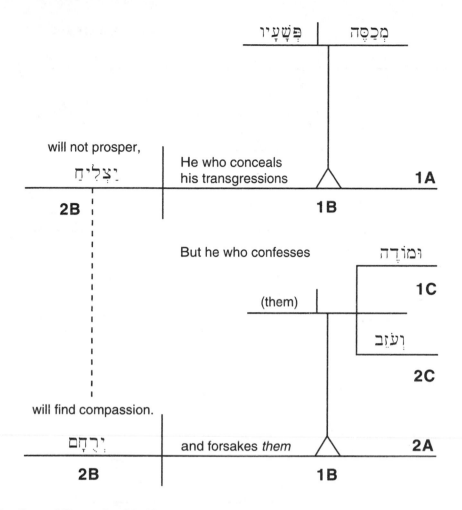

Outline of Proverbs 28:13:

Two differently rewarded RESPONSES in reference to rebellion against God:

1A. The One Who Responds Deviously Will Experience Frustration.
    1B. His Evasive Response
    2B. His Equitable Reward
2A. The One Who Responds Decisively Will Experience Forgiveness.
    1B. His Complementary Responses:
        1C. Acknowledgement
        2C. Abandonment
    2B. His Consoling Reward

Figure 9–3
Diagram of Proverbs 28:13

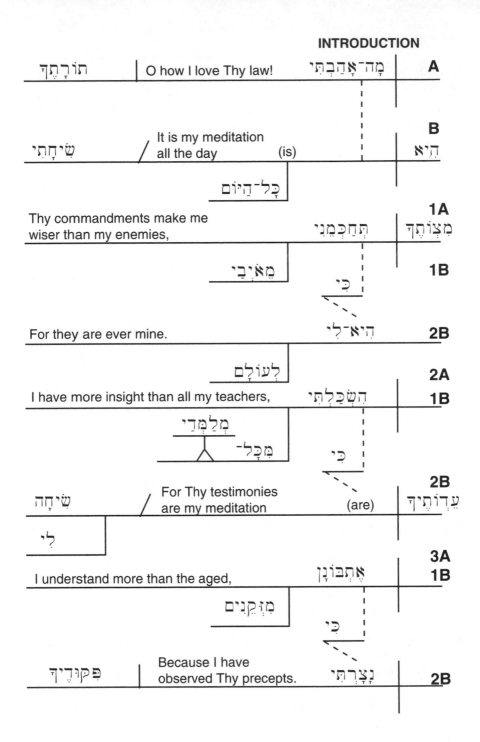

Figure 9–4
Diagram of Psalm 119:97–100

Outline of Psalm 119:97–100:

Three ASSERTIONS of the man of God illustrate how the Word of God can compensate for youthfulness:

Introduction (v. 97): The Underlying Bases of the Man of God's Assertions
    A. (97a) Desire for God's Word
    B. (97b) Diligence in God's Word
1A. The First Assertion (v. 98): The Word Gives Prudence to the Young Man in the Presence of his Foes.
    1B. (98a) The Substance of His Assertion
    2B. (98b) The Foundation of His Assertion: *Possession* of God's Word
2A. The Second Assertion (v. 99): The Word Multiplies the Insight of the Young Man in the Presence of Intellectuals.
    1B. (99a) The Substance of His Assertion
    2B. (99b) The Foundation of His Assertion: *Study* of God's Word
3A. The Third Assertion (v 100): The Word Increases the Discernment of the Young Man in the Presence of More Experienced Men.
    1B. (100a) The Substance of His Assertion
    2B. (100b) The Foundation of His Assertion: *Obedience* to God's Word

---

the diagram and outline, the reader should note the subtle progression of increasing human responsibility incorporated into the *kî* clauses of verses 98b, 99b, and 100b.

Hebrews 12:1, 2. The first two verses of Hebrews 12 comprise one complex sentence in the Greek New Testament. Therefore, the passage must be handled with grammatical and syntactical finesse if the message derived from it is to be inductive in nature. The place to begin is on the base line of the diagram. Both the leading verb, "to run" or "to race," and its object, an *agonizing* (that is ἀγών [*agōn*]) *athletic competition* (that is, [the] "race") suggest a background of the Greek games.[36] The first key term on the base line is the emphatic pronoun ἡμεῖς (*hēmeis*) which is tightly tied into the immediately preceding context (that is, the "Hall of Fame of Faith" in ch. 11) by an adverbial usage of καί (*kai,* "also"). Therefore, by recognizing how essential each of those base-line elements is and by combining them with the vivid metaphor which conveys their major burden, a plural-noun proposition of three points may be constructed (see the following outline).

The nature of the Christian life as a spiritual Olympics is defined more completely by an extensive adverbial substructure. It is as if God, as Coach, were reviewing the basics with a new team. These basics are summarized in the four adverbial statements that form an integral part of the Christian's running (note the various levels of substructure development and description by comparing the outline below). In addition, parallels in semantics and phraseology between the race of Christians and the ultimate example of Christ enrich the description.[37]

Figure 9–5
Outline of Hebrews 12:1–2

Hebrews 12:1, 2 Presents Three Essentials of the Christian's Spiritual Olympics:

1A. The Contestants
2A. The Competition: Some Basics from *the* Coach:
    1B. Our Incentive
    2B. Our Stamina
    3B. Our Preparation: Getting in Shape by Shedding:
        1C. All Impediments
        2C. Ensnaring Sin
    4B. Our Concentration: Focusing Our Eyes on *the* Example:
        1C. His Person:
            1D. As Identified by Name
            2D. As Identified by Association
        2C. His Performance
            1D. The Contest
            2D. The Consummation
3A. The Course
    1B. Its Nature
    2B. Its Layout

Habakkuk. A whole Bible book furnishes a final example of diagramming and outlining.[38] Like the Book of Job, the message of Habakkuk is developed through a ongoing dialogue. However, in this case it is restricted to the prophet and God only. This dictates that the major points correspond to the changes in speaker. When these points are located, five stages of discourse emerge. It remains to integrate these into a plural-noun statement that preserves the book's overarching message, to follow the same procedure at each successive level of development, to make sure that all the textual features (whether stylistic, rhetorical, grammatical, semantical, etc.) control the effort, and finally to strive for description and parallelism at each level of the outline's development. The following outline of Habakkuk should be examined alongside the Hebrew text and English translations.[39]

Figure 9–6
Outline of Habakkuk

Five progressive stages of discourse in the book of Habakkuk unfold the valuable doctrine of practical providence:

Introduction (1:1)

1A. (1:2–4) The FIRST STAGE Is Habakkuk's Lament Concerning Internal Injustice.
  1B. (1:2, 3b) His Appeal Addressed to the Divine Judge via Interrogation
  2B. (1:3c, 4) His Case Presented to the Divine Judge via Argument:
    1C. (1:3c–d) His Evidence
    2C. (1:4a–b) His Indictment
    3C. (1:4c–d) His Summation
2A. (1:5–11) The SECOND STAGE Is God's Decision in Reference to the Rectification of Internal Injustice.
  1B. (1:5, 6) The Pronounced Intention of This Decision
    1C. (1:5) The Awesomeness of This Pronounced Intention
    2C. (1:6) The Activation of This Pronounced Intention
  2B. (1:7–11) The Pronounced Instrument of This Decision
    1C. (1:7) Their General Reputation
    2C. (1:8–11) Their Military Reputation
3A. (1:12—2:1) The THIRD STAGE Is Habakkuk's Challenge of God's Justice.
  1B. (1:12–17) Habakkuk's Support for His Challenge:
    1C. In Verses 12–14, He Musters Theological Support:
      1D. (1:12a–b) His Theological Support Is Based upon the Person of God.
      2D. (1:12c–14) His Theological Support Is Also Based upon the Government of God.
    2C. In Verses 15, 16, He Musters Historical Support:
      1D. (1:15) He Points to the Insolence of the Chaldeans.
      2D. (1:16) He Especially Points to the Blasphemy of the Chaldeans.
    3C. In Verse 17, He Musters Ethical Support.
  2B. (2:1) Habakkuk's Summons Concerning His Challenge
4A. (2:2–20) The FOURTH STAGE Is God's Disclosure *to* and *through* Habakkuk Involving Divine Retribution.
  1B. (2:2, 3) The Importance of This Disclosure:
    1C. (2:2) From the Revelational Standpoint
    2C. (2:3) From the Temporal Standpoint
  2B. (2:4–20) The Lessons of This Disclosure:
    1C. (2:4) The Crucial Lesson Is That the Unrighteous One's Nature Is Perverted.
      1D. (2:4a–b) The Statement of This Crucial Lesson
      2D. (2:4c) The Application of This Crucial Lesson
    2C. (2:5–20) The Consequent Lesson Is That the Unrighteous One's Actions Are Perverted.

1D. (2:5) These Actions Are Evaluated Generally by God.

2D. (2:6–20) These Actions Are Verified Specifically by God *Through* the Taunting Cries of Victims:

    1E. (2:6b–8) The Unrighteous One's *Covetousness*

        1F. (2:6b) The Risk of Such Covetousness

        2F. (2:7, 8) The Recompense for Such Covetousness

            1G. (2:7) This Recompense Is Inevitable.

            2G. (2:8) This Recompense Is Equitable.

    2E. (2:9–11) The Unrighteous One's *Thievery*

        1F. (2:9) The Intention of Such Thievery

        2F. (2:10, 11) The Backfire of Such Thievery

            1G. (2:10) This Thievery Harms.

            2G. (2:11) This Thievery Haunts.

    3E. (2:12–14) The Unrighteous One's *Brutality*

        1F. (2:12) The Irreverence of Such Brutality

        2F. (2:13, 14) The Irony of Such Brutality

    4E. (2:15–17) The Unrighteousness One's *Exploitation*

        1F. (2:15) The Shamefulness of Such Exploitation

        2F. (2:16–17) The Sentence for Such Exploitation

    5E. (2:18–20) The Unrighteous One's *Idolatry*

        1F. (2:18) The Vanity of All Such Idolatry

        2F. (2:19, 20) The Tragedy of All Such Idolatry

            1G. (2:19) This Tragedy Is Expressed by Satire.

            2G. (2:20) This Tragedy Is Expressed by Comparison.

5A. (3:1–19) The FIFTH and LAST STAGE of Discourse Is Habakkuk's Psalm of Public Testimony to the Sovereign God of History.

(3:1) A Liturgical Preface + (3:19d) A Liturgical Postscript.

1B. (3:2) Habukkuk's Prayer in the Presence of the Sovereign God of History

    1C. (3:2a) The Prelude to His Prayer

    2C. (3:2b–d) The Purpose of His Prayer

2B. (3:3–15) Habakkuk's Dramatic Vision of the Sovereign God of History

    1C. (3:3, 4) The Awesomeness of His Demeanor

    2C. (3:5–12) The Awesomeness of His Dominion

        1D. (3:5, 6a) The Outline of His Dominion

        2D. (3:6b–11) The Effects of His Dominion

            1E. (3:6b) The Introduction to These Effects

            2E. (3:7–11) The Illustrations of these Effects:

                1F. (3:7) Historical Illustrations

                2F. (3:8–11) Metaphorical Illustrations

        3D. (3:12) The Summary of His Dominion

    3C. (3:13–15) The Awesomeness of His Deliverance

        1D. (3:13a–b) The Confirmation of His Deliverance

        2D. (3:13c–15) The Commemoration of His Deliverance

3B. (3:16–19c) Habakkuk's Response to a Heightened Understanding of the Sovereign God of History

    1C. (3:16) His Immediate Response of Reverence

    2C. (3:17–19c) His Irenic Response of Readiness

1D. (3:17, 18) The Reality of His Readiness
   1E. (3:17) The Underlying Circumstances of His Readiness
   2E. (3:18) The Unwavering Confession of His Readiness
2D. (3:19a–c) The Resources of His Readiness

Figure 9–6—*Continued*
Outline of Habakkuk

10

Study Tools for Expository Preaching

James F. Stitzinger

A solid theological library is essential to the careful exposition of God's Word. Those seeking to devote themselves to a life of biblical study and exposition must make the commitment to develop a solid library and view it as a high priority. This important goal will be the product of careful planning so that it meets the individual needs and budget constraints of the expositor. A well-balanced library should include books, periodicals, audio and video recordings, and software, all assembled and organized with careful planning and acquired at an affordable pace. A model library of tools for the expositor designed to assist the serious student or pastor as well as the dedicated layman will be recommended.

A biblical expositor must develop and maintain a strong core library of significant books and other materials to use in his preparation. Such a collection is the necessary response to Paul's instruction for Timothy to "be diligent to present yourself approved to God as a workman who does not need to be ashamed, handling accurately the word of truth" (2 Tim. 2:15). In seeking to become expository preachers, today's pastors need to change the sign on the door from "the minister's office" back to "the pastor's study."[1] An expositor must create a quiet room, a sacred place, where he can retreat to study and prepare diligently to expound the Word of God. This room must contain the tools necessary for that study.

The following discussion seeks to assist all who wish to build a library to help them in a pursuit of expository preaching. The principles set forth here, as well as the materials recommended, are designed to give clear direction to the student preparing for a life of preaching, the experienced pastor seeking to improve his library, and the layman seriously interested in the study of the Scriptures.

A carefully assembled collection of good study tools is as essential to the expositor as the tools of the profession are to a dentist or medical doctor. Without them, study is an exercise in futility. In his usual direct style, Charles Spurgeon wrote of the necessity of a sound library for a preacher:

In order to be able to expound the Scriptures, and as an aid to your pulpit studies, you will need to be familiar with the commentators: a glorious army, let me tell you, whose acquaintance will be your delight and profit. Of course, you are not such wiseacres as to think or say that you can expound Scripture without assistance from the works of divines and learned men who have labored before you in the field of exposition. If you are of that opinion, pray remain so, for you are not worth the trouble of conversion, and like a little coterie who think with you, would resent the attempt as an insult to your infallibility. It seems odd, that certain men who talk so much of what the Holy Spirit reveals to themselves, should think so little of what he has revealed to others.[2]

The biblical expositor cannot always be original and must be "content to learn from holy men, taught of God, and mighty in the Scriptures."[3] A well-constructed library will serve as the basis for being taught by others. If an aspiring expositor is not in position to acquire immediately such a collection of carefully selected tools, he must locate one and use it on a regular basis until he can build his own library.

The Priority of a Sound Library

A sound study-library must be a top priority. For many, such a library has been unimportant and the result has been an impoverished ministry, lacking depth, breadth, and stimulation. An excellent library is constructed by deliberate acquisition rather than "accidental" accumulation. Since an expository preacher's library is an integral part of his pulpit work, it should be assembled with an eye toward the highest quality.[4] A preliminary indication of what a core library is *not* will help understand what it should be:

1. It is not a collection of inferior books donated to the preacher by well-meaning friends and listeners.
2. It is not an accumulation of books offered on sale or at discount prices.
3. It is not simply a collection of materials that are highly recommended or found on standard lists of bibliographies.
4. It is not simply an accumulation of required texts used in seminary.
5. It is not an accumulation of material treating current religious trends or theological speculations.

Almost a hundred years ago John Fletcher Hurst described the deplorable condition of the average preacher's library. His perceptive comments are still relevant:

That the average library of the Christian layman and of the minister of the Gospel is poor beyond words, is a lamentable fact. Many of the books are of such inferior authorship as to unfit them for even storage in any home of people either intelligent or hoping to be intelligent. Such books have drifted in because they are radiant with glaring and realistic pictures, or are bound in captivating sheep or calf, or are presented by well meaning friends, or have been bought in lots at auction under the hallucination of cheapness, or because of some other apology for the existence of the trash. If two thirds of the shelves of the typical domestic library were emptied of their burden, and choice books put in their stead, there would be reformation in intelligence and throughout the civilized world. A poor book is dear, and a good one cheap, at any cost. One's best book is that which treats best the subject on which one most needs light, and which one can get only by planning, by seeking, and often by sacrificing. . . .

It is a friend for all seasons, and remains true to the eighties, and beyond, if they come. Better one shelf of such treasures than a shipload of literary driftings from the dead pyramids of publishers who sell slowly and of authors who fail quickly.[5]

In contrast, a sound study-library is a carefully selected and assembled collection of materials that an expository preacher needs to do his work. Every expositor should take time to identify, use, and obtain those items that will directly support his ministry and meet his specific needs in anticipation of a life of exposition, at the same time avoiding "excess baggage" that he will never use. As one preacher has written,

My books are my tools, and I use them. I cannot afford to be a book collector; neither the budget nor the diminishing shelf space . . . permits such a luxury. . . . I enjoy my library. Each book is a friend that converses with and teaches me. Better to have fewer of the best books than to clutter your shelves with volumes that cannot serve you well. Above all, love your books, use them, and dedicate all you learn to the service of Jesus Christ.[6]

THE ESSENTIAL ELEMENTS OF AN EXPOSITOR'S LIBRARY

A sound study-library has five essential elements. Each requires careful thought as to materials to be included, the priority in which they should be acquired, and the way they should be organized. Long before the student of Scripture begins to purchase materials, he should develop objectives and priorities with respect to each of the categories identified below.

A Book Collection

A book is a written record of the labors, views, or positions of a given author or authors. Books take a variety of forms and serve various purposes.

A quality book can greatly assist in the study of the Scriptures by concentrating one's study on a single topic. By providing historical, grammatical, and theological background material, it can save valuable study time. A worthwhile book will inform a reader of relevant issues, positions, and current research. Many books will also provide a spiritual challenge to readers.

The expositor must learn how to build a library of such books. Here are some suggestions for doing so:

1. *Practice "courtship before marriage."* Books should be purchased after they have been used and determined to fill a need. If possible, a book should be used in a library first to determine its value to the expositor. In a few instances, a new book can be purchased based on its author's reputation, the significance of its topic, or the book's relationship to other works.

2. *Evaluate authors and publishers.* Before buying a particular book, it is important to determine something about its author's basic point of view. In addition to a direct recommendation or a review article, much can be learned about the nature of a book from its introduction, footnotes, bibliography, conclusion, publisher, dust jacket, and author information.

3. *Decide if the book should be purchased in paper and/or electronic format.* A significant number of paper books are also published in electronic format. E-books are easier to search and paste into a document and they take up less space. On the other hand, paper books are easier to study out of and provide more consistency in quoting. Most electronic publishing is currently done by individual CD-Roms or by Bible software programs that include published books on CD-Roms.

4. *Prioritize book purchases.* Books should be purchased from a carefully prepared list. This type of acquisition will result in a quality library and will reduce compulsive buying.

5. *Purchase and consult the "best" book or books on a given subject first.* Remember, in theological studies the best is not always the newest or most expensive.

6. *Organize books by subject or use a library classification system such as the Dewey Decimal system.*[7] If books are classified, the system should be kept simple to avoid creating an ongoing project too involved to continue over a long term.

A Periodical Collection

Periodicals are issued in successive parts, usually at regular intervals, and as a rule, are intended to continue indefinitely. Various forms of serial literature include periodicals, journals, magazines, annuals, proceedings, and other ongoing publications. In the bibliographic chain, periodicals usually run five to ten years ahead of books, and thus provide a reader with the most up-to-date thought on a subject. This "cutting-edge" information is often not available in any other kind of source. Unless the expositor has access to a theological library, he should subscribe to a basic collection of periodicals that will keep him informed on biblical and theological issues as well as stimulate his thinking. The following suggestions are offered with respect to periodicals:

1. *Identify and subscribe to a basic collection of periodicals.*[8] Bradford's law states that in any given subject area, a large number of articles will appear in a small number of periodicals, while the rest of the articles on the subject will be in a large number of periodicals. Subscriptions to this small number of periodicals will produce the highest rate of return.
2. *Create a simple index of the articles covered in these periodicals either by a card system or a computer program such as Pro Cite or End Note (Pro Cite includes more technical features; End Note is easier to use).* These can be listed by topic or Scripture verse.
3. *Read periodicals selectively to avoid wasting time.* Reading choices should be balanced between current events and exegetical studies.
4. *Write for sample issues before subscribing.* Also, a number of periodicals are available free when requested.
5. *Use indexes available from periodical publishers as well as general religious indexes.* The two most helpful are *Christian Periodical Index* and the ATLA Religion Database. Paper and electronic versions are available at any theological library. The ATLA Religion Database is available either through OCLC First Search or by purchase of the *Biblical Studies Subset* CD-ROM directly from ATLA.

A Media Collection

In recent years, audio and video recordings have become distinct publishing formats. A significant amount of valuable material is available only in this type of media. For example, much expositional material is available in CD-ROM and MP3 formats. Audio recordings of other expositors can be both stimulating and encouraging. Other types of electronic data are helpful for documenting events and theological positions. The following recommendations apply to building a tape collection:

1. *Collect a limited number of media items from a variety of sources and formats.* This includes tapes, CD-ROMS, MP3s, WMAs, VHS, and DVDs. The building of this collection should follow a master

plan most helpful to the expositor. Include tapes in the following categories:

    a. Individual exegetical studies and courses

    b. Competent expository preachers

    c. Important meetings and events

    d. An area of the expositor's special interest.

2. *Organize this material by subject and author.* It is also very helpful to index the material by card file or computer program as mentioned above, because media is often overlooked as a viable source of information.

3. *Create a lending library of material to share with interested listeners as a support and expansion of the expositor's ministry.*

4. *The expositor should create a library of his own expositions for his own reference and for use by others.*

A Computer Software Collection

The personal computer has become a significant tool and a valuable asset in the hands of the Bible expositor. Students of Scripture are increasingly finding technology indispensable in their work. While computers are often purchased for a singular purpose or to perform a task better than is possible without one, the user normally moves to higher levels of proficiency, achieving results with the computer that he had never imagined possible. Expositors should consider acquiring several computer software programs to assist their work. Computer technology for expositors must include word-processing software, graphics software, database software, and presentation software such as Power Point. Basic web page design software may also be of great benefit in making the expositor's work available to others.

Beyond these, the expositor must also own a Bible searching and publishing software. Several excellent programs exist to enable a student to search the text of Scripture for a word, word variations, phrases, or a verse. Software for the King James Version, New International Version, or New American Standard Bible also allows the user to identify a Hebrew or Greek word behind an English word. The strongest PC Based grammatical concordance program for the Hebrew, LXX, and Greek texts is GRAMCORD which is available through The GRAMCORD Institute (www.gramcord.org). It permits a search for individual words, word inflections, word phrases, and grammatical constructions. The Macintosh version, known as *Accordance,* is exceptionally powerful and valuable for exegetical study. It is available from www.accordancebible.com.

In addition, there are two excellent Bible searching software tools of worth to the expositor. 1) Bible Works 6 New Version. This is a powerful exegetical tool for searching and analyzing the original languages through complex grammatical and syntactical searches. The program also functions as a publishing utility for an excellent collection of scholarly reference works. It is available at www.bibleworks.com. 2) Logos Bible Software Series X (in various versions). While not quite as strong in exegetical searching power or as extensive in exegetical reference tools, it is nonetheless a valuable and important study tool for the expositor. The great benefit of this program is the vast number of theological e-books published only in the Libronix Digital Library System. These can be searched and used in place of paper copies so that a good number of the tools recommended below can be purchased through Logos. The program is available from www.logos.com. Beyond this, there are many good individual e-books or collections of e-books available from individual publishers available on CD-Rom.[9]

A Subject File

An expositor needs a filing system to enable him to organize and retrieve vast amounts of information not found in book format. Such a system should be personal and simple so that materials are easily located. It must also be flexible to allow for expansion in any area. The system should include files for materials produced by others as well as materials produced by the expositor himself. Some suggestions concerning a file system include:

1. *A file system should be organized by numerically coded topics rather than in alphabetical order.* If a classification number is assigned to each topic, only one point of entry per topic is necessary. This system allows related topics to be filed together and provides room to expand or subdivide any given topic.
2. *Headings and structure should make sense to the individual using the system.* These headings should be the same as other headings used for topics of periodical files.
3. *Create an alphabetical index to the file either on cards or a computer.* This facilitates quick location of all the information on a given subject.
4. *Periodically purge the file of unneeded topics and materials so that it remains useful and manageable.*

DEVELOPING A "WANT LIST"

A dependable study library is the product of careful thought. Therefore, the expositor should develop objectives and priorities for his personal library. The purpose of Bible exposition should be clear, and materials should be selected with the purpose in mind. Barber identifies two major problems facing the contemporary expositor who sets out to build a reliable library.[10]

The first is the rising cost of books, which necessitates judicious purchases. The second is the astonishing number of new books being published every year. These two difficulties mean that a preacher needs advice in selecting library tools. The wise expositor will draw on the wisdom of Barber and others in planning a personal library. Here are several issues to resolve:

1. *What kinds of materials are to be acquired?* For example, will they be reference books, commentaries, theologies, periodicals, and items in areas of special interest?
2. *How many of each kind of resource will be collected?* The number and kinds of reference books, the balance between liberal and conservative authors, the number of commentaries per book of the Bible, and the number of books on various theological topics must be determined.
3. *An actual "want list" of basic materials to be purchased should be developed.* As the aspiring expositor learns of new items, he should add them to his list for future purchase.[11] Standard bibliographies are a great help in this,[12] as are recommendations. These can then be refined by personal inspection. A choice of paper or electronic format should be identified for each item.
4. *This buying list should then be prioritized to identify which items are most important to secure first in view of a limited budget.* Once the needs are clarified and prioritized, the effort and sacrifices necessary to purchase the material come easier.

Many Christians want to invest in the ministry of a biblical expositor. A prepared list of needed tools affords an excellent opportunity for others to make such an investment more meaningful. In this writer's experience, most preachers lack a quality library because they have not made it a top priority or because they have not specifically identified the materials they need. This, more than a lack of funds, is most often the reason for not having a good library.

FINDING MATERIALS ON A "WANT LIST"

After completion of a "want list," it must be sorted into in-print materials and those that are out of print. The two categories should be treated separately, and different sources for acquisition developed for each.

In-print items can usually be secured from a well-stocked seminary or Christian-college bookstore.[13] A working relationship with such a store facilitates ordering items in the future. The expositor should subscribe to several discount book houses and purchase needed items as they are put on sale. Most theological librarians can provide a list of discount houses.[14]

Out of print material is easier to locate if an expositor sends his list to various dealers. A "want list" sent periodically to a select group of major used-book dealers, both in America and in the United Kingdom, is the best procedure.[15] Sources in the United Kingdom are very likely to have the sought-after books because religious publishing is very extensive in these countries. Since these dealers will be able to furnish only a few items requested each time, the expositor's library will grow slowly and with moderate expenditure. The most difficult part of finding an out of print book is getting it on a list and writing to dealers. With a little effort and persistence, any book can be located.

Reportedly, Erasmus once said that if he had some money, he would first buy some books, then some clothes, and then some food! Erasmus loved books and considered them "the greatest of all inventions!"[16] In a day of great economic pressure, a similar level of commitment is required to build a sound library. Many expositors deeply committed to building such a library find the costs overwhelming. In light of this, the following proposals are offered to help locate needed material at reduced cost. These suggestions require extra effort and ingenuity, but should produce results.

1. *Put an ad in a local newspaper asking for religious books.* With persistence, good books can be found from former students, professors, or pastors. This technique works better in a denominational or organizational paper.
2. *Visit a major university, seminary, or college library and present a want list to the individual in charge of gifts or acquisitions.* Libraries always have unwanted duplicates. Almost every library has a room full of them.
3. *Inspect the bulletin board of a local seminary.* Opportunities to obtain personal libraries frequently will be noted. Also a "wanted" sign for used books posted on the bulletin board can be quite fruitful.

The First 600 Titles for an Expositor's Library

After the previous discussion of the importance of a solid library for an expository preacher, it seems appropriate to include a suggested list of materials and thereby identify a model library for one who has this goal. The works listed here are only suggestions. Each person will need to adapt the list to fit his own needs. "Books are like clothes: what fits one person's needs and style may not fit another person's at all."[17] Also, this list is limited to a basic collection in the fields of biblical studies and theology, and does not identify other items that an expositor may wish to acquire. The expositor should acquire a number of important items on current biblical and theological issues to assist him in his study and keep himself current. The purpose of this list is to assist a new generation of aspiring expository preachers in gathering a collection of tools for this worthy task. It includes books which have or will stand the test of time and tries to avoid items based on current theological speculation.

The list has a wider purpose, however. It is for a wide spectrum of readers who are seeking to assemble a well-rounded library. Serious expositors should consider the entire list as a model library. A reasonable goal is to acquire the 600 titles in ten years. The first items to purchase have been marked with an asterisk (*). These same ones can serve as a basic list for a serious layman or devoted pastor who wishes to accumulate fewer than the proposed 600 for assistance in Bible study. The following are clarifications regarding the list:

1. *Some of the volumes listed under individual commentaries are parts of sets that are also included in the list.* They have not been counted twice.
2. *When entire sets are recommended, it is understood that individual volumes within each set are of uneven quality because of a variety of authors.* The expositor should sometimes buy selectively from sets with this in mind. In other cases, he should own entire sets so that he has resources on the whole Bible.
3. *The expositor may choose to wait to purchase commentaries on individual books of the Bible until he needs them.* He should remember, however, that books are in and out of print and that he may not always have the time or be in the right place to secure good materials. *The key to building a good library is a good "want list" carefully pursued over a period of time.* Books tend to show up when least expected and often cannot be found when needed! They are often cheaper when the need for them is not so urgent.
4. *The list can also be used as a study guide for those with access to a theological library.* It can also be modified and made suitable as a basis for a church library in biblical studies.

I. Bibliographic Tools

Badke, William B. *The Survivor's Guide to Library Research*. Zondervan, 1990.

––––––. *Research Strategies, Finding Your Way Through the Information Fog* Writer's Club Press, 2000.

*Barber, Cyril J. *Best Books For Your Bible Study Library*. Loizeaux, 2000.

––––––. *The Minister's Library*. Moody, 1985. 2 vols.

————. and Robert M. Krauss, Jr. *An Introduction to Theological Research*. University Press of America. 2000.

*Barker, Kenneth L., Bruce K. Waltke, Roy B. Zuck. *Bibliography for Old Testament Exegesis and Exposition*. Dallas Theological Seminary, 1979.

Bollier, John A. *The Literature of Theology: A Guide for Students and Pastors*. Westminster, 1979.

*Carson, D. A. *New Testament Commentary Survey*. InterVarsity, 5th ed. 2001.

Childs, Brevard S. *Old Testament Books for Pastor and Teacher*. Westminster, 1977.

Danker, Frederick W. *Multipurpose Tools for Bible Study*. rev. and expanded ed. Fortress, 1993.

Glynn, John *Commentary and Reference Survey*. Kregel, 2003

Johnston, William M. *Recent Reference Books in Religion*. InterVarsity, 1996

Kiehl, Erich H. *Building Your Biblical Studies Library*. Concordia, 1988.

Longman III, Tremper. *Old Testament Commentary Survey* 3rd. ed. Baker, 2002.

Martin, Ralph P. *New Testament Books for Pastor and Teacher*. Westminster, 1984.

Rosscup, James E. *Commentaries for Biblical Expositors*. Grace Book Shack, 1993.

*————. *Commentaries for Biblical Expositors*. rev. ed. Grace Book Shack, 2003.

Spurgeon, Charles H. *Commenting and Commentaries*. Reprint. Banner of Truth, 1969.

*Wiersbe, Warren W. *A Basic Library for Bible Students*. Baker, 1981.

II. *Bibles*

American Standard Version. Nelson, 1901.

The Amplified Bible. Zondervan, 1965.

King James Version (or *Authorized Version*). Various publishers.

The Holy Bible, English Standard Version. Crossway, 2001.

The MacArthur Study Bible. Word, 1997.

The NASB Study Bible. Zondervan, 1999.

New American Standard Bible. Lockman, 1977.

New International Version. Zondervan, 1978.

New King James Version. Nelson, 1982.

The Nelson Study Bible. Nelson, 1997.

The New Scofield Reference Bible. Oxford, 1967.

The NIV Study Bible. Zondervan, 1985.

Ryrie Study Bible. Moody, 1978.

The Scofield Reference Bible. Oxford, 1917.
Spirit of the Reformation Study Bible. Zondervan, 2003.

III. Biblical Texts

*Aland, Kurt. *The Greek New Testament.* 4th ed. United Bible Society, 1993.

————. *The Text of the New Testament.* Eerdmans, 1987.

Biblia Hebraica Stuttgartensia. ed. by Ellinger and Rudolph; Deutsche Biblestiftung, 1984.

Brotzman, Ellis. *Old Testamant Textual Criticism.* Baker, 1994.

*Bruce, F. F. *The Books and the Parchments.* Revell, 1984.

*————. *The Canon of the Scripture.* InterVarsity, 1988.

————. *History of the English Bible in English.* 3rd ed. Revell, 1978.

Greenlee, J. Harold. *Introduction to New Testament Textual Criticism.* Eerdmans, 1964.

*Harris, R. Laird. *Inspiration and Canonicity of the Bible.* rev. and updated ed. Attic, 1995.

Jobes, Karen H., and Moises Silva. *Invitation to the Septuagint.* Baker, 2000.

Lewis, Jack P. *The English Bible From KJV to NIV: A History of Evaluation.* Baker, 1982.

Metzger, Bruce M. *The Canon of the New Testament.* Oxford, 1987.

————. *The Text of the New Testament: Its Transmission, Corruption, and Restoration.* Oxford, 1968.

*————. *A Textual Commentary on the Greek New Testament.* United Bible Society, 1971.

*Nestle-Aland. *Novum Testamentum Graece.* 27th ed. Deutsche Bibelstiftung, 1979.

*Rahlfs, Alfred. *Septuaginta.* Wuerttembergische, 1962.

Roberts, B. J. *The Old Testament Text and Versions.* U. of Wales, 1951.

*Ryken, Leland *The Word of God in English: Criteria for Excellence in Bible Translation.* Crossway, 2002.

*Thomas, Robert. *How to Choose a Bible Version.* Christian Focus, 2000.

Swete, Henry B. *An Introduction to the Old Testament in Greek.* KTAV, 1968.

White, James R. *The King James Only Controversy.* Bethany, 1995.

Wurthwein, Ernst. *The Text of the Old Testament.* Eerdmans, 1979.

IV. Old Testament Tools

*Armstrong, Terry A., Douglas L. Busby, and Cyril F. Carr. *A Reader's Hebrew and English Lexicon of the Old Testament.* Zondervan, 1989.

*Barrick, William and Irvin A. Busenitz, *A Grammar for Biblical Hebrew.* s.p., 2001.

Botterweck, G. Johannes, and Helmer Ringgren, eds. *Theological Dictionary of the Old Testament.* Eerdmans, 1974– . Vols. 1– .

*Brown, Francis, Samuel R. Driver, and Charles A Briggs. *A Hebrew and English Lexicon of the Old Testament.* Oxford, 1907.

Einspahr, Bruce. *Index to Brown, Driver, and Briggs Hebrew Lexicon.* Moody, 1977.

*Even-Shoshan, Abraham. *A New Concordance of the Old Testament.* Baker, 1989.

Girdlestone, Robert Baker. *Synonyms of The Old Testament.* Eerdmans, n.d.

*Harris, R. Laird, Gleason L Archer, and Bruce K. Waltke, eds. *Theological Wordbook of the Old Testament.* Moody, 1980. 2 vols.

Hatch, Edwin, and Henry A Redpath. *A Concordance to the Septuagint and the Other Greek Versions of the Old Testament.* Akademische, 1955. 2 vols.

*Holladay, William. *A Concise Hebrew and Aramaic Lexicon of the Old Testament.* Eerdmans, 1971.

Jenni, Ernst and Claus Westermann. *Theological Lexicon of the Old Testament.* Hendrickson, 1997. 3 vols.

Koehler, Ludwig, and Walter Baumgartner. *The Hebrew and Aramaic Lexicon of The Old Testament.* Brill, 1994–2000. 5 vols.

*Kohlenberger III, John R., James A Swanson. *The Hebrew English Concordance To the Old Testament.* Zondervan, 1998

Liddell, Henry G., and Robert Scott. *A Greek English Lexicon.* 9th. ed., rev. by H. S. Jones and R. McKenzie; Oxford, 1968.

Muravka, T. *Hebrew/Aramaic Index to the Septuagint Keyed to the Hatch-Redpath Concordance.* Baker, 1998.

*Owens, John Joseph. *Analytical Key to the Old Testament.* Baker, 1989. 4 vols.

Seow, C. L. *A Grammar for Biblical Hebrew.* Abingdon, 1987.

Unger, Merrill F., and William White. *Nelson's Expository Dictionary of the Old Testament.* Nelson, 1980.

Van Gemeren, Willem A. *New International Dictionary of Old Testament Theology And Exegesis.* Zondervan, 1997 5 vols.

Waltke, Bruce. *An Intermediate Hebrew Grammar.* Eisenbrauns, 1984.

————. and M. O'Connor. *An Introduction to Biblical Hebrew Syntax.* Eisenbrauns, 1990.

*Weingreen, Jacob. *Practical Grammar for Classical Hebrew.* Oxford, 1959.

Wilson, William. *Old Testament Word Studies.* Kregel, 1978.

*Wigram, George *The Englishman's Hebrew Concordance of the Old Testament.* Hendrickson, 1996.

V. New Testament Tools

*Abbot-Smith, George. *A Manual Greek Lexicon of the New Testament.* T. & T. Clark, 1936.

Alsop, John R., ed. *An Index to the Revised Bauer-Arndt-Gingrich Greek Lexicon.* 2nd ed. by Wilbur Gingrich and Frederick W. Danker; Zondervan, 1981.

Balz, Horst, and Gerhard Schneider, eds. *Exegetical Dictionary of the New Testament.* Eerdmans, 1978. 3 vols

Black, David A. *Linguistics for Students of New Testament Greek.* Baker, 1988.

————. *Linguistics and New Testament Interpretation.* Broadman, 1992.

Barclay, William. *New Testament Words.* Westminster, 1974.

*Bauer, Walter, W. F. Arndt, F. W. Gingrich, and F. W. Danker. *A Greek-English Lexicon of the New Testament and Other Early Christian Literature.* University of Chicago, 3rd ed, 2000.

Blass, F. W., A. Debrunner, and Robert W. Funk. *A Grammar of New Testament and Other Early Christian Literature.* University of Chicago, 1961.

Bromiley, Geoffrey. *Theological Dictionary of the New Testament.* ed. by Gerhard Kittel and Gerhard Friedrich, translated by Geoffrey W. Bromiley, abridged in 1 vol. Eerdmans, 1985.

*Brown, Colin, ed. *The New International Dictionary of New Testament Theology.* Zondervan, 1975–86. 4 vols.

Burton, Ernest DeWitt. *Syntax of the Moods and Tenses in New Testament Greek.* T. & T. Clark, 1898.

Cremer, Hermann. *Biblico-Theological Lexicon of New Testament Greek.* 4th ed. T. & T. Clark, 1962.

Dana, H. E., and Julius R. Mantey. *A Manual Grammar of the Greek New Testament.* Macmillan, 1955.

Gingrich, F. W. *A Shorter Lexicon of the Greek Testament.* 2nd ed., rev. by Frederick W. Danker. University of Chicago, 1983.

Hanna, Robert. *A Grammatical Aid to the Greek New Testament.* Baker, 1983.

Kittel, Gerhard, and Gerhard Friedrich. *The Theological Dictionary of the New Testament.* Translated by Geoffrey Bromiley. Eerdmans, 1964–76. 10 vols.

Kohlenberger III, John R., Edward W. Goodrick and James A. Swanson. *The Exhaustive Concordance to the Greek New Testament.* Zondervan, 1995.

*————. *The Greek English Concordance To the New Testament.* Zondervan, 1997.

Liddell, H. G., and R. Scott, *A Greek-English Lexicon*. 8th ed. Clarendon, 1897.

*Machen, J. Gresham. *New Testament Greek for Beginners*. Macmillan, 1923.

Moule, C. F. D. *An Idiom Book of the New Testament Greek*. Cambridge, 1963.

Moulton, James Hope. *A Grammar of New Testament Greek*. T. & T. Clark, 1908– . 4 vols.

———— and George Milligan. *The Vocabulary of the Greek New Testament Illustrated from the Papyri and Other Non-Literary Sources*. Hodder and Stoughton, 1952.

Moulton, William, and A. S. Geden. *A Concordance to the Greek Testament*. 6th ed., fully rev. by I. Howard Marshall. T. & T. Clark, 2002.

Richards, Lawrence O. *Expository Dictionary of Bible Words*. Zondervan, 1985.

*Rienecker, Fritz. *A Linguistic Key to the Greek New Testament*. Zondervan, 1980.

Robertson, A. T. *A Grammar of the Greek New Testament in the Light of Historical Research*. Broadman, 1923.

Rogers, Cleon L Jr. and Cleon L Rogers III. *The New Linguistic and Exegetical Key to The Greek New Testament*. Zondervan, 1998.

Smith, J. B. *Greek-English Concordance to the New Testament*. Herald, 1955.

Spicq, Ceslas. *Theological Lexicon of the New Testament*. Hendrickson, 1994. 3 vols.

Sturtz, Harry A. *The Byzantine Text-Type and New Testament Textual Criticism*. Nelsons, 1984.

*Thayer, Joseph H. *Greek-English Lexicon of the New Testament*. Zondervan, 1962.

Trench, Richard Chenevix. *Synonyms of the New Testament*. Eerdmans, 1953.

Turner, Nigel. *Christian Words*. Nelson, 1981.

————. *Grammatical Insights into the New Testament*. T. & T. Clark, 1977.

*Vine, W. E., Merrill F. Unger, and William White. *An Expository Dictionary of Biblical Words*. Nelsons, 1984.

*Wallace, Daniel B. *The Basic of New Testament Syntax: An Intermediate GreekGrammar*. Zondervan, 2000.

————. *Greek Grammar Beyond the Basics*. Zondervan, 1996.

*Wingram, George V. *The Englishman's Greek Concordance of the New Testament*. 9th ed.; Zondervan, 1970.

Zerwick, Max, and Mary Grosvener. *A Grammatical Analysis of the Greek New Testament*. Biblical Institute, 1981.

VI. *Hermeneutics and Exegesis*

Archer, Gleason L. *Encyclopedia of Bible Difficulties*. Zondervan, 1982.

Black, David A. and David Dockery, eds. *Interpreting the New Testament*. Baker, 2001.

Chisholm, Robert. *From Exegesis to Exposition*. Baker, 1998.

Couch, Mal. ed. *An Introduction to Classical Evangelical Hermeneutics*. Kregel, 2000.

Johnson, Elliott. *Expository Hermeneutics*. Grand Rapids: Zondervan, 1990.

Ferguson, Duncan S. *Biblical Hermeneutics, an Introduction*. John Knox, 1986.

*Kaiser, Walter C., Jr. *Toward an Exegetical Theology*. Baker, 1981.

Kuhatchek, Jack. *Taking the Guesswork out of Applying the Bible*. InterVarsity, 1990.

Linnemann, Eta. *Biblical Criticism on Trial*. Kregel, 2001.

_____. *Historical Criticism of the Bible*. Baker, 1990.

McKim, Donald. ed. *Historical Handbook of Major Biblical Interpreters*. InterVarsity, 1998.

Mickelsen, A. Berkeley. *Interpreting the Bible*. Eerdmans, 1963.

*Ramm, Bernard. *Protestant Biblical Interpretation*. Baker, 1970.

Sproul, R. C. *Knowing Scripture*. InterVarsity, 1977.

Tan, Paul Lee. *The Interpretation of Prophecy*. BMH, 1974.

*Terry, Milton S. *Biblical Hermeneutics*. Zondervan, 1974.

*Thomas, Robert L. *Evangelical Hermeneutics*. Kregel, 2002.

_____. *Introduction to Exegesis*. s. p., 1987.

Traina, Robert A. *Methodical Bible Study*. s.p., 1952.

Veerman, Dave *How to Apply the Bible*. Tyndale, 1993.

Virkler, Henry A. *Hermeneutics, Principles and Processes of Biblical Interpretation*. Baker, 1981

*Zuck, Roy B. *Basic Bible Interpretation*. Victor, 1993.

*_____. *Rightly Divided: Readings in Biblical Hermeneutics*. Kregel, 1996.

VII. *General Reference Works*

*Bromiley, Geoffrey W., ed. *The International Standard Bible Encyclopedia*. Eerdmans, 1979–88. 4 vols.

Buttrick, George A., and K. Crims, eds. *The Interpreter's Dictionary of the Bible*. Abingdon, 1962–76. 5 vols.

Cross, F. L. and E. A. Livingston. *The Oxford Dictionary of the Christian Church*. Oxford, 1997.

Desmond, T. Alexander and David W. Barker. *Dictionary of the Old Testament: Pentateuch*. InterVarsity, 2003.

Douglas, J. D.ed. *The New Bible Dictionary*. 3rd ed. IVP, 1986.

————., and E. E. Cairns, eds. *The New International Dictionary of the Christian Church*. Zondervan, 1978.

————, ed. *New 20th-Century Encyclopedia of Religious Knowledge*. Baker, 1990.

Elwell, Walter A., ed. *Encyclopedia of the Bible*. Baker, 1988. 2 vols.

*————, ed. *Evangelical Dictionary of Biblical Theology*. Baker, 1996.

*————, ed. *Evangelical Dictionary of Theology*. Baker, 2nd ed. 2001.

Evans, Craig A. and Stanley E. Porter, eds. *Dictionary of New Testament Backgrond*. InterVarsity, 2000.

Ferguson, Sinclair B., David F. Wright, and J. I. Paker. *New Dictionary of Theology*. InterVarsity, 1988.

Green, Joel B. and Scot McKnight, eds. *Dictionary of Jesus and the Gospels*. InterVarsity, 1992.

*Harrison, Everett F. *Baker's Dictionary of Theology*. Baker, 1960.

Harrison, R. K. *Encyclopedia of Biblical and Christian Ethics*. Nelsons, 1987.

Hastings, James, ed. *Dictionary of the Apostolic Church*. T. & T. Clark, 1915. 2 vols.

————. *Dictionary of the Bible*. T. & T. Clark, 1898. 5 vols.

————. *Dictionary of Christ and the Gospels*. T. & T. Clark, 1906. 2 vols.

Hawthorne, Gerald F. and Ralph Martin. Eds. *Dictionary of Paul and His Letters*. InterVarsity, 1993.

McClintock, John, and James Strong, eds. *Cyclopedia of Biblical Theological, and Ecclesiastical Literature*. Reprint. Baker, 1981. 12 vols.

Martin, Ralph and Peter H. Davids, eds. *Dictionary of the Later New Testament and its Developments*. InterVarsity, 1997.

*Orr, James, ed. *International Standard Bible Encyclopedia*. Eerdmans, 1939. 5 vols.

Palmer, ed. *The Encyclopedia of Christianity*. Wilmington, 1964. 4 vols.

Reid, Daniel G. *Dictionary of Christianity in America*. InterVarsity, 1990.

*Tenney, Merrill C., ed. *The Zondervan Pictorial Encyclopedia of the Bible*. Zondervan, 1975. 5 vols.

*Unger, Merrill F. *The New Unger's Bible Dictionary*. rev. and updated edition ed. by R. K. Harrison. Moody, 1988.

Youngblood, Ronald F., F. F. Bruce, and R. K. Harrison. eds. *Nelson's New Illustrated Bible Dictionary*. Nelson, 1995.

VIII. Concordances

Anderson, Ken. *The Contemporary Concordance of Bible Topics.* Victor, 1984.

Elder, F., ed. *Concordance to the New English Bible: New Testament.* Zondervan, 1964.

Goodrick, Edward, and John Kohlenberger III. *The NIV Complete Concordance.* Zondervan, 1981.

Hill, Andrew E., comp. *Baker's Handbook of Bible Lists.* Baker, 1981.

*MacArthur John F. *The MacArthur Topical Bible.* Word, 1999.

*Monser, Harold E. *Topical Index and Digest of the Bible.* Baker, 1983.

*Nave, Orville J. *Nave's Topical Bible.* Nelson, 1979.

The Phrase Concordance of the Bible. Nelson, 1986.

*Strong, James. *Exhaustive Concordance of the Bible.* Abingdon, 1980.

*Thomas, Robert L., ed. *New American Standard Exhaustive Concordance of the Bible.* Holman, 1981.

*Torrey, R. A. *The New Treasury of Scripture Knowledge.* revised and expanded. by Jerome H. Smith. Nelson, 1992.

*_____. *The New Topical Textbook.* Revell, n.d.

*Young, Robert., ed. *Analytical Concordance to the Bible.* rev. ed. Nelson, 1980.

IX. Works on Archaeology, Geography, and History

Aharoni, Yohanan. *The Land of the Bible: A Historical Geography of the Bible.* Westminster, 1979.

*_____, and Michael Avi-yonah. *The Macmillan Bible Atlas.* complete rev. 3rd ed. Macmillian/ Carta, 1993.

Arnold, Bill T. and Bryan E. Beyer. *Encountering the Old Testament.* Baker, 1998. with CD-ROM.

Baly, Denis. *The Geography of the Bible.* new and rev. ed. Harper, 1974.

Barrett, C. K. *The New Testament Background: Selected Documents.* SPCK, 1958.

Beitzel, Barry J. *The Moody Atlas of Bible Lands.* Moody, 1985.

Blaiklock, E. M., and R. K. Harrison eds. *The New International Dictionary of Biblical Archaeology.* Zondervan, 1983.

Bouquet, A. C. *Everyday Life in New Testament Times.* Scribner, 1953.

Bruce, F .F. *Israel and the Nations.* Eerdmans, 1963.

*_____. *New Testament History.* Doubleday, 1971.

Dowley, Tim. *Atlas of the Bible and Christianity.* Baker, 1997

*Edersheim, Alfred. *Bible History.* Eerdmans, 1954. 2 vols.

*_____. *The Life and Times of Jesus the Messiah.* Eerdmans, 1954. 2 vols.

Elwell, Walter A. and Robert W. Yarbrough. *Encountering the New Testament*. Baker, 1997. with CD-ROM.

Ferguson, Everett. *Backgrounds of Early Christianity*. Eerdmans, 1987.

Finegan, Jack. *Handbook of Biblical Chronology* rev. ed. Hendrickson, 1998.

*Gower, Ralph. *The New Manners and Customs of Bible Times*. Moody, 1987.

Harrison, Roland K., ed. *Major Cities of the Biblical World*. Nelson, 1985.

*_____. *Old Testament Times*. Eerdmans, 1990.

Heaton, E. W. *Everyday Life in Old Testament Times*. Scribner and Sons, 1956.

Jeremias, Joachim. *Jerusalem in the Times of Jesus*. Fortress, 1969.

Josephus, Flavius. *Complete Works*. Kregel, 1960.

Kaiser, Walter C. *A History of Israel*. Broadman, 1998.

Keener, Craig S. *The IVP Bible Background Commentary, New Testament*. InterVarsity, 1993.

King, Philip J., and Lawrence E. Stayer. *Life in Biblical Israel*. WJK, 2001.

Littell, Franklin H. *Historical Atlas of Christianity*. Continuum, 2001.

Lohse, Eduard. *The New Testament Environment*. Abingdon, 1976.

Merrill, Eugene H. *Kingdom of Priests*. Baker, 1987.

Metzger, Bruce Manning. *The New Testament, Its Background, Growth, and Content*. Abingdon, 1965.

Miller, Madeleine S., and J. Lane, rev. by Boyce M. Bennett and David Scott. *Harper's Encyclopedia of Bible Life*. Harper, 1978.

*Paker, J. I., Merril C. Tenney, and William White. *The Biblical Almanac*. Nelson, 1980.

*Pfeiffer, Charles F. *The Biblical World*. Baker, 1966.

*_____. *Old Testament History*. Baker, 1973.

*_____. and Howard F. Vos. *The Wycliffe Historical Geography of Bible Lands*. Moody, 1967.

Reicke, Bo. *The New Testament Era*. Fortress, 1968.

Schultz, Samuel J. *The Old Testament Speaks*. 6th. ed.; Harper, 2001.

Schoville, Keith N. *Biblical Archaeology in Focus*. Baker, 1978.

*Tenney, Merrill C. *New Testament Times*. Eerdmans, 1965.

Thompson, J. A. *The Bible and Archaeology*. Eerdmans, 1972.

*_____. *Handbook of Life in Bible Times*. InterVarsity, 1986.

Vos, Howard F. *Archaeology in Biblical Lands*. Moody, 1987.

Walton, John H., Victor H. Matthews and Mark W. Chavalas. *The IVP Bible Background Commentary, Old Testament*. InterVarsity, 2000.

Wood, Leon. *Israel's United Monarchy*. Baker, 1979.

_____. *The Prophets of Israel*. Baker, 1979.

*_____. *A Survey of Israel's History.* Rev. by David O'Brien. Zondervan, 1986.

_____. *Israel's United Monarchy.* Baker, 1979.

Yamauchi, Edwin M. *Pre-Christian Gnosticism.* 2nd ed. Baker, 1983.

X. *Survey and Introduction*

*Alexander, David, and Pat Alexander. *Eerdman's Handbook to the Bible.* Eerdmans, 1973.

Andrews, Samuel J. *The Life of Our Lord Upon the Earth.* Zondervan, 1954.

*Archer, Gleason L. *A Survey of Old Testament Introduction.* rev. ed. Moody, 1974.

Bock, Darrell L. *Jesus According to Scripture, Restoring the Portrait from the Gospels.* Baker, 2002.

*Bruce, A. B. *The Training of the Twelve.* Zondervan, 1963.

Bruce, F. F. *The Letters of Paul and Expanded Paraphrase.* Eerdmans, 1965.

_____. *Paul: Apostle of the Heart Set Free.* Eerdmans, 1977.

Bullock, C. Hassell. *An Introduction to the Old Testament Poetic Books.* Moody, 1988.

Chisholm, Robert B. *Handbook on the Prophets.* Baker, 2002.

Conybeare, W. J., and Howsen, J. S. *The Life and Epistles of Saint Paul.* Eerdmans, 1954.

Craigie, Peter C. *The Old Testament, Its Background, Growth, and Content.* Abingdon, 1986.

*Culver, Robert D. *The Life of Christ.* Baker, 1976.

Dillard, Raymond B. and Tremper Longman III. *An Introduction to the Old Testament.* Zondervan, 1994.

Farrar, Frederic W. *The Life of Christ.* Cassell, 1874. 2 vols.

_____. *The Life and Work of St. Paul.* Cassell, 1879. 2 vols.

Foakes Jackson, F. J., and Kirsopp Lake. *The Beginnings of Christianity.* Macmillian, 1920. 5 vols.

*Freeman, Hobart E. *An Introduction to the Old Testament Prophets.* Moody, 1968.

*Gundry, Robert H. *A Survey of the New Testament.* 4th ed. Zondervan, 2003.

Guthrie, Donald. *The Apostles.* Zondervan, 1975.

_____. *Jesus the Messiah.* Zondervan, 1972.

*_____. *New Testament Introduction.* rev. ed. InterVarsity, 1990.

*Gromacki, Robert. *New Testament Survey.* Baker, 1974.

*Harrison, Everett F. *Introduction to the New Testament.* Eerdmans, 1964.

Harrison, Roland K. *Introduction to the Old Testament*. Eerdmans, 1969.

*Hiebert, D. Edmond. *An Introduction to the New Testament*. Moody, 1975–77. 3 vols.

Kaiser, Walter C. *Classical Evangelical Essays in Old Testament Interpretation*. Baker, 1972.

Kidner, Derek. *An Introduction to Wisdom Literature, The Wisdom of Proverbs, Job, and Ecclesiastes*. InterVarsity, 1985.

Lange, John Peter. *The Life of the Lord Jesus Christ*. Zondervan, 1958.

*Lasor, William Sanford, David Hubbard, Frederic Bush, and Leslie C. Allen. *Old Testament Survey*. 2nd ed. Eerdmans, 1996.

MacArthur, John. *The MacArthur Bible Handbook*. Nelson, 2003.

Morgan, G. Campell. *The Crises of the Christ*. Revell, n.d.

————. *The Parables and Metaphors of Our Lord*. Revell, n.d.

————. *The Teaching of Christ*. Revell, n.d.

Pentecost, J. Dwight. *The Words and Works of Jesus Christ*. Zondervan, 1981.

Ramsay, William. *The Church in the Roman Empire*. Baker, 1954.

————. *The Cities of Saint Paul*. Baker, 1960.

————. *Saint Paul the Traveler and Roman Citizen*. Baker, 1949.

Robertson, A. T. *A Harmony of the Gospels for Students of the Life of Christ*. Harper, 1950.

Scroggie, William Graham. *A Guide to the Gospels*. Revell, 1948.

*————. *Know Your Bible*. Pickering, 1940.

————. *The Unfolding Drama of Redemption*. Zondervan, 1970.

Shepard, J. W. *The Christ of the Gospels, An Exegetical Study*. Eerdmans, 1957.

————. *The Life and Letters of Saint Paul*. Eerdmans, 1950.

Smith, David. *The Days of His Flesh, The Earthly Life of Our Lord and Saviour Jesus Christ*. New York: Doran, n.d.

*Tenney, Merrill C., rev. ed. by Walter M. Dunnett. *New Testament Survey*. Eerdmans, 1985.

Thomas, Robert L. *Charts of the Gospels and the Life of Christ*. Zondervan, 2000.

*————., and Stanley N. Gundry. *A Harmony of the Gospels with Explanations and Essays*. Harper, 1978.

————. *The NIV Harmony of the Gospels*. Harper, 1988.

————., ed. *Three Views on the Origins of the Synoptic Gospels* Kregel, 2002.

Trench, R. C. *Notes on the Parables*. Pickering, 1953.

Unger, Merrill F. *Introductory Guide to the Old Testament*. Zondervan, 1951.

*————. *Unger's Guide to the Bible*. Tyndale, 1974.

*Wiersbe, Warren W. *Wiersbe's Expository Outlines on the New Testament*. Victor, 1992.

*_____. *Wiersbe's Expository Outlines on the Old Testament*. Victor, 1993.

Willmington, H.L. *Willmington's Complete Guide to Bible Knowledge*. Tyndale, 1990–93. 6 vols.

_____. *Willmington's Guide to the Bible*. Tyndale, 1981.

Young, Edward J. *An Introduction to the Old Testament*. Eerdmans, 1960.

XI. *Theological Works*

Bahnsen, Greg L. *Always Ready*. American Vision, 1996.

_____. *Van Til's Apologetic, Readings and Analysis*. Presbyterian and Reformed, 1998.

*Berkhof, L. *Systematic Theology*. Eerdmans, 1941.

Bruce, F. F. *New Testament Development of Old Testament Themes*. Eerdmans, 1968.

Buswell, James Oliver. *A Systematic Theology of the Christian Religion*. Zondervan, 1962.

Cairns, Alan. *Dictionary of Theological Terms* 2nd ed. Ambassador, 2002.

Calvin, John. *Institute of the Christian Religion*. Westminster, 1960. 2 vols.

Chafer, Lewis Sperry. *Systematic Theology*. Dallas Seminary, 1947. 8 vols.

Elwell, Walter. *Handbook of Evangelical Theologians*. Baker, 1993

Enns, Paul. *The Moody Handbook of Theology*. Moody, 1989.

*Erickson, Millard J. *Christian Theology*. 2nd ed. Baker, 1998.

_____. *The Concise Dictionary of Christian Theology* revised ed. Crossway, 2001.

*Grenz, Stanley, et al. *Pocket Dictionary of Theological Terms*. InterVarsity, 1999.

Feinberg, Charles L. *Millennialism: The Two Major Views*. 3rd ed. Moody, 1980.

Garrett, James Leo. *Systematic Theology, Biblical, Historical, and Evangelical*. Eerdmans, 1990. 2 vols.

Gill, John. *Body of Divinity*. Lassetter, 1965.

*Grudem, Wayne. *Systematic Theology*. Zondervan, 1994, 2000.

Guthrie, Donald. *New Testament Theology*. InterVarsity, 1981.

Hastings, Adrian, ed. *The Oxcord Companion to Christian Thought*. Oxford, 2000.

Hastings, James, ed. *Encyclopaedia of Religion and Ethics*. Scribners, 1928. 13 vols.

Hodge, Charles. *Systematic Theology*. Clarke, 1960. 3 vols.

*Kaiser, Walter C., Peter H. Davids, F.F. Bruce, and Manfred T. Brauch. *Hard Sayings of the Bible*. InterVarsity, 1996.

―――. *Old Testament Theology*. Zondervan, 1978.

―――. *Toward an Exegetical Theology: Biblical Exegesis for Preaching and Teaching*. Baker, 1981.

*McClain, Alva J. *The Greatness of the Kingdom*. Moody, 1959.

Muller, Richard A. *Dictionary of Latin and Greek Theological Terms*. Baker, 1985.

Murray, John. *Collected Writings of John Murray*. Banner of Truth, 1976–82. 4 vols.

Oehler, Gustav Friedrich. *Theology of the Old Testament*. Funk and Wagnalls, 1884.

Packer, J. I., ed. *The Best in Theology*. Christianity Today, 1987. 3 vols.

Payne, J. Barton. *Encyclopedia of Biblical Prophecy*. Harper, 1973.

Reymond, Robert. *A New Systematic Theology of the Christian Faith*. Nelson, 1998

Ridderbos, Herman. *Paul: An Outline of His Theology*. Eerdmans, 1975.

Ryrie, Charles C. *Biblical Theology of the New Testament*. Moody, 1959.

Shedd, William G. T. *Dogmatic Theology*. Reprint. Zondervan, 3 vols. n.d.

Turretin, Francis. *Institutes of Elenctic Theology*. Presbyterian and Reformed, 1992. 3 vols.

Van Til, Cornelius. *The Defense of the Faith*. Presbyterian and Reformed, 1955.

―――. *In Defense of Biblical Christianity*. Presbyterian and Reformed, 1967–71. 6 vols.

Vos, Gerhardus. *Biblical Theology*. Eerdmans, 1948.

Walvoord, John F. *Lewis Sperry Chafer Systematic Theology*. Victor, 1988 2 vols.

Warfield, Benjamin B. *Biblical and Theological Studies*. Presbyterian and Reformed, 1968.

―――. *Selected Shorter Writings of Benjamin B. Warfield*. Presbyterian and Reformed, 1970. 2 vols.

―――. *The Works of Benjamin B. Warfield*. Reprint. Baker, 1981. 10 vols.

Zuck, Roy B. ed. *A Biblical Theology of the New Testament*. Moody, 1994.

―――. *A Biblical Theology of the Old Testament*. Moody, 1991.

XII. *One-Volume Commentaries*

Guthrie, Donald, J. A. Motyer, A. M. Stibbs, and D. J. Wiseman, eds. *The New Bible Commentary: Revised*. 3rd. ed. Eerdmans, 1970.

*Harrison, E. F., and Charles F. Pfeiffer. *The Wycliffe Bible Commentary*. Moody, 1962.

XIII. Commentary Sets

*Alford, Henry. *The Greek Testament*. Moody, 1958. 4 vols.

Barclay, William F. *The Daily Bible Series*. Rev. ed. Westminster, 1975. 18 vols.

Calvin, John. *Calvin's Commentaries*. Baker, 1981. 22 vols.

———. *Calvin's Commentaries*. ed. by David W Torrance and Thomas F. Torrance. 12 vols. Eerdmans, 1972.

Carson, D. A. gen. ed. *The Pillar New Testament Commentary*. Eerdmans, 1988– .

*Clendenen, E. Charles and David S. Dockery. *The New American Commentary*. Broadman, 1991

*Gaebelein, Frank E., ed. *The Expositor's Bible Commentary*. Zondervan, 1978– . 12 vols.

Harrison, R. K.and Robert L. Hubbard, Jr., eds. *New International Commentary on the Old Testament*. Eerdmans, 1952– .

*Hendriksen, William, and Simon J. Kistemaker. *New Testament Commentary*. Baker, 1954–2001. 12 vols.

*Henry, Matthew. *Matthew Henry's Commentary on the Whole Bible*. Reprint. Revell, n.d. 6 vols.

Hubbard, David, and Glenn W. Barker. *Word Biblical Commentary*. Word, 1972. 52+ vols.

Hughes, R. Kent. ed. *Preaching the Word Series*. Crossway, 1989–.

*Jamieson, Robert, A. R. Fausset and Brown. *A Commentary, Critical, Experimental, and Practical on the Old and New Testaments*. Eerdmans, 1945. 6 vols.

*Keil, C. F., and F. Delitzsch. *Biblical Commentary on the Old Testament*. Eerdmans, 1968. 11 vols.

Lange, John Peter. *Commentary on the Holy Scriptures, Critical, Doctrinal and Homiletical*. Zondervan, 1960. 12 vols.

Lenski, R. C. H. *Interpretation of the New Testament*. Augsburg, 1943. 12 vols.

*MacArthur, John. *The MacArthur New Testament Commentary*. Moody, 1983– .

Marshal, II. Howard and W. Ward Gasque, eds. *The New International Greek Testament Commentary*. Eerdmans, 1978. 11+ vols.

Meyer, H. A. W. *Critical and Exegetical Handbook to the New Testament*. Funk and Wagnals, 1884. 11 vols.

*Morris, Leon, ed. *Tyndale New Testament Commentaries*. Various eds; InterVarsity. 20 vols plus revised volumes.

*Nicoll, William Robertson. *The Expositor's Greek New Testament.* Eerdmans, 1970. 5 vols.

Perowne, J. J. S., ed. *Cambridge Bible for Schools and Colleges.* Cambridge, 1880. 60 vols.

Phillips, John and Jerry Vines. *The Exploring Series.* Loizeaux, 1994. 14 vols.

*Robertson, A. T. *Word Pictures in the New Testament.* Broadman, 1930. 6 vols.

Simeon, Charles. *Expository Outlines on the Whole Bible.* Reprint. Zondervan, 1956. 21 vols.

Stonehouse, Ned B., F. F. Bruce, and Gordon Fee., eds. *New International Commentary on the New Testament.* Eerdmans, 1952.

Vincent, Marvin R. *Word Studies in the New Testament.* Eerdmans, 1946. 4 vols.

*Walvoord, John F., and Roy B. Zuck. *The Bible Knowledge Commentary.* Victor, 1983. 2 vols.

Wilson, Tom and Keith Stapley. *What the Bible Teaches.* Kilmarnoch, Scotland: John Richie, 1984. 11+ vols.

*Wiseman, D. J., ed. *The Tyndale Old Testament Commentaries.* InterVarsity, 1964. 28 vols.

Wuest, Kenneth S. *Wuest's Word Studies From the Greek New Testament.* Eerdmans, 1973. 3 vols.

XIV. Individual Book Commentaries

Genesis

Aalders, G. Ch. *Genesis.* Zondervan, 1981. 2 vols.

*Davis, John J. *Paradise to Prison.* Baker, 1976.

Leupold, H.C. *Exposition of Genesis.* Baker, 1963.

MacArthur, John *The Battle for the Beginning.* Nelson, 2001.

Ross, Allen P. *Creation and Blessing.* Baker, 1988.

Stigers, Harold G. *A Commentary on Genesis.* Zondervan, 1976.

Waltke, Bruce. *Genesis, a Commentary.* Zondervan, 2001

Exodus

Bush, George. *Notes, Critical and Practical on the Book of Exodus.* Reprint. Klock and Klock, 1976. 2 vols.

Childs, Brevard. *The Book of Exodus: A Critical, Theological Commentary.* Westminster, 1974.

*Davis, John J. *Moses and the Gods of Egypt.* 2nd ed. Baker, 1986.

MacKay, John L. *Exodus.* Christian Focus, 2001.

Leviticus

Bonar, Andrew. *A Commentary on the Book of Leviticus.* Zondervan, 1959.

Noordtzij, A. *Leviticus*. Zondervan, 1982.

Ross, Allen P. *Holiness to the Lord*. Baker, 2002.

*Wenham, Gordon J. *The Book of Leviticus*. NICOT. Eerdmans, 1979.

Numbers

Bush, George. *Notes, Critical and Practical on the Book of Numbers*. Reprint. Klock and Klock, 1976.

Gray, George G. *A Critical and Exegetical Commentary on Numbers*. ICC. T. & T. Clark, 1912.

*Harrison, R. K. *The Wycliffe Exegetical Commentary: Numbers*. Moody, 1990.

Deuteronomy

*Craigie, Peter C. *The Book of Deuteronomy*. NICOT; Eerdmans, 1976.

McConville, J.G. *Deuteronomy*. AOT. InterVarsity, 2002.

Reider, Joseph. *The Holy Scriptures: Deuteronomy*. Jewish Publication Society, 1937.

Ridderbos, J. *Deuteronomy,* Zondervan, 1986.

Joshua

Davis, John J. *Conquest and Crisis*. Baker, 1969.

Goslinga, C. J. *Joshua, Judges, Ruth*. Zodervan, 1986.

Pink, Arthur. *Gleanings in Joshua*. Moody, 1964.

*Woudstra, Marten H. *The Book of Joshua*. NICOT; Eerdmans, 1981.

Judges

Bush, George. *Notes, Critical and Practical on the Book of Judges*. Reprint. Klock and Klock, 1976.

Moore, George F. *A Critical and Exegetical Commentary on Judges*. ICC; T. & T. Clark, 1901.

*Wood, Leon J. *Distressing Days of the Judges*. Zondervan, 1975.

Ruth

Atkinson, David. *The Message of Ruth*. InterVarsity, 1983.

Barber, Cyril J. *Ruth: An Expositional Commentary*. Moody, 1983.

*Hubbard, Robert L. *The Book of Ruth*. NICOT; Eerdmans, 1988.

Morris, Leon. *Ruth, an Introduction and Commentary*. TOTC; InterVarsity, 1968.

1 & 2 Samuel

Anderson, A. A. *II Samuel, Word Biblical Commentary*. Word, 1989.

Barber, Cyril J. *The Books of Samuel*. Loizeaux, 2000. 2 vols.

*Davis, John J., and John C. Whitcomb. *A History of Israel: From Conquest to Exile*. Baker, 1980.

Gordon, Robert P. *I & II Samuel: A Commentary*. Zondervan, 1986.

Keil, C. F., and F. Delitzsch. *Biblical Commentary on the Books of Samuel*. Eerdmans, 1971.

Klein, Ralph W. *I Samuel, Word Biblical Commentary*. Word, 1983.

1 & 2 Kings

DeVries, Simon J. *I Kings, Word Biblical Commentary*. Word, 1985.

Hobbs, T. R. *II Kings, Word Biblical Commentary*. Word, 1985.

*Keil, C. F. *Biblical Commentary on the Old Testament: The Books of the Kings*. Eerdmans, 1971.

Montgomery, James A. *The Book of Kings*. ICC; T. & T. Clark, 1951.

Newsome, James D., ed. *A Synoptic Harmony of Samuel, Kings and Chronicles*. Baker, 1986.

1 & 2 Chronicles

Braun, Roddy. *I Chronicles, Word Biblical Commentary*. Word, 1986.

Dillard, Raymond B. *II Chronicles, Word Biblical Commentary*. Word, 1987.

*Keil, C. F. *Biblical Commentary on the Old Testament: The Book of the Chronicles*. Eerdmans, 1971.

Pratt, Richard L. *1 and 2 Chronicles*. Mentor, 1998

Wilcock, Michael. *The Message of Chronicles*. InterVarsity, 1987.

Ezra, Nehemiah, Esther

Barber, Cyril J. *Nehemiah and the Dynamics of Effective Leadership*. Loizeaux, 1976.

Cassel, Paulus. *An Explanatory Commentary on Esther*. Edinburg, 1881.

Keil, C. F. *The Books of Ezra, Nehemiah, and Esther*. Eerdmans, 1970.

*Kidner, Derek. *Ezra and Nehemiah, An Introduction and Commentary*. TOTC. InterVarsity, 1979.

*Whitcomb, John C. *Esther: Triumph of God's Sovereignty*. Moody, 1979.

Williamson, H. G. M. *Ezra, Nehemiah, Word Biblical Commentary*. Word, 1985.

Job

*Anderson, Francis I. *Job*. TOTC. InterVarsity, 1976.

Caryl, Joseph. *Practical Observations on Job*. Dust and Ashes, 2001. 12 vols.

Delitzsch, Franz. *Biblical Commentary on the Book of Job*. Eerdmans, 1970. 2 vols.

Dhorme, Edouard. *A Commentary on the Book of Job.* Nelson, 1967.

Zuck, Roy B. ed. *Sitting with Job.* Baker, 1992.

Psalms

Alexander, J. A. *The Psalms Translated and Explained.* Zondervan, n.d.

Leupold, H. C. *Exposition on the Psalms.* Baker, 1969.

Scroggie, W. Graham. *The Psalms.* Pickering, 1965.

*Spurgeon, C. H. *The Treasury of David.* Zondervan, 1966. 3 vols.

Proverbs

*Alden, Robert L. *Proverbs.* Baker, 1983.

Bridges, Charles. *A Commentary on Proverbs.* Banner of Truth, 1968.

McKane, William. *Proverbs.* OTL; Westminster, 1970.

Delitzsch, Franz. *Biblical Commentary on the Proverbs of Solomon.* Eerdmans, 1970. 2 vols.

Steveson, Peter A. *A Commentary on Proverbs.* BJU Press, 2001.

Zuck, Roy B. ed. *Learning from the Sages.* Baker, 1995.

Ecclesiastes

Eaton, Michael. *Ecclesiastes An Introduction and Commentary.* InterVarsity, 1983.

*Kaiser, Walter C. *Ecclesiastes: Total Life.* Moody, 1979.

Leupold, H. C. *Exposition of Ecclesiastes.* Baker, 1952.

Song of Solomon

Burrowes, George. *A Commentrary on The Song of Solomon.* Banner of Truth, 1973.

*Carr, G. Lloyd. *The Song of Solomon.* InterVarsity, 1984.

Durham, James. *The Song of Solomon.* Banner of Truth, 1982.

Zuck, Roy B. *Reflecting with Solomon.* Baker, 1994.

Isaiah

Alexander, Joseph A. *Isaiah, Translated and Explained.* Zondervan, 1974.

Morgan, G. Campbell. *The Prophecy of Isaiah. The Analyzed Bible.* Hodder and Stoughton, 1910. 2 vols.

Motyer, J. Alex. *The Prophecy of Israel: An Introduction and Commentary.* InterVarsity, 1993.

*Young, Edward J. *The Book of Isaiah.* Eerdmans, 1965–72. 3 vols.

Jeremiah

*Feinberg, Charles L. *Jeremiah, A Commentary.* Zondervan, 1982.

Laetsch, Theodore. *Jeremiah.* Concordia, 1952.

Morgan, G. Campbell. *Studies in the Prophecy of Jeremiah.* Revell, 1969.

Ryken, Philip Graham. *Jeremiah and Lamentations.* Crossway, 2001.

Lamentations

*Harrison, R. K. *Jeremiah and Lamentations.* TOTC. InterVarsity, 1973.

Jensen, Irving L. *Jeremiah and Lamentations.* Moody, 1974.

Kaiser, Walter C., Jr. *A Biblical Approach to Personal Suffering.* Moody, 1982.

Ezekiel

Block, Daniel I. *The Book of Ezekiel.* 2 vols. NICOT. Eerdmans, 1997, 98.

*Feinberg, Charles L. *The Prophecy of Ezekiel.* Moody, 1969.

Keil, Carl Friedrich. *Biblical Commentary on the Prophecies of Ezekiel.* Eerdmans, 1970. 2 vols.

Taylor, John B. *Ezekiel, An Introduction and Commentary.* TOTC. InterVarsity, 1969.

Daniel

*Walvoord, John F. *Daniel, The Key to Prophetic Revelation.* Moody, 1971.

Wood, Leon J. *Commentary on Daniel.* Zondervan, 1972.

Young, Edward J. *The Messianic Prophecies of Daniel.* Eerdmans, 1954.

Minor Prophets

*Feinberg, Charles L. *The Minor Prophets.* Moody, 1976.

Keil, C. F., and Franz Delitzsch. *The Twelve Minor Prophets.* Eerdmans, 1961. 2 vols.

Laetsch, Theodore. *The Minor Prophets.* Concordia, 1956.

McComiskey, Thomas E. ed. *An Exegetical and Expositional Commentary: The Minor Prophets.* Baker, 1992–8. 3 vols.

Pusey, E. B. *The Minor Prophets, a Commentary.* Baker, 1956.

Hosea

Hubbard, David Allen. *Hosea.* InterVarsity, 1989.

Joel

Busenitz, Irvin A. *Commentary on Joel and Obadiah.* Christian Focus, 2003.

Finley, Thomas J. *Joel, Amos, Obadiah. Wycliffe Bible Commentary.* Moody, 1990.

Amos

> Finley, Thomas J. *Joel, Amos, Obadiah. Wycliffe Bible Commentary.* Moody, 1990.
>
> Smith, Gary V. *Amos.* Mentor, 1998.

Obadiah

> Busenitz, Irvin A. *Commentary on Joel and Obadiah.* Christian Focus, 2003.
>
> Finley, Thomas J. *Joel, Amos, Obadiah. Wycliffe Bible Commentary.* Moody, 1990.

Jonah

> Allen, Leslie. *The Books of Joel, Obadiah, Jonah, and Micah.* Eerdmans, 1976.
>
> Martin, Huge. *The Prophet Jonah.* Reprint. Banner of Truth, 1966.

Micah

> McKane Willaim. *The Book of Micah.* T. & T. Clark, 1998.

Nahum

> Maier, Walter. *The Book of Nahum.* Concordia, 1959.
>
> Patterson, Richard D. *Nahum, Habakkuk, Zephaniah. Wycliffe Bible Commentary.* Moody, 1991.

Habakkuk

> Patterson, Richard D. *Nahum, Habakkuk, Zephaniah. Wycliffe Bible Commentary.* Moody, 1991.

Zephaniah

> Patterson, Richard D. *Nahum, Habakkuk, Zephaniah. Wycliffe Bible Commentary.* Moody, 1991.

Haggai

> Moore, Thomas V. *A Commentary on Haggai and Malachi.* Reprint. Banner of Truth, 1960.

Zechariah

> Feinberg, Charles L. *God Remembers.* American Board of Missions to the Jews, 1965.

Malachi

> Moore, Thomas V. *A Commentary on Haggai and Malachi.* Reprint. Banner of Truth, 1960.

Matthew

> Broadus, John A. *Commentary on the Gospel of Matthew.* American Baptist, 1886.

Hendriksen, William. *The Gospel of Matthew*. Baker, 1973.

MacArthur, John. *The MacArthur New Testament Commentary: Matthew*. Moody, 1985–89. 4 vols.

Morgan, G. Campbell. *The Gospel According to Matthew*. Revell, n.d.

Morris, Leon. *The Gospel According to Matthew*. Eerdmans, 1992

*Toussaint, Stanley D. *Behold the King, A Study of Matthew*. Multnomah, 1980.

Mark

Gundry, Robert H. *Mark, A Commentary on His Apology for the Cross*. Eerdmans, 1993.

Hendriksen, William. *The Gospel of Mark*. Baker, 1975.

*Hiebert, D. Edmond. *The Gospel of Mark.*. Bob Jones, 1994.

Morgan, G. C. *The Gospel According to Mark*. Revell, n.d.

Swete, Henry Barclay. *The Gospel According to Saint Mark*. Eerdmans, 1952.

Luke

Hendriksen, William. *The Gospel of Luke*. Baker, 1978.

Morgan, G. Campbell. *The Gospel According to Luke*. Revell, n.d.

*Morris, Leon. *The Gospel According to St Luke*. TCNT; Eerdmans, 1974.

Plummer, Alfred. *A Critical and Exegetical Commentary on the Gospel According to St. Luke*. ICC; T. & T. Clark, 1922.

John

Carson, D. A. *The Gospel According to John*. Eerdmans, 1991.

Hendriksen, William. *Exposition of the Gospel According to John*. Baker, 1961.

Morgan, G. Campell. *The Gospel According to John*. Revell, n.d.

*Morris, Leon. *Commentary on the Gospel of John*. NICNT; Eerdmans, 1970.

Westcott, B. F. *The Gospel According to Saint John*. Eerdmans, 1950.

Acts

Bruce, F. F. *The Acts of the Apostles*. 3rd. ed. Eerdmans, 1990.

_____. *The Book of Acts*. NIC., Eerdmans, 1956.

*Harrison, Everett F. *Acts: The Expanding Church*. Moody, 1976.

Kistemaker, Simon J. *Exposition of the Acts of the Apostles, New Testament Commentary*. Baker, 1990.

Lloyd-Jones, D. Martyn. *Authentic Christianity, Studies in the Book of Acts*. Crossway, 2000. 2 vols.

MacArthur, John. *The MacArthur New Testament Commentary: Acts*. Moody, 1994–96. 2 vols.

Morgan, G. Campbell. *The Acts of the Apostles*. Revell, n.d.

Romans

*Cranfield, C. E. B. *A Critical and Exegetical Commentary on the Epistle to the Romans*. ICC; T. & T. Clark, 1975–77. 2 vols.

Lloyd-Jones, D. Martyn. *Romans*. Zondervan, 1971–2002. 13 vols.

MacArthur, John. *The MacArthur New Testament Commentary: Romans*. Moody, 1991 2 vols.

McClain, Alva J. *Romans, the Gospel of God's Grace*. Moody, 1973.

Murray, John. *The Epistle to the Romans*. NICNT; Eerdmans, 1968.

1 Corinthians

*Fee, Gordon D. *The First Epistle to the Corinthians*. NICNT; Eerdmans, 1987.

Godet, Franz. *Commentary on the First Epistle to the Corinthians*. Zondervan, 1957.

MacArthur, John. *The MacArthur New Testament Commentary: 1 Corinthians*. Moody, 1984.

Robertson, Archibald, and A. Plummer. *A Critical and Exegetical Commentary on the First Epistle to the Corinthians*. ICC; T. & T. Clark, 1914.

2 Corinthians

*Hughes, Philip E. *Commentary on the Second Epistle to the Corinthians*. NICNT; Eerdmans, 1962.

Kent, Homer A. *A Heart Opened Wide: Studies in II Corinthians*. Baker, 1982.

MacArthur, John. *The MacArthur New Testament Commentary: 2 Corinthans*. Moody, 2004.

Plummer, Alfred. *A Critical and Exegetical Commentary on the Second Epistle to the Corinthians*. ICC; T. & T. Clark, 1915.

Galatians

Bruce, F. F. *The Epistle to the Galatians, A Commentary on the Greek Text*. Eerdmans, 1982.

*Kent, Homer A., Jr. *The Freedom of God's Sons: Studies in Galatians*. Baker, 1976.

Lightfoot, Joseph Barber. *The Epistle of St. Paul to the Galatians*. Zondervan, 1966.

MacArthur, John. *The MacArthur New Testament Commentary: Galatians*. Moody, 1987.

Ephesians

*Bruce, F. F. *The Epistles to the Colossians, to Philemon, and to the Ephesians.* NICNT; Eerdmans, 1984.

Hendriksen, William. *Epistle to the Ephesians.* Baker, 1966.

Hoehner, Harold W. *Ephesians, An Exegetical Commentary.* Baker, 2002.

Lloyd-Jones, D. Martyn. *Expositions on Ephesians.* Baker, 1972–82. 8 vols.

MacArthur, John. *The MacArthur New Testament Commentary: Ephesians.* Moody, 1986.

Philippians

Hendriksen, William. *A Commentary on the Epistle to the Philippians.* Baker, 1962.

*Lightfoot, John B. *Commentary on the Epistle of St. Paul Philippians.* Zondervan, 1953.

MacArthur, John. *The MacArthur New Testament Commentary: Philippians.* Moody, 2001.

Vincent, Marvin R. *A Critical and Exegetical Commentary on the Epistles to the Philippians and to Philemon.* ICC. T. & T. Clark, 1897.

Colossians

*Bruce, F. F. *The Epistles to the Colossians, to Philemon, and to the Ephesians.* NICNT; Eerdmans, 1984.

Hendriksen, William. *Exposition of Colossians and Philemon.* Baker, 1964.

Lightfoot, Joseph Barber. *St Paul's Epistles to the Colossians and to Philemon.* Zondervan, 1959.

MacArthur, John. *The MacArthur New Testament Commentary: Colossians and Philemon.* Moody, 2002.

Philemon

See Philippians and Colossians above.

1 & 2 Thessalonians

Hendriksen, William. *Exposition of I and II Thessalonians.* Baker, 1955.

*Hiebert, D. Edmond. *The Thessalonian Epistles.* Moody, 1971.

MacArthur, John. *The MacArthur New Testament Commentary: 1 and 2 Thessalonians.* Moody, 2002.

Mayhue, Richard *1 and 2 Thessalonians.* Christian Focus, 1999.

Morris, Leon. *The First and Second Epistles to the Thessalonians.* NICNT; Eerdmans, 1959.

Thomas, Robert L. "1, 2 Thessalonians," *Expositor's Bible Commentary*. Vol. 11. Zondervan, 1978.

Wannamaker, Charles. *The Epistles to the Thessalonians: A Commentary on the Greek Text*. NIGTC. Earnmans, 1990.

1 & 2 Timothy, Titus

Fairbairn, Patrick. *Commentary on the Pastoral Epistles*. Zondervan, 1956.

Hendriksen, William. *Exposition of The Pastoral Epistles*. Baker, 1957.

*Kent, Homer A. *The Pastoral Epistles*. Moody, 1982.

Knight, George Knight, Jr. *The Pastoral Epistles*. NIGTC. Eerdmans, 1992.

MacArthur, John. *The MacArthur New Testament Commentary: 1 Timothy*. Moody, 1995.

————. *The MacArthur New Testament Commentary: 2 Timothy*. Moody, 1996.

————. *The MacArthur New Testament Commentary: Titus*. Moody, 1996.

Simpson, E. K. *The Pastoral Epistles*. Tyndale, 1954.

Hebrews

Bruce, F. F. *The Epistles to the Hebrews*. NICNT, rev. ed. Eerdmans, 1990.

Hughes, Philip Edgcumbe. *A Commentary on the Epistle to the Hebrews*. Eerdmans, 1977.

*Kent, Homer A. *The Epistle to the Hebrews*. Baker, 1972.

MacArthur, John. *The MacArthur New Testament Commentary: Hebrews*. Moody, 1983.

Westcott, Brooke Foss. *The Epistle to the Hebrews*. Eerdmans, 1970.

James

Adamson, James B. *The Epistle of James*. NICNT. Eerdmans, 1976.

————. *James, the Man and His Message*. Eerdmans, 1989.

*Hiebert, D. Edmond. *The Epistle of James, Tests of a Living Faith*. Moody, 1979.

MacArthur, John. *The MacArthur New Testament Commentary: James*. Moody, 1978.

Mayor, Joseph Bickersteth. *The Epistle of St. James*. Zondervan, 1954.

Moo, Douglas J. *The Letter of James*. Eerdmans, 2000.

1 Peter

*Hiebert, D.Edmond. *First Peter*. Moody, 1984.

Kistemaker, Simon J. *Exposition of the Epistles of Peter and of the Epistle of Jude*. Baker, 1987.

Selwin, Edward Gordon. *First Epistle of Saint Peter.* Macmillian, 1961.

2 Peter, Jude
*Hiebert, D. Edmond. *Second Peter and Jude.* Unusual Publications, 1989.
Kistemaker, Simon J. *Exposition of the Epistles of Peter and of the Epistle of Jude.* Baker, 1987.
Lawlor, George Lawrence. *The Epistle of Jude, a Translation and Exposition.* Presbyterian and Reformed, 1972.
Manton, Thomas. *A Commentary on Jude.* Banner of Truth, 1958.
Mayor, James B. *The Epistle of St. Jude and the Second Epistle of St. Peter.* Macmillian, 1907.

1, 2, 3 John
Candlish, Robert Smith. *The First Epistle of John.* Zondervan, n.d.
Kruse, Colin G. *The Letters of John.* Erdmans, 2000.
Findlay, George G. *Fellowship in the Life Eternal.* Eerdmans, 1955.
*Kistemaker, Simon J. *Exposition of the Epistle of James and the Epistles of John.* Baker, 1986.
Westcott, Brooke Foss. *The Epistles of Saint John.* Eerdmans, 1966.

Revelation
Beckwith, Isbon T. *The Apocalypse of John.* Macmillan, 1919.
MacArthur, John. *The MacArthur New Testament Commentary: Revelation.* Moody, 1999–2000. 2 vols.
Swete, Henry Barclay. *The Apocalypse of St. John.* Eerdmans.
*Thomas, Robert L. *Revelation.* Moody, 1999–2000, 2 vols.
Walvoord, John F. *The Revelation of Jesus Christ.* Moody, 1966.

A Study Method for Expository Preaching

John MacArthur

Careful and diligent Bible study is the key to effective expository preaching. Because the Bible is God's holy Word, it must be treated with respect, not expounded flippantly or carelessly. An effective method of sermon preparation is based on general rules for Bible study.

An expository preacher must be a diligent student of Scripture. Because the Bible is God's holy and sacred Word, it must be treated with respect, its purity protected, and its intended message never violated or misrepresented. It is not to be handled flippantly or carelessly, but great deliberation and industry must mark all efforts to discern its truths. A commitment to the inerrancy of the Bible carries with it a mandate to preach the Bible expositionally, as noted earlier (see ch. 2). A corollary to this principle is that preaching the Bible expositionally also carries with it the mandate of diligent study.

Fruitful expository preaching demands great effort. Since nothing is as important as the Word, no energy expended by anyone in any other field should even equal the effort of an expositor seeking to "rightly divide the Word." Adams identifies the number-one reason for poor preaching:

> I have had the opportunity to hear much preaching over the last few years, some very good, some mediocre, most very bad. What is the problem with preaching? There is no *one* problem, of course. . . . But if there is one thing that stands out most, perhaps it is the problem I mention today.
>
> What I am about to say may not strike you as being as specific as other things I have written, yet I believe it is at the bottom of a number of other difficulties. My point is that good preaching demands hard work. From listening to sermons and from talking to hundreds of preachers about preaching, I am convinced that the basic reason for poor preaching is the failure to spend adequate time and energy in

preparation. Many preachers—perhaps most—simply don't work long enough on their sermons.[1]

Much shallow contemporary preaching has led people to ask why it is necessary for an expositor to go into so much detail. They want to know why I refrain from just highlighting the practical points and featuring relevant illustrations. If one really believes God inspired every word of Scripture, how can he justify treating it in such a superficial manner? And if the Word is the most powerful sword (Heb. 4:12) and the power of God for salvation (Rom. 1:16) and sanctification (John 17:17), how can anyone invest more trust in stories and clever insights than in Scripture? A man once said to the Puritan preacher Richard Rogers, "Mr. Rogers, I like you and your company very well, only you are too precise." "Oh sir," replied Rogers, "I serve a precise God."[2] We, too, serve a precise God, and that requires diligence and precision on our part.

THREE BASIC PRINCIPLES FOR BIBLE STUDY

To be precise in preaching, hard work is not enough, however. One must also know *how* to work in productive study of the Bible. Being an effective expositor of God's Word depends on the understanding of three basic principles of Bible study.[3]

Observation

Observation is the initial step in Bible study. An interpreter must avoid the temptation to jump immediately into interpreting the specific elements of a passage. Traina defines observation as

> essentially *awareness* . . . the general function of observation is to enable one to become *saturated* with the particulars of a passage so that one is thoroughly conscious of their existence and of the need for their explanation. Observation is the means by which the data of a passage become part of the mentality of the student. It supplies the raw materials upon which the mind may operate in the interpretive process.[4]

Observation includes a broad awareness of the terms, structure, and literary form of the passage.

Observation should be *careful*. Traina relates the following story to illustrate the importance of exactness in observation:

> Sir William Osler, the eminent physician, always sought to impress upon young medical students the importance of observing details. While stressing this point in a lecture before a student group he indicated a bottle on his desk. "This bottle contains a sample for analysis," he

announced. "It's possible by testing it to determine the disease from which the patient suffers." Suiting actions to words, he dipped a finger into the fluid and then into his mouth. "Now," he continued, "I am going to pass this bottle around. Each of you taste the contents as I did and see if you can diagnose the case." As the bottle was passed from row to row, each student gingerly poked his finger in and bravely sampled the contents. Osler then retrieved the bottle. "Gentlemen," he said, "Now you will understand what I mean when I speak about details. Had you been observant you would have seen that I put my index finger into the bottle but my middle finger into my mouth."[5]

Observation also needs to be *systematic*. Martin Luther likened his Bible study to gathering apples: "First I shake the whole tree, that the ripest may fall. Then I climb the tree and shake each limb, and then each branch and then each twig, and then I look under each leaf."[6]

Observation must also be *persistent*. To repeat, extended time in observation is a must for an expositor. He must resist the temptation to plunge immediately into commentaries and other study helps. Nothing can replace firsthand observation. At the risk of seeming to violate my own guideline of keeping illustrations short, I offer the following lengthy story about the great nineteenth-century scientist Louis Agassiz and how he taught one of his students an unforgettable lesson about the importance of observation. The principles it teaches can be applied to our Bible study.

The Student, the Fish, and Agassiz
By the Student

It was more than fifteen years ago that I entered the laboratory of Professor Agassiz, and told him I had enrolled my name in the scientific school as a student of natural history. He asked me a few questions about my object in coming, my antecedents generally, the mode in which I afterwards proposed to use the knowledge I might acquire, and finally, whether I wished to study any special branch. To the latter I replied that while I wished to be well grounded in all departments of zoology, I purposed to devote myself specially to insects.

"When do you wish to begin?" he asked.

"Now," I replied.

This seemed to please him, and with an energetic "Very well," he reached from a shelf a huge jar of specimens in yellow alcohol.

"Take this fish," said he, "and look at it; we call it a Haemulon [pronounced Hem-yoo lon]; by and by I will ask what you have seen."

With that he left me, but in a moment returned with explicit instructions as to the care of the object entrusted to me.

"No man is fit to be a naturalist," said he, "who does not know how to take care of specimens."

I was to keep the fish before me in a tin tray, and occasionally moisten the surface with alcohol from the jar, always taking care to replace the stopper tightly. Those were not the days of ground glass stoppers, and elegantly shaped exhibition jars; all the old students will recall the huge, neckless glass bottles with their leaky, wax-besmeared corks half eaten by insects and begrimed with cellar dust. Entomology was a cleaner science than ichthyology, but the example of the professor, who had unhesitatingly plunged to the bottom of the jar to produce the fish, was infectious; and though this alcohol had "a very ancient and fishlike smell," I really dared not show any aversion within these sacred precincts, and treated the alcohol as though it were pure water. Still I was conscious of a passing feeling of disappointment, for gazing at a fish did not commend itself to an ardent entomologist. My friends at home, too, were annoyed, when they discovered that no amount of *eau de cologne* would drown the perfume which haunted me like a shadow.

In ten minutes I had seen all that could be seen in that fish, and started in search of the professor, who had, however, left the museum; and when I returned, after lingering over some of the odd animals stored in the upper apartment, my specimen was dry all over. I dashed the fluid over the fish as if to resuscitate it from a fainting-fit, and looked with anxiety for a return of the normal, sloppy appearance. This little excitement over, nothing was to be done but return to a steadfast gaze at my mute companion. Half an hour passed, an hour, another hour; the fish began to look loathsome. I turned it over and around; looked it in the face—ghastly; from behind, beneath, above, sideways, at a three-quarters' view—just as ghastly. I was in despair; at an early hour I concluded that lunch was necessary; so, with infinite relief, the fish was carefully replaced in the jar, and for an hour I was free.

On my return, I learned that Professor Agassiz had been at the museum, but had gone and would not return for several hours. My fellow students were too busy to be disturbed by continued conversation. Slowly I drew forth that hideous fish, and with a feeling of desperation again looked at it. I might not use a magnifying glass; instruments of all kinds were interdicted. My two hands, my two eyes, and the fish; it seemed a most limited field. I pushed my finger down its throat to feel how sharp its teeth were. I began to count the scales in the different rows until I was convinced that that was nonsense. At last a happy thought struck me—I would draw the fish; and now with surprise I began to discover new features in the creature. Just then the professor returned.

"That is right," said he; "a pencil is one of the best of eyes. I am glad to notice, too, that you keep your specimen wet and your bottle corked."

With these encouraging words he added,—

"Well, what is it like?"

He listened attentively to my brief rehearsal of the structure of parts whose names were still unknown to me: the fringed gill—arches and movable operculum; the pores of the head, fleshy lips, and lidless eyes; the lateral line, the spinous fin, and forked tail; the compressed and arched body. When I had finished, he waited as if expecting more, and then, with an air of disappointment,—

"You have not looked very carefully; why," he continued, more earnestly, "you haven't seen one of the most conspicuous features of the animal, which is as plainly before your eyes as the fish itself; look again, look again!" and he left me to my misery.

I was piqued; I was mortified. Still more of that wretched fish! But now I set myself to my task with a will, and discovered one new thing after another, until I saw how just the professor's criticism had been. The afternoon passed quickly, and when, towards its close, the professor inquired,—

"Do you see it yet?"

"No," I replied, "I am certain I do not, but I see how little I saw before."

"That is next best," he said earnestly, "but I won't hear you now; put away your fish and go home; perhaps you will be ready with a better answer in the morning. I will examine you before you look at the fish."

This was disconcerting; not only must I think of my fish all night, studying, without the object before me, what this unknown but most visible feature might be; but also, without reviewing my new discoveries, I must give an exact account of them the next day. I had a bad memory; so I walked home by Charles River in a distracted state, with my two perplexities.

The cordial greeting from the professor the next morning was reassuring; here was a man who seemed to be quite as anxious as I that I should see for myself what he saw.

"Do you perhaps mean," I asked, "that the fish has symmetrical sides with paired organs?"

His thoroughly pleased, "Of course, of course!" repaid the wakeful hours of the previous night. After he had discoursed most happily and enthusiastically—as he always did—upon the importance of this point, I ventured to ask what I should do next.

"Oh, look at your fish!" he said, and left me again to my own devices. In a little more than an hour he returned and heard my new catalogue.

"That is good; that is good!" he repeated, "but that is not all; go on." And so, for three long days, he placed that fish before my eyes, forbidding me to look at anything else, or to use any artificial aid. "Look, look, look," was his repeated injunction.

This was the best entomological lesson I ever had—a lesson whose influence has extended to the details of every subsequent study; a legacy the professor has left to me, as he has left it to many others, of inestimable value, which we could not buy, with which we cannot part.

A year afterward, some of us were amusing ourselves with chalking outlandish beasts upon the museum black board. We drew prancing starfishes; frogs in mortal combat; hydra-headed worms; stately craw-fishes, standing on their tails, bearing aloft umbrellas; and grotesque fishes, with gaping mouths and staring eyes. The professor came in shortly after, and was as amused as any, at our experiments. He looked at the fishes.

"Haemulons, every one of them," he said. "Mr. _____ drew them."

True; and to this day, if I attempt a fish, I can draw nothing but Haemulons.

The fourth day, a second fish of the same group was placed beside the first, and I was bidden to point out the resemblances and differences between the two; another and another followed, until the entire family lay before me, and a whole legion of jars covered the table and surrounding shelves; the odor had become a pleasant perfume; and even now, the sight of an old, six-inch, worm-eaten cork brings fragrant memories!

The whole group of Haemulons was thus brought in review; and, whether engaged upon the dissection of the internal organs, the preparation and examination of the bony framework, or the description of the various parts, Agassiz's training in the method of observing facts and their orderly arrangement was ever accompanied by the urgent exhortation not to be content with them.

"Facts are stupid things," he would say, "until brought into connection with some general law."

At the end of eight months, it was almost with reluctance that I left these friends and turned to insects; but what I had gained by this outside experience has been of greater value than years of later investigation in my favorite groups.[7]

The same kind of prolonged pondering of the Scriptures will eventually pay even more enduring dividends, stretching into eternity.

Interpretation

After observing in detail the various parts of a passage, the next logical step is to determine their meaning. That process is known as interpretation. Observation answers the question, "What does the passage say?" Interpretation answers the question, "What does the passage mean?"

One should interpret the Bible literally, in its normal and natural sense, seeking to understand its meaning and not to read his own into the text. Proper interpretation follows the rules and methods of hermeneutics and exegesis summarized in earlier discussions (see chs. 7—8). It is largely concerned with bridging the gaps that exist between the Bible writers and the present day. At least four such gaps exist:

1. *The language gap.* The Bible was written originally in Hebrew, Aramaic, and Greek. Therefore, to interpret it correctly, one needs

to understand the original languages. English-based word studies, such as *Vine's Expository Dictionary of New Testament Words* and Colin Brown's *The New International Dictionary of New Testament Theology* are helpful for those who do not know Greek.[8] *Vine's Expository Dictionary of Old Testament Words* and R. Laird Harris et al., *Theological Wordbook of the Old Testament* (which is keyed to Strong's Concordance) are useful for those who know no Hebrew or Aramaic. Commentaries are also a good source for word studies. Of course, no substitute is comparable to working in the original languages for those who know Greek and/or Hebrew.

2. *The cultural gap.* The cultural setting in which each part of the Bible was written is very different from our twenty-first century western culture. To interpret each part properly, one must understand the culture of its time. For example, understanding the Old Testament requires a knowledge of ancient Judaism and pagan culture, just as comprehending first-century Jewish culture is important in interpreting the Gospels. A comprehension of first-century Greek and Roman culture helps the interpreter grasp the New Testament Epistles correctly.

The Life and Times of Jesus the Messiah by Alfred Edersheim is an excellent source of background material on the Jewish culture of Jesus's day. *The Daily Study Bible Series* by William Barclay, although theologically blurred, is a very helpful source of information on the cultural background of the Gospels and the Epistles. Barclay's theology is suspect in many areas, but he provides good insights into the culture of the first-century world.

3. *The geographical gap.* Understanding the geography of Bible lands is sometimes essential in unlocking the meaning of a passage. In 1 Thessalonians 1:8, for example, Paul wrote to the Thessalonians, "For the word of the Lord has sounded forth from you, not only in Macedonia and Achaia, but also in every place your faith toward God has gone forth." The amazing part of that statement is that Paul had left Thessalonica only a short time before writing 1 Thessalonians. How had their testimony spread so rapidly through the surrounding area? A study of the geography of the region reveals that one of the major highways of the Roman Empire, the Ignatian Highway, ran right through Thessalonica. Thus, travelers along the Ignatian Highway could rapidly spread the Thessalonians' testimony far and wide.

A good Bible atlas, such as *The Macmillan Bible Atlas* or the *Wycliffe Historical Geography of Bible Lands,* is indispensable in understanding Bible geography.

4. *The historical gap.* Knowing the historical setting of a passage often helps immeasurably to understand its meaning. A major effort of research to develop the historical background of a passage often is the major key to its interpretation. For example, understanding the history of Pilate's relationship with the Jewish leaders helps explain why he gave in to their demands to crucify Jesus, though he had pronounced Jesus innocent. Pilate had already antagonized the Jews by some of his policies, and they had reported him to Caesar. Pilate feared that another complaint might get him into serious trouble with the Emperor. He was in no position to refuse their demands.

Bible encyclopedias, such as *The Zondervan Pictorial Encyclopedia of the Bible* or the *Baker Encyclopedia of the Bible,* contain helpful articles on matters of historical interest. *New Testament History* by F. F. Bruce and *The Bible as History* by Werner Keller are also helpful. Books on biblical archaeology are important sources for historical information as well.

Application

After observation and interpretation comes application. Bible study is not complete until the truth discovered is applied to life situations. Application answers the question, "How does this truth relate to me?" The following questions will help apply the truths discovered in Bible study:[9]

1. Are there *examples* to follow?
2. Are there *commands* to obey?
3. Are there *errors* to avoid?
4. Are there *sins* to forsake?
5. Are there *promises* to claim?
6. Are there *new thoughts* about God?
7. Are there *principles* to live by?

Meditation is an important, final step in the process.[10] Meditation entails focusing the mind on one subject, involving reason, imagination, and emotions. It is a natural overflow of the discovery process in Bible study. Concentrated meditation on the truths of God's Word weaves those truths into the fabric of our lives. Perhaps, Paul had this meditative process in view when he told Timothy to be "constantly nourished on the words of the faith and of the sound doctrine" (1 Tim. 4:6).

Excellent Bible study skills are the foundation upon which good expository sermons are built. The expository preacher is, by definition, a skilled Bible student. He interprets Scripture accurately, applies its truths in his own life, and then proclaims them to his congregation.

Studying for the Expository Sermon

An expositor needs to develop a plan of studying for his sermons. His method should be systematic and should include basic elements for effective, productive Bible study. The following method is the one I follow in my own study.

Read the Book

I usually preach through entire books of the New Testament, so I always begin by reading the whole book. You cannot begin your exposition of a Bible book until you have read and generally observed the message and flow of thinking through all of it. Maturing as an expository preacher, I have come to realize how important this step is. When I was less experienced, I sometimes found myself chasing down rabbit trails in my interpretation because I lacked familiarity with a book's theme. Skipping this step may lead to contradicting oneself later. For example, in 1 Thessalonians, God's eschatological wrath is mentioned in 1:10 and again in 5:9. We would want to make sure that our interpretation of wrath in those two passages is consistent.

Context is the most important hermeneutical principle. By reading and familiarizing ourselves with the entire book, the expositor can relate each passage to the overall context of the book. Putting together a general outline of the book and identifying key verses is also helpful in grasping the overall flow.

At this point I also read the introductory sections in several good commentaries. Through this I become familiar with the author of the book, the addressees, the book's theme or purpose, the date of its writing, and other important background material. General introductions, such as R. K. Harrison's *Introduction to the Old Testament* or Gleason Archer's *Survey of Old Testament Introduction* for Old Testament books and Everett Harrison's *Introduction to the New Testament* or Donald Guthrie's *New Testament Introduction* for New Testament books, also provide background material. Bible encyclopedias are another useful source of this kind of information.

Read the Passage

The first step in studying an individual passage is to read it. I read it repeatedly in my English Bible (I use the New American Standard Bible) until it is pretty well fixed in my memory. I try to do that early in the week of preaching it, or even before, so I have time to meditate on it. Before I get into actual preparation, I want to be mentally grappling with the passage. Once I begin concentrating on my sermon text, it dominates my thinking, conversation, and reading during my time of preparation. All this begins with becoming familiar with the text. I rarely consciously memorize Scripture, but by the time I finish preparing the sermon, I usually have the text fairly well memorized.

Find the Main Point

This concept is referred to as the "big idea," the thesis, or the proposition.[11] It is the main idea the passage is teaching. That main truth is very often connected with the main verb in the passage, though not necessarily so, especially in a parable or narrative passage. I ask myself, "What is the primary message of this passage? What is the central truth? What is the main expositional idea?" Once I have found it, I write it out in a complete sentence because it is crucial that the main idea of the passage be clear in my own mind. Subsequent development of the text hinges on it.

This becomes the target I aim for in the exposition. It is also the primary message I want my people to retain after they hear the sermon. So it is crucial that the proposition be carefully thought through and clearly stated. Everything else in the sermon builds to support, elucidate, convict, and confront the hearer with the main truth. This means every expository sermon is a unit with one main theme or topic, rather than a rambling through a text verse after verse.

Organize the Passage

Having found the main point, I begin to look for the subordinate points that support it. They will often be connected with the subordinate verbs, participles, or infinitives. This is the first step in outlining the passage. It also provides a confirmation of the main point. If the main thought I have determined for a passage is not broad enough to include all the other thoughts or is not fully supported by them, I need to rework it.

Let me illustrate the process of finding the main and subordinate points by looking at Matthew 28:19, 20. The main verb is "make disciples," while "go," "baptizing," and "teaching" are all participles modifying the main verb. The main point, then, might be "how to make disciples." The sub-points would be "going," "baptizing," and "teaching." The sermon explains how to make disciples by fulfilling those three duties.

Analyze the Structure

After reading the passage and discovering the main and subordinate points, the next step is a detailed analysis of its words and grammar.[12] I work through the passage in detail in the Greek text, taking notes on a legal-sized note pad. I look first of all for any problems in the passage, such as an important textual variant, an unusual word, or a difficult grammatical construction. At this point, I begin to use study tools. One very helpful tool is the *Linguistic Key to the Greek New Testament* by Fritz Rienecker and Cleon Rogers (Zondervan). This little book goes through every passage in the New Testament and gives key lexical and grammatical insights on nearly every verse. I also use a Greek concordance because I want to see how key words are used elsewhere in the New Testament. I do word studies of significant terms in Greek lexicons. I find Abbott-Smith's *A Manual Greek Lexicon of the New Testament* to be handy for the general meaning of words. For more definitive studies I turn to Bauer, Arndt, and Gingrich's *A Greek-English Lexicon of the New Testament and Other Early Christian Literature* or Moulton and Milligan's *The Vocabulary of the Greek Testament*. Liddell and Scott's *Greek-English Lexicon* contains detailed information on how words were used in classical Greek. For a thorough discussion on how a word was used in classical Greek, the Septuagint, and the New Testament, I turn to Colin Brown's *The New International Dictionary of New Testament Theology* or Kittel's *Theological Dictionary of the New Testament*. Commentaries, particularly those on the Greek text, also contain useful lexical and grammatical insights. A. T. Robertson's *Word Pictures in the New Testament* is another rich source of lexical and grammatical information.

I also find it helpful to diagram the passage.[13] While I no longer write out the diagram, since I can usually visualize it mentally, diagramming each sentence makes me aware of the grammatical structure. When studying the grammar of a passage, I pay special attention to prepositions and the case of the nouns. Finding the direct object, the indirect object, and whether something is in apposition to something else can be crucial to understanding the passage correctly. A knowledge of English grammar is essential for this process. During this phase, I read all the available good commentaries to assist in the interpretation and to garner cross-references and theological insights.

Put Together an Exegetical Outline

As the final step in the study process, I put together a preliminary outline. This is not the outline for the sermon. It is not alliterated, and I may write down several different ways of stating each point. I have purposely placed this step toward the end of the study process. Doing even a preliminary outline before the detailed study of the passage increases the danger of reading into a passage something that is not there. We must draw the outline from the passage, not bend the passage to fit some preconceived outline. We do not want to be like the preacher who said, "I've got a great sermon and I'm looking for a passage to put it in." Making the outline follow the other steps in the study process avoids this tendency.

Add Illustrations

After the outline is refined, I search for the best biblical illustrations. I prefer biblical illustrations because they teach the Word while they illustrate, because they are God's choice of illustrative material, in that Scripture interprets itself best, and because they have divine authority to go with human interest. Other illustrations can certainly be added to these. Finally, I write the introduction and conclusion—now that I know what I am introducing and concluding.[14]

THREE KEY WORDS

Expository preaching can be summed up in three key words: inductive, exegetical, and expositional.

Expository preaching is *inductive.* That means simply that we approach the text to find out what it means, to let it speak for itself. It is the opposite of the deductive method, which goes to Scripture with a preconceived idea and reads that idea into the text. A deductive approach may be valid sometimes, but extreme care must be taken to make sure the passage really does support an idea before using that approach.

Expository preaching is *exegetical.* The expository preacher must do his homework in the passage before he preaches it. That means following proper hermeneutical and exegetical principles and practice. That is really what this chapter has been about, laying out a study method that facilitates an exegetical approach to a text. An expository preacher is to be a man noted for "handling accurately the word of truth" (2 Tim. 2:15).

Expository preaching is *expositional.* It approaches the Word of God inductively, studies it exegetically, then explains it to the people expositionally. Expositional preaching seeks to clarify what is difficult to understand in a passage. It opens up the Word and exposes the less obvious meanings and applications it contains.

Part IV

Pulling the Expository Message Together

12

Central Ideas, Outlines, and Titles

Donald G. McDougall

Hard work is required to preach expository messages, especially in determining the central idea and outline of a passage. Word meanings alone will not yield the data needed to do this. Only a detailed analysis of a passage's grammatical structure, along with lexical information, will lead to a real understanding of a passage's contextual flow. A single statement, the larger context, or recurring ideas may be the key to discovering the central idea of a section. Various passages lend themselves to different types of outlines—some to a basic contextual outline, some to a "string-of-pearls" outline, and some to a "waves-of-the-sea" outline. Sermon titles should accurately reflect the sermon content; although they are not on the same level of importance as central ideas and outlines, they are nevertheless significant in support of the sermon through the "atmosphere" they create.

"I would like to be able to preach expository messages. What do you suggest I do?" Those were the words of a pastor following a Bible conference in his church. He reflects the feeling of many, but the path from desire to reality is not short or easy.

As a long-distance runner, my participation in the Boston marathon was a lifetime highlight. It was necessary to qualify to enter that race. Most who qualify to run in such races are not what you would term "great natural athletes." They are simply people who have exercised much personal discipline and have worked very hard and long to reach their desired goal.

The same can be said about good expositors of the Bible. They have disciplined themselves to work hard and long. Nowhere is that discipline and hard work more demanding and rewarding than in determining the central idea and structure of a passage. In this brief discussion only a few basic ideas can be developed, but if these are followed, they will cause the form of the sermon to reflect the essence of the passage and that is legitimate expository preaching.

A pastor recently suggested that exegesis classes in seminary should focus more on lexical studies[1] than syntax[2] since, according to him, "most pastors are concentrating on word studies these days." This philosophy leads to the conclusion that teaching based just on thorough etymological study of significant words is expository preaching. That is not true. The syntax and structure of a passage lie at the very heart of true expository preaching.

The meaning and significance of a given word is only comprehended through a clear understanding of its context. This should be evident to anyone who reflects on common usage of the English language. Extreme care is required to ensure that the meaning of a word in one book or by one author is not arbitrarily transferred to another book or author. The structure or flow of each passage is, therefore, of utmost importance in preparing a true expository or exegetical message. Understanding the argument of a passage and of an entire book is essential if one is to comprehend what the author is communicating.[3]

EXAMINING THE CONTEXT

Therefore, the first step in preparing to preach on a passage is to determine the parameters of its context. Failure to define the parameters usually results in the misunderstanding and misrepresentation of a passage's meaning. The only way to determine these boundaries is to study the syntax of a passage and determine where a section begins and ends. The standard chapter and paragraph divisions identified in various ways in Hebrew, Greek, and English Bibles cannot be used for this, because they are unreliable.

Many instances of unfortunate chapter and paragraph breaks occur and cause a casual reader to miss the point of a passage or obscure the full significance of a writer's meaning. For example, the chapter division at 2 Corinthians 7:1 has often hidden the connection between 6:11–13 and 7:2–4. Furthermore, many fail to see the broader contextual significance of the injunction not to be "bound together with unbelievers" in 6:14—7:1. Another example is the new paragraph marked at James 1:12 by both English and Greek texts (that is, Nestle-Aland 26th ed. and United Bible Society 3rd ed.). This has often led to a misunderstanding of the relationship between James 1:9–11 and the broader context of verses 2–12 and hidden the function of verse 12 as a conclusion to the preceding discussion (James 1:2–11).

The essential ingredient in dealing with central ideas, outlines, and titles in expository preaching is an understanding of the structure of the passage to be preached. The expositor should not communicate his own central idea, nor his own outline, nor his own title. He is, rather, to teach the central idea, outline, and theme of the author. Failure to reflect the author's theme, outline, and central idea is a departure from true exposition.

Recording and careful study of lexical and syntactical material for a passage is tedious and time consuming. But that process does not begin to compare with the time necessary to grasp the full significance of the material gleaned. Further, additional time and care are vital to assimilate the material and its practical significance to one's own personal life. It must be emphasized that the expositor does not "make" a message out of a passage. Rather, he interacts with the contextual material until the message of the author emerges. The first step of recording the material could take a day or two. The following steps of understanding the significance of the material and its relevance to one's life could take days or weeks or, in a fuller sense, even a lifetime.

It has been my practice over the years to begin studying a book of the Bible at least months, sometimes years, before preaching sermons on it. This study is for personal benefit and at a relaxed pace. Through the prolonged process I accumulate extensive notes so that when the week for preaching on a given passage arrives, much of the groundwork has been done. Initial thoughts for the following weeks' messages begin long in advance as introductory passages are studied. Then, in a good week, it usually takes Monday and sometimes part of Tuesday to record most of the information. The next few days are spent reviewing the data repeatedly, not trying to make a proposition, outline, or sermon title, but rather trying to grasp a fuller perception of the central thrust and outline of the passage.

The following discussion and illustrations show what is entailed in finding and communicating the central idea, outline, and theme of a passage. Three important elements are helpful to keep in mind throughout the process. Always remember that we are to preach from the passage, preach from our heart, and preach for changed lives.

Preach from the Passage

Many of the subsequent suggestions will repeatedly echo the importance of preaching from the passage. Years ago, while on a backpacking trip, we left the trail, lost our way, and had to make a path though tall grass in constant rain. It was difficult because we were forging a new path through the forest. On the way back, it was entirely different because we followed a well-beaten path. We even let the children run ahead. As long as they stayed on the path, they could not get lost.

This is important to remember while preparing to preach. The purpose of the expositor is to follow the path established by the biblical author and not to create his own trail. The reason why so many preachers struggle to remember where a sermon is going, and are therefore bound to their notes, is that they have created a path of their own and are not following the clearly marked path established by the author. For that reason, listeners have a similar problem when, at a later time, they try to retrace the steps of the message on their own.

Preach from Your Heart

Years ago in a college class, a girl gave a speech on Hawaii and was having a difficult time. The teacher stopped her and asked, "Weren't you born in Hawaii?" and "Weren't you raised there?" To both questions, she responded, "Yes." He then replied, "Then just tell us about it." If an expositor follows the path laid out by the author and wrestles long with God over the application of the truth to his own life, then when he finds himself struggling or stumbling in his delivery, he can go back to that path and his own personal interaction with truth and preach both from the passage and from his heart.

Preach for Changed Lives

A study of Scripture clearly shows that whether it was an Old Testament prophet, John the Baptist, Jesus, or Paul, the message was always given to achieve a desired change in belief or behavior. For instance, people who hurt need encouragement, that is, a changed outlook. An elderly preacher often recounts the time in his early years when a well-seasoned minister told him, "Remember, you are preaching to hurting people." That advice transformed both his life and his ministry. This is a good reminder as we prepare to preach.

Determining the Central Idea of a Passage

The central idea of a true expository message reflects the central idea intended by the Bible author himself. Sometimes the central idea is evident from a careful examination of the primary text. On the other hand, often only a study of the broader context that may even extend to the context of the whole book can reveal what it is.

Our task is NOT to create our own message;
    It is rather to communicate the author's message.
Our task is NOT to create a central theme;
    It is rather to
        1. find the author's central theme
        2. build a message around that theme, and
        3. make that theme the central part of all we have to say.

How does one identify the key thought and make it the main point of his expository message? Following are a few ways in which this can be done.

Find the Central Idea from a Single Statement in the Passage

The central idea can sometimes be found at a single point in the text. It is important to remember that in normal writings, whether Hebrew, Greek, or English, the main thought of a paragraph is not always found in its first sentence. As in any in-depth study of literature, it is important to identify the main thought or focus of a section. After this, it is imperative to make that the main focus of the message. A few examples will clarify.

1 Timothy 4:6–16. The main thought of 1 Timothy 4:6–16 is in verse 16, where Paul states, "Pay close attention to yourself and to your teaching." This is central to the entire passage. It helps if the expositor and his audience are aware of this principal thought from the very beginning of a message. It helps them piece the rest of the passage together. The first thought, "pay close attention to yourself," is developed in 4:6–10. The latter, "pay attention to your teaching," is the essence of 4:11–15. The impact is enhanced when one realizes that this is a twofold emphasis elsewhere in both 1 Timothy and Titus. These are two key reminders for all church leaders.

Galatians 6:1–10. The proposed chapter and paragraph divisions in Galatians 6:1–10 cause two problems. First, the chapter break makes it easy to study these verses separately from the verses immediately before. One may miss the relationship of these verses to walking in the Spirit and evidencing the fruit of the Spirit. The second problem occurs if one observes the paragraph separation of both Greek and English texts that sets verses 6–10 off from verses 1–5. With the passage divided in half, the uniting thought of the entire passage in verse 10, "let us do good to all men, and especially to those who are of the household of the faith," will probably go unnoticed. Another result of such a division is an obscuring of the close relationship between the three parallel commands and cautions found in 6:1–8.

1 Peter 5:1–11. The main thought of 1 Peter 5:1–11 is in the middle of verse 5. Verses 1–5 revolve about the command to "clothe yourselves with humility toward one another" in verse 5. This responsibility is applied first to leaders (5:2–4) and then to those who are led (5:5a). Once again, the new paragraph indicated by the texts at verse 6 should not cause the expositor to separate 5:6–11 from the first five verses. They are inseparably connected in thought and emphasis. This is evident in the references to "humility" in the middle of verse 5 and God's giving grace to "the humble" in the last part of verse 5 and the command "to humble oneself" under God's mighty hand in verse 6. The central thought of the message should somehow reflect the need for humility in attitude and service.

Matthew 5—7. In the Sermon on the Mount recorded in Matthew 5—7, Jesus laid a foundation in 5:1–16 upon which He built in 5:17–20. Verse 20 contains the key for understanding the verses that follow. Jesus there said, "Unless your righteousness surpasses that of the scribes and Pharisees, you shall not enter the kingdom of heaven." In the verses immediately following (5:21–48), He showed them how their righteousness must exceed that of the scribes. In 6:1–18 He described ways their righteousness must exceed that of the Pharisees.

Zechariah 4:1–14. The central idea of the Zechariah 4:1–14 is doubt-lessly found in 4:6 where the angel says, "This is the word of the LORD to Zerubbabel saying, 'Not by might nor by power, but by My Spirit,' says the LORD of hosts." This principle is given pictorially in 4:1–5, and its results are described in 4:7–10.

Zechariah 3:1–10. The central idea in Zechariah 3 is found in the state-ment, "See, I have taken your iniquity away" (v. 4). This is expanded later in the statement, "I will remove the iniquity of that land in one day" (v. 9). As in Zechariah 4, the picture is given in 3:1–5, and the further description is in 3:6–10.

Finding the Central Idea from the Larger Context

The central idea is sometimes found in a "sandwich-type" structure. Many examples of this structure exist both in broad and restricted contexts.

1 Corinthians 12—14. First Corinthians 12:31—14:1 provides an exam-ple of a sandwich-type structure in a broad context. Paul ends the twelfth chapter with the command to "earnestly desire the greater gifts" (12:31a). The list preceding this command (v. 28) indicates the greater gifts were "first apostles, second prophets, third teachers." Since the number of apostles was limited, the greatest gift available to most local churches was prophecy. The same form of the verb for "earnestly desire" comes again in 14:1 with the command to "*desire earnestly* spiritual gifts, but especially that you may prophesy" (emphasis added). This is a very slight variation of the same command. Sandwiched between those two commands is the thought best described in Paul's own words: "And I show you a still more excellent way. . . . pursue love." The central thought sandwiched between 1 Corin-thians 12:31 and 14:1 is that the church is to pursue the greater gifts, but in so doing is to manifest the spirit of love described in chapter 13.

Hebrews 10—12. Hebrews 10:32—12:1 provides another "sandwich" example in a larger context. Chapter 10 ends with the reminder of "the former days, when . . . you endured" (10:32) and the present days, when "you have need of endurance" (v. 36). This is followed by what is known as "the faith chapter" (Heb. 11). The chapter division is really "an interrup-tion to the thought" since the sense in chapter 11 "flows directly out of 10:35–39" and then flows naturally into chapter 12.[4] The thought continues in 12:1–7 with the reminder that we are to "run with endurance the race that is set before us" and are to fix "our eyes on Jesus . . . who . . . endured the cross" and "consider Him who endured such hostility" (12:1–3). The author then wrote that "it is for discipline that you endure" (v. 7). A message communicated in chapter 11, sandwiched (as it were) between the closing verses of chapter 10 and the opening verses of chapter 12, is that a genuine faith is one which endures. This is evident both in the admonition on either side of this chapter and in most of the examples within the chapter itself.

2 Corinthians 6:11—7:4. One of the prime examples of sandwiching in a smaller context is found in 2 Corinthians 6:11—7:4. Recognizing this corrects the misunderstanding that has often arisen when 6:14—7:1 is separated from the commands on either side of it. The emphasis on openness of heart and mouth is clearly seen in the two commands, "Open wide to us also" (6:13) and "Make room for us in your hearts" (7:2). Couple this with Paul's personal example of opening his heart and mouth to them in 6:11. Sandwiched between is the responsibility of not being unequally yoked together with unbelievers. This is accompanied by rhetorical questions to teach that we as believers have no partnership, fellowship, harmony, or agreement with unbelievers. In fact, we have nothing in common with them (vv. 14–16). Therefore, we must stop patterning our lives after the world. Instead, we need to "cleanse ourselves" from both the inner (spirit) and outer (flesh) defilement of sin so that such an openness of heart and mouth toward other Christians can exist (7:1).

Finding the Central Idea from Recurring Ideas

The central idea can sometimes be found by noting recurring ideas in a passage. As one reads and repeatedly rereads certain passages, an outstanding idea (or group of ideas) comes to the fore. By observing this, he can catch the emphasis of the author.

Ephesians 1:3–14. One of the key passages in which the central idea is found by merging recurring ideas of a context is Ephesians 1:3–14. As Robinson wrote,

> But as we read it again and again we begin to perceive certain great words recurring and revolving round a central point:
> "The will" of God: vv. 5, 9, 11.
> "To the praise of His glory": vv. 6, 12, 14.
> "In Christ": vv. 3, 4, 6, 7, 9, 10bis, 11, 12, 13bis.
> The will of God working itself out to some glorious issue in Christ—that is the theme.[5]

Using the words in the passage, these verses can be summarized in the statement that God is doing all things after the counsel of His will in and through the person of Christ for the praise of His glory.

Matthew 6:19–33. The portion of the Sermon on the Mount in Matthew 6:19–33 has both a mixture of recurring ideas and a related statement of the central idea. When taken together, the two conclusively convey the message of the passage. The twofold reminder by Jesus to "stop being anxious" (v. 25, author's translation) and "never be anxious" (vv. 31, 34, author's translation) frames the illustrations regarding anxiety (vv. 26–30). Then the contrasting command comes: "But seek first His kingdom and His righteousness; and all these things [the things over which we tend to become anxious as delineated earlier] shall be added to you" (v. 33). It is plain, then, that believers are to both stop being anxious and refrain from becoming anxious about physical needs. They are rather to seek God's kingdom and righteousness and trust Him for their provisions.

DETERMINING THE OUTLINE OF A PASSAGE

There is a need to determine not only the central idea of a passage but also the outline that reflects the thinking of the author. Three basic principles should guide us as we discuss outlining for expository preaching. These three will somehow recur time and time again in the following discussion of individual passages.

Communicate the message; don't just outline it. Concentrate on the communication of the message, not just its outline. We have such a penchant for nice, pat outlines. Having an outline is not bad. Nor is it bad to have an outline that people can remember, but creating an outline that inadequately reflects a passage's meaning is terrible. When having a special outline into which preconceived human ideas can fit usurps the importance of teaching the central idea of a section, then the would-be expositor has lost his bearings. At that point, the message ceases to be an exposition of Scripture and becomes an exposition of the preacher's thoughts.

Find the outline; don't create it. As illustrated by the backpacking trip described earlier, many preachers have trouble remembering the points of their message (causing them to refer to notes constantly) because they have made their own path through a passage and are not following the clear path dictated by a biblical author.

Let the passage dictate to you; don't dictate to it. A major danger for those who prefer neat, three- or four-point outlines with parallel points is that the passage may not lend itself to that luxury. When it does not, you dare not force it. One of the greatest compliments ever paid me was given inadvertently when a lady commented after a message, "I came to realize that you didn't have an outline; it just flowed." Actually I did have an outline I was following, but it was inconspicuous; that is how it should be. As will be discussed later, a book like James should not be made to fit into a simple, western thought-pattern since it reflects a different mind-set that should be honored by being communicated.

If space permitted, this same plea also could be made for the understanding of entire books of the Bible. Two examples must suffice. It is easiest to remember the contents of Genesis by focusing on four key activities and four key individuals, but it is better to emphasize the oft-repeated "the book of the generations of . . ." in outlining the book. In addition, Acts can be outlined in a number of ways. We would do well, though, to consider the progress reports which conclude six sections of that book (6:7; 9:31; 12:24; 16:5; 19:20; 28:30, 31). The reader who reflects on these divisions defined by Luke gains further insight into the meaning of the author.

Basic Contextual Outlining

It is indisputable that an expositor must concentrate on determining the outline that best reflects the thought pattern of the author. A few examples will illustrate the principles given above.

1 Thessalonians 1. The central idea of the first chapter of 1 Thessalonians revolves around the statement, "We give thanks" (v. 2). This clause is then followed by three participles (vv. 2b, 3, 4) that describe different aspects of that thanksgiving. The first participle (v. 2b) tells the manner of the thanksgiving, the second (v. 3) the time of the thanksgiving, and the third (v. 4) the reason for the thanksgiving. Verses 5 and following are connected with verse 4 by a causal particle that indicates the thoughts to follow are subordinate to verse 4. The author thereby distinctly indicates that, although other important thoughts occur in the chapter, the chapter's major thought or theme is thanksgiving with an explanation of (1) how it is done, (2) when it is done, and (3) why it is done.

With the syntactical flow of the chapter in mind, it is then possible to study a single section within that context in detail. Once again, the structure is of supreme importance. Verse 3, for example, has three parallel ideas that are indicated by three nouns of action: work, labor, and endurance. These three are connected with three Christian graces: faith, love, and hope. The nouns of action describe three characteristics of the Christians in Thessalonica that are needed in any church seeking to fulfill its God-given responsibility. The church needs workers, especially those who labor to the point of fatigue and do not give up in their labor for the Lord.

The words for faith, hope, and love can in turn be classified as subjective genitives.[6] This indicates that the needed work is produced by those who have faith; the needed labor to the point of fatigue is produced by those who have sacrificial love; and the much-needed endurance is seen in the lives of those who have directed their hope toward the Lord Jesus Christ. In the final analysis, what the church really needs to fulfill its mission are faith, love, and hope. Genuine faith, love, and hope will motivate those who possess them to work, to labor to the point of fatigue, and to endure to the end. These elements should be reflected in both the message and the outline of this verse.

2 Thessalonians 1. Thanksgiving is also the leading thought in 2 Thessalonians 1. Here Paul not only gives thanks but also reminds his readers that they are obligated "to give thanks" (v. 3; see also 2:13). This is important to remember when preaching on this chapter. Because several significant eschatological statements come in this portion, many think of this passage only as eschatological truth, but the author's primary purpose is not to present an eschatological treatise. He is, rather, expressing some of the major reasons for his thanksgiving for his readers. The two major parts of this chapter are the thanksgiving (1:3–10) and the prayer (1:11, 12). Thanksgiving for what God is doing for them [and us] in the present (vv. 4, 5) and what God will do for them [and us] in the future (vv. 6–10) should receive prime emphasis in an exposition of the former of the chapter's two sections.

Galatians 6:1–10. This text is an excellent example of a passage that plainly outlines itself. As mentioned earlier, the central thought of the passage is in verse 10. With that as a starting point, the section's development is obvious. Also, its relationship with the preceding context must be kept in view. This passage describes the lifestyle of an individual who is filled with the Spirit and manifests His fruit:

Central idea: As those who are walking by the Spirit and manifesting the fruit of the Spirit . . .

1A.   What are we to do? (6:10)
    "let us do good to all men"
  1B.   Do good to all men (stated but not developed)
  2B.   (Do good) especially to the household of faith
      What does this entail? This is developed in 6:1–8:
    1C.   Repair
        1D.   The command (6:1a)
        2D.   The caution (6:1b)
    2C.   Bear
        1D.   The command (6:2)
        2D.   The caution (6:3–5)
    3C.   Share
        1D.   The command (6:6)
        2D.   The caution (6:7–8)
2A.   When are we to do it? (6:10a)
    "while we have opportunity"
3A.   Why are we to do it? (6:9)
    "in due time we shall reap if we do not grow weary"

Figure 12–1
Galatians 6:1–10

Zechariah 4. Zechariah 4:1–14 is one of many Old Testament portions that naturally and easily outline themselves. The main thought of the passage, as noted above, is in verse 6. The verses before that (vv. 1–5; see also

vv. 11–14) describe in pictorial form the truth of verse 6. The verses which follow (vv. 7–10) present the outworking of the same truth in the life of God's servant.

The expositor should use care in outlining. Although some segments fall into an easily recognized and preachable outline, some are not so simple to outline, and a simple structure should not be imposed upon them. Two important passages illustrate where the thrust of an author and not a simple outline must be adhered to if the progression of thought is to surface accurately.

A String of Pearls

James 1:1–12 is most correctly viewed as a beautiful string of pearls. That is the best way to describe the progress of James's argument. Several considerations indicate that verse 12 is a summary of verses 2–11, one of the most significant being that the noun form of the word for "trial" found in verse 2 and again in verse 12 is used exclusively in these verses. This contrasts with the verb form of the same word (translated "tempt") which is found exclusively in verses 13 and 14. The shift in forms indicates a new subject.

Having concluded that the first section extends from verse 2 to verse 12, the passage can be divided roughly as follows:

1A. What we are to do—1:2
2A. Why we are to do this—1:3–4
3A. How we are to do this—1:5–8
4A. How this practically affects our lives—1:9–11
5A. What lies ahead for those who live this way—1:12

Figure 12–2
James 1:1–12

Even if this outline were used, however, the expositor could fail to convey adequately, if not personally understand, the author's logical development. This section of James 1, and indeed the whole book, is not outlined according to western standards. This structure, and therefore our preaching on the chapter, should be characterized more as "a string of pearls," since that is what it is. Even from the English text one can see that "endurance" is the closing thought of verse 3 and the opening thought of verse 4. The same pattern is followed with the use of "perfect" in verse 4a and verse 4b, "lacking" in verse 4b and verse 5a, "ask" in verse 5a and verse 6a, and "doubting" in verse 6a and verse 6b. Following a beautiful string of precious jewels like this is an important part of an exposition of this passage and others like it.

This is important to remember because James is not the only author to do this. On a broader scale, Paul has many examples of this structure. An understanding of this helps the expositor see not only the flow of an entire section, but also the interrelationship of thoughts in successive sections in a book.

Waves of the Sea

Another type of structure occurs in the first chapter of Ephesians. The person studying verses 3 through 14 is best served by realizing that Paul did not use a simple, balanced outline. In fact, to impose a symmetrical outline on this passage overlooks either the message or the feelings of the verses. The paragraph is emotion-packed. Paul had labored hard and fought many battles as God's servant and now that he and his ministry were well along in years, he reflected on all that God had done and was doing. As he did so, he could not even bring himself to pen the letter in his normal style, but rather broke out in ecstatic praise to God. The outpouring of praise is not smoothly structured, according to usual standards. To regard it as such is to miss the impact of his words. The thoughts expressed could best be compared to waves smashing against the seashore, one after another. The same thoughts kept coming back time and again, but each time with varying intensity.

This section recalls another picture: that of the finale in most fireworks displays. Burst after burst explodes in the sky. Without a replay, it is impossible at one viewing to define or appreciate fully any single burst. The entire experience must be fully appreciated, albeit with a sense of awe. That is the thrust of this passage. To pick it up, one needs to concentrate on the powerful waves that keep smashing upon the seashore or on the magnificent bursts of light that break out against a dark sky, or, if you will, on those deeply impressive, transcendent thoughts that keep presenting themselves.

Even so, some sections of Ephesians 1:3–14 may, and even should, be dealt with another way. After the overwhelming experience of viewing so much light exploding all at once against a darkened sky and of gaining an appreciation for the overall thrust of the passage, it is helpful to go back and look carefully at each segment of the magnificent display. After all, the words have so much beneficial information for healthy Christian living. More than one message is necessary if the expositor or his audience is to approach a full awareness of the significance of what Paul said.

The importance of each detail is evident as early as the first verse in this passage (Eph. 1:3). It has some of the book's major themes in capsulized form. When developing this verse, one needs simply to follow each word in sequence to find the outline. For outlining, the words of the verse can be used or headings with the same ideas can be adapted. Notice both in the following illustration.

As we look at the opening words of Ephesians 1:3, it is instantly apparent that Paul had, for some reason, interrupted his normal epistolary introduction. He usually began with thanksgiving and prayer for his readers. He had these here, but only after he completed this initial outburst of praise (see vv. 15, 16). What caused him (and will cause us) to break forth in such an outburst of praise? Undoubtedly it was reflecting on the unity God has brought to His church, but ultimately it was centered in Paul's understanding of:

1A. The Source of Our Blessings (1:3a)
"God . . . has blessed us"
(Incidentally, God's name only appears here in the twelve verses, and yet He is the agent of most of the active as well as passive actions referred to.)
2A. The Scope/Substance of Our Blessing (1:3b)
"with every spiritual blessing"
(It cannot be overemphasized that one of the greatest hindrances to understanding this book is that the blessings defined herein are not material, neither physical nor financial, but spiritual.)
3A. The Sphere of Our Blessing (1:3c)
    1B. "in heavenly places"
    (One cannot even begin to comprehend the message of the book without understanding the significance of this phrase and, one need not, in fact should not, go outside the bounds of the book to understand it.)
    2B. "in Christ"
    (Without this the message of Ephesians does not exist.)

Figure 12–3
Ephesians 1:3

CHOOSING A TITLE FOR A MESSAGE

Devising catchy titles for messages has become a highly developed skill for many preachers. But as important as titles are, coming up with great titles is not a primary criterion for a true expositor. It is possible to labor hard and long to come up with that special wording to attract the attention of many, only to find that very few people pay attention to it or even care. Title-searching can become a significant drain on a preacher's time. It is necessary to remember at least a few basic principles with respect to titles.

Titles Should Reflect the Content of the Message

Make the title reflect what the sermon will say. Recently a paper with a very catchy title was offered at a conference. One listener commented,

"The content of the paper was in no way reflected in the title." In another setting, a skilled musician, while discussing a certain cantata, said, "The problem with the works prepared by that composer is that too often 'the form transcends the message.' " These two thoughts should be kept in mind when choosing a title for a message. The title should reflect the sermon content and should in no way transcend or obscure it.

An example of having a title that reflects the message of a passage can be drawn from 1 Peter 2:1–10. These verses are a unit. The "therefore" in verse 1 indicates that the unit is a logical outgrowth of 1:22–25. Three distinct subsections compose the unit: 2:1–3; 2:4–8; and 2:9–10. The first centers around the command to crave the word with unquenchable thirst (see v. 2). The main emphasis of the last subsection is on proclaiming the excellencies of God (see v. 9). But what is the essence of verses 4–8?

A study of the titles given to 1 Peter 2:4–8 reveals that despite the fact that the rest of the verses speak primarily of Christ and not the believer, the focus is often placed on the spiritual sacrifices of verse 5. Yet the focus of even verse 5 is on Him. Believers are "living stones" (v. 5) only because of their relationship to Him who is by quality a "living stone" (v. 4). In addition, the only reason why the spiritual sacrifices please God is their channeling "through Jesus Christ" (v. 5). In the choice of a title, then, the focus must be on the person of Christ rather than the work of the believer, on Him to whom the believer continually comes (v. 4). Only then, secondarily, is attention drawn to the believer's relationship to and service for Him.

With this background, some preliminary titles come to mind that reflect the content of the subsections while showing their close relationship to each other.

1. Our relationship to the Word of God—2:1–3
2. Our relationship to the Son of God—2:4–8
3. Our relationship to those without God—2:9–10

An awareness of these three central ideas leads to the following titles for a series of messages on these three sections.

1. The Priority of the Child of God (thirst for the Word)—2:1–3
2. The Position of the Child of God (relationship to Christ)—2:4–8
3. The Privilege of the Child of God (proclamation)—2:9–10

Whatever the titles may be, they must reflect the meaning of the passage and hence the contents of the sermon.

The Time Spent Should Reflect the Importance of the Title

Allot time required for sermon-title preparation according to its importance in comparison with the importance of the sermon's content. On some special occasions a title could determine the number and nature of the people who attend. At such times, one does well to give more attention to the title, always, of course, assuring that it reflects the sermon content. On most occasions, however, the title has little to do with the nature or the number of those in attendance. Most people pay more attention to what is preached than to the sermon title. It is hoped that people will return every week because they know they will receive God's message, not because of a titillating title. Therefore, without neglecting the title altogether, concentrate most attention on the content of the message.

The Title Should Complement the Message

Make the title complement the message in its thoughtfulness and pattern. This suggestion needs to be applied in line with the two previous ones regarding sermon content and time spent. Most people will revisit a restaurant because of the food served—that is, sermon content—and not just because the table setting looks good. But on the other hand, it is uniquely rewarding when they can to go to a restaurant that provides both a nice atmosphere and a good meal. Therefore, it is important, in giving due regard to the content of and time spent on the message, to give some consideration to the setting in which you place your sermon. The title is what provides a sermon with its "atmosphere." One that measures up to the content of the message in thought and form is definitely beneficial.

THE NECESSARY DISCIPLINE

Undoubtedly, there are some great natural athletes. When it comes to the field of expositors, however, probably no such thing as a great natural expositor exists. To be a true and acknowledged expositor of the Word requires discipline. It takes hard work and thorough preparation for which there are no substitutes. A lot of time and effort must be spent establishing the central idea and determining the outline of a passage. Some time also should be given to the sermon title. All three phases must accurately reflect, and none should obscure or take precedence over, the message of both the human and divine authors of Scripture.

13

Introductions, Illustrations, and Conclusions

Richard L. Mayhue

The three "undervalued" components of expository sermon preparation include introductions, illustrations, and conclusions. Due to the complexities of pastoral ministry in general and message preparation particularly, pastors tend to let these three slide. The congregation, in contrast, eagerly looks forward to how its pastor will handle these elements of the message. This discussion, which intends to equip the preacher for a new level of expository excellence, is built around purposes, sources, variations, guidelines, and preparation tips for these three parts of an exposition.

The relationship of seasonings and sauces to gourmet cooking parallels the role of introductions, illustrations, and conclusions in preaching. The main meal, or the message, should never be eclipsed by secondary features; nonetheless, these garnishings can dramatically enhance the flavor/interest level of a meal/message well prepared in other respects.

None of these three elements can replace the Holy Spirit's work of impacting people with the power of God's Word. However, to ignore or minimize these proven features of good communication makes a preacher negligent in exercising his human responsibility to be as effective as possible.

You can usually tell how a pastor's week went by his introduction, illustrations, and conclusion; hectic times tend to crowd out or minimize his time spent on them. Whether they are deemed unimportant to the communication process, excessively time consuming in proportion to their perceived value, or unappealing hard work, slighting them can measurably lessen the potential impact of a message from a purely human perspective. Robinson reminds us, "Introductions and conclusions have significance in a sermon out of proportion to their length."[1] Avoid the deception of underrating their importance.

If a preacher fails to gain his audience's attention with a captivating introduction, he has probably lost them for the rest of the message. If his main points are not clarified or made memorable with quality illustrations, then the effect of his message can be short-lived. If he bypasses concluding his remarks with a review or exhortation, the purpose of the message will probably not be achieved. The ensuing discussion describes how to avoid these common pitfalls.

INTRODUCTIONS[2]

By definition, "to introduce" means to acquaint or to bring into play for the first time. The introduction is to a sermon as an opening kickoff and run-back are to a football game, as the initial volleys of gunfire are to a battle, or as a departure from a harbor is to an ocean voyage. It is a time for everyone to acclimate to what follows the initial situation and to gain a sense of direction.

> Someone has said that the introduction to a sermon may be likened to the prelude to a poem, the preface to a book, the portico to a building, or the preamble to the statement of a case in court. The prelude introduces us to a poem, suggests its method and meaning or message. The preface to a book also does that. . . . An introduction, then, must introduce.[3]

Purposes

The element of *ethos,* that is, the preacher's perceived credibility in the mind of his audience, can be markedly influenced by the kind and quality of his introduction.[4] This is especially true in cases where listeners have no previous acquaintance with their preacher. As the adage goes, "First impressions are lasting impressions." The initial impact of the introduction may even shape the final effect of a message.

Listed below are some of the major reasons why introductions are important and what a preacher can accomplish with them. Not every introduction will necessarily incorporate every reason. The setting, the relationship of the preacher to the audience, and the kind of message determine the appropriate combination of these purposes. Overall, the introduction will put the preacher and his hearers mentally in step with each other:

1. Capture and redirect the audience's attention to focus on the preacher and his message.
2. Enhance the audience's goodwill toward the preacher.
3. Create audience interest in and anticipation of the body of a message.
4. Demonstrate the biblical importance of a message.
5. Answer every listener's unspoken question, "Why should I listen to this message?"

6. Orient listeners to the preacher's wavelength.
7. Make the preacher's intended course of discussion clear to his audience so that they can follow along and not get lost on the preaching journey.

Variations

Only a preacher's imagination and creativity limit the kinds of effective introductions. The introduction used, however, should be tailored to fit a speaker's relationship to his audience, the occasion for the message, and the intended outcome of the sermon.

Consider the following examples of effective kinds of introduction.[5] These suggestions assume that the expositor reads continually for fresh ideas and insights into both the biblical text and life itself.

1. Current statistics which highlight a contemporary problem to be addressed in the message.
2. Historical illustrations that serve to acquaint listeners with the message theme.
3. Humor.
4. Current events that relate to the message.
5. Careful reading of the biblical text from which the message comes.
6. Real-life stories.
7. Biographical illustrations.
8. Striking quotations.
9. Rhetorical questions directed to the audience.
10. Personal experiences of the preacher.
11. References to current, well-known books.
12. Life-related problems for which biblical solutions will be forthcoming.
13. Contemporary confusion over biblical teaching to which the preacher will bring correction and clarity.
14. Highly interesting personal correspondence.
15. Appropriate prayer.
16. Fictional stories.
17. Modern-day parables.
18. Personal testimony.
19. Hymns related to the message.
20. Asking an audience for their response to a hypothetical situation.

Guidelines

Every introduction should have a clear purpose—both to the preacher and the congregation. It should never be hastily prepared or indiscriminately tacked on to a message. Use these factors to evaluate the appropriateness and effectiveness of your introduction:

1. Does it fit the occasion? For example, the introduction of a message at a banquet would be different than one in a worship service.
2. Does it connect with—that is, actually introduce—the subject of your message?
3. Do you deliver in the message what you promise in the introduction?
4. Is it short, like an appetizer in relation to the main course (generally no more than five to ten minutes)?
5. Do you avoid using humor just for humor's sake?
6. Do you create the highest possible level of interest to capture the audience's attention?
7. Is the introduction crisp and striking?

Preparation

As a general rule, development of introductions comes toward the end of message preparation. That way the message is pretty much in place and the introduction can have the highest level of relationship to the central focus of the exposition.

As I write this chapter, three sermons I plan to preach soon are before me. Let me use these to "flesh out" the guidelines just given. I selected a parishioner's personal note—"Brother, don't ever try to be a big preacher. Instead, preach a big Savior"—and a striking C. S. Lewis quote on pride to introduce the message on David's battle with ego in 1 Chronicles 21:1–7.

A moving letter from a severely discouraged pastor friend opened my message on Peter's "sifting" by Satan in Luke 22:31–34:

> I am presently looking for a second job in order to offset the possibility that the church might not be able to pay my salary in the near future. It is the most soul-destroying, wearisome activity I have ever endured. But it has given me a remarkable insight into the financial pressures and discouragements of men who cannot find work or are underemployed.
>
> Please pray for the church and its growth. Please pray for me; Satan regularly overwhelms me with fears and discouragement. And, taking God out of the equation, his fears and discouragements are perfectly logical. I do not know when I last had a full night's sleep without waking up in the midst of one of these satanic attacks. It has worked out for good, however, in that I have learned the value of incessant supplication before God's throne, even though much of that time occurs when I would rather be sleeping.

Surprising words from psychologist Carol Tavris's book *Anger: The Misunderstood Emotion* started my message "How to Control Your Anger" from James 1:19–20. Her book disagreed with the consensus of psychologists on anger and essentially confirmed what Scripture teaches. I did not use it to prove the Bible true, but rather to demonstrate that the field of psychology was being challenged by one of its own members to rethink the emotion of anger. I wanted to dislodge abruptly the mistaken notion that psychologists have all the answers and are in agreement on everything.

ILLUSTRATIONS[6]

"To illustrate" means to enlighten or to make clear. Few have expressed the value of illustrations as well as Spurgeon:

> Mr. Paxton Hood once said, in a lecture that I heard him deliver, "Some preachers expect too much of their hearers; they take a number of truths into the pulpit as a man might carry up a box of nails; and then, supposing the congregation to be posts, they take out a nail, and expect it to get into the post by itself. Now that is not the way to do it. You must take your nail, hold it up against the post, hammer it in, and then clinch it on the other side; and then it is that you may expect the great Master of assemblies to fasten the nails so that they will not fall out." We must try thus to get the truth into the people, for it will never get in of itself; and we must remember that the hearts of our hearers are not open, like a church door, so that the truth may go in, and take its place, and sit upon its throne to be worshipped there. No, we have often to break open the doors with great effort, and to thrust the truth into places where it will not at first be a welcome guest, but where, afterwards, the better it is known, the more it will be loved.
>
> Illustrations and anecdotes will greatly help to make a way for the truth to enter; and they will do it by catching the ear of the careless and the inattentive. We must try to be like Mr. Whitefield, of whom a ship-builder said, "When I have been to hear anybody else preach, I have always been able to lay down a ship from stem to stern; but when I listen to Mr. Whitefield, I cannot even lay the keel." And another, a weaver, said, "I have often, when I have been in church, calculated how many looms the place would hold; but when I listen to that man, I forget my weaving altogether." You must endeavour, brethren, to make your people forget matters relating to this world by interweaving the whole of divine truth with the passing things of every day, and this you will do by a judicious use of anecdotes and illustrations.[7]

The emphasis that writers of Scripture place on illustrations should be a most compelling motivation for us to walk in their footsteps. We delight in the imagery and illustrations of Old Testament prophets in such passages as Isaiah 20, Amos 5, and Ezekiel 1. Jesus also captivated His audience with illustrations from nature and with parables. Revelation becomes intensely memorable because of the numerous illustrations and imagery from the Old Testament. Wise is the contemporary preacher who emulates his ancient predecessors, not to mention using their materials as a primary source of illustrations.

Purposes

Here are the major "whys" of illustrating.[8]

1. To interest the mind and secure the continuing attention of the audience.
2. To make our preaching three dimensional and lifelike.
3. To explain Christian doctrine and duties in a clear understandable manner.
4. To communicate convincingly to those who respond better to pictures than to facts.
5. To ensure that the message is unforgettable.
6. To involve all the human senses in the communication process.
7. To catch the hearing of the disinterested.

Sources [9]

Illustrations can be found everywhere. The keys to having good illustrations are continual searching, constant collecting plus filing, easy retrieval, and keen discernment to select just the right illustration.

Some of the most important places to look for illustrations include:

1. Your pastoral experience (used with great discretion).
2. The lives of other people (autobiographies, biographies, or personal acquaintances).
3. Newspapers and periodicals.
4. Illustration books.
5. Books and magazines, both Christian and secular.
6. Scripture.
7. Books of quotation.
8. Almanacs.
9. Specialty books like *Guinness Book of World Records*.
10. Hymnals and histories behind particular hymns.
11. Other men's preaching, whether in person, in print, or on tape.
12. Hebrew, Aramaic, or Greek word studies.
13. Pastoral magazines such as *Leadership* or *Pulpit Helps*.
14. Biblically oriented archaeology, customs, or history books.
15. People in your congregation who help you by looking for illustrations.
16. Dictionaries and encyclopedias.
17. Science.
18. Devotional guides such as *Our Daily Bread*.

19. Biblical geography books.
20. Your personal and family life (use sparingly).

Guidelines

First, consider some "don'ts": Don't use canned, trite, or commonplace illustrations. Don't use an illustration just because it is a great illustration; make sure it illustrates your point from the biblical text. Don't betray personal or congregational confidences when illustrating from your pastoral experiences. Don't use an illustration merely to move the congregation emotionally. Don't be dishonest with personal illustrations by exaggerating or manufacturing an experience. Don't repeatedly use your favorite illustrations.

Now, the "do's": Do be diligent in searching for and collecting the best illustrations. Do use just the right illustration to make your point. Do keep your congregation in mind; for example, illustrations from our American culture would not have worked when I preached in the Soviet Union. Do use illustrations to clarify the biblical text. Do be discriminating and use only choice illustrations. Do consult a wide variety of sources for your illustrations.

Preparation

Collecting and filing illustrations will only be as fruitful as your ability to retrieve them quickly, months or years later. No preferred method used by most expositors exists. Instead, each one develops a system that works for him.

Some of the ways to file include:

1. Alphabetically by topic.
2. Sequentially by biblical text.
3. Randomly in a general file of illustrations.

With experience, each preacher must decide what method or combination of methods is best for him. Remember the bottom line: being able to retrieve just the right illustration quickly when needed. Generally, you develop introductions and conclusions in the final stages of sermon preparation. In contrast, you collect illustrations months or years before you use them.

To illustrate the message on David's pride in 1 Chronicles. 21:1–7, I used

1. A story told by a personal friend about an experience he had serving as a naval officer in Vietnam.

2. A quote about Satan from Goethe's *Faust*.
3. A personal experience I had as a guest on a nationally broadcast Bible question-and-answer show.
4. A quote from a well-known Old Testament scholar.
5. Numerous biblical texts incorporating similar content or experiences to reinforce my point.

With Luke 22:31–34, I had these:

1. A list of famous people who at one time in their lives had been considered failures.
2. Abraham Lincoln's less-than-illustrious career in politics prior to his excellent presidency.
3. The story of a British naval captain whose ship had a near collision.
4. Quotes from *When Smart People Fail*.
5. Numerous biblical citations to parallel the text in content or experience.

To shed light on the James 1:19–20 treatment of anger, I chose

1. A newspaper report of a medical study which linked excessive anger with disease.
2. A Chinese proverb on anger.
3. A quote by Thomas Jefferson on anger.
4. Parallel material on anger from Proverbs.
5. Old Testament characters who misused anger.
6. A quote from a secular physician on the destructive nature of anger.
7. Quotes from ancient literature on anger.
8. A *Reader's Digest* story about a hot-headed man who murdered four people in an angry rage.
9. Numerous parallel passages in Scripture.

CONCLUSIONS[10]

"Ending," "bringing to a close," and "shutting up" all describe what the word "conclude" means. Most students of preaching agree that it is the most-likely-to-be-neglected aspect of proclamation. However, just as an athlete needs to finish strong at the end of a race or game, the preacher must be at his best in the closing minutes.

A conclusion must conclude. And in order to conclude well it must include. In order to conclude perfectly, it must also preclude. When we are concluding we are concluding. We are bringing everything to an end. A conclusion must include the things which have been said, as to their spiritual and moral impact and appeal; and it must preclude the possibility that those who listen may escape from the message, so far as is possible.[11]

Purposes

A conclusion should be tied directly to the end result that the biblical text requires of the audience. Multiple purposes for a conclusion because of diverse needs among the listeners are also possible.

Commonly, one or more purposes will help develop a conclusion:

1. Review or summarize the message content.
2. Explain the sermon's application.[12]
3. Exhort the audience to obey the sermon's appeal.
4. Call for some sort of decision to mark the beginning of the required obedience (this should be a part of all messages).
5. Encourage, comfort, or in some other way build up the flock with the message.

These purposes can normally be achieved directly. Other times they will be built into a real-life story or a prayer. Careful discrimination must dictate the most effective means.

When preachers desire to identify people who have made decisions in order to follow them up, several options in closing the message or the service are open. People can fill out decision cards in the pew or be asked to respond to an altar call. Also, trained counselors can be available and a prayer room open after every service where people know they can come in response to a concluding appeal.

Guidelines

Frequent neglect of conclusions has been compared to the game of golf. "The tee shot (introduction) is straight and true, the fairway game (body of the sermon) is skillfully played, but the preacher 'blows' his putt (the conclusion)."[13] Here are some "putting" tips to help "break par" with your conclusion.

1. Do not add new material in a conclusion.
2. Make a conclusion clear and specific.
3. Let your conclusion reflect the demands of the passage you just preached.
4. Avoid prolonging your conclusion, especially with calls for decisions, thus usurping the Holy Spirit's role in the appeal.

5. Be direct and brief (no more than five minutes as a general rule).
6. When you begin a conclusion, avoid lapsing back into the message. **Conclude.**
7. Direct the conclusion to cause people to change their beliefs and/or behavior.
8. Try to conclude with something for everyone: unbelievers and believers, young Christians and mature Christians.

Preparation

The idea of conclusion should be in mind all the way through the preparation process. A pertinent question is, "As a result of this message, what changes does God want in my life and the lives of those who hear it?" Then as "processing and principlizing" ends, the conclusion should start to take shape in your thinking. As you pull the message together, continue to sharpen and focus the pointedness of your conclusion.

The message on David's pride (1 Chr. 21:1–7) concluded this way:

True humility will be marked by these qualities:

- A greater desire to serve than to be lord (Matt. 20:26, 27).
- Peace in being last rather than first (Matt. 20:16).
- Contentment in living low instead of high (Phil. 4:11, 12).
- More satisfaction in giving than receiving (Acts 20:35).
- A compulsion to forgive rather than to exact punishment (Matt. 18:21–35).
- A desire for exaltation only by the hand of God (Matt. 23:12).

These qualities marked the One who walked this earth as the model of humility, the Lord Jesus Christ. Let's be like Him. "Blessed are the gentle, for they shall inherit the earth" (Matt. 5:5).

David's confession in Psalm 32:1–7, a personal illustration from ministry, plus a quotation from Theodore Roosevelt closed the message on Peter's near defeat in Luke 22:31–34. A key question with a practical answer capped off the message on anger from James 1:19–20: "If I sin with anger, how can I recover?"

ENCOURAGING EXCELLENCE

John Stott reminded us,

It is an enormous privilege to be called to preach in the contemporary world, and to be a biblical expositor! For one then stands in the pulpit, with God's Word in his hands, God's Spirit in his heart, God's people before his eyes, waiting expectantly for God's voice to be heard and obeyed.[14]

With this great privilege comes an equally important responsibility. We all need to carry out our sacred duty to exposition at the highest level of excellence, an excellence that extends even to our introductions, illustrations, and conclusions.

14

Thematic, Theological, Historical, and Biographical Expository Messages

Irvin A. Busenitz

To be truly biblical, preaching must be expository, even if it is thematic, theological, historical, or biographical. Expository sermons of these types must be thoroughly biblical, not only in their foundation but in their superstructure as well. The effectiveness of the messenger and the power of the message depend upon a close attention to the Word presented with grammatical, historical, literary, and contextual accuracy. For these special kinds of expository messages, certain guidelines must prevail, and many tools are available to assist the research process; but there are no shortcuts. The path to powerful preaching inevitably demands diligence in the Word.

Just as verse-by-verse preaching is not necessarily expository, preaching that is *not* verse-by-verse is not necessarily *non*-expository. Granted, some topical approaches are not expository, but such *need not* and certainly *should not* be the case. No book deals with topics that directly impact daily life more than the Bible. Thus, to be effective, all topical preaching and teaching, whether the topic be thematic, theological, historical, or biographical, must be consumed with expounding the Word.

Jesus expounded the Scriptures powerfully (Mark 1:22), but not always verse by verse. As an expositor, He sometimes spoke topically, using many different Old Testament Scriptures as the basis of His teaching. Sometimes He touched on a specific theme or aspect of theology, such as the nature of the kingdom of heaven (Matthew 13), divorce (Matthew 19), or how to pray (Matthew 6; Luke 11). At other times He employed a historical event (Luke 13:4–9) or character (Matt. 12:41–45). Yet He always used the Word as the foundation and building blocks of His instruction. On the basis of Jesus' example, it can be unequivocally asserted that all truly biblical preaching is also expository and is not necessarily restricted to a verse-by-verse format. It can take alternative forms, too.

Topical preaching has many benefits. First, used at the end of one book study and before starting another, it provides variety. The change from one type of presentation to another often contributes freshness and causes increased attentiveness. Preaching on a theme or salient point of doctrine can give people a greater understanding of a particular subject, resulting in a greater impact on their lives. Larsen observed,

> Topical preaching has a venerable place in the history of the craft. Its legitimacy is seen in the validity of biblical and systematic theology. While this should not be the first choice of the pastor-teacher, every pastor will preach topically on occasion. . . . Because the topical sermon can be more relentlessly unitary, one discovers that any list of the ten sermons which have most decisively influenced world culture and society consists mostly if not entirely of topical sermons.[1]

Second, restricting preaching solely to the verse-by-verse method without including any kind of didactic treatment of major biblical themes, doctrines, and ethical teachings is to make an unbiblical distinction between preaching and teaching, thereby withholding from a congregation essential perspectives on the Word. Stevenson asked,

> Is there any reason why he should meet them week after week but leave them ignorant of doctrinal meanings . . . ? The didactic and kerygmatic sides of the gospel cannot be separated, one to be assigned to the pulpit, the other to the church school. To separate one from the other is to kill both.[2]

PRECAUTIONS

Contrary to what is frequently thought (and, by the preponderance of its usage, apparently taught), topical preaching is not always the easiest. In many respects, it is the most difficult when done with correctness and accuracy. Consider these reasons. First, the biblical text often used for topical homilies is merely a springboard for launching a selected topic and has no inherent relationship to the topic of the message. When this happens, the preacher draws from his own personal perspectives, ideas, principles, and world view to develop the subject. This is not expository preaching. The preacher's proper task is to *deliver* the goods, not to *manufacture* them. He is the waiter, not the chef. Therefore, the biblical text must be his resource, the fountain of truth to which he constantly resorts, from which he himself continually drinks and from which he faithfully draws to satisfy the thirst of others. Exercising this kind of control over topical preaching is hard work.

Second, the Scriptures garnered to support the emphasis of a topical message are many times wrested from their context and forced to teach something they do not espouse. The memorization of selected verses of the Bible, beneficial in and of itself, frequently exacerbates the problem. For example, how often has Matthew 18:20 ("For where two or three have gathered together in My name, there I am in their midst") been employed to console the faithful few at poorly attended prayer meetings, rather than to assure divine presence and enablement in implementing church discipline? This type of pitfall is most common, often capturing its victims unwittingly. Noting its dangers, Stevenson asserts, "To the extent that this kind of preaching uses the Bible at all, it does so to exploit or devour it and not to listen to it, let alone to stand under it and be guided by it."[3] In such cases, pastors "are using the text as its masters rather than serving the text as its ministers."[4] Avoiding this type of danger is very time-demanding. Whether the subject is thematic or theological, each Scripture must be thoroughly researched so as to do justice to its historical and literary context.

Third, though "problem preaching" or "life-situation preaching" may bring much contemporaneity to the pulpit and thus capitalize on relevant issues, it often generates greater focus on the problem than on the solution. It may also occasionally expose the preacher to a "he's-preaching-at-me" accusation. Broadus cautioned against a restricted focus on one's immediate concerns:

> Subject preaching is the orator's method par excellence. It lends itself to finished discourse. But it has its dangers. The preacher easily becomes interested in finding subjects that are interesting and readily yield a good oration rather than such as have a sure Christian and scriptural basis or such as come close home to the needs of his people. He is tempted to think more of his ideas and his sermons than of "rightly dividing the word of truth" and leading men into the Kingdom of God. He is in danger also of preaching in too narrow a field of truth and human need, since of necessity he will be drawn to those subjects that interest him personally or with which he is already familiar. Unless, therefore, he is constantly widening his horizon by diligent study, he will soon exhaust his resources.[5]

Consequently, great diligence is required to avoid a "problem-only" orientation when using this method. With a reasonably broad coverage of the Bible in one's preaching, a wide variety of problems and life situations can be addressed naturally and delicately without violating expository boundaries in employing a "topical" approach.

When preaching on a theme, a theological doctrine, or a historical event or character, the expositor must endeavor to utilize Scripture fully in his preaching. His task is to *unfold* the Scriptures, not merely to *enfold* them into a topic. The latter will bend the Word to conform to the preacher's perspective; the former will bend the preacher's perspective to conform to the Word. This is important, because it is the Word that is "living and active and sharper than any two-edged sword" (Heb. 4:12). It is the Scriptures that bear witness about Christ (John 5:39). It is the Gospel that is "the power of God for salvation" (Rom. 1:16). Desire to be relevant or current must not prevail over biblical authority. *Through the knowledge of the Word,* the Spirit of God convicts, directs, and strengthens for Christian living.

Consequently, unless the Scriptures constitute the basis for all the structural elements of a sermon and unless the expositor labors diligently in the context of each of the texts he cites, a sermon will inevitably lack the power of the Word of Truth rightly divided, and hearers will be misled, both in the substance of what is taught and in the example of Bible study methodology. As Koller has poignantly noted, "The preacher must lead his people *into* the text, not *away* from it."[6]

GENERAL PRINCIPLES

Sermons are classified in different ways, so it is not always evident what category a sermon falls into. Some are categorized on the basis of content and others according to homiletical style. Most classifications must be viewed as nothing more than a skeleton, rough sketches around which the artist crafts the findings of his study. Consequently, the *type* of sermon chosen depends on which type will match the message to be preached. The sermon-type is to serve, not dominate. Hence the underlying commitment must not be to the class of sermon, but to the *sine qua non* dictated by biblical hermeneutics and the sermon-preparation process. As a respected authority has noted, these must guide the craftsman:

> [Sermon structures] are always secondary to purpose and utility. They are tools, and in the shaping of tools and the techniques for handling tools experimentation and invention are desirable. But these require intelligence and faithfulness to underlying principles.[7]

Some underlying principles are well defined and very specific, applying more directly to one type of sermon structure than to another. Other guidelines are more generic and give equally significant direction for all types. General principles will be reviewed next and, after this, specific guidelines will be outlined.

When?

The times when a preacher may wish to present an expository sermon with a thematic, theological, historical, or biographical structure are many and varied. A most effective, and probably the easiest, time is when one is preaching through a book and arrives at a subject requiring greater depth of explanation. For example, when preaching through the Gospel of John, one may pause at 1:1 for an extra message (or extra messages) on the deity of Christ, including a discussion of the related Jehovah's Witness errors; at 1:12, 13 to treat the subject of divine election; at 1:14 to discuss the incarnation of Christ; or at 4:24 for a series on worshiping God.

A pastor must be careful, however, not to become too involved with every topic that stems from the text. Too many topical messages along the way cause the audience to lose the train of thought of the ongoing consecutive exposition. In the return to book exposition after a topical study, it is imperative to review the structural and thematic flow of the book.

Other occasions for topical sermons include times of significant events in the life of a church, a community, or the world. The death of a church-family member or a tragedy in the community are also suitable occasions for topic-centered messages. Wars (especially those in the Middle East) give unsurpassed opportunities to focus on subjects like eschatology, the return of the Lord, the omnipotence and sovereignty of God, and the holiness and judgment of God. Major earthquakes give similar openings to treat earthquakes of the Bible, including the significance of such an event and the time frame of its biblical occurrence.

Special days like Christmas, Easter, and Mother's or Father's Day are the most obvious times for topical sermons. Such special occasions often generate increased church attendance and greater attentiveness to the teaching of the Word. They can be strategic occasions for greater effectiveness. However, though one does not want to miss the opportunities such times afford, it is not necessary to produce a special sermon for every special occasion. Pressure to generate something new every time can lead to eisegesis[8] rather than exegesis. Unger warned,

> Topical sermons most readily suggest themselves for special days and events of the year. But the faithful preacher must beware that the incessant clamor of special days and events of the year for recognition does not prove a temptation to lure him from true Bible exposition. [Special days] tend to crowd out solid exposition of the Bible and to displace it with superficial preaching deficient in Biblical content and appeal.[9]

Special days and events bring with them significant beneficial effects, both to the process of sermon preparation and to the hearers. People are often caught up with the significance of the day or moment, allowing the pastor to build his sermon from the foundation already in place. The joy of Mother's Day or the excitement generated at Christmas often enhances the impact of a message.

How?

Some very basic principles must undergird all preaching of God's Word. Because it is *His* Word, it must be studied and presented with care and accuracy. James 3:1 is an ever-present warning and should not be overlooked or underestimated! These underlying principles are, in many respects, the same for all sermons, regardless of their homiletical structure or manner of textual focus. However, sermons that focus on particular subjects or issues are by their very nature extremely vulnerable to particular shortcomings. Consequently, the fundamental principles of preparation require constant attention in this type of preaching.

The first of these principles is *contextual analysis*. Whether one is preaching thematically, theologically, historically, or biographically, he must give close attention to the context of each verse or phrase used in preaching. This is especially true if he is using other passages and cross-references to develop a subject. It is dangerously easy to slip into "proof-texting"[10] when developing this kind of message. A verse in support of a sermon point may contribute to great oratory, but be wrong for expository preaching! As Haddon Robinson puts it, "A text cannot mean what it has not meant."[11]

Contextual analysis requires attention to both the immediate and the remote contexts. Focusing on the remote context draws attention to the thematic unfolding of an entire book. For example, understanding 1 John as setting forth various tests which people may apply to see whether they are in the faith, as Robert Law convincingly demonstrates it does,[12] will significantly influence the interpretation of individual texts within the epistle.

A study of the immediate context will yield equally significant benefits. For example, Hebrews 13:5b ("I will never desert you, nor will I ever forsake you") is frequently quoted meaninglessly and applied inaccurately, because it has been detached from verse 5a ("Let your character be free from the love of money, being content with what you have"). This principle is often paid lip service, but the actual expending of energy toward its true implementation is far more difficult and too rarely practiced. Researching the context of narrative and biographical passages, especially of the Old Testament, can demand extra effort because they are frequently lengthy.

The second principle is *historical analysis*. While often overlooked or summarily passed over, this kind of study can generate tremendous insight into a passage and result in a significantly improved comprehension of the text. For example, a historical study of the Feast of Tabernacles and the ritual reenactment of God's provision of water from a rock in the wilderness furnishes a sharpened perception of John 7:37–38: "If any man is thirsty, let him come to Me and drink. He who believes in Me, as the Scripture said, 'From his innermost being shall flow rivers of living water.' " In the preaching of Matthew 19:1–12, the text comes alive with the observation that the Pharisees' query regarding divorce takes place in Perea, the precise region where Herod Antipas beheaded John the Baptist after being confronted by John regarding his divorce (Matt. 14:1–12). It is obvious that the Pharisees were attempting to lure Jesus into a situation where Herod might kill him, too.

A third general principle is *literary analysis,* which basically looks at the type of literature in which the text is found. Is it biography, history, letter, proverb, parable, or what? Aune noted the importance of carefully observing the literary form of a passage:

> Literary genres and forms are not simply neutral containers used as convenient ways to package various types of written communication. They are social conventions that provide contextual meaning for the smaller units of language and text they enclose. The original significance that a literary text had for both author and reader is tied to the genre of that text, so that the meaning of the part is dependent upon the meaning of the whole.[13]

Each genre embodies characteristics that are distinctive; thus, each requires attention to its own unique interpretive principles. For instance, Jesus's teaching on prayer in Luke 18:2 is prefaced with these words: "Now He was telling them a parable" (v. 1). The interpreter is informed that the teaching is to be construed in keeping with principles of parabolic hermeneutics. Therefore, the interpretive strategy has obvious differences from one adopted in Exodus 20:15: "You shall not steal." Recognizing and understanding the genre of a given passage prompts a reading strategy, rules out false expectations, and represents an *entrée* to the meaning of the text.[14]

In the final analysis, placing the preaching text within the broader contextual, historical, and literary framework of the biblical author simply extends to the Bible the same courtesy that we extend to the morning newspaper. Only when that is done will one grasp the authorial intent and release the power of the "rightly divided" Word. These principles elicit a commitment of time and energy, and generally do not yield instant results. Yet their fruit is sweet and the rewards great for using them.

SPECIFIC PRINCIPLES

Thematic Preaching

Guidelines. As a safeguard against selecting a text that does not accurately undergird the subject under consideration, the first principle for thematic preaching requires that the primary text for the sermon be chosen contextually—that is, as faithfully reflecting what the text means in its own context. Too often in thematic preaching, a sermon is prepared on a purely topical basis, and the text chosen as a "motto" to sound the theme and bless the preacher's ideas.

Unfortunately, this is an exploitation of the biblical text. The text "simply serves as a catalyst; the actual content of the sermon is derived elsewhere and frequently could have been suggested just as well by a fortune cookie."[15] Instead of accurately expounding the Scriptures, the would-be expositor heralds nothing more than personal or cultural values saturated with randomly chosen Bible verses.

> Preachers are called to be ministers of the word of God. This means that the sermon should be much more than 'one man's opinion'; the sermon should be the word of God. . . . A sermon is the word of God only to the extent that it faithfully proclaims the word of God in the Bible.[16]

The Word of God rightly divided brings authority to the sermon, thereby protecting the preacher from heresy and, at the same time, giving the audience a means to validate and defend the instruction.

A second principle for thematic preaching is to focus on biblical word (or sometimes, short-phrase) studies, researching in particular those words around which the theme is built. For example, when preaching on 1 Thessalonians 5:16 ("rejoice always"), one researches the meanings and biblical usage of the words "rejoice," "joy," and the general exhortations in Scripture to be glad. In the process, various aspects of rejoicing will emerge, such as its source(s), its hindrances, its rewards, and so on. This method incorporates the important element of using Scripture directly to obtain guidance and teaching for a sermon and avoids the danger of falling into wayward philosophical abstractions. Where an abundance of biblical information exists on a given theme, the expositor will need to sift and select the parts with more significant suitability. At the same time, thoroughness should not be sacrificed.

A third thematic principle requires that a subject of appropriate size be chosen. The broader the topic, the more difficult it is to cover the pertinent material with justice and cohesiveness, and the more difficult it is to instruct people, generate understanding, and foster retention. Alexander noted,

> The more *special* the subject, the more you will find to say on it. Take it as a general rule, the more you narrow the subject, the more thoughts you will have. . . . It requires vast knowledge and a mature mind to treat a general subject, such as virtue, or honor, and it is much better to begin with particular instances.[17]

It is sometimes desirable to preach on a broad subject, such as an exposition of a whole book of the Bible in one sermon. The benefit of this type of message is that it affords people a comprehensive grasp of the contents and significance of the whole before it is broken into its parts.

This "macro" approach, however, intensifies the preparation demands on the expositor, for unless he understands the constituent parts, he cannot present the whole accurately. Furthermore, the temptation of a busy pastor is to present the obvious, reciting facts and details already known to his people, thereby sacrificing the primary value of exposition, that is, telling the audience more than they can glean from a casual reading. This has the disastrous effect of leaving both himself (in the preparation process) and the audience without meaningful interaction with the Word and thus without instruction, increased comprehension, and opportunity for spiritual growth.

To restrict the scope to be covered allows for depth of research and precision in instruction. Broadus added, "It is usually better that the subject should not be general but specific. This not only promotes variety in successive sermons but really makes each subject more fruitful."[18]

Ultimately, such preaching can and should be expository—a rich development and presentation of the Word of God. Regardless of one's specific homiletical approach, preaching must be biblical or it is not expository. It must be filled with teachings from the Word, not with humanistic perspectives or cultural philosophies.

Tools. The expositor has many tools at his disposal when researching a particular theme. Listed below are just a few of the basic ones:

a. A good English concordance.
b. *Theological Dictionary of the New Testament,* 10 vols., ed. by Gerhard Kittel and Gerhard Friedrich (Eerdmans).
c. *Theological Wordbook of the Old Testament,* 2 vols., ed. by Archer, Harris, and Waltke (Moody).
d. *Treasury of Scripture Knowledge* (Revell).
e. W. E. Vine, *Expository Dictionary of New Testament Words* (Revell).
f. *Dictionary of New Testament Theology,* 3 vols., ed. by Colin Brown (Zondervan).
g. Numerous books on preaching for special occasions, such as Herbert Lockyer's *All the Holy Days and Holidays* (Zondervan).
h. Your own file is one of the best, if you have been faithfully reading, clipping, and storing away. It is imperative that you have a good filing system, one that permits you to retrieve the appropriate materials quickly.

Theological Preaching

Guidelines. Preaching a theological expository sermon is very similar to thematic preaching. For the most part, the principles given there apply here, too. However, some additional elements apply specifically to theological topics and thus require separate explanation.

Theological instruction transpires continually within a verse-by-verse expository sermon in brief excurses, paragraphs, or sentences. Nevertheless, to furnish perspective, expand theological understanding, and provide greater appreciation for the nature and character of God, such doctrinal teaching occasionally requires specific unified attention in a sermon devoted exclusively to it. Theological preaching is often shunned because of a pastor's lack of theological acumen and his unwillingness to pay the cost of preparation. But despite its high price tag, it needs to be done. The health of the church necessitates it.

> Doctrine, that is, teaching, is the preacher's chief business. To teach men truth, or to quicken what they already know into freshness and power, is the preacher's great means of doing good. The facts and truths which belong to the Scripture account of sin, Providence, and redemption, form the staple of all scriptural preaching. But these truths ought not simply to have a place after a desultory and miscellaneous fashion in our preaching. The entire body of Scripture teaching upon any particular subject, when collected and systematically arranged, has come to be called the "doctrine" of Scripture on that subject . . . ; and in this sense we ought to preach much on the doctrines of the Bible. We all regard it as important that the preacher should himself have sound views of doctrine; is it not also important that he should lead his congregation to have just views?[19]

Theological sermons need not be dry. Broadus observes that it " all depends on the way in which it is done. The dry preacher will make all subjects dry; dull anecdotes and tame exhortations have sometimes been heard of."[20] Conversely, theological sermons can and should be as fresh and vibrant as the pastor's own zeal for knowing God, his zest for discovering the deep riches of God's Word, and his passion for preaching the whole counsel of God. Much more than a theological lecture is required; mandated is a treatise passionately delivered and overflowing with evidence that the subject has captured the heart and life of the pastor and now begs to infiltrate the innermost being of the hearer.

By way of caution, the expositor must avoid making a single doctrine his hobby horse. The Word of God in its entirety is to be explained, not just one favorite portion of it. Nor should one avoid those doctrines which may be controversial with some audiences. They, too, must be taught.

> It would seem to be a just principle that a preacher should never go out of his way to find a controversial matter or go out of his way to avoid it. He who continually shrinks from conflict should stir himself up to faithfulness; he who is by nature belligerent should cultivate forbear-

ance and courtesy. When the text or topic naturally leads us to remark upon some matter of controversy, we should not, save in exceptional cases, avoid it. We should of course be mainly occupied with the advocacy of positive truth; but . . . in many cases we cannot clearly define truth save by contrasting it with error. And since errors held and taught by good men are only the more likely to be hurtful to others, we are surely not less bound to refute them in such cases than when advocated by bad men. . . . While faithfully and earnestly opposing error, even as held by Christian brethren, let us avoid needlessly wounding the cause of our common Christianity.[21]

Elsewhere Broadus appropriately cautioned, "Be faithful and fearless, but skillful and affectionate."[22]

Tools. Topics on which to preach theological sermons are seemingly innumerable. Included in the great doctrines of the faith would be the attributes of God, the doctrine of the church, the Holy Spirit, and the inerrancy and trustworthiness of the Bible and its transmission to us. One could preach on each of the key points in the doctrinal statement of his church, and so on.

Resources for this type of preaching are many, including the following:

a. John Gill, *A Body of Divinity* (Sovereign Grace).
b. John MacArthur, *The Ultimate Priority* (Moody)
c. John MacArthur, *The Gospel According to Jesus* (Zondervan).
d. John MacArthur, *God, Satan, and Angels* (Moody).
e. John MacArthur, *God With Us* (Zondervan).
f. John MacArthur, *Heaven* (Moody).
g. John MacArthur, *Charismatic Chaos* (Zondervan).
h. John MacArthur, *The Master's Plan for the Church* (Moody).
i. Thomas Watson, *A Body of Divinity* (Sovereign Grace).

However, it is best to begin with the Scriptures themselves and thereby, in essence, write one's own theology. This cannot be encouraged too strongly! The freshness of the material and the rewards of discovery will exceed what can be gained from a study of theology books. After one's own study, theology books become an excellent source for reinforcement and enhancement. As Unger has wisely admonished, "The best work in this field will carefully expound what the Scriptures themselves reveal more than what might be gleaned from books of theology."[23]

Historical Preaching

History rightly presented has tremendous attractiveness to an eager-to-learn mind. Nor does it lack power to impact and generate understanding.

History is the ultimate teacher, patiently waiting in the wings of life until one opens to its persistent knocking. Unfortunately, the old saying is all too applicable: "The only thing we have learned from history is that we have learned nothing from history."

But this need not be the case. To a greater degree than secular history, biblical history generates great attraction to the truth and is imbued with great power to produce spiritual discernment and influence. Most appropriate are the words of Paul in 1 Corinthians 10:11: "Now these things happened to them as an example, and they were written for our instruction."

> In the Bible the designs of Providence are not left to be judged of by our sagacity but are often clearly revealed, so as to show us the meaning of things obscure and the real co-working of things apparently antagonistic. Thus the Bible histories act like the problems worked out in a treatise of algebra, teaching us how to approach the other problems presented by the general history of the world. The oft-quoted saying of an ancient writer that "history is philosophy teaching by example" applies nowhere so truly as to the inspired records, which are God himself teaching by example.[24]

Consequently, with so much valuable data at his disposal, it behooves the expositor to research the biblical archive and expound the biblical histories that were sovereignly commenced and which have providentially transpired.

Guidelines. Historical preaching requires an acquaintance with the physical surroundings of a context. A Bible expositor should review geography and topography together with the manners and customs of Israel and her neighbors. He should study them industriously so that he can visualize the scenes so as to recreate them vividly in the minds of the hearers. When preaching from historical books such as Ruth, Esther, Jonah, or Acts, for example, he should incorporate both the setting and the substance of the text in his sermon. Included with the content, the setting provides an expositor with a wealth of historical information from the surrounding physical realm and with an opportunity to present the sermon in dramatic story-book fashion.[25]

Tools. Commentaries will generally include some historical and geographical information. Topographical and archaeological assistance is usually more difficult to retrieve. However, a number of excellent works are available for the expositor researching the historical.

   a. Merrill C. Tenney, ed., *The Zondervan Pictorial Encyclopedia of the Bible* (Zondervan).
   b. James B. Pritchard, ed., *The Harper Atlas of the Bible* (Harper & Row).

c. Paul L. Maier, trans. & ed., *Josephus, The Essential Writings* (Kregel).
d. Alfred Edersheim, *The Life and Times of Jesus the Messiah* (Eerdmans).
e. J. Alberto Soggin, *A History of Ancient Israel* (Westminster).
f. Michael Grant, *The History of Ancient Israel* (Scribners).
g. F. F. Bruce, *New Testament History* (Doubleday).
h. Richard L. Niswonger, *New Testament History* (Zondervan).
i. Everett Ferguson, *Backgrounds of Early Christianity* (Eerdmans).

Biographical Preaching[26]

It seems that nothing interests people more than stories about other people. News (or gossip, for that matter) about another person is like honey to flies. It rarely fails to attract a crowd. When tirelessly researched and skillfully presented, an invitation to peer into the life and character of a biblical personage brings with it an unveiling of sin and motivation toward maturity. Biblical principles are not abstract; they occur on the stage of living history displayed in biblical personification. Since this is true, biographical preaching is a powerful true-to-life instrument eagerly waiting to be used as an effective tool in an expositor's repertoire.

Guidelines. Generally speaking, biographical sermons are constructed and delivered in one of two ways. One way is to tell the story of the person and then to follow it with the lessons drawn from his experience. Another is to draw one lesson from each point/stage of a biblical character's life. The lesson is extracted and applied at each stage of the description before moving on to describe the next stage. The reverse is equally effective. The lesson is stated and then followed with a portion of the life story to illustrate it. "If the story has been properly told, the truths one wishes to enforce will already be so clear that they can be driven in and clinched quickly."[27]

Biographical preaching faces the same primary concern that confronts all topical preaching: being true to the context. Because of the ease with which one can extract a "juicy" vignette for a sermon, preachers may be tempted (often unconsciously) to make the life of a biblical character teach lessons it does not teach. The temptation is especially strong when illustrating from a single incident or characteristic from a biblical individual's life. Such temptations should be vigorously avoided since biblical biographies are generally descriptive, not prescriptive.

Consequently, it is generally safer to use the biblical character's entire life as an illustration rather than extracting a single point. And since the Bible frequently furnishes only brief and incomplete sketches, filling in the gaps must be strictly compatible with known or recorded facts. Biblical biographical preaching must be seen first within the context of the Bible's theme. Biographies form an integral part of the whole of sacred history and serve a very specific purpose in the delineation of that history. For this reason, they must be seen first as a part of the larger picture.

Some preachers abuse biographical preaching by shunning it, because they feel they have little talent for description and storytelling. Others abuse it by focusing only on the historical person without teaching anything substantial. A chief benefit of describing lives in the Bible is from character analysis, a study of God's sovereign, providential workings in their motives and actions, both good and bad. Koller has aptly cautioned,

> It must be remembered that the Bible was not given to reveal the lives of Abraham, Isaac, and Jacob, but to reveal *the hand of God* in the lives of Abraham, Isaac, and Jacob; not as a revelation of Mary and Martha and Lazarus, but as a revelation of *the Savior* of Mary and Martha and Lazarus.[28]

Furthermore, biographical preaching must have more substance than just a rereading of the text in a Sunday school fashion. It must teach insight into the sovereign workings of the hand of God, insight that comes only through diligent research and faithful study.

Tools. The pages of Scripture abound with men and women from every walk of life, such as, kings, beggars, housewives, zealots, and servants. Biblical material from which to preach is not lacking in this area. Though tools to assist in preparation are not quite as numerous, many are still available. In addition to Bible encyclopedias that generally provide good historical background material, the following are quite helpful:

a. John MacArthur, *Twelve Ordinary Men* (Word).
b. John MacArthur, *In the Footsteps of Faith* (Crossway).
c. Richard Mayhue, *Fight the Good Fight* (Christian Focus).
d. Gene Getz, *Joseph* (Regal).
e. Elmer Towns, *History Makers of the Old Testament* (Victor).
f. Herbert Lockyer, *All the Apostles of the Bible* (Zondervan).
g. Herbert Lockyer, *All the Men of the Bible* (Zondervan).
h. Herbert Lockyer, *All the Women of the Bible* (Zondervan).
i. Herbert Lockyer, *All the Children of the Bible* (Zondervan).
j. Herbert Lockyer, *All the Kings and Queens of the Bible* (Zondervan).
k. J. D. Douglas & Merrill C. Tenney, *The New International Dictionary of the Bible* (Zondervan).

SUMMING UP

Whether preaching thematically, theologically, historically, or biographically, the bottom line is that the Scriptures must be the primary resource and contextual guidelines must be observed. They are the expositor's chief source of spiritual insight and teaching, the place to which he turns first before studying the many available helps. And once in the Scriptures, the expositor must take great pains to utilize them in a fashion that will reflect the authorial intent.

15

Expository Preaching from Old Testament Narrative

David C. Deuel

A significant part of the Bible is devoted to sections of narrative literature, also referred to as "story." The advantages of preaching from this type of passage have not been fully realized because preachers have not preached the sections just as they are in the text. Advantages to be capitalized on include the intrinsic interest involved in such stories, the patterned nature of the stories, the timeless truths illustrated, and the way the stories lend themselves to easy application. Yet certain precautions are necessary in preaching narrative sections. An artificial structure must not be imposed on them. They must not be used solely as a resource of illustrations for the rest of the Bible. They are not just examples of obeying or disobeying God's law. By observing these guidelines and precautions, the expository preacher can utilize narrative sections to great advantage in his preaching.

Song titles such as "I Love to Tell the Story," "Tell Me the Old, Old Story," and "Tell Me the Story of Jesus" reflect the important role of stories in a Christian's life. For example, evangelistic efforts commonly include the use of stories, just as Stephen and others told (for example, Acts 7:2–50). A "testimony" is *the believer's* story about how Jesus has worked in his life. It is the essence of the gospel message: *Jesus'* story about His exemplary life and substitutionary death. In Christian educational programs, teachers instruct children in one of the most effective ways possible: they tell them stories, both biblical and contemporary.

If all the above examples are true, then why do preachers usually not preach biblical narratives (that is, stories[1]) as stories? Often expositors use an illustration (that is, a story) to clarify a point, apply a principle, or wake up a sleepy congregation. They do this because stories make sermons clear, relevant, and interesting.[2] Yet many seem uncomfortable in preaching narrative as story, perhaps fearing to appear ridiculous or sound condescending. Consequently, they either refrain from preaching narrative, or in preaching it, they reduce the narrative to the stereotypical, three abstract propositions or points without dealing with the story's plot or allowing the story to have its full impact on the reader. Either of these reactions is unnecessary. Narrative makes its own point(s) in an interesting and effective manner, while the selection and arrangement of the story's details provide clues for finding them.[3]

Nearly one-third of the Bible is narrative. Because the story format of biblical narrative hinders expositors from preaching this large proportion, two general suggestions in understanding and preaching Old Testament narrative will help the expositor capitalize on this gold mine of preaching material.

PREACH THE STORY LINE

Following the story line[4] facilitates a grasp of some of the characteristics of narrative. "Narrative, in its encompassing sense, is an account of events and participants moving over time and space, a recital with beginning and ending patterned by the narrator's principle of selection."[5] Biblical narratives are stories in which the message is "embodied in a structure of events and persons, rather than in a structure of verbal generalizations."[6] Why change the format when preaching them? If the preacher's goal is to be expositional, what is more expositional than preaching the text in its story-line form?

The following are characteristics that mark biblical narrative as storylike. These features of narrative are best preserved by preaching narrative as God gave them, that is, in story form.

Narrative Has Literary Power

"Story" means story-like history. Biblical narrative combines qualities of literature and history. From a literary standpoint, narrative is very carefully written and employs a set of conventions not combined in other types of biblical literature.[7] Even many of the dialogues embedded in narratives display unique literature-like features.[8] On the other side, history focuses on the cause-and-effect relationships of events. Understanding the cause of an event enhances one's understanding of the event itself.

Comparing biblical narrative with a history of Israel shows that the literary features of narratives do more than inform historically. So a narrative's concentration is not so much on historicity versus fictionality as it is on how biblical writers chose to recount historical events.[9] Spirit-inspired writers were not trying to report all that happened, because most biblical narrative is narrowly focused. God led these writers to include what He wanted recorded and to do it in the way He wanted it recorded and without error. Because narrative blends features of history and literature, the story is the best format for preaching the narrative's message in the form God gave.

Biblical narrative, then, is neither history, strictly speaking, nor is it prose.[10]

Prose does appear in the Old Testament in letters (such as, 2 Sam. 11:15), proclamations (such as, Ezra 1:2–4), some dialogues (such as, 2 Sam. 9:1–4), and other forms, but it does not share many of the characteristics of biblical narrative.[11] The latter is a different type of literature and should be preached in a way that maintains its distinctiveness.[12] One of the qualities that separates biblical narrative from prose and provides clues for its interpretation and preaching is the thoughtful structuring displayed in its symmetrical format and patterns of expression.

Narrative Is Patterned

Patterning, a primary characteristic of Old Testament narrative that notes its formation into a specific literary plan, offers two advantages in preaching. First, it presents a unifying framework essentially marking the narrative's parameters. The story follows a prescribed but general pattern that identifies it as a story.[13] A more complex pattern occasionally unites the entire story, giving it a deliberate symmetry. For example, some narratives form an "X" or chiastic pattern, where the middle through the last episodes parallel closely the first through the middle ones, but in reverse order. One oft-used saying illustrates this pattern: "When the going gets tough, the tough get going."

A second aspect of patterning is its provision of a form for the sermon. This helps in capturing the text's intended emphases, one of the hardest, but most important parts of sermon preparation. One of the most difficult decisions for a preacher before preaching is determining the form of his message. Expository preaching purposes to preach the *message* of the biblical text. But what about the *form* of the scriptural message? Form is part of the text, too.

In a sense, preaching requires the messenger to make at least minimal changes of the message from one form, say a psalm, a letter, or a narrative, into another form called a sermon. In other words, a preacher must structure his sermons, unless he merely reads the text.[14] His message, then, may be in a form or forms inconsistent with the text treated.

Both the preacher who moves verse by verse through a well-studied passage and the one who preaches without a preplanned text or message have decided on the form of their sermons. The former chooses to follow a commentary-application format, probably because he feels that it is the truest to the original. The latter follows a stream-of-consciousness format, perhaps because he feels that he must rely directly on the Holy Spirit. Part of the frustration of expositors in trying to preach narrative comes in attempting to translate the form of the text into a sermonic structure. What form should it assume?

If the sermon needs to represent the entire message of the original, will the usual point-by-point outline suffice? What will constitute the individual points? Summaries of the separate episodes? Behaviors or attributes of the characters in the narratives? Theological propositions inferred from the text? No wonder would-be expositors are often perplexed by narrative.

The structuring stage is greatly simplified by selecting the story line as the format to represent the narrative passage and by following the emphases in the patterning of the narrative for deriving emphases for the sermon. This requires deliberate effort by the preacher, because narrative sermons should stress the message of the narrative. A simple retelling of the story may not do this. As one homiletician suggests, the preacher must "move in and out of the story with analogues, explanations, and interpretations as the plot line of the story moves along."[15] Whether he does this with points of the sermon or with pauses for elaboration at the text's points of emphasis is a matter of individual judgment. But by preaching the story, the expositor can simplify a potentially complex task of representing patterns and preserve the narrative's patterned quality most effectively.

Narrative Is Timeless and Universal

Biblical narrators concern themselves with relaying facts; that is, they do, indeed, convey historical information.[16] Yet they also guide perspective and responses to events.[17] It is this subtly prescriptive quality of biblical narrative that makes it inherently "sermonic." Biblical narrative assumes "that what happens to the characters in the story is somehow a model of the enduring human situation"[18] and that the characteristics of God in the story are timeless, as well. When people hear or read a biblical narrative, they have a strong tendency to say, "I can relate to that." Preachers sometimes refer to the generalizations drawn from such passages as "timeless principles" and the activity of drawing such generalizations as "principlizing" the text.[19]

But not all that occurs in narrative is truly timeless. In fact, much of the detail is culture-specific, such as the festivals and offerings prescribed for Israel under the law. Issues of this type are affected by progressive revelation, for example, the nexus between Israel and the church. All such items that fall under the continuity/discontinuity rubric must be considered carefully. The tendency to become overly prescriptive or exemplary to the exclusion of the Bible's forward movement in redemption history must be avoided. Each passage must be interpreted carefully to learn its intended message before being taught and applied. But one of the best formats for bringing out either the narrative's timeless and universal character or its redemption-historical development is the story-line sermon.

Narrative Relates Experience

A natural tendency in preaching narrative is to sound like a historian. Extreme manifestations exasperate congregations as, for instance, when the sermon becomes a lecture on cultural anthropology. This extreme points once again to confusion regarding the major distinction between historical writing and biblical narrative. Historiography, as traditionally conceived, seeks to reconstruct historical events based on facts. The objective is to tell what *happened*. Biblical narratives aim to impact readers with what *happens*, that is, "they provide a vicarious *experience* of the truth to be taught, and thus they move persons to identify with and live by that truth."[20] In short, narrative as story is very application-oriented. For this reason, the story line in the sermon tends to preserve the narrative's experiential quality more cogently than most other formats.

On the other hand, because narrative impacts its audience in such subtle ways, it is difficult to codify fully into a set of interpretive principles or procedures. In the Joseph story, for example, the listeners' sympathy for poor Joseph being led off as a slave could be lost unless time for audience reaction is allowed at that point. For this reason, reduction or cutting the story down in size and scope, is a great challenge. Some would say this is impossible, but it is not if one presents the story line carefully.

Narrative Is Difficult to Reduce

Reduction is the process whereby the expositor takes a larger and more detailed block of text and summarizes it, perhaps in a brief single sentence, clause, or word. A question could be raised regarding the wisdom of reducing biblical narratives to sermon propositions and points. After all, if the biblical writer intended a strictly propositional format to communicate his message, why did he employ narrative?

Perhaps the answer is that narrative communicates that particular message better. This does not mean that the preacher may never use summary points, propositions, or theological abstractions. It seems that the message of a narrative must be reduced somehow, either by the preacher or the listener, before it can become contemporary. If nothing else, time requires this. So the process of generalizing requires at least some reduction.

Even from the standpoint of pedagogy, when some might contest the narrative's capacity to teach, the story line can hold its own. This is the lesson of the Old Testament itself. Much of Old Testament religious symbolism and many Old Testament rituals, monuments, feasts, etc., were designed to prompt the children to ask questions like "What does this rite mean to you?" (Ex. 12:26) or "What do these stones mean to you?" (Josh. 4:6). The teaching response was almost always a story.

The issue remains, "What is the best way to preach biblical narrative?" In most cases, presenting the narrative as story is technically the easiest, ꓱegetically the safest, rhetorically the most effective, and lends itself to the most natural application. "Moreover, developing the sermon in the same form as the text will enable the congregation all the better to follow the exposition of the text and to test and remember the sermon."[21] Attempts to handle narrative sections in other than a story-line format may account for the frustration of expositors in trying to preach narrative.

LOOK TO THE TOTAL THEOLOGICAL MESSAGE

A second general suggestion in handling narrative revolves around three possible ways of mishandling such portions. Special precautions are necessary to avoid overlooking major theological emphases.

Substituting the Preacher's Conceptual Structure for the Narrative's Unifying Structure

Biblical narratives are complete stories. Even the Joseph story (Genesis 37—50),[22] although part of a larger complex of narrative, has its own introduction and conclusion. Unifying patterns, in joining together parts of the story, give it a cohesiveness that makes it a story. The preacher sometimes ignores a narrative's inherent unity, however, by focusing on some of its tantalizingly colorful details.

Does the following exemplify a familiar title, proposition and outline of a narrative sermon?

> *Text:* Genesis 37—50
> *Title:* "Joe Christian"
> *Proposition:* BE LIKE JOSEPH: Respond Correctly
>   A. *Flee Immorality:* Potiphar's wife enticed Joseph.
>   B. *Work Hard:* The jailer and the Pharaoh assigned work to Joseph.
>   C. *Forgive Others:* The brothers mistreated Joseph.

This arrangement is right as far as it goes. The title, proposition, and outline focus on the attributes and behavior of Joseph. All three outline points are supportable by clear, didactic passages elsewhere in Scripture. They are not unbiblical. But they do not go far enough.[23]

Sermons that focus primarily on the behavior or character of an individual in the narrative (sometimes called "biographical sermons") *may* miss the passage's broader theological teaching. Some narratives do prescribe behavior, but the Joseph story does not merely present a model of how young people should be or behave. If the preacher is looking for an exemplar and settles on the Joseph story, he has exchanged the story's unifying structure for his own conceptual structure. He chooses the narrative only for the sake of certain details within the story. Joseph's behavior may well be part of the message, but the preacher has made it the whole message. This inevitably leads to no more than prescriptive mimicry.

A simple corrective for this is to focus on the entire message to its original audience instead of having the congregation identify with specific characters in the story.

Searching for Details in the Narrative to Illustrate
New Testament or Other Old Testament Passages

A second mistaken approach preaches Old Testament narrative only to illustrate New Testament or other Old Testament principles. Illustrations, if not overdone, perform an important function in teaching or preaching situations. Using Old Testament stories as illustrations of either good or bad behavior is not wrong. Joseph's behavior toward Potiphar's wife, his ten brothers, and God is exemplary.[24] Using Old Testament narrative *only* to illustrate New Testament teaching, however, results in ignoring much Old Testament instruction that may serve as background for New Testament theology, or else as teaching not repeated in the New Testament. Creation, law, and covenant are in Old Testament narrative which, if ignored or used for illustrations only, will create many problems of biblical imbalance. An adequate theological framework must include the whole Old Testament (see 2 Tim. 3:16, "All Scripture . . .").

New Testament writers used characters, events, and all kinds of phenomena from the Old Testament as illustrations (such as Hebrews 11, etc.). Nevertheless, this does not prove that the incorporation of details of an Old Testament narrative for illustrative purposes is the way to *preach* that Old Testament narrative. An Old Testament narrative as a textual unit presented an entire theological message to its original audience. Through theological abstraction, it may have called for an ethical change, either directly or indirectly. Or it may move the history of redemption forward, demonstrating how God's redemptive purpose is at work in the world. Should it not do the same in sermons today? To preach the message of a narrative passage is to take it in its entirety, not to dwell just on character/behavior traits of individuals in the narrative.

An expositor should use great caution in proving a theological or ethical principle by employing an Old Testament narrative. He should find clear admonitions of "do or believe this" or "do not do or believe this" elsewhere in Scripture before drawing on narrative illustrations to elaborate on the point. Adopting the theology of Job's counselors indiscriminantly, for example, is not wise. Similarly, a blind following of the ethical example in narrative portions of Scripture is unsafe. In other words, the expositor wants to assure that the Bible advocates a certain doctrine, attribute, or behavioral quality *before* illustrating it with an Old Testament narrative. Professing Christians have at times wrongly justified bad theology or immoral actions on inferior grounds, that "so and so, an otherwise virtuous Bible character, spoke/did it."[25]

Limiting the Narrative to an Ethical Reflex of the Law

A different, but related, way of mistreating narrative is to use it to show what happens when God's people obey or disobey His law.[26] Following this assumption is a way of strengthening ethical norms not specifically stated in Scripture. In this third interpretive scheme, Joseph's good behavior and subsequent reward are viewed as part of the complex of the blessing and cursing which came as a result of his obeying or disobeying the law. A case in point is his ascendancy to the role of second-in-command in Egypt because of his obedience to God's law. Preaching of this type often dwells on disobedience as a cause of lost blessing or punishment. Using narrative thus seems to make good sense, for characters in the narratives are demonstrating either good or bad ethical behavior. In a certain sense, it is correct. Yet the question is the same: "Is this *all* that the narrative teaches?" or more significantly, "Is this what the narrative was intended to teach?" Clearly, some narratives have more to say.[27] A problem here is that the sovereign grace of God, clearly prominent in the Joseph story, is omitted because of exclusive attention to human works.

The three misuses of Old Testament narrative just summarized emphasize the need for caution in preaching. *What the Bible itself teaches* often differs considerably from *the ways one uses the Bible to teach*. Without special precautions, the expositor may use narrative characters to teach something that is only supported in another part of the Bible, whether it be through substituting the preacher's propositions/points, careless use of illustrations, or ill-advised choice of legal-case exemplars. The Joseph story does not merely affirm this young man's exemplary behavior. A sermon reflecting the story's true emphasis must take the complete message, the theological dynamic of Joseph's character within God's sovereign plan— salvation history.

Joseph's response to his brothers' pleas for forgiveness pointedly summarizes the details of the whole story. The God-given dream (Gen. 37) was fulfilled by God when the brothers, upon recognizing Joseph, fell before him (Gen. 50:18). Thus, the dream marks the beginning and ending of the preaching unit *and* provides clues to an interpretation featuring God's providential care and guidance. Joseph's two statements to his fearful brothers are also part of the narrative patterning. These two emphasize God's sovereign control over all that has happened as a result of their sin: "You sold me. . . . God sent me" (Gen. 45:5; see 45:7–8) and "You meant evil against me, but God meant it for good" (Gen. 50:20a). The brothers had evil intentions and bad behavior. God allowed the latter, but curtailed the former so that His purpose to build a nation, even from such a poor breed as slave traders, might not be thwarted.

The point is that the expositor should not indiscriminantly use Joseph or any other biblical character as an example. Far more importantly, he should not neglect to preach and teach such portions for their truth intentions as represented in the entire textual unit. Or, more boldly, if he focuses on Joseph's behavior only, he has not preached Genesis 37—50.

The question remains, "How does one preach narratives like the Joseph story?" Perhaps the easiest, most effective way, the way truest to the biblical form, is just to retell the story, allowing the story itself to heighten points of application. Is this not the way that Sunday school teachers teach children these stories? Why stop at age eight or nine? Why reduce the story to three points (often just three examples of good behavior), when telling the whole story brings honor to the sovereign hand of God? Homiletically speaking, which has more impact, hearing an abstract proposition about God's sovereignty (such as, "God is sovereign") or seeing it borne out in the experience of God's people? When a preacher states an abstraction, he usually follows it with an illustration to enhance comprehension of the abstraction. Narrative preached as narrative has already incorporated the illustration.

Who Is Sufficient?

One final question may enter the preacher's mind when approaching Old Testament narrative. Who is sufficient for the task of preaching Old Testament narrative? It is true that identifying the conventions of narrative, then formulating them into interpretive guidelines, is as complex as it is important,[28] but those who read and study the narrative portions of Scripture come to understand these conventions intuitively. Not only does understanding come through careful reading, but also "there is a certain commonality among narrative traditions of whatever age and culture, just as there is a certain commonality among different language systems."[29] Readers "tend to apply most of these rules intuitively, simply as close readers to the biblical text."[30]

Preaching narrative is important. If the expositor has committed himself to preaching "the whole counsel of God," he will soon discover that a large portion of Scripture is either narrative or narrative-like. Because narrative follows a story line, (1) it has literary power, (2) it is patterned, (3) it is timeless and universal, (4) it relates experience, and (5) it is difficult to reduce. In light of these factors, the expositor does well to maintain the story format.

Preaching the story line in its entirety has the advantage of guarding against at least three common shortcomings in the interpretation of narrative: (1) ignoring the narrative's unifying structure for the sake of the preacher's conceptual format, (2) searching for details in the narrative merely to illustrate New Testament and other Old Testament passages, and (3) limiting the narrative to an ethical reflex of the law. None of these methods handles the entire textual unit or looks for the complete theological and ethical message.

When preaching narrative, one should take the spotlight off the Joseph-like heroes and shine it on the only praiseworthy character in the story—God. Perhaps because of such a focus, those to whom he preaches will make God the focus of their life stories. As a byproduct, human behavior will probably improve also, and not in just a threefold way to correspond to a three-point message.

16

Moving from Exegesis to Exposition

John MacArthur

Preaching an expository sermon involves more than merely repeating the technical results of one's Bible study. True expository preaching involves transforming technical details into principles or doctrines so that the expositor preaches theologically with appropriate applications. This discussion focuses on how to bridge the gap from exegesis to a Bible exposition.

Careful and diligent Bible study is the foundation of the expository sermon. This compels the expository preacher to be first of all a student of Scripture with a reverence and awe for God's Word that makes him diligent in his study (see Is. 66:2, 5; 2 Tim. 2:15). He examines the Bible inductively, letting it speak for itself by using a systematic study method, correct rules of hermeneutics, and skillful exegesis. He employs all the appropriate study tools to enhance his understanding of a passage. These necessities have been discussed earlier (see chs. 7—11).

But preaching an expository message involves far more than standing in the pulpit and reviewing the high points, details, and components unearthed through research. Neither a word study nor a running commentary on a passage is, in itself, an expository sermon. An expository sermon does more than simply explain the grammatical structure of a passage and the meanings of its words. A true expository message sets forth the principles or doctrines supported in the passage. True expository preaching is doctrinal preaching.[1]

The proper elements in an expository sermon may be summed up as follows:

1. *Preaching is expository in purpose.* It explains the text.
2. *Preaching is logical in flow.* It persuades the mind.
3. *Preaching is doctrinal in content.* It obligates the will.
4. *Preaching is pastoral in concern.* It feeds the soul.

5. *Preaching is imaginative in pattern.* It excites the emotion.
6. *Preaching is relevant in application.* It touches the life.

The task of the expository preacher is to take the mass of raw data from the text and bridge the gap between exegesis and exposition. The following is the process I follow in doing that.

DEVELOPING THE MAIN BODY OF THE SERMON

Proper communication in preaching involves taking people through a logical, systematic, and compelling process.

Be Aware of the Logical Flow of the Message

As I begin to develop the main body of the message, I am concerned first with logical flow. I want to take the people step by step through the process of interpreting the passage. I often state my main idea in the form of a question and then show how the passage answers it. If I raise a question that is critical to their spiritual lives, they will stick with me to get the full answer.

After developing that question or compelling theme, I begin to refine the outline, making sure the points all relate clearly to the main idea. The outline is the road map that takes people through the logical flow of a passage to the destination of doctrine to be applied. It is critical that this flow be clear.

As I move through the passage, I not only give the correct interpretation, but enough of the interpretive process to show them how reasonable that interpretation is. It is not enough to tell people what a passage means; you also must show them *why* it means that. Avoid pontificating; show listeners how you arrived at your interpretation. For example, I cannot just state that the messenger of Satan that tormented Paul in 2 Corinthians 12:7 was a demon-inspired person. I must also give my reasons for interpreting the passage that way. This also teaches them an interpretive method they need to apply in their own study of Scripture.

Include Discussions of Problematic Interpretations

I devote a major part of my study time on a passage resolving the problems it poses. The first time I preached through Romans 6, early in my ministry, it took me a month of studying before I could fully grasp the argument. And when I began my study of 1 John, I felt almost like abandoning the ministry! It is an extremely difficult epistle to outline, and some of its passages offer hard challenges to the interpreter. Avoid the temptation to ignore problems. Every devoted Bible student has been frustrated with commentaries that ignore obvious difficulties. The expositor should not frustrate his people this way. They can often interpret the obvious parts of a passage for themselves. They need a leader to explain the difficult ones. The faithful preacher knows he must deal with the whole text, avoiding nothing, since all is inspired and intended for the understanding of God's people. Frequently, the richest nuggets lie buried in the deepest places.

Taking the people through interpretive steps in solving a problem teaches them a basic Bible-study process. Involving them in the discovery process also excites them about Bible study. It is not necessary to overwhelm them with all the details, but do show them enough of the process to enable them to defend the conclusions drawn. Do not put them in a position where they have just your word to lean on. They are going to share your conclusions with other people. Give them some hard data to offer in defense of the conclusions, so that they will have more than just "I believe it because my pastor said it." Consciously preach to a second generation of hearers who will be a target for your hearers.

I first define clearly an interpretive problem or difficulty in the text. Then I briefly state all alternatives. Finally, I explain why I chose the alternative I did. I find that explaining problems generates high interest. By raising a provocative question, I get people's attention because they want to know the answer. So do not avoid problems; rather, draw your people into the adventure of discovery.

The expositor's primary goal is to teach the Word accurately and completely, not to move people's emotions independently of a comprehension of the text. Their only wholesome emotional response comes through understanding the text's meaning. Most speakers try to motivate, excite, and generate emotion through either rousing stories, oratorical manipulations, or histrionics of some sort. Without a comprehension of divine truth, this produces a short-lived reaction that cannot sustain a lasting transformation. People live out their theology. The stronger the hearer, the more well defined and biblically framed his belief system is, the more his conduct will conform to the Word and to truth. So teach people the deep things of God, avoiding nothing.

Connect the Passage with the Rest of Scripture

After tracing the logical flow of a passage, I show how it fits the rest of Scripture. I do that by cross-referencing each point. In my notes, I list all the cross-references I find that clarify, illuminate, or expand the truth, although I do not necessarily share them all when I preach. Listing them in my notes gives me a permanent record of my thoughts on a given point. Explaining to your people the significance of essential cross-references supporting and clarifying your points adds credibility to your interpretation and strengthens the doctrine. It shows its harmony with the rest of Scripture. Make sure, however, that the verses used really support your point when properly interpreted in their own context. Traina warned of those who "fail to take the time to examine each unit to discover its singular meaning, and . . . therefore frequently make erroneous associations. The result is much faulty interpretation."[2] He added,

> The danger to which attention is being called is the failure to interpret each unit in its own right before blending various units together. If each passage is first expounded as a literary entity, then valid associations will be made, and such associations will be beneficial. But if there occurs an amalgamation of material before each unit is expounded in view of its own context, then errors in exposition will be the inevitable result.[3]

Commentaries, lexicons, and concordances are good sources for cross references. Perhaps the best source, however, is *The Treasury of Scripture Knowledge.* It gives extensive cross-references for nearly every verse in the Bible. Its format is similar to marginal references found in most Bibles, but the citations are far more extensive. The book *10,000 Biblical Illustrations* contains another helpful collection of references to aid in using the Bible to explain the Bible. Also consult *The MacArthur Topical Bible.*

By reinforcing the truths of a passage with other Scriptures, you acknowledge the *analogia Scriptura,* the analogy of Scripture. This hermeneutical principle states that Scripture does not contradict itself, but is consistent in its teaching. Scripture is its own best interpreter. Obscure passages should always be interpreted in light of clear ones. Packer wrote,

> The Bible appears like a symphony orchestra, with the Holy Ghost as its Toscanini; each instrumentalist has been brought willingly, spontaneously, creatively, to play his notes just as the great conductor desired, though none of them could ever hear the music as a whole. . . . The point of each part only becomes fully clear when seen in relation to all the rest.[4]

People love to see the big picture. They want to know how everything fits together. It is sometimes difficult for them to grasp a truth presented in isolation, but bringing analogous passages to bear on a text enriches its truths by viewing them from different angles. The more times you illustrate a truth from Scripture, the more you fix it in your listeners' minds. Cross-references help etch truths deeply into your people's consciousness.

When looking for cross-references, start with the book your passage is in, then move on to other books by the same author, then to the same testament, and finally to the whole Bible. Remember to check parallel accounts of the same story in the Gospels. Look for passages containing the same word or words, as well as conceptual cross-references—those teaching the same doctrine.

Finding Appropriate Biblical Illustrations

Having put together the main body of the sermon, I then concentrate on illustrations. I first return to illustrations that have come to mind and have been recorded in my notes as I worked through the main body of the message, to refine them and add others where needed.

Illustrations are critical to a good expository message. Spurgeon likened them to windows in a building. They do not support the structure, but they do let in light. He wrote,

> A building without windows would be a prison rather than a house, for it would be quite dark, and no one would care to take it upon lease; and, in the same way, a discourse without a parable is prosy and dull, and involves a grievous weariness of the flesh. . . . Our congregations hear us with pleasure when we give them a fair measure of imagery: when an anecdote is being told they rest, take breath, and give play to their imaginations, and thus prepare themselves for the sterner work which lies before them in listening to our profounder expositions.[5]

Illustrations serve several purposes:

1. Illustrations make an exposition *interesting*. People will often say to me after a sermon, "That was a great sermon!" when what they really meant was that it had a couple of good illustrations. Illustrations also keep the listeners' attention. Spurgeon pointed out that

> A house must not have thick walls without openings, neither must a discourse be all made up of solid slabs of doctrine without a window of comparison or a lattice of poetry; if so, our hearers will gradually forsake us, and prefer to stay at home and read their favourite authors whose lively tropes and vivid images afford more pleasure to their minds.[6]

2. Illustrations make an exposition *memorable*. People often remember a sermon because of a striking illustration in it. In fact, when I preach a sermon and use an illustration I have used before, people sometimes tell me they have heard the sermon before, when all they really remember is the illustration. Even years later, people still remember some illustrations.

3. Illustrations make an exposition *convincing*. People will not be persuaded by what they do not understand. Sometimes a good illustration, by showing how a principle works in a life situation, will convince people of its truth.

4. Illustrations make an exposition *clear*. People sometimes are dazed by the minutiae of an exposition. An illustration opens a window and gives them relief from the stark facts. Spurgeon said,

To every preacher of righteousness as well as to Noah, wisdom gives the command, "A window shalt thou make in the ark." You may build up laborious definitions and explanations and yet leave your hearers in the dark as to your meaning; but a thoroughly suitable metaphor will wonderfully clear the sense.[7]

5. Illustrations make an exposition *motivating*. Giving examples (especially biblical ones) of people whose experience illustrates a biblical principle will motivate hearers to put it into practice in their own lives.

Too few illustrations make a sermon dull and hard to follow, but at the other extreme, use of too many illustrations is also undesirable. The purpose of an expository message is to teach the meaning of a biblical passage. Too many illustrations or illustrations that are too long will water down the doctrinal content of a sermon. Once again, Spurgeon's warning is timely:

Illustrate, by all means, but do not let the sermon be all illustrations, or it will be only suitable for an assembly of simpletons. A volume is all the better for engravings, but a scrap-book which is all woodcuts is usually intended for the use of little children. Our house should be built up with the substantial masonry of doctrine, upon the deep foundation of inspiration; its pillars should be of solid Scriptural argument, and every stone of truth should be carefully laid in its place; and then the windows should be ranged in due order, "three rows" if we will: "light against light," like the house of the forest of Lebanon. But a house is not erected for the sake of windows, nor may a sermon be arranged with the view of fitting in a favourite apologue. A window is merely a convenience subordinate to the entire design, and so is the best illustration.[8]

I look primarily for biblical illustrations. The New Testament writers used the Old Testament for illustrations more than any other source. It is appropriate to use illustrations from other sources, but I prefer biblical ones for two reasons. Biblical illustrations, unlike nonbiblical ones, have authority. Illustrations from other sources may be interesting and help hearers grasp a point better, but they are not the inspired Word of God. A second reason I prefer biblical illustrations is that they teach, as well as illustrate. They expand your people's knowledge of the Bible.

The best source of biblical illustrations is *10,000 Illustrations from the Bible*. Other helpful sources include topical Bibles such as Nave's or the *Topical Index and Digest of the Bible*. Since the Old Testament was written for our instruction and as an example of truth illustrated in the lives of other people (1 Cor. 10:11), it is the first place to look. The next place I go is to the Gospels to see if Jesus's life or teaching illustrates the doctrine I am preaching.

Many sources of nonbiblical illustrations are available, but the expositor should always be alert to finding good illustrations of his own. Developing an illustration file can be beneficial, especially if it is well indexed.

It is very important for an expository preacher to develop a "parable perspective," that is, learn to think in analogies. The most effective communicators are those who have learned how to use analogies to provide windows to what they say. They take abstract truths and make them concrete and thus more easily understood. Practice in inventing parables or analogies is helpful. When I taught a seminary course in homiletics, I required students to compose a parable each week. Learning to think in analogies saves time looking for illustrations. Do not, however, use analogies as a source for truth, because doctrine comes from Scripture, not from analogies. Analogies illustrate truth, but do not establish it. Disregard for this axiom is widespread and has led to all kinds of error.

Putting Together the Final Sermon Outline

After developing the main body of a sermon, cross-referencing it, and adding biblical illustrations, the next step for me is to complete the final form of my outline.

I prefer to keep my outlines simple. I do not like complicated ones with a lot of subpoints. Outline points are hooks to hang thoughts on. They are lights along the pathway to enable listeners to stay on the path. They help retain listener attention and facilitate comprehension. An imbalanced, confusing, or complicated outline is self-defeating.

Outline points must be parallel in structure, that is, all built around the same part of speech, such as all nouns, all verbs, or all adjectives. They should all be either questions or declarative statements. An example of a nonparallel outline from Matthew 28:19–20[9] is as follows:

What Is Involved in Making Disciples?

I. Going
II. Baptizing
III. Instruction

The first two key words are verbs, but the third is a noun. The correct way of formulating these points is:

I. Going
II. Baptizing
III. Teaching

Subpoints, in addition to being parallel, must relate to their main point. In the following example, the third subpoint is not only unparallel, but also does not relate to its main heading:

I. God's love for us
  A. Seen in His sending of Christ into the world
  B. Seen in His forgiving of our sins
  C. Sin results in death

As you preach a message, periodically reviewing its outline reminds your people where you are. Their minds often wander during a message. They tune out and then tune back in. Frequent reminders of your location in the outline help them return quickly to your flow of thought. If they cannot get back into the context of your remarks, they may become lost and tune out altogether.

WRITING THE INTRODUCTION AND CONCLUSION

This is the final step in preparing an exposition. Only after the rest of the sermon is put together can you know what to introduce and conclude. Writing the introduction first tempts one to bend the passage to fit the introduction. My introductions tend to be somewhat lengthy, because I have to set the historical and cultural background of a text and review the context. Make sure your introductions do not disclose too much of what is to come, or the rest of your sermon will be like watching a replay of a football game when you already know the final score. Do not allow an introduction to undermine the discovery process that you want your people to experience in the main body of your message.

The conclusion should summarize the main points of a message, and leave the people with a challenge to put what they have learned into practice in their lives. Always preach in the second person to make it personal and preach for a verdict. Force people by the logic, clarity, and power of your exposition to make a life-changing decision based on what they have heard.[10] I want them to leave knowing so clearly what God requires of them that they also know whether they have obeyed or refused to submit to that requirement. A summary statement, illustration, or parallel passage of Scripture can reinforce the need for them to respond.

SEVEN "BE'S" OF EXPOSITORY PREACHING

After the hard work of exegesis and the development of the sermon, the message is ready to preach. But before stepping into the pulpit to preach it, remember the following general guidelines:

1. Be Prepared

I cannot emphasize this enough. The Word of the living God is the source of our messages, and its truths are inexhaustible. There is simply no excuse for a man stepping into the pulpit without having something profound, insightful, and rich to share with his people.

My father is an expositor, and one thing he hammered into me when I was young was the importance of preparation. He told me again and again, "Don't you ever go into a pulpit unprepared. And if you say 'The Bible says . . .' you make sure to the best of your ability that it truly does say that." Lack of preparation leads to poor preaching, offends God, and leads people to weakness, not strength.

People often ask me if I get nervous before I preach. That only happens when I am not sure what I will say. If I know what I am going to say, I do not get nervous, no matter what the subject is. Confidence is directly linked to preparation.

Too many men enter the pulpit without working the results of their study and exegesis into an expository message. As a result, they are unsure where they are going, and the sermon is unfocused. Still others fail to spend enough time in study and message preparation. Make sure you are thoroughly prepared before you get into a pulpit to expound God's holy Word.

It is very easy to be hard to understand, just be unfamiliar with your subject and the listeners will share your lack of understanding. They may think you were too deep for them, but that is not true. You had not grasped your own subject, or they would have grasped it, too. It is very difficult to be clear; you have to master your subject.

2. Be Interesting

Refrain from boring people with the Bible. Preach more than what is obvious in a passage, what your people can see for themselves. The way to avoid preaching just the obvious is to work hard in preparation. Make sure your well is a lot deeper than their buckets. Make your sermons an adventure in discovery for your people.

3. Be Biblical

The Word is "living and active and sharper than any two-edged sword, and piercing as far as the division of soul and spirit, of both joints and marrow, and able to judge the thoughts and intentions of the heart" (Heb. 4:12). Stories, analogies, anecdotes, or discussions of current events do not have the power or authority of the Word of God. Power in expository preaching comes from the Word, not from slighting it in favor of other themes.

4. Be Prayerful

After all is said and done, after all our diligent study and careful preparation, if we are not energized by the Holy Spirit, our preaching will be in vain. I once read of a godly pastor who years ago kept repeating, "I believe in the Holy Spirit. I believe in the Holy Spirit," from the time he left his office until he stepped into the pulpit. He acknowledged his total dependence on the Holy Spirit's power.[11]

We need to bathe our sermons in prayer. Generally speaking, prayer is a way of life. Specifically, I begin praying for the sermon the moment I begin preparation and then pray particularly for my Sunday-morning message on Saturday night, often falling asleep in prayer. I pray Sunday morning, first privately in my study, then with some of the elders, thus surrounding the message with prayer. Then in the afternoon I pray directly for the evening message. Afterward, I have a season of prayer with other pastors before preaching.

5. Be Enthusiastic

If you cannot get excited about what you are to say, you cannot expect your people to get excited, either. The message God gives should be like fire in our bones so that we *have* to preach because we are weary of holding it in (see Jer. 20:9). When I step into the pulpit on Sunday after a week of study and preparation, I am excited about what I will say. People sometimes ask me how far in advance I prepare my messages. I prepare each week for that Sunday. That is where my intensity comes from. The thrill of fresh discovery generates my enthusiasm.

Some years ago we had a Christmas outreach at our church. I asked one of the men at my table how long he had been coming to the church. "A year," he replied. "And how long have you been a Christian?" I inquired. He answered that he was not a Christian. "Why do you come?" I asked. "I'm in sales, and you're so enthusiastic that you get me pumped up for my week of selling." I politely told him there was more to my messages than just enthusiasm. Yet, I was grateful to learn that I was not boring. There must be an enthusiasm, an excitement, and an intensity in our preaching.

6. Be Authoritative

Preach with conviction. The Bible is God's authoritative word to man. As someone remarked, "God didn't give us the Ten Suggestions; He gave us the Ten Commandments." We could define authority as "soft confidence." If we believe what we say is true, we should say it with confidence and authority. We say *soft* confidence, because we cannot resemble a spiritual drill sergeant, barking commands at our people.

Preach in the second person. Say "you," not "we" or "they." You are God's spokesman from Him to them, so you must be direct in the use of "you."

I remember hearing several years ago that the Los Angeles Police Department had to flunk a man out of its police academy because he had a weak, high-pitched voice. They felt it inappropriate for him to tell people, "You're under arrest!" in a voice that did not sound authoritative. We must preach with conviction, and people must sense it. As Paul wrote to Timothy, "Preach the word . . . reprove, rebuke, exhort, with great patience and instruction" (2 Tim. 4:2).

7. Be Relevant

Avoid being oblique, obscure, pedantic, or using outdated illustrations to which people cannot relate. Show how the timeless truths of the Word of God touch their everyday lives.[12]

True expository preaching is actually the most effective kind of applicational preaching. When Scripture is accurately interpreted and powerfully preached, the Spirit takes the message and applies it to the peculiar needs of each listener. Apart from explicit general application in principlizing the main parts in the exposition, the expositor is not compelled to give a set number of points of specific application before a sermon can have an applicational impact. That is not to say he should not make some illustrative applications, but if the text is allowed to speak fully, applications will multiply far beyond what he can anticipate as the Spirit of God takes His Word and applies it to each listener.

If hundreds or even thousands are present, the expositor by proposing his own specific applications may place unnecessary restrictions and run the risk of eliminating many other applications to the lives of his hearers. Rather, he should concentrate on giving the correct meaning of the text and be content with general applications. This grants the Holy Spirit, who is most capable in applying the Word to every heart, His rightful place in speaking to individual lives.

God's high and solemn calling to preach His Word demands our best study and careful exposition. The spiritual food of God's Word causes our hearers to grow in grace, so we must be sure that it is properly prepared before we serve it to a congregation, and we must serve it in a manner befitting its unique authority.

Part V

Preaching the Exposition

Bible Translations and Expository Preaching[1]

Robert L. Thomas

Expository preaching presupposes the goals of teaching an audience the meaning of the passage on which the sermon is based and urging obedience to that meaning properly applied. Two types of Bible translations are available as "textbooks" the preacher may use in accomplishing this task. One type follows the original languages of Scripture in form and vocabulary insofar as possible without doing violence to English usage. The other type is not so much governed by phraseology in the original languages, but accommodates itself to contemporary usage of the language into which the translation is made. It is possible, with a fair degree of objectivity, to measure how far each translation deviates from the original languages. The greater degree of deviation inevitably reflects a higher proportion of interpretation on the translator's part. Regardless of the accuracy of the interpretation, the preacher will at times disagree with it and have to devote valuable sermon time to correcting the text. The best choice of translations on which to base expository preaching is, therefore, one which more literally follows the original languages and excludes as much human interpretation as possible.

English versions of the Bible can be classified in different ways. They can be classified in regard to historical origin, in regard to textual basis, in regard to theological bias, and in regard to usage of the English language. These areas of consideration are not without relevance to exegesis and expository preaching, but for purposes of the current study, a fifth classification will be examined, that of the philosophies of translation used in producing Bible versions.[2]

This category of analysis is chosen because of its very close connection with exegesis and exposition. In such an investigation as this these two terms, exegesis and exposition, must be clearly defined. "Exegesis" is the critical or technical application of hermeneutical principles to a biblical text in the original language with a view to the exposition or declaration of its meaning. "Exposition" is defined as a discourse setting forth the meaning of a passage in a popular form. It is roughly synonymous with expository preaching. In a comparison of these two it is to be noted that exegesis is more foundational and more critically and technically oriented. Exposition is based upon exegesis and has in view a more popular audience. The exposition under consideration here is public and spoken exposition rather than written exposition.

In the practice of exposition or expository preaching it is assumed that the preacher's goals include the teaching of his passage's meaning to the audience.[3] Such teaching points out items in the text that are obvious but may never have been noticed. It also calls attention to items that may be completely hidden from the reader of an English translation. It will, in addition, explain passages that are difficult to interpret. In the process of imparting new teaching, the expositor also will remind his listeners of truth previously learned. Based on all this instruction, the preacher will apply the principles of his passage to listeners with a view to producing spiritual growth and transformation in their lives.

It is obvious that the above aims are much more attainable if the congregation has an English version of the Bible in which to follow the sermon, preferably the same translation as that used by the leader of the meeting. The question to be addressed in the following discussion is, with what type of translation can the minister of the Word best accomplish his goals? In other words, what kind of connecting link between exegesis and exposition is the most desirable? Stated still another way, what type of translation is most advantageous for use in the practice of expository preaching? But before this question receives an answer, several important issues regarding translation must be discussed.

TWO PHILOSOPHIES OF TRANSLATION

In search for an answer to this question about the kind of version needed, it is necessary first to understand, in some detail, features of the two major philosophies of translation.

One philosophy focuses most of its attention on the original text or the source of the translation. This is called the literal or formal equivalence method of translation. The other is more concerned with the target[4] audience of the translation. This is referred to as the free or dynamic equivalence method of translation. A literal translation seeks a word-for-word equivalency, trying also to retain the grammatical structure of the original insofar as the destination language will permit. A free translation aims for communicative effectiveness or an effect upon the reader in the receptor language comparable to that produced upon the original readers and listeners.[5]

According to dynamic-equivalence advocates, literal translations, which are for the most part the traditional and older ones, have not allowed adequately for cultural and social factors that affect readers of a translation.[6]

The formal-equivalence advocate responds that the translator of a free trans-lation has not shown sufficient respect for the inspired text.[7]

Translating freely is not a new idea. Jerome, who produced the Latin Vulgate at the end of the fourth century, purposed to translate the sense, not the words, of the original whenever translating anything other than Scripture.[8] John Purvey, an associate of John Wycliffe, expressed much the same sentiment in the late fourteenth century when he said that the unit in translation cannot be the word, but at the very least the clause or sentence.[9] Yet, the degree of freedom advocated by these scholars is inapplicable to many modern English versions. Jerome did not apply these standards to the Vulgate, and the second edition of the Wycliffe version, in which Purvey was most influential, would now be classed as a literal translation. A major breakthrough in free translating came at the very beginning of this twentieth century with the publication of the Twentieth Century New Testament. Though translated by those of a basically non-scholarly orientation, this project paved the way for a flow of scholarly works geared more to modern English practice than to the precise wording of the original text.[10] These have in-cluded undertakings by Weymouth, Moffatt, Goodspeed, and Knox as well as the New English Bible and the Good News Bible.

In connection with the last of these, there finally developed a philo-sophical rationale for what the free translator had been doing for many decades already.[11] It was at this point that the title "dynamic equivalence" was applied to the practice.[12] Many of the principles of modern communica-tions theory were then integrated into translation practice.

Side-by-side with the newer emphasis in translation, the traditional philosophy of literal translation, labeled "formal equivalence" and then "formal correspondence" by the theorists of the American Bible Society,[13] continues to present its candidates: the Revised Standard Version, the Mod-ern Language Bible, the New American Standard Bible, the New American Bible, the New King James Version, the New American Standard Bible Up-date, and the English Standard Version.

Among English translations, the roots of this philosophy are deep. The first English translation done by associates of John Wycliffe was a very literal translation, corresponding word-for-word, whenever possible, with the Latin text on which they based their translation.[14] The principle of literality was observed so scrupulously in the Douai-Rheims version that the English prod-uct is unintelligible in some places. The goal of the King James Version transla-tors was to be "as consonant as possible to the original Hebrew and Greek."[15]

The contemporary preacher is thus faced with a choice between these two types of English translations. The reaction of some might be to question whether there is that much difference between the two. They would want to know whether the differences are measurable. Of interest also is the nature of the differences and how they affect expository preaching.

MEASUREMENT OF DIFFERENCES BETWEEN FREE
AND LITERAL TRANSLATIONS

Evaluations of translations in regard to the philosophies of their translation techniques have usually been general in nature. For example, "The NEB [New English Bible] is a free translation, tending to paraphrase and, in some instances, to wordiness."[16] "The NIV [New International Version] is also too free in its translation."[17] "The NASB [New American Standard Bible] is a literal approach to the translation of the Scriptures."[18] "The NAB [New American Bible] is more faithful to the original than is either the JB [Jerusalem Bible] or the NEB [New English Bible]."[19] The Modern Language Bible sought to avoid paraphrase, and so is a "fairly literal" translation.[20]

General appraisals such as these are helpful as far as they go, but are at best vague in their connotation and at worst open to question as to their accuracy. Can they be made more definitive and defensible? In other words, can tests of dynamic equivalence and formal equivalence be applied to various versions so that equivalency of effect and conformity to the original can be measured? The answer in the case of dynamic equivalence is a qualified "no," and in regard to formal equivalence it is "yes."

Testing the communicative effectiveness of translations and thereby determining their degrees of dynamic equivalence is a very inexact task. According to Nida, a translation should stimulate in a reader (in his native language) the same mood, impression, or reaction to itself that the original writing sought to stimulate in its first readers.[21] This is an unattainable goal and one that can be only approximately achieved.[22] Impressions of different people will vary widely after reading the same biblical passage. Also "equivalent effect" is difficult to quantify, because no one in modern times knows with certainty what the effect on the original readers and listeners was. To assume that a writing was always clear to them, as is frequently done, is precarious.[23] Yet tests have been devised to measure how well modern readers comprehend what they read. One of the most successful of these is called the "Cloze Technique."[24] It consists of reproducing portions of literature with words intentionally omitted at regular intervals. A representative group of people who are unfamiliar with the literature are given these portions and asked to insert the missing words. On the basis of their success in doing so, statistical data are compiled on the readability of the literature in question. By using comparable sections of different English versions, one can formulate an estimate of the comparative communicative effectiveness of these versions.

The limitations of this test are several. They center in the difficulty of assembling a sufficiently representative group of people.[25] Vocabulary aptitudes vary widely even among members of the same family. Backgrounds and experiences differ to the point that members of the same socio-educational group reflect wide discrepancies in scoring on such a test. Devising a pattern of meaningful results is next to impossible because of the extreme subjectivity of the quantity or quality being tested.

The test of formal equivalence is more successful, however. It is a test of "deviation values." First formulated by Wonderly,[26] this procedure consists of five steps.[27]

The first of these steps is to take a passage of suitable length, say from thirty to fifty Hebrew or Greek words, and number the words consecutively.

Second, each word is translated into its nearest English equivalent, in accord with standard lexical tools based on principles of literal interpretation. This stage, known as the "literal transfer," is carried out without rearranging the word order. In cases where alternative English renderings are possible, both choices are included. The consecutive numbers from step one remain in their proper sequence. Of course, the result of this step is incomprehensible English. Nevertheless, this is an important intermediate stage.

The third step consists of changing the English word order and making any other changes necessary to produce a readable English format. Changes thus made are kept to a minimum, being only those absolutely necessary to make the sense of the English comprehensible. This process is known as the "minimal transfer." In this rearrangement each word or phrase retains its original sequential number, the result being that the numbers no longer fall into their previous consecutive sequence. The result of this step is called the "closest equivalent" translation. This closest equivalent constitutes a standard to which various published translations may be compared.

The fourth part of the procedure for determining deviation values of English versions is the comparison of these versions, one by one, with the closest equivalent translation in the section of Scripture under consideration. Such a comparison will reflect five types of differences: changes in word order, omissions from the text, lexical alterations, syntactical alterations,[28] and additions to the text. Each time a translation differs from the closest equivalent, an appropriate numerical value is assigned, depending upon the degree of difference between the two. When the values for the five kinds of differences are totaled, a deviation value for the section is established. From this deviation value for the thirty to fifty words is extrapolated a deviation value per one hundred words.

The fifth and last step is to repeat the whole process in other passages until a sufficient sampling of the whole book is obtained. The deviation values from all the passages are then averaged together to obtain a single deviation value per one hundred words for the whole book. This can be done for each book of the Bible in any selected version.

The deviation values obtained through this test have no significance as absolute quantities, but when the value for one version is compared to that of another, the versions that are closer to the original text can be identified, as can the versions that differ more extensively from the original.

From such relationships as these a diagram can be constructed to reflect the profile of each English translation in relation to the others.[29] A range of deviation values for literal translations, free translations, and paraphrases[30] can also be established to show in which category each translation belongs and how it compares with other translations within the same category. (See Figure 17–1.)[31]

A comment is needed about the dividing point between literal and free translations and between free translations and paraphrases. These are somewhat arbitrary, but not completely so. The NIV is taken as the bottom

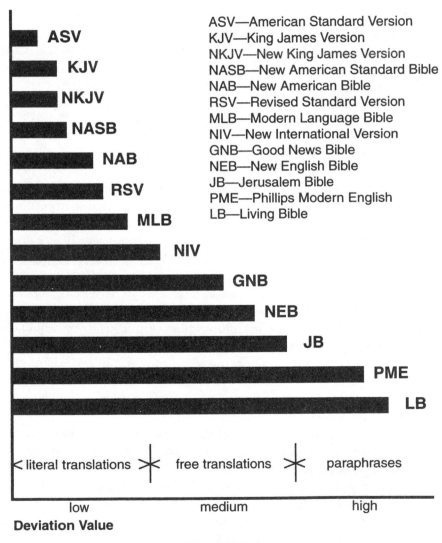

ASV	ASV—American Standard Version
KJV	KJV—King James Version
NKJV	NKJV—New King James Version
NASB	NASB—New American Standard Bible
NAB	NAB—New American Bible
RSV	RSV—Revised Standard Version
MLB	MLB—Modern Language Bible
NIV	NIV—New International Version
GNB	GNB—Good News Bible
NEB	NEB—New English Bible
JB	JB—Jerusalem Bible
PME	PME—Phillips Modern English
LB	LB—Living Bible

‹ literal translations ✕ free translations ✕ paraphrases

low   medium   high
Deviation Value

Figure 17–1
Deviation Values in Romans

of the range of free translations because of its own claim to follow the method of dynamic equivalence.[32] Yet it is more literal than other versions that are also based on the dynamic equivalence principle. Phillips Modern English (PME) is taken as the bottom of the range of paraphrases because Phillips's initial purpose was not to produce something that would be scrutinized as closely as a translation.[33]

The advantage of this test is that it lends a degree of objectivity to general evaluations of the various versions. For example, when Lewis says that the Jerusalem Bible is rather paraphrastic in nature,[34] we would take issue with him on the basis of its difference from Phillips. While the JB is one of the freest of the free translations, it is not so free as to be called a paraphrase. We would likewise question the propriety of Kubo and Specht in calling the New English Bible "paraphrastic."[35] Though these reviewers may be correct about some of its renderings, the translators claimed to have refrained from paraphrase,[36] and an application of the deviation test places the NEB well within the category of free translations.

On the other hand, when Lewis says that the NIV uses "dynamic equivalence" renderings in a number of places[37] or that the NEB is a free translation or when Kubo and Specht say that the New American Standard Bible and Modern Language Bible are literal translations,[38] the accuracy of their words is borne out. Lewis is also correct when he says that the New American Bible is more faithful to the original than the Jerusalem Bible or the New English Bible.[39]

Bruce is almost correct when he states that the NASB retains the precision in rendering that made the ASV (American Standard Version) of such great value as a handbook for students.[40] A comparison of deviation values for the two versions reflects that actually the ASV is more literal than the NASB, but that the NASB still falls low in the range of deviation values set for literal versions. In other words, Lewis's opinion is confirmed: the NASB is relatively literal, but is not entirely free from paraphrasing.[41] Van Bruggen is also proven correct when he notes the distinct difference in literality between the King James Version, the Revised Standard Version, and the New American Standard Bible on the one hand, and the New International Version, Good News Bible, and the Living Bible on the other.[42]

Deviation values can be used in a variety of ways to detect translation trends. For example, a comparison of deviation values for different books reflects differing degrees of deviation within the same version. Subsequent reviews by committees notwithstanding, when a different translator is assigned to each book, there is a good chance that a given version will vary from book to book in its deviation values. The Jerusalem Bible is a case in point. In Romans, it is close to the top in deviation value among free translations but, in 1 Corinthians, its value locates it at the bottom of that range. (See fig. 17–2.) The Modern Language Bible in Romans and 1 Corinthians show translator tendencies that are in reverse of the Jerusalem Bible. In Romans the version falls into the literal translation range, but in 1 Corinthians it reflects substantial characteristics of a free translation. (See again Figure 17–2.)

Kubo and Specht are right when they observe that the Jerusalem Bible is not a homogeneous translation.[43] The same observation applies to the Modern Language Bible when comparing deviation values in Romans and 1 Corinthians.

Another point to be made is that a line between literal translations and

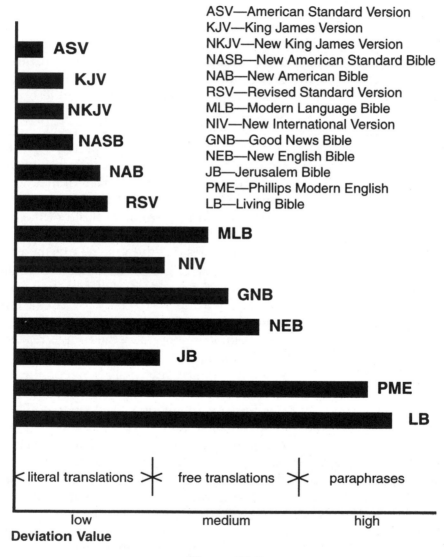

Figure 17–2
Deviation Values in 1 Corinthians

those that are free cannot be precisely drawn. Therefore, there is not a great deal of difference between a translation at the top of the literal range and one at the bottom of the free range. For example, the philosophy behind the RSV (Revised Standard Version) is not radically different from that of the NIV, even though the former is classed as literal and the latter as free. On the other hand, there is a significant difference between a translation in the lower range of literal, such as the ASV, and one in the lower range of free translations.

Of further interest are the deviation values of versions in the Tyndale tradition. (See fig. 17–3.)

Tyndale's work was near the top of the literal translation range, but subsequent revisions moved closer and closer to the zero base, until the twentieth century. Since then, deviation values have both decreased and increased.

INTERPRETATION AS A FACTOR IN TRANSLATION

The above discussion of degrees of deviation from the form of the original text raises a question about what factor or factors account for the higher deviation of some versions in comparison with others. In more general

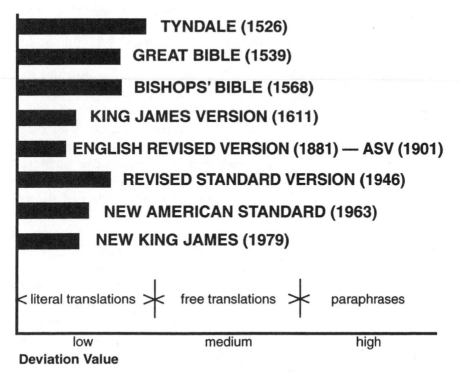

Figure 17–3
Deviation Values in Romans

terms, what are distinctives of free translations and paraphrases that set them apart from literal translations?

The largest single distinction lies in the area of interpretation. To be sure, some interpretation must accompany any translation effort.[44] In this connection Barclay is right,[45] and the editor of the *Churchman* is wrong in saying that translation and interpretation must be kept rigidly separate.[46] For example, one cannot translate 1 Corinthians 7:36–38 without adopting a view as to whether the passage is referring to the virgin's father or to her male companion. Still, the largest difference between translations of a relatively low deviation value and those of a high value lies in the quantity of interpretation behind the renderings. In free translations and paraphrases this element is, as a rule, substantially higher.[47]

This highlights a difficulty inherent in free translation and paraphrase. The translator must choose one interpretation from the possible alternatives, thus leaving the English reader at the mercy of his choice.[48] The translator of a literal translation can often retain the ambiguity of the original text and thus allow the English reader to interpret for himself.[49]

For example, the reader of Galatians 5:12 in the New King James Version (NKJV) will need the help of a commentary to understand the verse.[50] What does it mean, "I could wish that those who trouble you would even cut themselves off"? The readers of free translations and paraphrases will not need a commentary, however, because translators have interpreted for them. In the GNB (Good News Bible), NIV, JB, and NEB "cutting off" is interpreted as referring to a deprivation of the male reproductive glands.[51] In the PME and the LB (Living Bible), a different interpretation is adopted. The statement is made to mean separation from the Christian assembly.

The added responsibility of a dynamic-equivalence translator is made apparent by this comparison. He has also become a commentator. It is to this added role that some have objected.[52] Without acknowledging that he has done so, such a translator has attached his own personal interpretation to the text, thereby excluding from the reader a consideration of the other possible meanings of the text. A literal translation can, on the other hand, often leave the same obscurity in the English text as is found in the original.

Similar dilemmas arise in numerous passages.[53] Which interpretation is right in 1 Thessalonians 4:4, the one which says that Paul speaks of control over one's own body, as in the JB, NEB, NIV, PME, or the one that says he speaks of taking a wife in marriage, as in the LB, RSV, and GNB? Or should the translator shun the responsibility of making a choice, as is done in the KJV, the NKJV, and the NASB?

Does 1 Timothy 3:2 prohibit appointment of an overseer who is a bigamist, as strongly implied by the NIV, LB, PME, and the GNB through the addition of the word "only"? Or does it forbid appointment of a man who is a divorcé, as the JB indicates? Or perhaps the verse speaks of the quality of faithfulness without dealing with marital history, as is the choice of the NEB. But maybe the decision in this matter should be left to the expositor or the English reader, as indicated by the noncommittal rendering of the KJV, NKJV, RSV, and NASB.

Kubo and Specht, as well as Lewis, are among those who seriously question whether a translator has the right to read his own interpretations into the text.[54] They would be joined by many in this objection when the translator's interpretations are blatantly wrong. Such is the case in John 1:1, where Moffatt's "the Logos was divine" and the GNB's "he was the same as God" both miss the point that the verse intends to teach, the Deity of the Word.[55]

Some translations have evidenced an awareness of the problem of excessive interpretation in succeeding editions of their works. For example, in earlier editions the RSV gave "married only once" in 1 Timothy 3:2, but in the 1959 edition it was changed back to "the husband of one wife." Phillips has also removed some of the extreme interpretive elements in a more recent edition of PME.[56] The 1978 edition of the NIV is more literal and less interpretive than the 1973 edition.[57]

THE EFFECT OF INTERPRETIVE VERSIONS ON PREACHING

With the above discussion in mind, it is time to answer the question of what type of translation is the best basis for expository preaching. For some preachers, the communicative effectiveness of a free translation or paraphrase is very important. This advantage should not be underestimated.[58] Yet, if the ultimate goal of the expositor is to teach the meaning of his passage as the foundation for applications to his congregation's practical experiences, he is seriously hindered if he uses a version with excessive interpretive elements. It is a copout to use a free translation or paraphrase under the pretext that all translations are interpretive. The fact must be faced that some versions are more interpretive than others, and a choice must be made in this light.

Upon encountering an interpretation different from his own, as he is bound to do,[59] the expository preacher must tell his listeners that the meaning is not what their Bibles say it is. This is a procedure quite different from explaining an ambiguous statement. It will assume the character of a reversal of what the translation says. This practice, when repeated too frequently, increases confusion and reduces pedagogical effectiveness.

The situation is analogous to teaching a subject in the classroom with a textbook that expresses viewpoints opposite to those held by the teacher. The class time is consumed with refutations of what the textbook teaches. Such an unsound teaching technique greatly diminishes the success of the learning process, especially in the situation where people are led to believe they hold an authoritative book in their hands. They have been taught that this is the "Bible," not a commentary on the Bible.

It is far more advantageous to use and encourage the audience to follow in a more literal translation, one the translator has transmitted from the original language in such a way as to give the church an accurate translation on which to do its own exegesis, and not one that subjects the church to limitations in the translator's understanding of what the text means.[60] It is the job of the expositor, not of the translator, to explain the meaning of the passage under consideration. When a servant of the Lord imposes on the people of God his personal interpretation, he is morally obligated to clarify his role, that it is one of an expositor, not a translator. In any work that is precisely called a translation, interpretation should be kept to a minimum. Otherwise, the role of the expositor is usurped, and the work becomes a commentary on the meaning of the text, not a translation into the closest equivalent of the receptor language.

Byington has reflected this view of translation:

> To say in my own words what I thought the prophet or apostle was driving at would not, to my mind, be real translation; nor yet to analyze into a string of separate words all the implications which the original may have carried in one word; the difference between conciseness and prolixity is one difference between the Bible and something else. So far as a translation does not keep to this standard, it is a commentary rather than a translation: a very legitimate and useful form of commentary, but it leaves the field of translation unfilled.[61]

Commentaries are much needed, but it is a mistake to assume that a translation can function in that role without ceasing to be a translation. Preaching from an interpretive free translation or paraphrase is almost tantamount to preaching from a commentary, not from a translation. It is not the translator's job to mediate between God's Word and modern culture as the commentator or expositor does.[62]

This is why a strong consensus exists that free translations and paraphrases do not furnish English texts that are suitable for Bible study.[63] This is why the general recommendation to follow a literal translation for study purposes is widespread.[64]

CONCLUSION

While it must be granted that a sermon is not the same as a classroom lecture, it is still similar to it in that edification of sermon listeners takes place only when learning takes place. To this end, insofar as philosophy of translation is concerned, it is proposed that the best link between exegesis and expository preaching, the best textbook to use in public exposition of the Word, is a literal translation of the Bible, one in which the interpretive element is kept to a minimum.

The final choice of a translation must not be based on translation techniques alone. It must take into account historical origin, textual basis, theological bias, and usage of the English language also. Among these, however, the philosophy followed in the translation process remains a major factor for consideration in the choice of a version on which to base effective Bible exposition.

18

Delivering the Exposition

John MacArthur

It is not enough just to have a message; you must also deliver it powerfully. Although "delivery" cannot be taught, per se, it can be improved by practicing some basic principles. Recommendations include establishing a disciplined routine before you preach and working diligently to be natural in the pulpit. Attention to methods of delivery, voice use, eye contact, and gestures can also improve delivery.

It is the most difficult element in teaching men about expositional preaching to teach someone to become skilled in the actual delivery of an expository sermon. Some expositors feel quite at home in the pulpit immediately, but others experience continuing uneasiness. However, by following some basic principles, anyone can improve his effectiveness in public presentation as an expositor of God's Word.

Careful preparation is only part of the expository preaching experience. The climax comes in what Martyn Lloyd-Jones calls "the act of preaching." Thorough exegesis and clear organization are crucial to an effective message. But a good sermon poorly preached is no better than a poor sermon properly preached. One has light but no heat; the other heat with no light.

Message content is the most important part of any sermon. What value is knowing how to preach with the eloquence of Apollos if you have nothing worthwhile to say? You cannot make up in zeal what you lack in substance. Good preaching techniques may be in evidence throughout a message, but without significant substance in the remarks, the result is inferior.

Conversely, worthwhile substance can be ineffective if communicated in an unskillful fashion. The congregation deserves to hear God's message preached in both spirit and truth. The manner of delivery is also important, as Jefferson reminded us:

It is surprising how stoutly and stubbornly the churches insist upon preachers knowing how to preach. They will forgive almost everything else, but they will not forgive inability to preach. . . . No man who knows how to preach with grace and power need stand idle in the market-place a single hour. Churches are scouring the country in search of such a man, and he cannot escape if he would![1]

The demand for qualified preachers in Charles Jefferson's day is, unfortunately, not as strong now as it was then. Yet, God's standards have not changed. An expositor must have the message right and then preach it with a zeal and passion befitting divine truth.

The expositor who faithfully prepares and then energetically delivers his exposition week after week will stand out in both heaven's notice and the church's attention.

AFTER PREPARATION—BEFORE PREACHING

An expositor is like an athlete who has finished his last practice, but now must endure the tedious wait until the game. True champions can maintain their concentration and intensity; other athletes cannot. The best expositor, like the winning athlete, must not forget why he prepared—to deliver a soul-searching, life-changing exposition of Scripture with all of the authority and power of a spokesman for God.

To build this kind of bridge between the study and the pulpit, three principles help keep the preacher on track:

Purpose

Begin by focusing on the reality that your sermon is an offering to the Lord. Be driven by the truth that the Lord is your highest judge. Then your consciousness will compel you to deliver the truth as a holy offering to Him. This gives you the proper frame of mind for your solemn responsibility.

What your colleagues or congregation may think or say is not your major concern. Know that delivering the message the Lord has given you is your service to the Him for His satisfaction. That is why Paul charged Timothy "in the presence of God and of Christ Jesus" (2 Tim. 4:1) to preach the Word. Let your thoughts after preparation and before delivery dwell on the Lord and His response to your expositional offering to Him. In the hours immediately before you preach, face the serious reality that you must deliver up a sacrifice that will be acceptable to the divine author of Scripture.

Passion

Feel deeply about the truth you are to preach.[2] If you were giving a book review or reciting an autobiographical vignette, it would be different. Remember that expositors have a mandate from God to preach the truth and that eternal consequences hang in the balance.

This mandate is not easy to obey, nor is it a light load to carry. It is difficult and demands our best effort and utmost concentration. Taking this charge seriously produces an inner compulsion to reach the pulpit better prepared than when leaving the study.

Pattern

In addition to the essential foundations of realizing a heavenly purpose and maintaining a holy passion, implementation of a carefully planned procedure can bring the preacher to a spiritual crescendo as he stands in the pulpit. I follow four conscious and disciplined steps to ensure that on the Lord's day I will deliver the best exposition possible:

1. I prefer to allow some time between doing my rough draft (exegetical notes) and writing out the preaching manuscript. This gives time for the message to settle in and reach a fresh level of clarity in my own thinking. If possible, I like to sleep on it for a night before the final touches are added. Sometimes this is not possible, but even in the most pressing of times, I try to allow a period of several hours.

2. Once both Sunday messages are in their final form, I usually take Friday evening to relax, relieve the mental fatigue, and remove the cobwebs. I often don't pay much attention to my message until around 6 P.M. Saturday.

3. After the Saturday-evening meal, I retire to my study at home for several hours and go through the morning message, marking up the preaching manuscript with a red pen. I really go over it with a fine-tooth comb so that I become intimately familiar with it. This way I will not be tied to the preaching notes on Sunday. If I do any refining, it is usually minor. I go through the same process Sunday afternoon for the evening message. I rarely do anything Saturday night other than review my notes. This helps to keep my mind focused and my thinking process clear. I then can close out Saturday night with my message thoroughly internalized so that I've recaptured the same flow of presentation and grasp of content that I had when the message was completed several days before. I go to bed reasonably early.

4. I fall asleep with my mind on the message. I drift off to sleep praying through my message and awaken Sunday to pray again. As I dress to go to church, I pray with my mind focused on the message and trying not to let anybody or anything distract me. Our elders pray with me before the service and then I am free to enter into the worship and praise of the service before I begin preaching.

Everyone will differ in how he bridges the time span between a finished message in the study and the preaching of it on Sunday. It will depend on his personality, family life, and other responsibilities. Yet, the general framework of (1) remembering that the ultimate *purpose* in preaching is to present an acceptable sacrifice to the Lord, (2) allowing the sacredness of preaching to be your *passion,* and (3) establishing a *pattern* of lifestyle that optimally prepares you to preach in prime mental and spiritual condition on Sunday allows a preacher to rest in God to accomplish His divine purposes through the preaching experience.

A COMPELLING DELIVERY

Every man who enters the pulpit must be conscious that his delivery will either enhance the exposition or detract from it. What makes the act of preaching effective? What qualities characterize the sermon delivery of forceful expositors?

Good preaching begins with *clarity* of content. And clarity begins with a single, easy-to-recognize theme. In his book *Preaching and Preachers* Martyn Lloyd-Jones recounted an event from his first year of preaching:

> It was the custom in Wales at that time, on special occasions, to have two preachers who preached together in a service, the younger man first and the older one following. . . . The old man was kind enough to listen to me in the afternoon, and it was the first time he had heard me trying to preach. As we were being driven in a car together to have some tea at the house of the minister of the church, the old preacher, who was exactly sixty years older than I was, very kindly and with a desire to help and to encourage me gave me a very serious warning. "The great defect of that sermon this afternoon was this," he said, "that you were overtaxing your people, you were giving them too much. . . . You are only stunning them, and therefore you are not helping them." And then he said, "You watch what I shall be doing tonight. I shall really be saying one thing, but I shall say it in three different ways." And that was precisely what he did, and most effectively.[3]

Your exegetical study should have identified a theme. The key in delivering the exposition is to make that theme stand out. Stress your theme and your major points as you preach. Avoid complex outlines; they cause your listeners to miss your major points. The most helpful way of emphasizing your theme and outline is repetition. As you move from one point to the next, use brief transitional sentences to review the points you have already covered. Restate the central idea of the message as often as appropriate. One way to ensure that your listeners comprehend your theme and development is to print it in the church bulletin with room for them to take notes.

Use *clear language*. Clear ideas need to be communicated in understandable ways. If ten people in your congregation will not understand the word "felicity," use "happiness" instead. Being scholastically impressive at the expense of listener understanding is counterproductive.

G. Campbell Morgan argued that *passion* is an essential ingredient for an effective delivery. In explaining what he meant by "passion," he recalled a discussion the English actor Macready had with a well-known pastor. The pastor was trying to understand why crowds flocked to fictional plays but few came to hear him preach God's changeless truth. Macready responded, "This is quite simple. . . . I present my fiction as though it were truth, you present your truth as though it were fiction."[4]

Morgan added,

I am not arguing for mere excitement. Painted fire never burns, and an imitated enthusiasm is the most empty thing that can possibly exist in a preacher. Given the preacher with a message . . . , I cannot understand that man not being swept sometimes right out of himself by the fire and the force and the fervency of his work.[5]

So what is passion? Kaiser answered,

From the beginning of the sermon to its end, the all engrossing force of the text and the God who speaks through that text must dominate our whole being. With the burning power of that truth on our heart and lips, every thought, emotion, and act of the will must be so captured by that truth that it springs forth with excitement, joy, sincerity, and reality as an evident token that God's Spirit is in that word. Away with all the mediocre, lifeless, boring, and lackluster orations offered as pitiful substitutes for the powerful Word of the living Lord. If that Word from God does not thrill the proclaimer and fill [him] . . . with an intense desire to glorify God and do His will, how shall we ever expect it to have any greater effect on our hearers?[6]

Often in the midst of some deep theological discussion, the apostle Paul

seems to forget his argument and bursts forth into one of his flights of great eloquence. . . . A theology which does not take fire, I maintain, is a defective theology; or at least the man's understanding of it is defective. Preaching is theology coming through a man who is on fire. A true understanding and experience of the Truth must lead to this. I say again that a man who can speak about these things dispassionately has no right whatsoever to be in a pulpit; and should never be allowed to enter one.[7]

In his own inimitable way, Spurgeon said of those who lack passion,

When I have thought of the preaching of certain good men, I have wondered, not that the congregation was so small, but that it was so large. The people who listen to them ought to excel in the virtue of patience, for they have grand opportunities of exercising it. Some sermons and prayers lend a colour of support to the theory of Dr. William Hammond, that the brain is not absolutely essential to life. Brethren, . . . you will, none of you, covet earnestly the least gifts, and the dullest mannerisms, for you can obtain them without the exertion of the will. . . . Labour to discharge your ministry, not with the lifeless method of an automaton, but with the freshness and power which will render your ministry largely effectual for its sacred purposes.[8]

Another quality always found in great preaching is *authority*.[9] One of the things that so impressed those who heard our Lord was that He spoke "as one having authority," unlike the Scribes and Pharisees (Matt. 7:29). The effect of an authoritative message is dependent on the character of the messenger.

If the life of the preacher does not harmonize with his words, the resultant discord will drown out the message, regardless of how well prepared and delivered it is. Thus Paul commands Timothy to give heed to himself as well as to the message (1 Tim. 4:16). It is equally true, however, that a man with a flawless reputation who is openly careless in his handling of God's Word does not—indeed, cannot—preach with authority. Both pure character and competent performance are necessary.

Authority comes from the preacher's mandate to proclaim the King's Word as a herald with all the authority of the throne behind him (2 Tim. 4:2). A herald has authority as long as he faithfully presents his King's message. The preacher's authority also rests on an accurate relaying of the message of God's Word.

Using Scripture to illustrate and support the points of a sermon also strengthens the authority of a message. And do not fear using the second person. Say, "*You* can't serve God and money," instead of "*We* can't serve God and money."[10] Morgan expressed it thus:

The preacher should never address a crowd without remembering that his ultimate citadel is the citadel of the human will. . . . The preacher comes with good news; but he does not come with something to be trifled with. His message has in it an insistent demand, because he comes from a King.[11]

Clarity of thought, clear language, passion, and authority are all characteristic of good preaching. But ultimately only one thing can make the act of preaching effective in changing lives: *the power of the Holy Spirit*. Paul wrote to the Corinthians, "My message and my preaching were not in persuasive words of wisdom, but in demonstration of the Spirit and of *power*, that your faith should not rest on the wisdom of men, but on the *power of God*" (1 Cor. 2:4, 5, italics added).

IMPROVING YOUR PREACHING

Every man, regardless of his current level of skill, can significantly improve his delivery by following a few practical steps.

It is not the time to stop working when exegesis is complete, illustrations are in hand, and final touches on an exposition have been added. Several important steps remain.

First, the expositor must select a *method of delivery*. If he has preached more than a few times, he has probably already chosen a method or perhaps constructed a hybrid that works best for him.

Most homileticians identify four basic methods of delivery.[12]

1. Reading—The preacher takes his manuscript into the pulpit and reads from it.
2. Reciting—The speaker repeats from memory what has been written and learned.
3. Extemporizing—The plan of the discourse is drawn out on paper and all the principal points are stated or suggested, but the language is extemporaneous.
4. Freely delivering—After thorough preparation, the preacher goes into the pulpit without notes or manuscript and without conscious effort to memorize the sermon.

The most common method among evangelicals is some form of the extemporaneous. It has the advantage of permitting freedom for the Spirit to direct, unlike reading and recitation, but avoids the risk of free delivery, which is forgetting some important point or perhaps a whole message!

The method chosen determines the quantity of preaching notes used. We especially encourage preachers to write out their sermons. Robinson wrote,

> A good part of the preparation for delivery lies in the use of a manuscript. For me, writing a sermon is a way of thinking. When I have thought myself clear, delivery is much more natural. Sometimes the greatest flaws in delivery come because the speaker is not completely sure of what he wants to say.[13]

He continued,

> I believe it is absolutely essential that a minister have his introduction clearly in mind when he stands to speak. While other parts of the sermon may be outlined, the introduction ought to be written out. It is in the introduction that the preacher establishes contact with the people in the pew. . . . If there is ever a time that the mind will go blank, it is in the first moment or two when you get on your feet.[14]

The benefits of writing out your expository message in some level of detail are many. The positive results will accrue over the expositor's lifetime of expositional ministry. Here are a few to convince you that the increased value is worth the additional effort.

1. Insures that your best thoughts in the study are retained for later as your best thoughts in the pulpit.
2. Clarifies the preacher's thinking through the extra refining step of writing.
3. Crafts the expositor's verbal expressions in a more memorable way for both the preacher and pew-sitter.
4. Captures and preserves the cumulative effect of your studies, that is, there is a previous foundation on which to build the next time the text is studied.
5. Provides already-studied reference material when the same word, concept, or theological concept is encountered in another text studied in the future.
6. Enables the message to be used again for other future occasions, such as, Bible conferences, magazine articles, books, or special teaching opportunities.
7. Guarantees consistency when you are preaching in a multiple-service setting.

Once you have written the notes you intend to take into the pulpit, repeatedly go through your sermon in that note form to make sure you know how to verbalize your outline. Working through your message will force you to put your exposition into words, and enable you to identify any problem areas. That will translate into a much smoother flow of words during the delivery. Although such effort requires time and discipline, it will pay rich dividends on Sunday when you preach.

In *Lectures on Preaching* Phillips Brooks defined preaching as the communication of divine truth through human personality.[15] Lloyd-Jones's definition was very similar: "a proclamation of the truth of God as mediated through the preacher."[16] Thus, speaking to a congregation from the pulpit should be no different than speaking with them individually in the pastor's office. The larger audience merely requires enlarged speaking intensity, facial expressions, and gestures so that all get the same message. In the words of Broadus,

Delivery should be the spontaneous product of the speaker's peculiar personality, as acted on by the subject which now fills his mind and heart. . . . Delivery does not consist merely, or even chiefly, in vocalization and gesticulation, but it implies that one is possessed with the subject, that he is completely in sympathy with it and fully alive to its importance, that he is not repeating remembered words but setting free the thoughts shut up in his mind. Even acting is good only in proportion to the actor's identification with the person represented—he must really think and really feel what he is saying. The speaker is not undertaking to represent another person, to appropriate another's thoughts and feelings, but aims simply to be himself, to speak what his own mind has produced.[17]

The Spirit cannot work through a preacher while he is imitating the external style of other preachers, even those he admires. Spurgeon's advice is wise:

Let every man, called of God to preach the Word, be as his Maker has fashioned him. . . . The good and the evil in men of eminence are both of them mischievous when they become objects of servile imitation; the good when slavishly copied is exaggerated into formality, and the evil becomes wholly intolerable. If each teacher of others went himself to the school of our one only Master, a thousand errors might be avoided.[18]

Concerning the *voice,* the key word is "variety." Before the modern microphone, preachers had to shout to be heard by everyone in the congregation. Tales about the volume of some of the great leather-lunged preachers of the past border on the superhuman. Today, however, sound systems in even the smallest churches make the softest-spoken man clearly heard, so shouting is unnecessary.

Several elements characterize every word we speak: pitch, resonance, inflection, volume, rate, and tone. It is helpful to study the common pitfalls of each by examining a good book on speech.

An easy way to learn your own irritating vocal habits is to record yourself on tape and ask a local speech or voice specialist to analyze it. In all of this, avoid *any* artificiality; your goal is a natural conversational style.

Another important aspect of a natural delivery is *eye contact.* The goal is to know the message well enough to allow more time to look at the audience than at sermon notes. A congregation grows restless quickly if they do not sense that the preacher is speaking to them. Eye contact with a single individual can be very distracting to the preacher, however, so a balanced view of the whole audience is needed to give greatest freedom for a dynamic delivery.

Gestures should be limited and natural. During delivery,

Be natural; forget yourself; be so absorbed in what you are doing and in the realization of the presence of God, and in the glory and the greatness of the Truth that you are preaching . . . that you forget yourself completely. . . . Self is the greatest enemy of the preacher, more so than in the case of any other man in society. And the only way to deal with self is to be so taken up with, and so enraptured by, the glory of what you are doing, that you forget yourself altogether.[19]

With time and diligence your delivery can improve dramatically. But improvement means change, and change requires honest evaluation. Your family, church staff, and flock will provide feedback for you. Learn to listen to their suggestions.

A FINAL CHARGE

When you mount the steps to the pulpit and are about to speak God's Word on His behalf, let these exhortations come to mind:

- Preach to honor God's Word.
- Preach to reach the unconverted.
- Preach to please God.
- Preach to equip Christians for the work of the ministry.
- Preach to lift up the downhearted.
- Preach to be more effective this time than last.
- Preach to bring conviction of sin and repentance.
- Preach to compete with no one but yourself.
- Preach to refresh the spiritually weary.
- Preach to exalt the Lord Jesus Christ.

Then let this prayer of a past generation come forth afresh from you:

O MY LORD,

Let not my ministry be approved only by men,
    or merely win the esteem and affections of people;
But do the work of grace in their hearts,
    call in thy elect,
    seal and edify the regenerate ones,
    and command eternal blessing on their souls.
Save me from self-opinion and self-seeking;
Water the hearts of those who hear thy Word,
    that seed sown in weakness may be raised in power;
Cause me and those that hear me
    to behold thee here in the light of special faith,
and hereafter in the blaze of endless glory;
Make my every sermon a means of grace to myself,
    and help me to experience the power of thy dying love,
    for thy blood is balm,

thy presence bliss,
thy smile heaven,
thy cross the place where truth and mercy meet.
Look upon the doubts and discouragements of my ministry
and keep me from self-importance;
I beg pardon for my many sins, omissions, infirmities,
as a man, as a minister;
Command thy blessing on my weak, unworthy labours,
and on the message of salvation given;
Stay with thy people,
and may thy presence be their portion and mine.
When I preach to others let not my words be merely elegant and masterly,
my reasoning polished and refined,
my performance powerless and tasteless,
but may I exalt thee and humble sinners.
O Lord of power and grace,
all hearts are in thy hands, all events at thy disposal,
set the seal of thy almighty will upon my ministry.[20]

19

Frequently Asked Questions about Expository Preaching[1]

John MacArthur

John MacArthur's thoughts about miscellaneous phases of preaching do not fit under any main heading of *Preaching: How to Preach Biblically,* but have come in response to questions asked him in pastors' conferences and expository preaching classes at The Master's Seminary. The current discussion reproduces his brief but suggestive answers to these questions.

How long does it take you to prepare a sermon?

I spend less time now than I did earlier in my ministry. I used to spend about fifteen hours on a sermon, but now it is about eight or ten hours. Over the years of my ministry, I have accumulated more information, more knowledge of the Scriptures, and more Bible-study skills. These allow me to dig deeper into a text in ten hours than I could in fifteen hours earlier in my ministry.

The big challenge facing me now is not just in the area of interpretation, but in communication. I have been at the same church for more than thirty-five years, so I have to fight to keep from falling into a pattern of similarity. It is a challenge for me to be fresh, and not just say the same things over and over in the same way.

Do you find it easier now to develop a sermon from a passage?

I never study to make a sermon. I study to understand the text. As I have grown in the Lord and in the knowledge of the Word, I have been able to dig deeper into the passages I study. I just keep studying until I have discovered all the rich truths I can from a text. I only preach part of what I find in my study process. Even doing this, however, I often wind up with a three- or four-week series from what began as a single message.

Preaching is a science, an art, and an adventure. It is a science in that it is based on the well-defined and absolute rules of hermeneutics and skills of exegesis. Interpretation is not whimsical, but implements literal, historical, grammatical, and contextual principles.

But preaching is also an art. Preaching a passage is similar to painting a picture. No two artists, though they use the same tools and techniques, will paint exactly the same picture. In the same way, no two preachers, even using the same principles of interpretation, will develop the same sermon. Applying the principles of sermon preparation and delivery is an art whose application depends on the skill, experience, and perspective of the preacher.

Preaching is also an adventure. A spiritual dynamic is at work when I step into the pulpit. I find myself saying things I had not planned to say as the data from my study come together in a way I had not seen before. When this happens, I may depart from my notes and amplify the new thought. That is why it sometimes takes me several weeks to preach through notes originally designed as one sermon.

How do you guard your preparation time?

I use a system I call "planned neglect": I plan to neglect everything else until my studying is done. I set aside Wednesday, Thursday, and Friday to prepare for my Sunday messages. Not until I have accomplished what I need to on those days do I then stop and care for other matters. I have an assistant and two secretaries who help shield me from the affairs of a large ministry that would deluge me and rob me of my study time. Of course, I am available when I need to be.

I realize all pastors do not have a personal assistant or a large staff to share the responsibilities of their ministry. Neither did I in the early years. But my commitment to studying the Word has never changed. If other details take my time, I simply put in longer hours that week. Our goal as pastors is not to do all the work of the ministry ourselves, but to equip our people for ministry (see Eph. 4:11–16). We can only accomplish this effectively through preaching based on thorough study. So I know that time spent in preparation will result in more sharing of my load by a maturing church.

Since notable expositors are avid readers, what are your reading preferences?

The irony of it is that when I was in college, I did not want to read. I was a typical athletic guy who was usually outdoors, and I preferred not to be indoors reading. I arrived at seminary and had no choice. So I just began to read and, of course, it was all about what I wanted to know. I really fell in love with reading theology. So now I read theology—books on doctrine— and commentaries. Every week of my life, I read all of the commentaries on any passage I am preaching, and then I just read theology. This comes in many volumes that deal with divine issues or divine themes, not just in theology textbooks, but also in books that deal with particular doctrines and doctrinal issues like the Holy Spirit, Christ, sin, or salvation. For variation, I then sprinkle in biographies of spiritual men and occasionally a really "hot" book on important contemporary issues.

To what extent do you use notes? Do you write a manuscript?

During my study I write out the flow of my sermon. Then, from that rough draft, I write out notes to take into the pulpit. I usually have about ten half-sheets of notes for each message. I have everything written out that I want to cover. I have some statements written exactly the way I want to phrase them. Certain truths need to be stated accurately or in fresh terms, so that I am not misunderstood or repetitious.

Since I preach in the same church week after week, I do not want to phrase the same truths in exactly the same way time after time. To keep my messages new, I need to guard against falling back into habitual ways of saying things. Extensive notes help me avoid that. They also assure that I do not forget something important I wanted to say. Since I use many cross-references, I need to write down their chapter and verse as well.

My notes are the record of my study of a passage, so I try to make them thorough. If they are too cryptic, I will not remember my flow of thought later when I review them. For example, if my notes say, "Tell story of boy and dog," six months later I may not remember what boy and what dog. Even referring to an Old Testament story requires some notes, so I can recall later what nuance of that story was relevant. I am also writing a commentary series on the entire New Testament. Sometimes the commentary on a book is written several years after I have preached through the book. My notes need to have enough of my exegesis to reflect how I interpreted a passage for the sake of this later use.

I am not really bound to my notes when I preach. I do not read a manuscript. On Saturday evening (or Sunday afternoon for the Sunday-evening message) I read through my notes and highlight key points with a red pen. These red notations are a visual crutch if I need them. I have learned through experience how to look at my notes while I am preaching without it being obvious to the congregation. I could preach my sermons without my notes. I might forget a few things, or not say something exactly the way I wanted to, but the main thrust of my message would be there.

How important is the size of your pulpit?

I want my pulpit to be about forty-two inches high and to have a very slight slant. I like that height because I can look across my notes at the audience. I can literally glance at my notes while I am looking at them without them seeing my eyes drop. When I move my eyes from side to side or front to back, I spot my notes and pick up what I want.

I don't like a pulpit that is deeply slanted because it forces me to raise my head noticeably to see the congregation; similarly, a pulpit that is too low makes me look down, showing the congregation the top of my head when I slip a look at the sermon notes. I prefer to stand back from the pulpit so I can look across the notes at the audience. They can hardly sense that I use notes. In fact, they always ask me whether I use notes when preaching.

One of the techniques that I have developed is to do everything that I can to divert their attention when I turn a page. It will come while I am making a very strong point, telling a very special story, giving a clear analogy, or speaking very passionately about some issue. At this point I turn a page. I want to shield them from any impression that I am only giving them my notes. I want them to know that I am giving them my heart.

What use do you make of quotes and illustrations?

I never quote someone just because he is an authority. The Scripture is authoritative and does not need outside support. The only time I quote an authority is on a matter about which Scripture is silent. Usually when I quote a commentator or theologian, it is because he has stated the truth in a clear, definitive, prosaic, or graphic manner. I only quote someone who has said something in a unique way worthy of quoting. I would not quote him just because what he said was true, since I could do this in my own words.

Of course, when I quote someone, I am careful to credit him. To quote someone else as though it were your own words is wrong. Yet I read so many different discussions and pour so many things through my mind as I prepare my sermons that it is next to impossible to document the source of each thought. As long as I phrase the thoughts in my own words and combine them with other thoughts, it is not necessary to footnote them. Extensive footnoting is proper in a book. I am careful in my books to document my sources, but too many references to sources would be distracting in a sermon.

A balance is the ideal. We cannot document every thought in our sermons. On the other hand, we should give credit where due. Pastors sometimes ask me if they can use my material. I have given blanket permission for anyone to use my sermons and preach them in whole or in part if they wish, and I do not want any credit as the source. If what I say has value to someone, I am honored for him to use it for God's glory. The truth is all His.

Yet if someone re-preaches one of my sermons without enriching it by going through the discovery process, that sermon will inevitably be flat and lifeless. The great Scottish preacher Alexander Maclaren once went to hear another man preach, a young man with a reputation for being a gifted preacher. Much to Maclaren's surprise, the young man said at the outset of his message, "I've had such a busy week that I had no time to prepare a sermon of my own, so I'm going to preach one of Maclaren's." He did not know Maclaren was in the audience until Maclaren greeted him afterward. He was very embarrassed and became even more so when Maclaren looked him in the eye and said, "Young man, I don't mind if you are going to preach my sermons, but if you are going to preach them like that, please don't say they are mine."

To rely too heavily on the sermons of others robs one of the joy of discovering biblical truth for himself. Such sermons will lack conviction and enthusiasm. Sermons by other preachers should be another study tool, like commentaries or illustration books.

Do you practice your sermons before you deliver them on Sunday?

I have no trial run or dress rehearsal of my sermons. I know that some men vocalize their sermons in advance and find it very helpful. Part of the adventure of preaching for me is getting into the pulpit and hearing what comes out. While I am preaching, my mind is working at its highest level, and it is in the pulpit that my sermon takes its final form. To rehearse sermons in advance would not do me much good, since I would probably say things differently once I stepped into the pulpit.

I do read through my notes several times and think through the sermon before I preach it. I try to ask myself, "What do I want the people to learn from this sermon?" I tend to apply the truths in a situation relevant to my own life. I trust that I am similar enough to everyone else that those truths will apply to others also.

How long should a sermon be?

As long as it takes to cover the passage adequately! I do not think the length of the sermon is as important as its content. At times I have preached fifty minutes and it has been ten minutes too long. Other times, I have preached an hour and twenty-five minutes and it has been just right. The important thing is to cover the main point so that people are convinced of its truth and comprehend its requirements. If you have nothing worthwhile to say, even twenty minutes will seem like an eternity to your people. If you are interesting, they will stay with you. Do not mistake persuasion for long-windedness, however. If you preach longer than you should, you will sacrifice persuasiveness.

I am convinced that biblical exposition requires at least forty minutes. Less than this just is not sufficient to probe the text deeply. If it takes fifteen to twenty minutes to give the setting, ten to fifteen minutes to draw out the principles, five to ten minutes to cross-reference them, and five to ten minutes for a conclusion, you already have about fifty minutes. Rarely does a man preaching twenty-five to thirty minutes do doctrinal exposition.

That is why developing the logical flow of a sermon is crucial.[2] If your message is clearly outlined and you lead your people through the process of discovery, you will hold their attention. Your sermon must be going somewhere. You cannot merely give a number of assorted truths unrelated to each other. If your sermon lacks interest because it is disjointed, your people will lose interest.

If you are going to be a Bible expositor, forget the twenty- and thirty-minute sermons. You are looking at forty or fifty minutes. In any less than that, you can't exposit the Scripture. The purpose of a sermon is not to get it over, but rather to explain the Word of God. My goal is not accomplished because I am brief. My goal is accomplished when I am clear and I have exposited the Word of God.

Won't people get bored if you preach too long in the same book?

I think people will be bored if you are boring. It is not related to how much time you spend in a book. As long as you are saying things that capture their interest and challenge their lives, they will not care what book you are in or for how long.

I think, however, that a balance is desirable. If you are preaching through a heavily doctrinal book like Romans or Hebrews, it is good to give your people a break from that periodically. If you are preaching through one of the Gospels, such may not be necessary. When I preached through Matthew over an eight-year period, I rarely felt the need to take a break. Matthew contains such a mixture of doctrinal passages, parables, and narrative passages that it changes pace frequently on its own.

At times, too, you will need to deal with a specific topic. You may find that people in your church are being influenced by an unbiblical teaching that you must combat. Or they may be confused over a Bible passage or a theological issue. Also, you may occasionally see a need to preach about the biblical view of a significant world event. In general, though, preaching through a book will not bore people if you are an interesting preacher. This is the purest form of expository preaching.

Why are you compelled to preach verse by verse through books of the Bible, unlike other notable preachers such as C. H. Spurgeon?

Spurgeon was not a pure expositor. He frequently preached topically. He was a great writer of sermons and was masterful in his prose and his insights, plus he possessed tremendous creativity. His mind had tremendous imaginative capacities. He could also hold an audience.

One of the reasons I preach verse by verse is because I could never produce such inspiring, clever, creative, topical sermons week in and week out as he did. He had an immensely creative imagination. I just don't have that, nor do many other preachers that I know. Where creativity is strong, so is the danger that it can turn a preacher away from the exposition of Scripture. We need to guard against this without suppressing legitimate creativity.

I could wish that Spurgeon had preached the book of Romans verse by verse. If he had done with Romans or Hebrews what he did with the book of Psalms, which resulted in *The Treasury of David,* his expositional legacy would be unsurpassed.

Most of all, however, preaching verse by verse through books of the Bible is the most reasonable way to teach the whole counsel of God. If I am obligated to teach the whole new covenant message and all of the mystery unfolded, the only systematic way that I know to teach it all is to take it the way it comes, one book at a time from beginning to end. If I were to approach the goal of teaching the whole New Testament in random fashion, it would be a hopeless maze to lead people through. On the other hand, if I am committed to teaching the Word of God systematically so that all of the revelation of God is brought before His people, the only reasonable way of doing that is to go through it one book at a time.

Also, the only effective way of seeing the significance of a passage is in its context. Going through an entire book sets the passage in its context on its widest, deepest, and richest level. One other thought: neither the Old Testament nor the New Testament was written as a collection of verses to be thrown into the air and allowed to fall back wherever they might. Rather, each book has a reasonable, logical, inspired flow of thought going from point A to point Z, with all stops in between. Each was designed by the Holy Spirit so that you have the Holy Spirit communicating something powerfully and clearly in the whole letter: you dare not miss a single part!

If I received five letters in the mail one day, it would make no sense to read a sentence or two out of one, skip two, read a few sentences out of another, and go to the next one and read a few out of that, and on and on. If I really want to comprehend the letter—what is going on, the tone, the spirit, the attitude, and the purpose—I must start from the beginning and go to the end of each one. If that is true of personal correspondence, then how much more is it so of divine revelation.

If we are to proclaim the "whole counsel of God," why do you preach predominately from the New Testament?

Paul said that he was a minister of the new covenant. Since he was responsible to preach the new covenant, I think it is compelling for us to herald the new covenant, too. What we find then is that we must primarily preach Christ and herald the new covenant, which is New Testament literature, the mystery now unfolded that was hidden in the past.

At the same time, we draw on the illustrative material in the Old Testament. I think the Old Testament material can be summed up like this: first, it describes God; then, it gives His law for life, His rules for righteous behavior; third, it shows how God blesses those who obey; and fourth, it tells how God punishes those who don't. The Old Testament also becomes the great source of illustrative material as we reach back to get some of the magnificence and fullness of God before the cross.

Another personal component for me is that when I was in seminary I realized that I could not be expert in Greek and Hebrew at the same time. Having had twenty-four units of Greek in college, I decided to follow that up and pursue New Testament studies as a primary objective for my own life and ministry.

The third little piece for me is that I have a personal goal in my life to preach through the whole New Testament. I desire to herald faithfully all the counsel of God and the revealed mystery of the new covenant. Occasionally, for variety I will sprinkle in an Old Testament series such as a study of Daniel or a character study.

When preaching through a book, how much of the text
do you cover in each sermon?

Basically, I cover one unit of thought. The number of verses will vary, depending on how I divide it. For example, I covered 1 Thessalonians 5:12, 13 in one sermon, verses 14, 15 in another, and verse 16 in a third. I could have preached the entire passage 5:12–16 as one message, since it is all related. Instead, I chose to subdivide it so as to give more emphasis to each section.

As you remember from the earlier discussion of "A Study Method for Expository Preaching" (chapter 11), the first step in my study is to read and become familiar with the entire book. That helps me separate the book into units of thought. Observing the outlines of passages in various commentaries is also helpful. Ultimately, each preacher must decide for himself how to organize the text. That is part of the art of preaching.

Where does storytelling fit into expository preaching?

I am not into storytelling. I fail to see the value of multiple, long, drawn-out illustrations. I think you can make a point effectively with a simple analogy. After all, the only value a story has is to put a window into an otherwise somewhat darkened truth. You pull up the shades so somebody can see a teaching more clearly. If you can do that with a brief analogy, you can keep the flow going better than by inserting a long story.

Stories have emotional impact, but they are lightweight compared with Scripture. People respond to a story with the idea, "Now I can sit back and hear this nice story." I call it communication in the light vein. I would rather find a concise analogy or an Old Testament illustration and keep the sermon moving than get caught in some long story that might send the wrong signal to people.

I want them to stay at my level of intensity. When I think they need a few relaxing moments, I will break in with a breather such as a funny statement or something that is simple. I try to pace the message that way. In my mind, stories tend to shut down the level of intensity that I prefer people to maintain. I tell a story when it is appropriate, but this happens only rarely. I like to think that I can say the same thing as effectively with a brief comparison.

*I've heard it said that 50 percent of a sermon should be application.
Could you comment?*

I think that is arbitrary. I prefer to say that all of a sermon should be applicable. If I preach the Word of God powerfully and accurately, everything I say should apply. Obviously, not all will apply to everyone in the same way, but it is my intent to speak what is life-changing for all.

I believe the goal of preaching is to compel people to make a decision. I want people who listen to me to understand exactly what God's Word demands of them when I am through. Then they must say either, "Yes, I will do what God says," or "No, I won't do what God says."

While I believe in the importance of illustrations, I do not believe that 50 percent of a sermon must be applications.[3] If I preach that we should love our neighbors, I need not devote half of my sermon to telling my people in exhaustive detail how to love this way. It is the Spirit who applies the truths of Scripture to each person.[4] But if we fail to give our hearers some clear principles they can apply, we have failed to present God's Word properly. Remember, people live out their theology or beliefs, but they forget your exhortations. They will apply what they genuinely believe to be true.

*How do you find the balance between instructing people
and playing to their emotions?*

Emotions are important. They were given to us by God, and they often move the will. People do not usually make decisions in an emotional vacuum. I do want to stir people's emotions when I preach, because truth that warms the heart can move the will.

When Jesus spoke of true worship, He described it as worship "in spirit and truth" (John 4:23–24).[5] What He meant was that emotion and truth in combination constitute true worship. Our worship of God must be based on truth, yet should also involve the emotions. It should be our goal to encourage the proper components in worship. The hymns and special music, as well as the pastoral prayer and sermon, must articulate truth. Yet they should also stir the emotions and activate the will.

What I oppose is artificially stimulating the emotions in isolation or separation from truth. This practice smacks of manipulation and peddling the Word of God (see 2 Cor. 2:17). Two extremes must be avoided: truth without emotions and emotions without truth. The two are seen in Jesus' discussion with the Samaritan woman in John 4. The Samaritans' worship was enthusiastic and emotional, but not based on truth. On the other hand, the Jews' worship was based on truth, but was cold, unemotional, and dead. Both were wrong. True worship is based on truth, and involves the emotions.

How do you differentiate between persuasion and manipulation?

The difference lies in the means we use to persuade. The Word of God is the only legitimate means of persuasion. Legitimate persuasion is cognitive, stirring the mind with reasonable truth. Convincing with tear-jerking stories, histrionics, and emotional outbursts takes an unfair advantage of people and wrongly muddles their thinking. That does not mean we cannot use all the communication skills available to us, but we should avoid playing on people's emotions, even by repeated singing or playing of hymns. These are artificial and should be avoided because they bypass the reason.[6]

Our goal in preaching is to constrain people to choose change because it is reasonable and right before God, not because they have been manipulated into some momentary feeling or action. We persuade them from the Scriptures to choose the right course of action. We do not pile on emotional pressure until they break. We want them to know clearly what the alternatives are and that they must choose. If after hearing our sermon someone does not know what he is supposed to do about it, we did not reach that person. I believe the legitimate point of persuasion ends with the clear presentation of the truth and must not move beyond that to artificial emotional stimuli for eliciting a response. This latter kind of appeal has produced false Christians and weak believers bouncing from one emotional high to another without a theology to live by.

In 1 Timothy 4:13, Paul wrote to Timothy, "Until I come, give attention to the public reading of Scripture, to exhortation and teaching." What he told Timothy was to read the text, explain the text, and apply the text. That verse is a call to persuasive, expository preaching. Paul himself was a very persuasive preacher, but he never tried to manipulate emotions to move people artificially. At the end of one of his messages, King Agrippa exclaimed, "In a short time you will persuade me to become a Christian" (Acts 26:28). Agrippa clearly understood the message. Unfortunately, he made a wrong decision in spite of his understanding.

Ultimately, however, our sermons will only be as persuasive as our lives. A traveling speaker who does not remain in one place long enough for people to get to know him may be able to "fake" it without a consistent life to back up his message, (though this is regrettable). Those of us who preach to the same people week after week, however, cannot do that. Our people know us, and our persuasiveness depends on the quality of our lives. Paul's preaching was persuasive; but it was his *life* that won the hearts of people. The Ephesian elders cried when Paul left them, but not because they would not hear him preach anymore. They were "grieving especially over the word which he had spoken, that they should see his face no more" (Acts 20:38). The integrity of the preacher's life is a key element in persuasiveness.

What are your thoughts on drama in the pulpit?

I was at a pastors' conference where one of the speakers came out in diapers with a doll under one arm, a pacifier around his neck, and a baby bottle in his hand. He proceeded to talk about baby Christians. In my judgment I would have to say that such a performance appears to be a crutch, and it seems that only a weak preacher would need such a crutch. You have to believe that the power of God's Word will be more effective than any human drama or communication gimmick. Nothing is as dramatic as the explosion of truth on the mind of a believer through powerful preaching.

How do you get yourself up for a sermon when you've been down during the week?

I often work harder on my sermons when I am not doing so well. Feeling good and excited about my message tends to carry me. When I feel bad, which is very rare, I know I have to give it everything I have, and I turn up the effort. It is similar to athletics. Many athletes exert themselves more when they feel below par.

The same is true when I think my message is not too exciting. I work harder to find ways to make it exciting. Often those sermons turn out to be better than others in which the material is great.

Do you have an illustration file?

If I find a good illustration, I usually use it right away. I do have a file, but in the years I have been in the ministry, it has grown large and cumbersome. So much material is in it that it is tedious and time-consuming to go through it. Keeping track of illustrations is one area where a personal computer is of immense help.

Do you use a personal computer?

In recent years people have tried to get me to begin using one, but I have a system that I am comfortable with. I do all my own research and write out all my sermon material from my rough notes. No one types it for me. This allows me to pour it through my mind one more time. My administrative assistant and my secretaries use computers to help me in all other areas of my ministry outside sermon preparation.

Do you use a preaching calendar to schedule your messages?

I have a general plan in that, before I finish the books I am currently preaching from, I decide what books I want to preach through next. But I cannot schedule what to cover week by week. As I mentioned earlier, I do not always know what I will cover until I begin preaching. This makes preaching an adventure, but it also means a preaching calendar would have to be revised so frequently that it would be useless.

Since I generally preach through books of the New Testament, a preaching calendar for me is unnecessary. I know what passage I will be preaching each Sunday. A preaching calendar is useful for those who preach topically. Wasting precious study time each week trying to figure out what to preach on should be avoided.

Even when I re-preach an old set of expositions, I cannot set a fixed schedule because I may encounter a theme that takes more time than I planned.

Do you ever get nervous when you preach?

In preaching, I can honestly say I am never nervous. The only thing I feel in my heart is this continual prayer: "Lord, please help me to get this truth across clearly, authoritatively, and passionately so that You are rightly represented here. Help me in the process of doing this!" I am never nervous because I am always prepared. If I was unprepared or if I thought I was facing something I could not handle, then I would have a reason to be nervous. I think nervousness is sort of an ego-defense mechanism because one is afraid he will be embarrassed or fall on his face. To be honest, I do not feel involved personally in what I do. I don't even think about myself. I only want to honor the Lord and avoid embarrassing Him in any way.

What two or three books on preaching have profoundly impacted your thinking?

The first book that affected my thinking was John Broadus's *On The Preparation and Delivery of Sermons*. A second book that really hit me hard was John Stott's book *The Preacher's Portrait* in which he explained five New Testament words that pictured the preacher's vast responsibility and duty. Then I read D. Martyn Lloyd-Jones's *Preachers and Preaching*. Those three have influenced me greatly.

What abiding lessons would you teach men who are committed to expository preaching, that will sustain them for a lifetime of ministry?

First of all, make sure that every expository message has a single theme that is crystal clear so that your people know exactly what you are saying, how you have supported it, and how it is to be applied to their lives. The thing that kills people in what is sometimes called expository preaching is randomly meandering through a passage. Second, when you go into a church that is not accustomed to exposition, realize that a period of training the listeners is needed. You must move your flock from whatever they have been hearing into thinking logically, rationally, and even deeply about the Word of God. This is the process of weaning them from whatever they have been on and whetting their appetites for the meat of God's Word.

Next, you need to go in with a long-term perspective. My dad said to me years ago, "I want you to remember a couple of things before you go into the ministry. One, the great preachers, the lasting preachers who left their mark on history, taught their people the Word of God. Two, they stayed in one place for a long time." These were two good pieces of advice. Everybody used to say, when I first came to Grace Community Church, that I would only last about a year or two, because they saw me as a communicator. But in my heart, I knew I wanted to do two things: one was to teach the Word of God systematically and the other was to do it in the same place over the long haul. I knew that was the only way I could nourish people who would be really doctrinally solid.

Fourth, realize that as you begin to unfold the Scripture, your ministry is going to change. You cannot know everything that the Bible is going to say unless you have dug deeply into it. You may think you have everything wired, but four or five years into your ministry, you will come to a passage that will change the way you think about a certain issue and the way your church does things. You and your people must allow the Word to shape your church.

What is the ultimate key to effective preaching?

Very simply, stay in your study until you know that the Lord will gladly accept what you have prepared to preach because it rightly represents His Word. Let me close with an unforgettable plan suggested by an unknown parishioner as to how to accomplish this.

> Fling him into his office. Tear the "Office" sign from the door and nail on the sign, "Study." Take him off the mailing list. Lock him up with his books and his typewriter and his Bible. Slam him down on his knees before texts and broken hearts and the flock of lives of a superficial flock and a holy God.
>
> Force him to be the one man in our surfeited communities who knows about God. Throw him into the ring to box with God until he learns how short his arms are. Engage him to wrestle with God all the night through. And let him come out only when he's bruised and beaten into being a blessing.

Shut his mouth forever spouting remarks, and stop his tongue forever tripping lightly over every nonessential. Require him to have something to say before he dares break the silence. Bend his knees in the lonesome valley.

Burn his eyes with weary study. Wreck his emotional poise with worry for God. And make him exchange his pious stance for a humble walk with God and man. Make him spend and be spent for the glory of God. Rip out his telephone. Burn up his ecclesiastical success sheets.

Put water in his gas tank. Give him a Bible and tie him to the pulpit. And make him preach the Word of the living God!

Test him. Quiz him. Examine him. Humiliate him for his ignorance of things divine. Shame him for his good comprehension of finances, batting averages, and political infighting. Laugh at his frustrated effort to play psychiatrist. Form a choir and raise a chant and haunt him with it night and day—"Sir, we would see Jesus."

When at long last he dares assay the pulpit, ask him if he has a word from God. If he does not, then dismiss him. Tell him you can read the morning paper and digest the television commentaries, and think through the day's superficial problems, and manage the community's weary drives, and bless the sordid baked potatoes and green beans, *ad infinitum,* better than he can.

Command him not to come back until he's read and reread, written and rewritten, until he can stand up, worn and forlorn, and say, "Thus saith the Lord."

Break him across the board of his ill-gotten popularity. Smack him hard with his own prestige. Corner him with questions about God. Cover him with demands for celestial wisdom. And give him no escape until his back's against the wall of the Word.

And sit down before him and listen to the only word he has left— God's Word. Let him be totally ignorant of the down-street gossip, but give him a chapter and order him to walk around it, camp on it, sup with it, and come at last to speak it backward and forward, until all he says about it rings with the truth of eternity.

And when he's burned out by the flaming Word, when he's consumed at last by the fiery grace blazing through him, and when he's privileged to translate the truth of God to man, finally transferred from earth to heaven, then bear him away gently and blow a muted trumpet and lay him down softly. Place a two-edged sword in his coffin, and raise the tomb triumphant. For he was a brave soldier of the Word. And ere he died, he had become a man of God.

Epilogue

The Listener's Responsibilities

In an age when shallow preaching is common, both shallow hearing and personal application are also common.

> Too many laymen speak about the preaching event as if it were a one-way street, as if the responsibility for what transpires when the Bible is proclaimed rests solely on the shoulders of the preacher. But that's not so! Effective communication demands competence from all parties.[1]

Preaching: How to Preach Biblically would not be complete without a word about the listener's responsibilities in the expository process. Everything culminates in the hearers. The science and art of producing an expository sermon are empty efforts if no one hears and assimilates the message. Three vital principles will aid the listener who wishes to gain the most from an expository message. They are at the same time his responsibilities as well as his privileges.

ANTICIPATION

The listener must be prepared to receive the preacher's message. Some components of anticipation to enhance the listening experience are basic and obvious, though often overlooked.

1. Be Personally Ready

The basic outlook of the listener must be to identify himself as the target of the message. The whole purpose of sitting in the listener's seat is exposure to the message for the purpose of personal confrontation, information, conviction, motivation, and transformation. The hearer's thoughts should not be concerns about how well the preacher is doing, how clever or interesting he is, or how well structured his sermon is. The listener is not there to admire or criticize a piece of oratorical art, but to be spoken to personally by God's representative. The object of the preaching event is a change in thinking, attitude, and behavior. The hearer must prepare himself with this anticipation.

2. Be Physically Ready

A basic key to good listening is being in good physical condition. This depends on adequate rest, well-balanced meals, and proper exercise. Each of these varies with different individuals, but all are essential to being alert and ready to comprehend what is spoken.

People do not listen well when they are tired or hungry. Their minds drift to other things because of improper care of their bodies. On the other hand, being awake and attentive is essential for one to hear God's message in a refreshing and dynamic way. The way one spends Saturday evening and Sunday morning, for example, will directly affect the expository exchange between expositor and listener.

Just before Jesus was betrayed, He asked His disciples to stand watch while He prayed in anticipation of the cross. Apparently they were not physically ready to comply, because Jesus "came to the disciples and found them sleeping, and said to Peter, 'So, you men could not keep watch with Me for one hour? Keep watching and praying, that you may not enter into temptation; the spirit is willing, but the flesh is weak'" (Matt. 26:40, 41). After leaving them to pray two more times, Jesus again "found them sleeping, for their eyes were heavy" (v. 43). He commented, "Are you still sleeping and taking your rest?" (v. 45). In a somewhat different situation, a listener does well to be alert and to watch also as he prepares to hear God's Word.

3. Be Prayerfully Ready

Expository preaching can be defined as a spiritual event through which Almighty God Himself speaks His Word to the hearts of men and women so that they might know and understand His will and obey it. So prayer is an essential element in readying one's heart to hear what God wants to communicate through His appointed messenger.

Two distinct, yet inseparable, objects summarize the format for preparatory prayer: Pray for the preacher as he communicates God's message, and pray for the ability to comprehend what God communicates, as the psalmist prayed: "Deal bountifully with Thy servant, / That I may live and keep Thy Word. Open my eyes, that I may behold / Wonderful things from Thy law" (Ps. 119:17, 18).

Scripture implores Christians to pray for their preachers. For Paul, faithful prayer by believers for those who proclaim God's Word boldly was foundational (see Rom. 15:30–32; 1 Thess. 5:25; 2 Thess. 3:1; Eph. 6:19; Col. 4:2–4).

> If a people are looking for rich sermons from their minister, their prayers must supply him with the needed material; if they seek for faithful sermons, their prayers must urge him, by a full and uncompromising manifestation of the truth, to commend himself to every man's con-

science in the sight of God (see 2 Cor. 4:2). If God's people are going to expect powerful and successful sermons, their prayers must make him a blessing to the souls of men![2]

The Puritan John Angell James offered this insightful call for prayer.

Prayer is a means of assisting the minister which is within the reach of all. They who can do nothing more, can pray. The sick, who cannot encourage their minister by their presence in the sanctuary, can bear him upon their hearts in their lonely chamber: the poor who cannot add to his temporal comfort by monetary donations, can supplicate their God "to supply all his needs according to His riches in glory by Christ Jesus" (Phil. 4:19): the timid, who cannot approach to offer him the tribute of their gratitude, can pour their praises into the ear of Jehovah, and entreat him still to encourage the soul of His servant: the ignorant, who cannot hope to add one idea to the stock of his knowledge, can place him before the fountain of celestial radiance: even the dying, who can no longer busy themselves as in former times for his interests, can gather up their remaining strength, and employ it in the way of prayer for their pastor.[3]

To receive the message from God's messenger with greatest benefit, believers must pray for their pastor's ability to impart it.

ATTENTION

Expository preaching is and always has been God's chief tool for producing growth in grace. Therefore, it deserves the closest attention. Though every Christian should read, study, and meditate on Scripture, God uses Bible exposition for the optimal enhancement of his spiritual growth. It is not overstating the case that preaching should be the chief means of dispensing strengthening grace in a believer's life. Spiritual advancement, then, will hinge on how determined one is to assemble with other Christians when God's Word is faithfully proclaimed (see Heb. 10:25).

Preaching is one of God's chief means of sowing seed and helping fruit grow; it is a way of watering and fertilizing the crop. But you must break up the hard clods that have formed in your soul over the week, turn under the weeds, and prepare the good soil to receive the good seed.[4]

Nothing has changed since Jeremiah Burroughs wrote,

In the hearing of God's Word we profess our dependence upon God, for the knowing of His mind, and the way to eternal life. . . . Remember that you come to tender up your homage to God, to sit at God's feet, and there to profess your submission to Him. That is one end of your coming to hear sermons.[5]

God has called, equipped, and gifted godly pastors and teachers to preach His Word faithfully. Because He has done this, we need to fulfill our responsibility in gathering to hear what He says through His servants.

Attitudes

Confessing all known sin removes hindrances and opens one's heart to hearing the truth (see 1 Pet. 2:1, 2). Exposure to the inspired "sword" of the Word (see Heb. 4:12) allows the Spirit of God to bring conviction of sin and to demand true repentance. Repentance will inevitably bring an increased desire to hear more of God's truth and will promote more spiritual growth. Growth, then, is contingent on how much a believer allows God to teach him through His herald.

Adams observed, "Like disobedient children, people do not want to listen. Even believers, habituated in ways of disobedience, have great difficulty listening to God. . . . It has been easier for sinners to blame preachers than to admit their own reluctance to listen."[6]

Moses told the children of Israel in his day about the required readiness: "God says to us today, 'Take to heart all the words with which I am warning you today, which you shall command your sons to observe carefully, even all the words of this law. For it is not an idle word for you; indeed it is your life'" (Deut. 32:46, 47). Failure to measure up to this requirement as a hearer leads inevitably to shallow listening.

Actions

It is not enough to talk about *wanting* to hear the preached Word; we must implement these desires regularly. Nothing substitutes for regular attendance in the weekly services of a local church. Though the writer of Hebrews was emphasizing the mutual encouragement of believers among themselves, he also warned them not to forsake their corporate gathering for worship and preaching: "Let us consider how to stimulate one another to love and good deeds, not forsaking our own assembling together, as is the habit of some, but encouraging one another; and all the more, as you see the day drawing near" (Heb. 10:24, 25).

APPLICATION

Many contemporary critics decry expository preaching as lacking relevance and clear personal application. This kind of criticism reflects a misunderstanding of or disbelief in the inherent power of the Word of God. Since the expositor's first concern is to clarify the *meaning* of the text, it may be granted that expository preaching is not driven by the same kind of obsession with illustrations and applicational formulas that characterize most topical and textual preaching. The expositor depends on the power of the text itself when rightly explained, and is assured that application of the truth in a personal and individual way is ultimately the responsibility of the listener, in concert with the Holy Spirit, of course.

One historian comments, "Calvin sought to make the biblical message clear so that under the power of the Holy Spirit it could make hearers alive to God's presence."[7] How much better it is to allow God the Holy Spirit to shape and mold us into Christ's image, rather than limiting the application of Scripture to human ingenuity! Jay Adams suggested that the listener "constantly seek to discover God's message in the verse or verses from which it was preached, going so far as to summarize it in one sentence. . . . Unless you can do this, it is doubtful whether you got the message."[8] If a listener cannot grasp the principles taught by the text of the sermon, he will fail to understand their application to his own life. If he does understand them, he will be unable to escape their specific application made by the Spirit to his own life.

When Jesus declared to His disciples, "He who has ears, let him hear" (see also Revelation 2—3), He was setting forth a general principle. Leith has written, "For Calvin as for Luther ('Lectures on Hebrews') 'The ears alone are the organ of the Christian man.' Hearing the Word of God makes one worthy of the name Christian."[9] Those who have their ears trained to hear the Word of God must take the responsibility of understanding the truth taught and applying it to their lives.

SUMMARY

What is the listener's responsibility to expository preaching? He must prepare with the right anticipation, give undivided attention, and under the leadership of the Holy Spirit apply what he learns from Scripture to his own life. Only by these means can he maximize the spiritual benefits to himself and others with whom he will share the truth.

Additional Reading

Bryson, Harold T. *Expository Preaching*. Nashville: Broadman & Holman, 1995.

Carrick, John. *The Imperative of Preaching*. Edinburgh: Banner of Truth, 2002.

Chapell, Bryan. *Christ-Centered Preaching*. Grand Rapids: Baker, 1994.

Kaiser, Walter C., Jr. *Toward An Exegetical Theology*. Grand Rapids: Baker, 1981.

Larson, David L. *The Anatomy of Preaching*. Grand Rapids: Baker, 1989.

Lloyd Jones, D. Martyn. *Preaching and Preachers*. Grand Rapids: Zondervan, 1972.

Logan, Samuel T., Jr., ed. *The Preacher and Preaching*. Phillipsburg, N.J.: Presbyterian and Reformed, 1986.

Morgan, G. Campbell. *Preaching*. Reprint, Grand Rapids: Baker, 1974.

Piper, John. *The Supremacy of God in Preaching*. Grand Rapids: Baker, 1990.

Stott, John R. W. *Between Two Worlds*. Grand Rapids: Eerdmans, 1982.

Appendix A

John MacArthur's Preaching Notes

The following pages contain a close approximation of the handwritten preaching notes used by John MacArthur, Jr. in his preaching of the message entitled "The Man of God" (1 Tim. 6:11–14). In the interests of space conservation and clarity, they have been carefully recopied to furnish an example of how an expositor can prepare for and preach an expository message (see Preface).

The Man of God

[Introduction:]   I Timothy 6:11-14

This passage contains one of my favorite descriptive phrases — "Man of God"

> That title, by which Paul identifies Timothy, is a simple yet immeasurably wonderful & Rich Designation.

> What a Privilege to be called "GOD'S MAN." The Man who personally belongs to GOD!

No other Person in the NT is given that title — AND that makes it unique.

→ The fact is, however, that it was a very common term in the OT — the use of which Paul & Timothy were surely very familiar, so they would both understand its Rich significance

NOTE: Paul uses it to put emphasis on Timothy's Responsibility TO FULFILL HIS MINISTRY.

* [How could he do less who is GOD'S MAN?]

→ It first appears in Dt. 33:1, where (Moses) the Great Prophet is the first one called "the Man of God" (cf. also 1 Chron 23:14 / 2 Chron 30:16 / Ezra 3:2).

→ It was used to describe the angelic messenger sent with a message from God to the wife of Manoah, announcing the birth of Sampson (Jud 13:6,7).

→ It was used to describe a prophet who spoke for God to Eli, the High Priest, predicting the severe divine judgment on his sinful family (1 Sam 2:27).

→ It was used to describe Samuel as "the man of God" who spoke divine truth (1 Sam 9:6f).

⇒ Anyone who was the Prophet of God was God's man — the one who belonged to God in a unique way so that He represented Him in the Proclamation of His Word. ... And there were more...

→ It was used of the prophet Shemaiah who was to prophesy against Rehoboam (1 Kings 12:22 / 1 Chron 11:2).

→ It was used again for a prophet who spoke the Word of God to Jeroboam Re: his being replaced & judged (1 Kings 13:1ff).

→ It describes Elijah (1 Kings 17:18f) & Elisha (2 Kings 4ff).

→ It entitles David (2 Chron 8:14 / Nehemiah 12:24, 36).

→ The prophet who confronted Amaziah is called "the Man of God" (2 Chron 25:7).

→ It identifies the Prophet Igdaliah in Jer 35:4.

⇒ (Key) The sum of all the uses in the OT tell us unequivocally that it is a Reference to a Messenger / a prophet who speaks for God!
*
*

(Note:) The one other NT usage confirms this... 2 Peter 1:21. God always had His Spokesman! Prophets! Preachers!

[" Men of God" are those who have been uniquely called
to proclaim His Word!

IMP → The only other NT usage of the term in 2 Tim 3:14-17
* allows us to broaden the title to include others beyond
just Timothy (who is the "man of God" in that context
primarily).

* { When Paul labels Timothy as a "man of God" it places him
in a long line of elite company!

(Key) The Historic Spokesman for God — and when the term
is made generic-for the only time in scripture in 2 Timothy
3:17, it can be extended to all who speak for the Lord —
including us!

(NOTE:) There is also a sense in which the truth of the passage
applies to all believers -- who are also Perfected by the Word

(IMP) Any man of God is dependent on the Word of God for His
Perfecting and His Proclaiming

* [So the title characterizes particularly those who speak for
God — those who belong to Him as His special messengers -- (ILL.)
Pilgrim's Progress calls them "the King's Champions" — They are men
whose lives are lifted above worldly aims & devoted to divine service.
"A man belonging to the spiritual order w/which things temporal
transitory, perishing have no permanent relationship" (ex. Grk T.)

[→ Such men are no longer the "world's men" — but are raised
beyond earthly things — becoming God's possession, property!

→ As Paul writes to Timothy, he recognizes the difficulty
of his pupil's circumstances — having to confront false teachers,
sinful leaders & doctrinal error & ungodliness in the church @

<u>Ephesus</u> which they have effected.

The whole <u>epistle</u> is a <u>call</u> for Timothy to get things in proper spiritual order.

THREE times Paul REFERS to the FALSE TEACHERS – 1:3-7 / 4:1-5 / 6:3-10 –

And each time that exposure is followed by a PERSONAL <u>word</u> to Timothy to <u>Resist</u> them – 1:18-20 / 4:6-16 / 6:11-16 – And in each case, there is also a clear REFERENCE to <u>Tim's spiritual beginnings</u> as one <u>called</u> & <u>ordained</u> & <u>sent</u> by <u>God</u> – 1:18 / 4:14 / 6:11,12

All that points to the <u>fact</u> that the <u>responsibility</u> of the MINISTRY <u>Revolves</u> around one <u>having been called</u> by <u>God</u> to be "HIS MAN" for the TASK.

NOTE: "<u>But then</u>" – emphatic contrast to False Teachers – You are <u>different</u> – You are God's Man! "O" – Personal appeal! Emotion (very Rare in personal greeting)

As a Man of God you should be easily identifiable & by what Marks? How is the Man of God Recognized? The ANSWER comes in the text, & can be easily summed up in the following 4 features:

The Man of God is MARKED By...
   – what He <u>flees from</u>
   – WHAT HE follows AFTER
   – WHAT HE fights for
   – WHAT HE is faithful to

I. <u>What He flees from</u> – v. 11A –
v. 11a "<u>flee these things</u>" – pres. imp v. – KEEP ON FLEEING – being a continual Running from

The word is φεύγε - from which we take our word fugitive.

It pixes one Running from a Plague, a poisonous serpent, an attacking enemy!

➡ The man of God Learns to Run w/ALL HIS MIGHT FROM CERTAIN THINGS — in general,

Note - I Cor 6:18 / 10:14
    "Flee Forn." "Flee idolatry"
Here the issue is to be constantly fleeing — "these things" —
→ WHAT DOES HE HAVE IN MIND?
The antecedents to this phrase are contained in (vv. 9, 10 —
(IMP) the evils (NEG.) attached to the love of money.
(NOTE) There are other things Paul tells Timothy to avoid —
* 1:4 / 4:7 / 6:20 / 2 Tim 2:22 — but here it is the love for money —
greed & all its associated vices!
➡ This is the sin of False Teachers & Liars who pervert the
truth for gain, who make merchandise of people, who seek
↘ filthy lucre, who preach for money!
→ From Balaam, the prophet who was bought by the highest
to Judas the apostle who sold Jesus for 30 pieces of silver..
→ From the false prophets of Israel who were "greedy dogs"
that never had enough & were concerned "everyone for his own gain"
(Isa 56:11) & the covetous prophets & priests of Jeremiah's time
(6:13; 8:10) & the prophets of Ezekiel's time who could be bought by
handfuls of barley & pieces of bread (13:19) & the prophets who
divined for money (Mic 3:11) to the false teachers who spoke "good
words" & gave "fair speeches" to the Romans to deceive the
innocent for the satisfaction of their own bodies, (Rom 10:18) &
"the unruly & empty talkers & deceivers of Crete, who
subverted whole houses, teaching things which they ought not
for filthy lucre's sake (Titus 1:10, 11).

The love of money has PERVERTED Many — cf. 2 Pet 2:1-3 /14
Paul was so Careful to avoid this!

(ILL) Acts 20:33-35 / I Cor 9:1-15 / Phil 2:20-22 /4:11-13 19/ I Thess 2:7-12

→ You may be a PREACHER, but if you love MONEY — you are
not a Man of God!

You cannot be God's Man if you are MONEY'S MAN — You
have PROSTITUTED the Call of God into Personal gain!

→ Never Put a Price on your Calling or MINISTRY — or you have
devalued yourself to (O)

A man of God is Known by what he flees from — love of money &
all that goes w/it!

He is Also Known By . . .

II. WHAT He Follows AFTER — v.11b —

(v.11b) "and follow after" — pres imp v. —
Continual Pursuit is in view —

→ We are always fleeing (neg) & alway following (pos) after . . .

(cf. 5:10) Paul says "never let them out of your sight!"

(IMP) The Christian life is not only an effort to run from
(EVIL) but to PURSUE good! — cf. 2 Tim 2:22

(ILL) Psa 34:14 / I Pet. 3:11
"The Lord loves him that pursues Righteousness" (Prov 15:9).

→ What Do You Pursue? What occupies your mind?
What goals call you to attainment?

. . . Success, fame, ESTEEM, Promotion, Money & Possessions?

→ What are you really after?

* The Man of God is to Pursue 6 VIRTUES . . .

(Key) The 1st 2 ARE Really general & contain the other 4 —

(1) "Righteousness" —

NOTE: The Remnant of faithful in Israel were called by Isaiah "you that follow after righteousness" (51:1).

The writer of Hebs. says the only people who will see the Lord are those "who follow after holiness" (12:14).

> The Righteousness Paul has in mind is NOT IMPUTED Right., but PRACTICAL RIGHTEOUSNESS —

➤ Doing what is Right before God & Man! Right behavior, Right Conduct —

* ┃Obeying God's Standards in the Matters of Living!┃

This is the MOST COMPREHENSIVE summary term for all virtues.

The Man of God follows after righteous behavior —
He pursues it! He likes to do what is Right, Good, Obedient to God's commands!

➤ The partner to this is the next spiritual virtue...
"Godliness" — this moves inside to direct our thought to the spirit of reverence, holiness. Piety in the heart.

> Behind THE RIGHT BEHAVIOR IS A RIGHT ATTITUDE! Reverence for God —

→ A worshipping heart! (Phil 3:3)
All of Life must be lived in the consciousness of God's Presence. We are to "SERVE God acceptably w/ REVERENCE & Godly fear!" (Heb 12:28)

NOTE: "Godliness" is a key to the Pastorals — 9 times in the 3 letters.

(IMP/ILL) I Cor 4:1-5 — motive, heart attitude is essential — & the only thing that produces the Righteous behavior.
— These are the 2 overarching virtues the "man of God" pursues.

KEY — They are at the CORE of usefulness & Power in ministry — & are the ESSENCE of TRUE character.

⇒ Watch your heart, your motives, your desires — & watch your conduct — Don't Be An Unsanctified Preacher! cf Psa 50: 16, 17 — (Read)

(ILL) Richard Baxter (p. 54) "Many a tailor goes in Rags, that makes costly clothes for others; & many a cook scarcely licks his fingers, when he has dressed for others the most costly dishes."

Paul was so concerned w/ the matters of right. & godliness.

(ILL) Acts 20:28 / I Cor 9:24-27 — buffet
⇒ He knew his sinful tendencies cf. I Tim 1:12-15 / Rom 7:18-25
No wonder he called for godliness — 2 Cor 7:1
⇒ I Tim 4:12-16 / II Tim 2:20-22

(IMP) People will feel the power of a godly, righteous life in the effect & impact of your ministry.
⇒ The sad reality is that we see few men of God, whose lives are marked by such power!

(ILL) John Flavel, the Puritan wrote: "It is easier to cry against a thousand sins of others, than to mortify one sin in ourselves."

John Owen wrote: "A minister may fill his pews, his communion Role, the mouths of the Public, but what he is on his knees in secret before almighty God — that he is & no more."

⇒ Unholiness, sin in the heart & life of God's servant disgraces the ministry & the Savior's glorious name —
« The man of God, then, pursues what is right to the glory of the Lord.

He employs all the means of grace in his Personal life — The Word, Prayer, discipline, self denial, accountability, worship, Communion — To strengthen his own life — then his people.

"For if we should study the Bible more as Ministers than as Christians—more to find matter for the instruction of our people, than food for the nourishment of our own souls; we neglect to place ourselves at the feet of our Divine Teacher; our communion with Him is cut off; and we become mere formalists in sacred profession . . . We cannot live by feeding others; or heal ourselves by the mere employment of healing our people."

Isn't that a profound statement? 'We cannot feed ourselves by feeding others, or heal ourselves by the mere employment of healing our people.' Bridges continues:

" . . . and therefore by this course of official service our familiarity with the awful realities of death and eternity may be rather like that of the grave digger, the physician, and the soldier, than of the man of God, viewing eternity with deep seriousness and concern, and bringing to his people the profitable fruit of his contemplations. It has well been remarked—that 'when once a man begins to view religion not as of personal, but merely of professional importance, he has an obstacle in his course, with which a private Christian is unacquainted.' It is indeed difficult to determine, whether our familiar intercourse with the things of God is more our temptation or our advantage."[2]

Stalker, in his book in the Yale Series on preaching, speaking to this very matter, says this:

"Brethren, study God's Word diligently for your own edification; and when it has become more to you than your necessary food, sweeter than honey or the honeycomb, it will be impossible for you to speak of it to others, without a glow passing into your words which will betray the delight with which it has inspired your own heart."

FALL OF LEADERS INTO SIN TEACHES:
① UGLINESS OF HYP
② DOMINANCE OF PRIDE
③ POWER OF SELF DECEPTION
④ ONLY TRUE TO CAN RESTRAIN FLESH
⑤ FRAGILE NATURE OF INTEGRITY
⑥ Inability to isolate SIN

So the man of God pursues these 2 general virtues & others that correspond.... dominant inner virtues "faith" - confident trust in God for everything - loyalty to the Lord! - unswerving confidence in Gods power, purpose plan & provision - He lives in the light of God's promises!

(10) Sovereignty is the real issue - His life is lived in the consciousness that everything is controlled by the Lord!

No FRUSTRATION, NO FORCING, NO MANIPULATION - just diligence & trust. And ... "love" - volitional love - unrestricted & unrestrained - toward God & man!

(11) Mt. 22:37-39

(KEY) The "man of God" is a lover of God - consumed w/devotion
* to the Lord & committed to self sacrificing service!
And he is a lover of men who uses the "love of God shed abroad in his heart" (Rom 5:5).

cf. II Cor 6:11-13; 12:15 / Phil 2:25f / Col 1:27, 28; 4:12, etc

He is known for his great & humble affection for God & men!

(12) And as Richard Baxter said: "Pretend not to love them if you favor their sins."

Even God chastens every son

Then, "the man of God" pursues 12 outward virtues...
"patience" ὑπομόνη - from verb "to remain under" - refers to enduring trouble - victorious endurance, not passive acquiescence.

The idea is unswerving loyalty to the Lord, the people & the truth.

Even in severe suffering - no wavering or compromising marks "the man of God."

Outer circumstances provide this opportunity -
II Cor 10:1, 23f / Phil 4:11f

No effort is made to focus on one's Rights under Persecution or Trial — The NOBLE VIRTUE is the ability to ENDURE INJUSTICE, Pain, battle, grief — whatever — "SPIRITUAL STAYING POWER" — That enabled Man to ENDURE EVEN to death! cf. Jas 1:3 (same term)

The spirit that takes what comes, not in anger, or PASSIVE RESIGNATION — But w/Hope Blazing!

IT motivates THROUGH EVERYTHING — TO STAY AT THE TASK — ACTS 14:19-21 - PERSISTENCE!

George Matheson, who was blind & lost the woman he greatly loved — wrote a prayer in which he pleads that he might accept God's will "not w/dumb Resignation but w/holy joy; not only w/ the absence of murmur, but w/ a song of praise." Only ὑπομονη DOES THAT!

The Man of God faces the INEVITABLE & constant trials of Ministry w/that virtue ... And this can be a very practical virtue as BAXTER points out ... (p. 119)

> When we have studied for them, and prayed for them, and exhorted them, and beseeched them with all earnestness and condescension, and given them what we are able, and tended them as if they had been our children, we must look that many of them will requite us with scorn and hatred and contempt, and account us their enemies, because we 'tell them the truth.' Now, we must endure all this patiently, and we must unweariedly hold on in doing good, 'in meekness instructing those that oppose themselves, if God, peradventure, will give them repentance to the acknowledging of the truth.' We have to deal with distracted men who will fly in the face of their physician, but we must not, therefore, neglect their cure. He is unworthy to be a physician, who will be driven away from a phrenetic patient by foul words.

So the Man of God is known by what He FLEES FROM
& WHAT HE Follows AFTER ... And ...

III. What He FIGHTS FOR - v.12 -

(V.12) It is so essential to say that the man of God is a
Fighter, a CONTENDER, a BATTLER, a soldier, a protagonist —
& that the MINISTRY IS WAR — cf. II Tim 4:7

➡ We battle the world, the flesh & the devil — sin — in us & all
we reach! We battle the Kingdom of darkness — that
yields to us reluctantly!

§ Sadly, many feel that if things don't go well — they must
§ quit — God wants them to leave — that may be AWOL!
"Many
adversaries"   cf. I Cor 16:8-9

➡ We must expect a battle — cf. II Tim 3:12 / 2:3-4 Explain
(KEY)
✻ Admit to a BATTLE — & to the possibility that you might have
to lay down your life for the SHEEP! (cf. Mt. 10:24ff)
      Many HAVE DONE it !!!

> "fight" — ΔΓΩΝΙΖΟΜΑΙ — PRES IMP V.
KEEP ON CONTINUALLY fighting ... cf. I Tim 1:18 - "BE ALWAYS BATTLING"
The term is from the world of athletics & describes the
Concentration & effort coupled w/ discipline & conviction
required of a winning athlete. cf. uses in Phil 1:30 / Col 2:1 /
II Thess 2:2 / II Tim 4:7
"the fight" — spiritual conflict w/ sin, unrighteousness
of the Kingdom of satan. ΔΓΩΝ —
➡ Play your part — "man of God — in the noble contest for
the truth!
(IV) Wrest — "When we find that the glories of the GRK

boxers were fur lined on the inside, but made on the outside
of oxhide w/ lead & iron sewed into it, & that the loser
in a wrestling match had his eyes gouged out, we come to
some appreciation of what the GRK athletic contest
consisted of!" (p. 47)

cf. II Cor 6:1-10 | 10:3-5

In spite of the intensity & anger it is a "good" fight —
know because it is a battle for the preservation of ...
"the faith" — the contest you enter when you become a XN — OBJECTIVE
The fight for the faith is the battle for God & His
Kingdom in which we are called to serve!

→ THE HIGHEST CAUSE IN THE WORLD!!

In order to fight effectively for the faith — the truth of
the Word & the place of the gospel & the glory of the Lord —
it is essential to do something ...
"lay hold on eternal life" — Aor this is essentially in
opposition to all 3 verbs → flee, follow, fight
To do this it is necessary to

→ "GET A GRIP ON ETERNAL LIFE" —

✱ What does that mean ????
   · NOT GET SAVED — they are
   · NOT GO TO HEAVEN — they will

Grasp it Now Paul says — while in the race from sin
to godliness, fighting as you run!

✱ In other words — get a grip on eternal things — Col 3:4 —
"set your affections ..." Phil 3:20 — "Recognize your citizenship..."
Live & Minister in the light of eternity — that keeps your
focus in the battle!
Be divorced from the temporal, transitory, passing
world — II Tim 2:3

We can make any sacrifice in this life if we are
fighting in the light of eternity!
Ill. 4:6-10 —

"the Promise of life to come" v.8
"the living God" — v.10 — who gives life now & forever!
— IN FACT, Paul says — it is this eternal life ...
"unto which they are also called"—
This Refers as always in the Epistles to the divine &
effectual call to salvation cf. II Tim 1:9 (Rom 8:29)
IMP ➤ He was called to eternal life & must get a grip on it as
the driving force in his life & ministry!
This Phrase looks at Tim's salvation from God's side —
the next one from Tim's side ... "and have confessed a
good confession" cf. Rom 10:9,10 / Phil 2:11 — Refers to Tim's
Confession Publicly of faith in the LJXT for salvation — a
Confession Reinforced by his consistent Life!
"before many witnesses"— At his conversion cf., No doubt, his
ordination to ministry — 1:18 / 4:14 / II Tim 1:6
Key ➤ "The Man of God" who has been called to eternal life &
* confessed JXT as Lord & Savior has entered into a battle
with the forces of sin & hell — a fight for the faith — which
demands all he has — & that he will give if he has the
eternal Perspective — cf. Rom 8:18 ff
Acts 20:24
➤ The "man of God" Rises above the pitiful struggles for things
Perishable & useless — to fight for the things eternal!

Finally, ... the man of God is known by fleeing, following,
fighting And ...
IV. What He is Faithful to — vv 13-14 —
Here is a solemn command to guard, Keep the Word of God.

(v.v. 13, 14) "that you KEEP this commandment"—

Την ἐντολην — the word "KEEP" means to guard by observing...

What is meant by "this commandment?"

Much has been suggested — the gospel, the teaching in this epistle, the whole of the New Covenant, the complete Revealed Word of God.

* — I prefer that last one, since there is no way to limit it —

It could be translated — KEEP this commission — that is the deposit of truth you are to guard & obey —

"KEEP this commission" — Preserve the truth intact by your living & Preaching.

IMP: Commitment to the truth — faithful to the word in life & lip.

cf. 1:18,19 / 4:6,16 / 6:20 / II Tim 1:13 / 2:15-18 / 4:7,8 / Tit. 3:9-11—

This is so basic "the Man of God" — cf. Mt 28:20 / Jn 15:10,14 / II Cor 2:17 / Phil 1:27-30 / II Thess 2:2 etc. → Guard the TREASURE!

> Paul begins the section w/ "I Command you" — not a new approach to Tim — cf 1:3,18 / 4:11 / 5:17

And calls for obedience, faithful adherence to the truth of God in light of observing witnesses!

"In the sight of God" — All seeing, omniscient God!

He is the One to whom we must look in spiritual service — not "Men pleasers" but "Seeing the Lord!"

That is the proper focus for maintaining faithfulness — God is watching! ⟨ POINT IS POS. NOT NEG! ⟩

"Who makes all things alive" Creator, sustainer of all life!

KEY: Including the life of Timothy! In other words — we are called to faithfulness to the truth w/out fear — since God is watching who is in charge of our life

* Protective power — eliminates fear! (Neh 9:6)

NOTE: The verb is used generally in resurrection — so Death has no real power because it has no consequence other than Resurrection!

(III) HEB 11:17-19

Confidence in the God of life & Resurrection Power!
We serve under His Careful & Concerned eye!
→ What Comfort!
And a 2nd witness... "and Christ Jesus"
IMP The One who displayed God's Power to Create, sustain
Preserve & Restore life!
"who before Pilate witnessed a good confession" — why this?
Key * Because it was before Pilate that Jesus, on trial for
His life facing the Horrible death on the Cross —
Courageously in the face of the enemy — Claimed to
* be King! And Knew it would mean His Death by
EXECUTION

cf. Mt 27:11 / Lk 23:2,3 / Jn 18:36,37
He confessed to being King, Messiah, Son of God — & that
IMP unwavering Confession of His Lordship & Sovereign authority
cost Him His life!
IMP But God Raised Him from the dead! — And thus He is
Living Testimony to the Power of the God who makes/
Preserves & Restores Life!
When we take a Courageous stand — ax XT did —
God is Pleased!
The Man of God should demonstrate the same
unflinching Courageous Commitment to the truth that his
Beloved Lord did — who is Watching!
And his Keeping of the truth in life & doctrine is to be
total "w/out spot" — No Blemish, cf Js 1:27
"unrebukable" — cf 3:2 — above accusation by anyone!
What an obligation!!
→ For How Long? ARE WE TO BE FAITHFUL... PERMANENT!
"until The appearing of our L/XT"
As long as the CHURCH EXISTS — As long AS WE LIVE —

UNTIL **JESUS RETURNS IN GLORY!**

"appearing" - "Shining forth" EITIΦVΕΦS Refers to the visible
& glorious display when XT Returns

(ILL) Acts 1:7ff / II Pet 3 / I Thess 3:11-13, 5:23

The Great Motive — Jesus is Coming — Rev 22:12 / I Cor 4:5

Until He Comes — which of course begins w/ the Rapture & then
glorious 2nd Coming, 7 years later - all men of God are to be
faithful to guard the truth at all costs — courageously fearing
nothing & no one for the God of life & the XT who possesses
that life are even witnesses to us —
    Protective Power!

→ What a Pix of the "Man of God"

    FLEEING / Following / FIGHTING & Faithful

Con: A Warning to close —
    I KINGS 13:20-24

DO WE HAVE TO
BE PERFECT TO BE
THE LORDS MAN?
NO - ILL MARK

This is Your MANDATE —
    MAN OF GOD
And the RESOURCES ARE THERE — Col 1:28 (ILL) MARK
* God continually involved in my prayer life!

Appendix B

Preaching Is an Adventure!

Teaching on the subject of preaching at the seminary is always a special treat. As you would expect, that is a topic about which the students are eager to learn: how to organize, prepare and structure the message, and how to build the introduction, the conclusion, the outline and all the things so important when preparing to preach the Word of God.

Inevitably it turns into a question and answer session as they try to pick my brain after having done this for so many years. Whenever I get into a setting like this I always have to confess that the ideal in preparing a sermon would be to study a passage of scripture, pick a unit of truth out of the text, develop the interpretation of it, get a good outline so people can follow the flow, create an introduction and a conclusion, and preach it. That is the ideal; that would be a real sermon.

As I teach that, however, I recognize the fact I am probably one of the poorest examples of structure in a sermon. And that is because, no matter how carefully I craft a sermon with somewhat equal parts that are both discernable and clearly identified by an outline, it rarely works out that way. In the study, it all seems to fit together very well.

But then, as is often the case, I only get a third of the way through it! I always prepare everything as a unit, but I rarely preach it as a unit. That, of course, blows the outline and the conclusion. Consequently, what the congregation gets is a long introduction and a point or two. A few years ago I was in Montreal, doing a week-long series of lectures on expository preaching with a group of French-speaking pastors. During a question and answer time, one of the students asked, "Dr. MacArthur, we understand what you are teaching us, but we also listen to your tapes (those of us who can understand English), and we wonder why you don't do what you're telling us to do?"

And so I always have to confess to the students that as hard as I endeavor to take the sermon that I've prepared and give it in one setting, I generally find myself unable to pull it off. Preaching is a science. That is to say, there are fixed laws of interpretation that cannot be violated if you are going to understand the text the way God intended. There is a scientific way to approach the Word of God. The process is not mystical, esoteric or intuitive. There are laws of language—syntax, lexicography, context, history, philosophy, background, etc.—that inform the text so that you can accurately interpret it.

But having done all that, the fact remains that teaching is also an art. It is an art and the art depends upon the adventure of the moment. When you get all the colors on the palette and you get the outline of how the painting should be, there is still that element of inspiration that comes out of you in the midst of the adventure. If that sounds like a rather muddled defense of why I cannot finish a sermon, that is exactly what it is intended to be.

Part of the joy of preaching is the very adventure of it. No matter how carefully I prepare, there is a serendipitous element to my preaching that is formed and guided by the Holy Spirit. The well of my mind—a lifetime of Scripture that has been poured into my soul—is so much deeper than what is in my notes. Informed by the Word and energized by the Holy Spirit, the preaching experience is a dynamic adventure that is too precious to me to submit to the rigid structure of an outline.

The objective is not to give you information in a perfectly clean little package that you will never forget, because you will forget! Preaching is more of a spiritual event that is intended to grip your heart and shake you loose from your comfort. It is designed to take you where you haven't gone in terms of your thinking and understanding of the Word of God. It is intended to create a spiritual response in that very moment and to deposit some things that will shape, over a long period of time, a fixed set of convictions in the fabric of your life.

And so all of that simply to say that I wanted to finish last Sunday's message but I did not.

Endnotes

Introduction

1. John White, *Flirting with the World* (Wheaton: Shaw, 1982), 114–17.

Chapter One—Rediscovering Expository Preaching

1. E.g., Haddon W. Robinson, *Biblical Preaching* (Grand Rapids: Baker, 1980); Walter C. Kaiser, Jr., *Toward an Exegetical Theology* (Grand Rapids: Baker, 1981); John Stott, *Between Two Worlds* (Grand Rapids: Eerdmans, 1982); Samuel T. Logan, ed., *The Preacher and Preaching* (Phillipsburg, N.J.: Presbyterian and Reformed, 1986); Al Fasol, *Essentials for Biblical Preaching* (Grand Rapids: Baker, 1989); Don Kistler, ed. *Feed My Sheep: A Passionate Plea for Preaching* (Morgan, Penn.: Soli Deo Gloria, 2002). Steven J. Lawson, *Famine in the Land: A Passionate Plea for Expository Preaching* (Chicago: Moody, 2003).
2. This pattern is not unique to The Master's Seminary but rather reflects the time-honored manner in which God's Word has been proclaimed by Christian preachers through the centuries. (See Chapter 3.)
3. William Gouge, *Commentary on Hebrews* (reprint, Grand Rapids: Kregel, 1980), 577–78.
4. C. H. Spurgeon, "Sermons—Their Matter," Lecture 5, Book 1, *Lectures to My Students* (reprint, Grand Rapids: Baker, 1977), 72.
5. John A. Broadus, *On the Preparation and Delivery of Sermons* (reprint, Grand Rapids: AP, n.d.), *x*.
6. G. Campbell Morgan, *Preaching* (reprint, Grand Rapids: Baker, 1974), 11.
7. Jeff D. Ray, *Expository Preaching* (Grand Rapids: Zondervan, 1940), 14.
8. Merrill F. Unger, *Principles of Expository Preaching* (Grand Rapids: Zondervan, 1955), 11–15.
9. Nolan Howington, "Expository Preaching," *Review and Expositor* 56 (January 1959): 56.
10. Klyne R. Snodgrass, "Exegesis and Preaching: The Principles and Practice of Exegesis," *Covenant Quarterly* 34 (August 1976): 3. For other comments on the decline of expository preaching in America, see Lloyd M. Perry, *Biblical Preaching for Today's World* (Chicago: Moody, 1973), 9–12.
11. Brian Bird, "Biblical Exposition: Becoming a Lost Art?" *Christianity Today* 30, no. 7 (18 April 1986): 34.
12. Ibid.
13. John F. MacArthur, Jr., " The Mandate of Biblical Inerrancy: Expository Preaching," *The Master's Seminary Journal* 1, no. 1 (Spring 1990): 4.
14. Siegfried Meuer, "What Is Biblical Preaching?" *Encounter* 24 (Spring 1963): 182.
15. Harry Emerson Fosdick, "What Is the Matter with Preaching?" *Harper's Magazine* 47 (July 1928): 133–41.

16. Bill Hybels, et al., *Mastering Contemporary Preaching* (Portland, Oreg.: Mult-nomah, 1989), 27. A similar comment is, " The wise interpreter begins with a human need today, and chooses a passage that will enable him to meet this need" (Andrew W. Blackwood, *Expository Preaching for Today* [New York: Abingdon-Cokesbury, 1953], 13).

17. Kaiser, *Exegetical Theology,* 242.

18. Gerhard Friedrich, "κηρύσσειν, et al.," *Theological Dictionary of the New Testament* 3 (Grand Rapids: Eerdmans, 1966): 703.

19. For further information on κηρύσσω, εὐαγγελίζω, and μαρτυρέω, see Klaas Runia, "What Is Preaching According to the New Testament?" *Tyndale Bulletin* 29 (1978): 3–48.

20. For an expanded discussion of *did–sjy,* see Homer A. Kent, Jr., "A Time to Teach," *Grace Theological Journal* 1, no. 1 (Spring 1980): 7–17.

21. Horton Davies, "Expository Preaching: Charles Haddon Spurgeon," *Founda-tions* 66 (January 1963): 14, calls exposition "contextual preaching" to distin-guish it from the textual and topical types.

22. These ten suggestions are derived from Faris D. Whitesell, *Power in Expository Preaching* (Old Tappan, N.J.: Revell, 1963), *vii–viii.*

23. *Webster's Ninth New Collegiate Dictionary* (Springfield, Mass.: Merriam-Webster, 1988), 438.

24. John H. Leith, "Calvin's Doctrine of the Proclamation of the Word and Its Significance for Today in the Light of Recent Research," *Review and Expositor* 86 (1989): 32, 34.

25. Merrill F. Unger, *Principles,* 33. See also William G. Houser, "Puritan Homilet-ics: A Caveat," *Concordia Theological Quarterly* 53, no. 4 (October 1989): 255–70. Houser proposes that the power of the Puritan pulpit diminished as the mechanical form of the message took precedence over the process of forming the message. Coupled with boring deliveries and exceedingly long messages, the Puritan preaching influence quickly declined when these factors became dominant.

26. Haddon W. Robinson, "What Is Expository Preaching?" *Bibliotheca Sacra* 131 (January–March 1974): 57. For other definitions, see Broadus, *On the Prepara-tion,* 119–20 and J. Ellwood Evans, "Expository Preaching," *Bibliotheca Sacra* 111 (January–March 1954): 59.

27. Iain H. Murray, *D. Martyn Lloyd-Jones: The Fight of Faith 1939–1961* (Edin-burgh: Banner of Truth, 1990), 2:261.

28. R. B. Kuiper, in "Scriptural Preaching," *The Infallible Word,* 3rd rev. ed., ed. by Paul Woolley (Philadelphia: Presbyterian and Reformed, 1967), 253, "asserts strongly, "Exposition of Scripture, exposition worthy of its name, is of the very essence of preaching. It follows that it is a serious error to recommend expository preaching as one of several legitimate methods. Nor is it at all satisfactory, after the manner of many conservatives, to extol the expository method as the best. All preaching must be expository. Only expository preach-ing can be Scriptural." A. Duane Litfin, " Theological Presuppositions and Preaching: An Evangelical Perspective" (Ph.D. dissertation, Purdue University,

1973), 169–70, concurs, stating, "Anything less than expository preaching is technically not really preaching at all."

29. Greer W. Boyce, "A Plea for Expository Preaching," *Canadian Journal of Theology* 8 (January 1962): 18–19.

30. D. Martyn Lloyd-Jones devotes a whole chapter to this subject in *Preaching and Preachers* (Grand Rapids: Zondervan, 1972), 100–20.

31. James Stalker, *The Preacher and His Models* (New York: Hodder and Stoughton, 1891), 95–99; see also John Piper, *The Supremacy of God in Preaching* (Grand Rapids: Baker, 1990), 37–46.

32. Louis Goldberg, "Preaching with Power the Word 'Correctly Handled' to Transform Man and His World," *Journal of the Evangelical Theological Society* 27, no. 1 (March 1984): 4–5.

33. Kaiser, *Exegetical Theology,* 236.

34. Charles H. Spurgeon wrote, "If you do not understand a book by a departed writer you are unable to ask him his meaning, but the Spirit, who inspired Holy Scripture, lives forever, and He delights to open the Word to those who seek His instruction" (*Commenting and Commentaries* [New York: Sheldon and Company, 1876], 58–59).

35. Nicholas Kurtaneck, "Are Seminaries Preparing Prospective Pastors to Preach the Word of God?" *Grace Theological Journal* 6, no. 2 (Fall 1985): 361–71.

36. See Snodgrass, "Exegesis," 5–19 for a basic, nine-step approach.

37. John A. Sproule, "Biblical Exegesis and Expository Preaching" (unpublished lecture at Grace Theological Seminary, Winona Lake, Ind., 1978), 1.

38. Spurgeon, *Commenting,* 47.

39. H. Cunliffe-Jones wrote, "We must be able to say not only 'This is what this passage originally meant,' but also 'This passage is true in this particular way for us in the twentieth century'" ("The Problems of Biblical Exposition," *Expository Times* 65 [October 1953]: 5). This is certainly true in the twenty-first century as well.

40. It is helpful to distinguish between a sermon, a homily, and an exposition. "Homily" comes from the Greek ὁμολία, which, like the Latin *sermo,* means "conversation" or "talk." The Latin word is the basis of the English "sermon," so in a general sense, all three are the same. For the purpose of this discussion, however, we choose to use the phrase "expository message" or "exposition" so that its source, process, and purpose are unmistakably distinguishable from the other two terms.

41. Howington, "Expository," 62.

42. F. B. Meyer, *Expository Preaching Plans and Methods* (New York: George H. Duran, 1912), 100.

43. Stalker, *The Preacher,* 121.

44. J. I. Packer, "Why Preach?" *The Preacher and Preaching,* ed. by Samuel T. Logan (Phillipsburg, N.J.: Presbyterian and Reformed, 1986), 9.

45. William W. Ayer, " The Art of Effective Preaching," *Bibliotheca Sacra* 124 (January–March 1967): 41.

46. Jerry Vines and David Allen, "Hermeneutics, Exegesis, and Proclamation," *Criswell Theological Review* 1, no. 2 (Spring 1987): 333–34.

47. For a thorough discussion of this point, see George J. Zemek, "First Corinthians 2:1–5: Paul's Personal Paradigm for Preaching," in *New Testament Essays* (Winona Lake, Ind.: BMH, 1991), 265–88.

48. James W. Alexander, *Thoughts on Preaching* (reprint, Edinburgh: Banner of Truth, 1988), 228–53, develops some of these advantages in more detail. See also the unsigned, reprinted article, "Expository Preaching," *The Banner of Truth* 31 (September 1963): 9–28.

49. Broadus, *On the Preparation,* 124.

50. Mark J. Steege, "Can Expository Preaching Still Be Relevant in These Days?" *The Springfielder* 34 (March 1971): 261.

51. Robert L. Dabney, *Sacred Rhetoric* (reprint, Edinburgh: Banner of Truth, 1979), 78–79. See also Walter L. Liefeld, *New Testament Exposition* (Grand Rapids: Zondervan, 1984), 3–25.

Chapter Two—The Mandate of Biblical Inerrancy: Expository Preaching

1. This chapter was initially given as a response at the International Council on Biblical Inerrancy, Summit II (November 1982). It was subsequently published under the title "Inerrancy and Preaching: Where Exposition and Exegesis Come Together" in the book *Hermeneutics, Inerrancy, and the Bible,* ed. by Earl Radmacher and Robert Preus. Copyright (c) 1984 by the Zondervan Corporation. Used by permission. An updated revision was published under this same title in *The Master's Seminary Journal* 1, no. 1 (Fall 1990): 13–15. The essay has been adapted for inclusion in this volume.

2. Over a ten-year period (1977–1987), the International Council on Biblical Inerrancy held three summits for scholars (1978, 1982, 1986) and two congresses for the Christian community at large (1982, 1987) to formulate and disseminate the biblical truth about inerrancy.

3. Paul D. Feinberg, "Infallibility and Inerrancy," *Trinity Journal* 6, no. 2 (Fall 1977): 120, crisply articulates critical inerrancy as "the claim that when all facts are known, the scriptures in their original autographs and properly interpreted will be shown to be without error in all that they affirm to the degree of precision intended, whether that affirmation relates to doctrine, history, science, geography, geology, etc."

4. James I. Packer, "Preaching As Biblical Interpretation," *Inerrancy and Common Sense,* ed. by Roger R. Nicole and J. Ramsey Michaels (Grand Rapids: Baker, 1980), 189.

5. D. Martyn Lloyd-Jones, *Preaching and Preachers* (Grand Rapids: Zondervan, 1971), 222.

6. Walter C. Kaiser, Jr., *Toward an Exegetical Theology* (Grand Rapids: Baker, 1981), 7–8.

7. R. B. Kuiper, "Scriptural Preaching," *The Infallible Word,* 3d rev. ed., ed. by Paul Woolley (Philadelphia: Presbyterian and Reformed, 1967), 217. Also see R. Albert Mohler, *Preaching: The Centrality of Scripture* (Edinburgh: Banner of Truth, 2002).

8. See Norman Geisler, "Inerrancy Leaders: Apply the Bible," *Eternity* 38, no. 1 (January 1987): 25, for this compact syllogism:

> God cannot err;
> The Bible is the Word of God;
> Therefore, the Bible cannot err.

9. Packer, "Preaching," 203.

10. Ibid., 187.

11. Bernard Ramm, *Protestant Biblical Interpretation,* 3d rev. ed. (Grand Rapids: Baker, 1970), 11.

12. Ibid. See also Jerry Vines and David Allen, "Hermeneutics, Exegesis and Proclamation," *Criswell Theological Review* 1, no. 2 (Spring 1987): 309–34.

13. This definition has been adapted from John D. Grassmick, *Principles and Practice of Greek Exegesis* (Dallas: Dallas Theological Seminary, 1974), 7.

14. Al Fasol, *Essentials for Biblical Preaching* (Grand Rapids: Baker, 1989), 41.

15. Merrill F. Unger, *Principles of Expository Preaching* (Grand Rapids: Zondervan, 1955), 33.

16. "Inerrancy: Clearing Away Confusion," *Christianity Today* 25, no. 10 (29 May 1981): 12.

17. These arguments have been adapted from Richard L. Mayhue, "Biblical Inerrancy in the Gospels," unpublished paper (Winona Lake, Ind.: Grace Theological Seminary, 1977), 12–15.

18. Benjamin Breckinridge Warfield, *The Inspiration and Authority of the Bible* (reprint, Philadelphia: Presbyterian and Reformed, 1948), 175.

19. Jill Morgan, *A Man of the Word: Life of G. Campbell Morgan* (Grand Rapids: Baker, 1978), 39–40.

20. Andrew A. Bonar, *Memoir and Remains of Robert Murray McCheyne* (Grand Rapids: Baker, 1978), 94.

21. John R. W. Stott, *The Preacher's Portrait* (Grand Rapids: Eerdmans, 1961), 30–31.

22. See 1 Timothy 6:20, 21 and 2 Timothy 2:15.

23. These central truths about the inerrant Bible, hermeneutics, exegesis, and preaching reflect the heart of The Master's Seminary curriculum and the faculty's commitment to prepare faithful expositors of God's Word in the twenty-first century.

Chapter Three—The History of Expository Preaching

1. No work in the English language is devoted specifically to the history of expository preaching. This includes dissertations, definitive monographs, and surveys. The reader is referred to the works of Edwin Charles Dargan, *A History of Preaching,* 2 vols. (reprint, Grand Rapids: Baker, 1968); Ralph G. Turnbull, *A History of Preaching,* vol. 3 (Grand Rapids: Baker, 1974); and Frederick Roth Webber, *A History of Preaching in Britain and America,* 3 vols. (Milwaukee: Northwestern, 1957), for their indexed references to expository preaching. Warren W. Wiersbe and Lloyd M. Perry, *The Wycliffe Handbook of Preaching and Preachers* (Chicago: Moody, 1984) have a limited treatment of the history of expository preaching. The recent works of Hughes Oliphant

Old, *The Reading and Preaching of the Scriptures in the Worship of the Christian Church* (Grand Rapids: Eerdmans, 1:1998) and David L. Larsen, *The Company of the Preachers, A History of Biblical Preaching from the Old Testament to the Modern Era* (Grand Rapids: Kregel, 1998) offer useful studies on the broad subject of biblical preaching with some material on expository preaching; yet, these works are still inconclusive. See also William Toohey and William D. Thompson, *Recent Homiletical Thought, A Bibliography, 1935–1965* (Nashville: Abingdon, 1967) and A. Duane Litfin and Haddon W. Robinson, *Recent Homiletical Thought, an Annotated Bibliography, Vol. 2, 1966–1979* (Grand Rapids: Baker, 1983).

2. Dargan, *History,* 1:12. See also Edwin Charles Dargan, *The Art of Preaching in the Light of Its History* (Nashville: Southern Baptist Convention, 1922), 14–15.

3. Ibid.

4. R. W. Dale, *Nine Lectures on Preaching* (London: Hodder and Stoughton, 1890), 93–94.

5. Alfred Ernest Garvie, *The Christian Preacher* (London: T. & T. Clark, 1920), 22.

6. John R. W. Stott, *Between Two Worlds: The Art of Preaching in the Twentieth Century* (Grand Rapids: Eerdmans, 1982), 47.

7. John A. Broadus, *Lectures on the History of Preaching* (New York: Sheldon, 1886), 7.

8. See Charles H. Spurgeon, *The Treasury of David,* 3 vols. (reprint, Grand Rapids: Zondervan, 1966). Note his "hints to preachers" under each psalm.

9. Larsen, *Company,* 26–30.

10. Broadus, *History,* 11.

11. Ibid., 12. See also Leon J. Wood, *The Prophets of Israel* (Grand Rapids: Baker, 1979), 94.

12. Benjamin B. Warfield, *The Lord of Glory* (reprint, Grand Rapids: Baker, 1974), 8–9. See also H. E. W. Turner, *Jesus Master and Lord* (London: Mowbray, 1954), 129–55, and Robert A. Guelich, *The Sermon on the Mount, a Foundation for Understanding* (Waco, Texas: Word, 1982), 43–46.

13. Warfield, *Lord of Glory,* 33–34.

14. Garvie, *Christian Preacher,* 43.

15. William Barclay, "A Comparison of Paul's Missionary Preaching and Preaching to the Church," *Apostolic History and the Gospel* (Grand Rapids: Eerdmans, 1970), 170.

16. See Benjamin B. Warfield, "The Christ that Paul Preached," *The Person and Work of Christ* (reprint, Grand Rapids: Baker, 1970), 73–90; R. H. Mounce, *The Essential Nature of New Testament Preaching* (Grand Rapids: Eerdmans, 1960); and Ralph Martin, *Worship in the Early Church* (Grand Rapids: Eerdmans, 1974), 66–71.

17. Broadus, *History,* 40.

18. William R. Estep, "A Believing People: Historical Background," *The Concept of the Believers' Church* (Scottsdale, Ariz.: Herald, 1969), 35–58; Franklin Hamlin Littell, *The Origins of Sectarian Protestantism* (New York: Macmillan, 1964);

Earl D. Radmacher, *The Nature of the Church* (Portland, Oreg.: Western Baptist, 1972); Johannes Warns, *Original Christian Baptism* (reprint, Grand Rapids: Kregel, 1962); E. C. Whitaker, *Documents of the Baptismal Liturgy* (London: SPCK, 1970); Kurt Aland, *Did the Early Church Baptize Infants?* (Philadelphia: Westminster, 1963); Dom Gregory Dix, *The Shape of the Liturgy* (Westminster: Dacre, 1945); J. B. Lightfoot, *The Christian Ministry* (New York: Whittaker, 1879).

19. Edwin Hatch, *The Influence of Greek Ideas and Usages Upon the Christian Church* (London: Williams and Norgate, 1914), 1.

20. Ibid., 30.

21. Ibid., 113–14.

22. Kevin Craig, "Is the 'Sermon' Concept Biblical?" *Searching Together* 15 (Spring/ Summer 1968): 25.

23. Ibid., 28. See also Lawrence Wills, "The Form of the Sermon in Hellenistic Judaism and Early Christianity," *Harvard Theological Review* 77 (1984): 296– 99.

24. Ibid., 24.

25. G. Wright Doyle, "Augustine's Sermonic Method," *Westminster Theological Journal* 39. (Spring 1977): 215, 234–35.

26. Some have concluded that he wrote commentaries on the entire Bible, e.g., Philip Schaff, *A Selected Library of the Nicene and Post-Nicene Fathers* (reprint, Grand Rapids: Eerdmans, 1983), 9:17.

27. Ibid., 22.

28. He emphasized grammar and history rather than the allegory of the school of Alexandria.

29. Schaff, *Selected Library,* 9:22.

30. James Philip, "Preaching in History," *Evangelical Review of Theology* 8 (1984): 300.

31. Erwin R. Gane, "Late-Medieval Sermons in England: an Analysis of Fourteenth- and Fifteenth-Century Preaching," *Andrews University Seminary Studies* 20 (1982): 201; see also 202–3.

32. Dargan, *History,* 218; Garvie, *Christian Preacher,* 108; Peter Allix, *Some Remarks upon the Ecclesiastical History of the Ancient Churches of Piedmont* (Oxford: Clarendon, 1821); Peter Allix, *Remarks upon the Ecclesiastical History of the Ancient Churches of the Albigenses* (Oxford: Clarendon, 1821); F. C. Conybeare, *The Key of Truth, a Manual of the Paulician Church of Armenia* (Oxford: Clarendon, 1898).

33. John Stacey, "John Wyclif and the Ministry of the Word," *The London Quarterly and Holborn Review* 190 (1965): 53.

34. William Tyndale, "The Obedience of a Christian Man," *Doctrinal Treatises* (Cambridge, 1848), 303–4. See also J. W. Blench, *Preaching in England in the Late Fifteenth and Sixteenth Centuries* (Oxford: Blackwell, 1964), 1–48.

35. James M. Hoppin, *Homiletics* (New York: Funk and Wagnalls, 1883), 123–24.

36. Frederick Roth Webber, *A History of Preaching in Britain and America,* 3 vols. (Milwaukee: Northwestern, 1957), 1:150.

37. David F. Wright, "Protestantism," in *Evangelical Dictionary of Theology,* ed. by Walter A. Elwell (Grand Rapids: Baker, 1984), 889.

38. Martin Luther, *Table Talk* (Philadelphia: Fortress, 1967), 63.
39. Martin Luther, "A Treatise on Christian Liberty," *Three Treatises* (Philadelphia: Muhlenberg, 1947), 23.
40. Roland H. Bainton, *Here I Stand* (New York: Abingdon-Cokesbury, 1950), 60–67.
41. Ibid., 65.
42. Luther, *Table Talk,* 235.
43. Ibid., 378–79.
44. Ibid., 382–84.
45. Ibid., 393.
46. R. C. Sproul, *The Holiness of God* (Wheaton: Tyndale, 1985), 111–12.
47. As quoted by Ernest Gordon Rupp, *Luther's Progress to the Diet of Worms 1521* (London: SCM, 1951), 99.
48. G. R. Potter, *Zwingli* (Cambridge: Cambridge University, 1976), 92.
49. Ibid., 61.
50. H. Wayne Pitkin and John H. Yoder, trans. and ed., *Balthasar Hubmaier, Theologian of Anabaptism* (Scottsdale, Ariz.: Herald, 1989).
51. T. H. L. Parker, *Calvin's Preaching* (Edinburg: T&T Clark, 1992), 1. See also, John Piper, "The Divine Majesty of the Word: John Calvin, The Man and His Preaching," *The Southern Baptist Journal of Theology* (Summer, 1999): 13–14.
52. John Calvin, *Institutes of the Christian Religion,* trans. and annotated by Ford Lewis Battles (reprint of 1536 ed.; Grand Rapids: Eerdmans, 1975), 195.
53. John Calvin, *Institutes of the Christian Religion,* XX and XXI in *The Library of Christian Classics,* ed. by John T. McNeill, trans. by Ford Lewis Battles (Philadelphia: Westminster, 1960), 4:1:9 (XXI: 1,023).
54. Ibid., 4:2:1 (XXI: 1,041).
55. John Calvin, *The Epistles of Paul the Apostle to the Romans and to the Thessalonians,* ed. by David W. Torrance and Thomas F. Torrance (Grand Rapids: Eerdmans, 1973), 1.
56. T. H. L. Parker, *Calvin's New Testament Commentaries* (Grand Rapids: Eerdmans, 1971), 50.
57. Ibid., 51.
58. Calvin, *Romans,* 1.
59. John Calvin, *Commentary on the Book of the Prophet Isaiah,* 22 vols. (reprint, Grand Rapids: Baker, 1981), 8, 2, 172. See also Ronald S. Wallace, *Calvin's Doctrine of the Word and Sacrament* (Grand Rapids: Eerdmans, 1957), 82–95.
60. Marvin Anderson, "John Calvin: Biblical Preacher (1539–1564)," *Scottish Journal of Theology* 42 (1989): 173.
61. Ibid., 176.
62. Calvin, *Institutes in Christian Classics,* 1:13:21 (1, 146).
63. Heiko A. Oberman, "Preaching and the Word in the Reformation" *Theology Today* 18 (1961): 26.
64. John Knox, *The Works of John Knox,* 6 vols. (Edinburg: Thin, 1845); see also Dargan, *History,* 1:513–14.
65. Clyde E. Fant and William M. Pinson, *Luther to Massillon 1483–1742.* 20 Centuries of Great Preaching, 13 vols. (Waco, Texas: Word, 1971), 2:189.

66. Erwin R. Gane, "The Exegetical Methods of Some Sixteenth-Century Anglican Preachers: Latimer, Jewel, Hooker, and Andrewes," *Andrews University Seminary Studies* 17 (1979): 33.

67. Ibid., 32.

68. Erwin Gane, "Exegetical Methods of Some Sixteenth-Century Puritan Preachers: Hooper, Cartwright, and Perkins," *Andrews University Seminary Studies* 19 (1981): 32–33.

69. D. M. Lloyd-Jones, *The Puritans: Their Origins and Successors* (Edinburgh: Banner of Truth, 1987), 375, 378.

70. Ibid., 379.

71. Ibid., 380.

72. Christopher Hill, *The Century of Revolution 1603–1714* (New York: Norton, 1980), 68. See also Gane, "Puritan Preachers," 27, and Ian Breward, ed., *The Work of William Perkins* (Sutton Courtenay, 1969), 331–49.

73. M. William Perkins, *The Works of that Famous and Worthy Minister of Christ in the Universitie of Cambridge, M. William Perkins,* 3 vols. (Cambridge: 1608–09), 2:762.

74. Gane, "Puritan Preachers," 34.

75. Webber, *History,* 1:204.

76. Ibid., 1:202–3.

77. Lloyd-Jones, *Puritans,* 388.

78. Joseph Hall, *Works of Joseph Hall,* 12 vols. (Oxford: 1837–39).

79. Thomas Goodwin, *Works of Thomas Goodwin,* 12 vols. (Edinburgh: 1861–66).

80. Richard Baxter, *The Practical Works of Richard Baxter,* 23 vols. (London: 1830).

81. John Owen, *The Works of John Owen,* 16 vols., ed. by William Goold (reprint, Edinburgh: Banner of Truth, 1965); see also John Owen, *An Exposition of the Epistle to the Hebrews,* 4 vols. (reprint, Wilmington, Del.: Sovereign Grace, 1969).

82. John Brown, *Puritan Preaching in England* (London: Hodder and Stoughton, 1901), 101.

83. Cited in Fant, *Luther to Massillon,* 238–39.

84. Thomas Manton, *The Complete Works of Thomas Manton,* 22 vols. (London: Nisbet, 1870–75).

85. John Bunyan, *Complete Works,* 3 vols., ed. by George Offer (London: 1853).

86. Stephen Charnock, *The Works of the Late Reverend Stephen Charnock,* 9 vols. (Leeds: Robinson, 1815).

87. William Greenhill, *An Exposition of the Prophet Ezekiel* (Edinburgh: 1863).

88. John Gill, *An Exposition of the Old Testament,* 4 vols. (London, 1852) and *An Exposition of the New Testament,* 2 vols. (London: 1852).

89. Matthew Henry, *Matthew Henry's Commentary on the Whole Bible,* 6 vols. (New York: Revell, n.d.).

90. Andrew Fuller, *Works of Andrew Fuller* (London: 1838).

91. Robert Hall, *The Works of Robert Hall,* 6 vols. (London: Holdsworth and Ball, 1832).

92. John Brown, *Analytical Expositions of Saint Paul to the Romans* (1857); *Expository Discourses on First Peter,* 3 vols. (1848); *Expository Discourses on Galatians* (1853); and *Exposition of the Epistle to the Hebrews* (1862).

93. Webber, *History,* 2:631.

94. Ibid., 3:350.

95. Nolan Howington, "Expository Preaching," *Review and Expositor* 56 (1959): 60.

96. John A. Broadus, *A Treatise on the Preparation and Delivery of Sermons* (1870); see John A. Broadus, *On the Preparation and Delivery of Sermons,* rev. ed. by Jesse Burton Weatherspoon (New York: Harper, 1943).

97. Broadus, *History,* 232. See also Turnbull, *History,* 108–9,

98. John C. Ryle, *Expository Thoughts on the Gospels,* 7 vols. (1856–1873), often available in reprint editions.

99. Joseph Parker, *Preaching Through the Bible,* 28 vols. (1896–1907; reprint, Grand Rapids: Baker, 1956–61).

100. L. E. Elliott–Binns, *Religion in the Victorian Era* (London: Lutterworth, 1946), 336–37.

101. Webber, *History,* 1:575.

102. E. T. Maclaren, *Dr. Maclaren of Manchester, a Sketch* (London: Hodder and Stoughton, 1911), 151.

103. Alexander Maclaren, *Expositions of Holy Scripture,* 32 original vols. reprinted in 16 vols. (reprint, Grand Rapids: Eerdmans, 1932); William Robertson Nicoll, ed., *The Expositor's Bible,* 25 original vols. reprinted in 6 (Grand Rapids: Eerdmans, 1965). Maclaren contributed Psalms and Colossians in the latter work.

104. Horton Davies, "Expository Preaching: Charles Haddon Spurgeon," *Foundations* 6 (1963): 15.

105. *C. H. Spurgeon Autobiography,* vol. 2: *The Full Harvest 1860–92* (reprint, Edinburgh: Banner of Truth, 1976), 50, 346–47.

106. Webber, *History,* 1:602. Also note the careful analysis in Davies, "Expository Preaching," 18–25.

107. Davies, "Expository Preaching," 17–18.

108. C. H. Spurgeon, *Treasury of David,* 7 original vols. reprinted in 3 (Grand Rapids: Zondervan, 1966).

109. For a brief description of the following preachers see Turnbull, *History;* Horton Davies, *Varieties of English Preaching 1900–1960* (London: SCM, 1963); Wiersbe and Perry, *Preaching and Preachers;* and William Preston Ellis, "A Study of the Nature of the Expository Sermon in the United States from 1940–1968" (Th.D. dissertation, New Orleans Baptist Theological Seminary, 1971).

110. Stephen F. Olford with David L. Olford, *Anointed Expository Preaching* (Nashville: Broadman & Holman, 1998).

111. See R. Albert Mohler, Jr. "Expository Preaching: Center of Christian Worship," in *Give Praise to God,* ed. by Philip Graham Ryken, Derek W.A. Thomas, and J. Ligon Duncan III. (Phillipsburg, PA.: Presbyterian and Reformed, 2003) 107–21. Also R. Albert Mohler, Jr. *Preaching: The Centrality of Scripture* (Edinburgh: Banner of Truth, 2002).

112. Ibid., 435.

113. G. Campbell Morgan, *Preaching* (New York: Revell, 1937), 17–21. See also G. Campbell Morgan, *The Study and Teaching of the English Bible* (London: Hodder and Stoughton, 1910), especially 72–95.

114. Jill Morgan, *A Man of the Word, Life of G. Campbell Morgan* (New York: Revell, 1951), 39–40.

115. G. Campbell Morgan, *The Westminster Pulpit,* 10 vols. (New York: Revell, 1954). See also, *Studies in the Four Gospels,* 4 vols. (Old Tappan, N.J.: Revell, 1929), along with his various other biblical expositions. Note also Don M. Wagner, *Expository Method of G. C. Morgan* (Westwood: Revell, 1957).

116. Turnbull, *History,* 442–43.

117. James Melvin Keith, "The Concept of Expository Preaching as Represented by Alexander Maclaren, George Campbell Morgan, and David Martyn Lloyd-Jones" (Th.D. dissertation, Southwestern Baptist Theological Seminary, 1975).

118. D. Martyn Lloyd-Jones, *Preaching and Preachers* (Grand Rapids: Zondervan, 1971), 9.

119. Ibid., 26–44.

120. Ibid., 63, 75–76. See also Robert L. Penny, "An Examination of the Principles of Expository Preaching of David Martyn Lloyd-Jones" (D.Min. dissertation, Harding Graduate School of Religion, 1980).

121. Iain H. Murray, *David Martyn Lloyd-Jones* (Edinburgh: Banner of Truth, 1990), 697–713. This book is worthy of special attention, along with Iain H. Murray, *David Martyn Lloyd-Jones, The First Forty Years, 1899–1939* (Edinburgh: Banner of Truth, 1982).

122. Stott's recently declared rejection of an orthodox doctrine of eternal punishment for the lost (David L. Edwards and John Stott, *Evangelical Essentials* [Downers Grove, Ill.: InterVarsity, 1988], 319–20) illustrates the need for caution in endorsing contemporary expositors. It is hoped he will repudiate his approval of annihilationism and turn back to the orthodox view he seems to have espoused earlier.

123. Stott, *Two Worlds,* 92.

124. Ibid., 125–26.

125. John F. MacArthur, Jr., *The MacArthur New Testament Commentary* (Chicago: Moody, 1983–).

126. Ibid., *Matthew 1–7,* vii.

127. Ben E. Awbrey, "A Critical Examination of the Theory and Practice of John F. MacArthur's Expository Preaching" (Th.D. dissertation, New Orleans Baptist Theological Seminary, 1990), 17; see R. Keith Willhite, "Audience Relevance and Rhetorical Argumentation in Expository Preaching: A Historical-Critical Comparative Analysis of Selected Sermons of John F. MacArthur, Jr., and Charles R. Swindoll, 1970–1990" (Ph.D. dissertation, Purdue University, 1990).

128. John F. MacArthur, Jr., "Principles of Expository Preaching," audio tape GC2001 (Panorama City, Calif.: Word of Grace, 1980), 1.

129. John F. MacArthur, Jr., *Our Sufficiency in Christ* (Dallas: Word, 1991), 129–37.

Chapter Four—The Priority of Prayer and Expository Preaching

1. Phillips Brooks, *The Joy of Preaching* (Grand Rapids: Kregel, 1989), 47.

2. "Nothing" defined by its context is the opposite of "fruit." The person abiding in Christ bears *some* fruit and can bear *more* fruit (John 15:2b) and *much* fruit (John 15:5, 8).

3. E.g., Don M. Wardlaw, *Preaching Biblically* (Philadelphia: Westminster, 1983); John E. Baird, *Preparing for Platform and Pulpit* (New York: Abingdon, 1968). Wardlaw focuses on good things such as learning biblical structure, style, content, and imagery as crafted and managed by the preacher. Prayer and dependence on the Spirit are not integrated in any way to show the whole picture. Baird correctly refutes the logic that the Spirit prepares a man, so the man needs no study (p. 8). Yet he offers no balance when emphasizing a one-sided picture, preparation by human skills alone.

4. E.g., R. E. O. White, *A Guide to Preaching* (Grand Rapids: Eerdmans, 1973). He covers preaching as worship, values of biblical preaching, hermeneutics, technique, and gathering and shaping materials, aids to style, zeal, etc. Prayer is given little place. "Of the preacher's private preparation for the pulpit little need be said. [Why?] Most men find they must have opportunity before every service for quiet prayer, recollection, and mental rehearsal . . ." (p. 152). White surely must not have intended it, but the weight of details suggests dependence on what the *preacher* can do. More attention to what only *God* can do (see Acts 6:4) would give a better perspective.

5. E.g., Dwight Stevenson and Charles Diehl, *Reaching People From the Pulpit. A Guide to Effective Sermon Delivery* (New York: Harper and Brothers, 1958). This book says it covers all topics essential to effective oral communication (p. 81), but prayer is not in the table of contents, subheadings, or index. There may be a vague reference in the statement that the preacher can help others because he has found a power not of himself to give him sobriety (p. 81). An opportunity to include prayer comes in "Preparing the Man" (pp. 100–102), but the focus on full sleep, good health, full vigor, freedom from distractions, and bringing "all his powers to bear" (p. 99) crowd out prayer. Among these excellent suggestions, one wonders why prayer was not added to balance the preacher's power with the power of God.

6. Compare two books by Andrew W. Blackwood. In *Preaching From the Bible* (New York: Abingdon-Cokesbury, 1941), he gives no arresting focus to the Holy Spirit, power, holiness, or prayer. A terse comment at the end of the foreword says the Holy Spirit should be our teacher (p. 9). The statement that the preaching in the apostolic church was in a spirit of prayer (p. 18) is rather buried in other emphases. Prayer gets brief mention in the last paragraph of chapter 11 (p. 196), and brief words about prayer are elsewhere (pp. 207–8, 218, 222). More is made of prayer in *The Preparation of Sermons* (New York: Abingdon, 1948), e.g., pages 36 and 208, and in the statement "the Scriptures and prayer go together as inseparably as the light and heat of the sun . . ." (p. 45).

7. E.g. Asa Cummings, *A Memoir of the Rev. Edward Payson* (New York: American Tract Society, 1830) and Andrew Bonar, ed., *Memoirs of McCheyne* (Chicago: Moody, 1947).

8. E.g., R. A. Bodey, ed., *Inside the Sermon. Thirteen Preachers Discuss Their Methods of Preparing Messages* (Grand Rapids: Baker, 1990), 28–35. Bodey says "faithful, earnest prayer and long hours of diligent, believing study of the Word of God" are more necessary than anything else (p. 28).

9. Roger Martin, *R. A. Torrey, Apostle of Certainty* (Murfreesboro, Tenn.: Sword of the Lord, 1976). J. I. Packer rightly applauds Richard Baxter's words: "Prayer must carry on our work as well as preaching: he preacheth not heartily to his people, that prayeth not earnestly for them. If we prevail not with God to give them faith and repentance we shall never prevail with them to believe and repent" (Richard Baxter, *The Reformed Pastor* [London: Banner of Truth, 1974], 120–23, cited by J. I. Packer, *A Quest For Holiness: The Puritan Vision of the Christian Life* [Wheaton: Crossway, 1990], 289).

10. Gardiner Spring, *The Power of the Pulpit* (1948; reprint, Edinburgh: Banner of Truth, 1986), especially "Ministers Must Be Men of Prayer," 137–44; W. E. Sangster, *Power in Preaching* (1958; reprint, Grand Rapids: Baker, 1976). Chapter 7 is "Steep It in Prayer," 96–107.

11. Prayer was frequent in Moses' life. Some instances are Ex. 3:1–4:17; 5:22–23; 6:12, 30; 8:12, 30; 9:33; 15:1–18, 25; 17:8–13; 19:23; 32:7–14, 30–34; 33:18; Num. 11:2, 11–15, 21–22; 12:13; 14:13–19; 16:15, 22; 27:15–17; and Deut. 3:23–28; 9:7–29; 32:1–43.

12. See Charles E. Hoekstra, "An Examination of the Prayer Life of Jesus to Ascertain the Relation of Prayer to the Pastor's Work" (D.Min. dissertation, Covenant Theological Seminary, St. Louis, Mo., 1987). Besides surveying instances in Jesus' ministry, Hoekstra relates prayer to pastoral work and suggests applications.

13. Compare with Hermann Wang, "The Prayers of Acts" (unpublished Th.M. thesis, Talbot School of Theology, La Mirada, Calif., 1988), a treatment of most prayers in Acts. In Warren Wiersbe's *Something Happens When Churches Pray* (Wheaton, Ill.: Victor Books, 1984), Wiersbe sees God's Word as the source of wisdom in prayer, successful efforts stemming from prayer, the Spirit's power through prayer, etc.

14. Without drawing a conclusion, Sinclair Ferguson wonders about the significance of the mention of prayer before preaching in Acts 6:4 (Bodey, *Inside,* 82).

15. Jesus and Paul used introductory devices, good organization, vivid examples, appeals for a verdict, etc.

16. J. B. Lightfoot, *Saint Paul's Epistle to the Philippians* (reprint, Grand Rapids: Zondervan, 1953), 160.

17. Lightfoot, *Philippians,* 160.

18. Walter Bauer, William Arndt, and F. W. Gingrich, *A Greek-English Lexicon of the New Testament and Other Early Christian Literature* (Chicago: University of Chicago Press, 1957), 715.

19. Lightfoot, *Philippians,* 160.

20. Ibid.

21. Ibid.

22. R. Kent Hughes, personal conversation, 21 December 1990; compare with Kent and Barbara Hughes, *Liberating Ministers from the Success Syndrome* (Wheaton, Ill.: Tyndale, 1987). The chapter "Success Is Prayer," pages 71–81, especially page 77, emphasizes the primacy of prayer; also see R. Kent Hughes,

Ephesians, The Mystery of the Body of Christ (Wheaton, Ill.: Crossway, 1990), where he discusses Eph. 6:18–20.

23. All have been published in recent editions by Baker Book House. See E. M. Bounds, *Purpose in Prayer* (Grand Rapids: Baker, n.d.). A biographical sketch on Bounds is given on pages 5–7 and the back cover.

24. Lyle W. Dorsett, *E. M. Bounds, Man of Prayer* (Grand Rapids: Zondervan, 1991). The second part of Dorsett's book has selections from Bounds's writings, especially some long-lost essays in Christian papers. He has data, including pictures, from Bounds's descendants.

25. E. M. Bounds, *Power Through Prayer* (Grand Rapids: Baker, n.d.), 74.

26. Ibid., 31.

27. David Larsen, *The Anatomy of Preaching. Identifying the Issues in Preaching Today* (Grand Rapids: Baker, 1989), 53–54. Chapter 4 is helpful on spiritual preparation, stressing identity in Christ, the Word, prayer, the Spirit's power, and personal holiness.

28. Ibid., 55.

29. G. F. Barbour, *The Life of Alexander Whyte* (New York: George H. Doran, 1923), 296–97.

30. Ibid., 307.

31. Ibid., 309.

32. Ibid., 388–89.

33. E. S. English, *H. A. Ironside, Ordained of the Lord* (Grand Rapids: Zondervan, 1946), 176.

34. H. A. Ironside, *Praying in the Holy Spirit* (New York: Loizeaux, n.d.), 59.

35. Stopford A. Brooke, *Life and Letters of Frederick W. Robertson, M.A.* (New York: Harper & Brothers, 1865), 60.

36. Ibid., 60.

37. Ibid., 60–61.

38. L. G. Parkhurst, *Charles G. Finney's Answers to Prayer* (Minneapolis: Bethany, 1983). See, for example, chapter 25.

39. Ibid., 126–27.

40. Ibid., 59; see John 15:5: inability without Christ to do anything that will bear fruit. Bearing fruit (doing what counts as success before God) is related closely to prayer (vv. 7, 8).

41. William Sangster, *The Approach to Preaching* (London: Epworth, 1951), 18; see also note 10 earlier in this chapter.

42. Joe W. Burton, *Prince of the Pulpit* (Grand Rapids: Zondervan, 1946), 26.

43. Ibid., 27.

44. Ibid., 65.

45. P. W. James, *George W. Truett. A Biography* (New York: Macmillan, 1945), 267–68.

46. Thomas Armitage, *Preaching: Its Ideals and Inner Life* (Philadelphia: American Baptist Publication Society, 1880), 170.

47. Faris D. Whitesell, *The Art of Biblical Preaching* (Grand Rapids: Zondervan, 1950), 86; see the essentials of preaching in chapter 3.

48. Sinclair B. Ferguson, cited by Bodey, *Inside* , 82–83.

49. Personal letter, 14 January 1991.
50. Personal letter, "Expository Preaching," 16 January 1991.
51. John R. W. Stott, *The Preacher's Portrait* (Grand Rapids: Eerdmans, 1961), 98–99.
52. Andrew W. Blackwood, *The Preparation of Sermons* (New York: Abingdon, 1948), 36.
53. Blackwood, *Preaching,* 196.
54. Asa Cummings, *Memoir,* 13–14.
55. Ibid., 65.
56. Ibid., 71.
57. Ibid., 242.
58. Ibid., 74.
59. Ibid., 75.
60. Ibid., 81.
61. Ibid., 59.
62. Ibid., 106.
63. See Ps. 119:25b, 37, 88.
64. Cummings, *Memoir,* 255–56.
65. Helmut Thielicke, *Encounter With Spurgeon* (Philadelphia: Fortress, 1963), 117.
66. Ibid., 118.
67. Ibid., 119.
68. Ibid.
69. Ibid.
70. E. G. Carré, ed., *Praying Hyde* (South Plainfield, N.J.: Bridge, 1982), 13–14.
71. R. A. Torrey, *Why God Used D. L. Moody* (Chicago: Moody, 1923), 16–17.
72. Martin, *Torrey,* 139; for the impact after people prayed, see pages 110, 131–32, 134, 144, 169–70, 173, 186.
73. Martin, *Torrey,* 279.
74. Ibid., 166.
75. R. A. Torrey, *The Power of Prayer and the Prayer of Power* (New York: Revell, 1924), 35.
76. Torrey, *Prayer,* 17.
77. Martin, *Torrey,* 110.
78. Cummings, *Memoir,* 180.
79. Ibid., 256.
80. Ibid., 260–61.
81. Ibid., 122.
82. Charles H. Spurgeon, *The Quotable Spurgeon* (Wheaton, Ill.: Harold Shaw, 1990), 207.
83. Spurgeon, *Metropolitan Tabernacle Pulpit* (1874; reprint, Pasadena, Texas: Pilgrim, 1971), 19:169.
84. Susannah Spurgeon and Joseph Harrald, *The Full Harvest, 1860–1892,* rev. ed., vol. 2 of *C. H. Spurgeon Autobiography* (reprint, Edinburgh: Banner of Truth, 1987), 321.
85. Ibid.
86. Ibid., 322.

Chapter Five—The Man of God and Expository Preaching

1. For a development of other themes such as steward, herald, witness, and servant, see John R. W. Stott, *The Preacher's Portrait* (Grand Rapids: Eerdmans, 1961).
2. Richard Baxter, *The Reformed Pastor* (reprint, Edinburgh: Banner of Truth, 1979), 63–64.
3. Baxter, *Reformed Pastor*, 54.
4. Cited in Warren Wiersbe, *Walking With the Giants* (Grand Rapids: Baker, 1976), 92.
5. Baxter, *Reformed Pastor*, 67–68.
6. Cited in I. D. E. Thomas, *A Puritan Golden Treasury* (Edinburgh: Banner of Truth, 1977), 191.
7. C. H. Spurgeon, *Lectures to My Students: First Series* (reprint, Grand Rapids: Baker, 1977), 12–13.
8. Andrew A. Bonar, ed., *Memoirs of McCheyne* (reprint, Chicago: Moody, 1978), 95.
9. Cited in Thomas, *Treasury*, 192.
10. Spurgeon, *Lectures*, 41, 49. The lecture from which these quotes are taken, "The Preacher's Private Prayer," is well worth reading.
11. Ibid., 11.
12. Charles Bridges, *The Christian Ministry* (reprint, Edinburgh: Banner of Truth, 1980), 163.
13. Baxter, *Reformed Pastor*, 74.
14. Cited in Francis A. Schaeffer, *The God Who Is There* (Downers Grove, Ill.: InterVarsity, 1973), 18.
15. Elisabeth Elliot, *Shadow of the Almighty* (San Francisco: Harper & Row, 1979), 108.

Chapter Six—The Spirit of God and Expository Preaching

1. C. H. Spurgeon, *An All-Round Ministry* (reprint, Pasadena, Texas: Pilgrim, 1973), 339.
2. The generally recognized classic essay on illumination has been done by John Owen in William H.
   Goold, ed., *The Works of John Owen*, vol. 4 (reprint, Edinburgh: Banner of Truth, 1967), 121–73.
3. Initial illumination that occurs at conversion will be discussed later in this chapter.
4. See also Ps. 119:12, 26, 27, 66, 68, 73, 125, 135, 144, 169, and 171.
5. *Institutes*, 1:9, 1.
6. Ibid.
7. Ibid.
8. J. Theodore Mueller, "The Holy Spirit and the Scriptures," *Revelation and the Bible*, ed. by Carl F. H. Henry (Grand Rapids: Baker, 1959), 278.
9. Bernard Ramm, *Questions About the Spirit* (Waco, Texas: Word, 1977), 85.
10. Wilber T. Dayton, "A Response to The Role of the Holy Spirit in the Hermeneutic Process," in *Summit II: Hermeneutic Papers* (Oakland: International Council on Biblical Inerrancy, 1982), A8–9.

11. Such is the confession of H. Beecher Hicks, Jr., in Richard Allen Bodey, *Inside the Sermon* (Grand Rapids: Baker, 1990), 111.

12. Paul Woolley, "The Relevancy of Scripture," in *The Infallible Word,* ed. by N. B. Stonehouse and Paul Woolley (Phillipsburg, N.J.: Presbyterian and Reformed, 1978), 201–2.

13. John Dillenberger, ed., *Martin Luther: Selections From His Writings* (Garden City, N.Y.: Anchor, 1961), 174–75.

14. *Institutes,* 1:7, 4–5.

15. For a defense of the biblical doctrine of creation, see Henry M. Morris, *The Biblical Basis for Modern Science* (Grand Rapids: Baker, 1984). For a defense of the sufficiency of Scripture, see John F. MacArthur, Jr., *Our Sufficiency in Christ* (Dallas: Word, 1991).

16. Ramm, *Questions,* 84.

17. Ibid., 85–86.

Chapter Seven—Hermeneutics and Expository Preaching

1. W. B. Catton, *Bruce Catton's Civil War* (New York: Fairfax, 1984).

2. Tobin (1822–1904) is perhaps best known for tracking as a service to Fort Garland in southwest Colorado, ca. 1863. The post commander said Tobin could track a grasshopper through brush (*The Pueblo Star-Journal and Sunday Chieftain,* 11 March 1984, 2G, 3G).

3. See good paths/trails (Ps. 17:5; 23:3; Prov. 4:11) and bad trails (Ps. 17:4; Prov. 2:15). The Old Testament has various words for "paths," as does the New Testament. One is applied to Jesus Christ who is "the way" (John 14:6).

4. Note the terms for streams used in Ps. 1:2; Is. 44:3; John 7:37–39.

5. John F. MacArthur, Jr., "The Mandate of Biblical Inerrancy: Expository Preaching," *The Master's Seminary Journal* 1, no. 1 (Spring 1990): 3–15, especially 9–10.

6. Among many books on principles some stand out such as: Elliott Johnson, *Expository Hermeneutics* (Grand Rapids: Zondervan, 1990); A. B. Mickelsen, *Interpreting the Bible* (Grand Rapids: Eerdmans, 1963); Bernard Ramm, *Protestant Biblical Interpretation* (Grand Rapids: Baker, 1970); Milton Terry, *Biblical Hermeneutics* (reprint, Grand Rapids: Zondervan, 1969). Some of the better books on Bible study in general are: Richard Mayhue, *How to Interpret the Bible for Yourself* (Fearn, Ross-shire, Great Britain: Christian Focus, 1999); A. B. Mickelsen, *Better Bible Study* (Glendale, Calif.: Regal, 1977); Roy Zuck, *Basic Bible Interpretation* (Wheaton, Ill.: Victor, 1991). Two helpful works on how to apply meaning are: Jack Kuhatschek, *Taking the Guesswork Out of Applying the Bible* (Downer's Grove, Ill.: InterVarsity, 1990); J. R. McQuilkin, *Understanding and Applying the Bible* (Chicago: Moody, 1983).

7. See chapter 10 of this book for additional study tools.

8. H. E. Dana and Julius R. Mantey, *A Manual Grammar of the Greek New Testament* (New York: Macmillan, 1958), 101–02. W. E. Vine has the idea that this meaning arises from a person hurling words across or through, as in a verbal assault, e.g., in Luke 16:1 a servant was *accused* before the man he

served (*Expository Dictionary of New Testament Words* [Westwood, N.J.: Revell, 1959], I, 26).

9. Dana and Mantey, *Manual Grammar,* 112.

10. Bauer, et al., *A Greek-English Lexicon,* 181; see also Vine, *Expository Dictionary,* I, 306, under "Devil." Even a person who knows no Greek finds Vine easy to use. A recent edition of Vine ties in with the numbering system in James L. Strong, *The Exhaustive Concordance of the Bible* (New York: Abingdon-Cokesbury, 1890) and in the *New American Standard Exhaustive Concordance,* Robert L. Thomas, gen. ed. (Nashville: Holman, 1981), e.g. Vine, M. F. Unger, and William White, *Vine's Expository Dictionary of New Testament Words* (New York: Nelson, 1985). The numbering system for Hebrew and Greek words is different in *The NIV Exhaustive Concordance,* ed. by Edward W. Goodrick and John R. Kohlenberger, III (Grand Rapids: Zondervan, 1990).

11. See Harold Hoehner, *Chronological Aspects of the Life of Christ* (Grand Rapids: Zondervan, 1977), 65–66, 72–74.

12. The better grammars for the Old Testament are by E. Kautsch (1910), J. Weingreen (1959), and R. J. Williams (1967). The best for the New Testament are by F. W. Blass and A. Debrunner (1961), E. D. Burton (1965), Dana and Mantey (see note 8 in this chapter), C. F. D. Moule (1963), J. H. Moulton, W. F. Howard, and N. Turner (1908–76), and A. T. Robertson (1934). For most purposes, preachers will find what they need in Weingreen, Dana/Mantey, and Robertson.

13. Charles Dyer, "Ezekiel," in *Bible Knowledge Commentary,* ed. by John Walvoord and Roy Zuck (Wheaton, Ill.: Victor, 1983–85) I, 1262; John Taylor, *Ezekiel* (Downers Grove, Ill.: InterVarsity, 1969), 153.

14. This statement has often been used to support the gap theory in Gen. 1:2. Many who favor that theory are aware that darkness does *not* always mean evil in usage (see Ps. 18:9; 97:2; 104:20, etc.), so they find support for it elsewhere. Of course, many others see no gap *or* evil in Gen. 1:2.

15. This principle has been used to prove that birds in the mustard plant represent evil (Matt. 13:31, 32). But birds are *not* always related to evil (see Ps. 104:12; Matt. 6:26, etc.). In Old Testament passages with a tree/birds picture analogous to Matt. 13:31, 32, birds simply help picture the idea of a tree large enough to furnish lodging or shelter. A large tree for birds is like a kingdom providing resources for its subjects (Ezek. 17:23, the Messiah's kingdom; 31:6, the Assyrian kingdom; Dan. 4:12, Nebuchadnezzar's rule). This seems to be the point Jesus is making about God's kingdom, and where Old Testament texts mean evil, they make it clear by using other details.

16. One needs to qualify such a statement, for God does hear the unsaved when they cry for mercy (Luke 18:9–12). See O. Hallesby, *Prayer* (Minneapolis: Augsburg, 1975), 159–60: God does not necessarily *promise* to answer prayers of the unsaved, but He sometimes *chooses* to respond favorably to them for His own purposes.

17. Cyril J. Barber, *The Minister's Library* (Chicago: Moody, 1985), I, 130 (Old Testament), 167–69 (New Testament).

18. Francis Brown, S. R. Driver, and C. A. Briggs, *A Hebrew and English Lexicon of the Old Testament* (Oxford: Clarendon, 1952); William Holladay, *A Concise*

Hebrew and Aramaic Lexicon of the Old Testament (Grand Rapids: Eerdmans, 1970); L. H. Koehler and W. Baumgartner, *Lexicon in Veteris Testamenti Libros* (Leiden: Brill, 1953).

19. G. Abbott-Smith, *A Manual Greek Lexicon of the New Testament* (Edinburgh: T. & T. Clark, 1937); see Bauer, et al., *A Greek-English Lexicon*.

20. Figures of speech are treated in detail by E. W. Bullinger, *Figures of Speech Used in the Bible* (1898; reprint, Grand Rapids: Baker, 1974). A good book on the significance of numbers is John J. Davis, *Biblical Numerology* (Grand Rapids: Baker, 1968).

21. This writer regards the following works as most accurate in handling prophetic themes: Alva J. McClain, *The Greatness of the Kingdom* (Chicago: Moody, 1968); John Walvoord, *The Revelation of Jesus Christ* (Chicago: Moody, 1966); Leon Wood, *A Commentary on Daniel* (Grand Rapids: Zondervan, 1973); and *The Bible Knowledge Commentary,* 2 vols., ed. by John Walvoord and Roy Zuck (Wheaton, Ill.: Victor, 1983–85).

22. A church leader may want to consider the practical jeopardy of expressing indecision in a public presentation. It could be that he will want to admit how difficult an interpretive problem is and state his intention to continue studying it, but rather than leave his audience "hanging" and without an answer for the meaning of a passage, he can express a tentative solution as his opinion until he receives clearer light. This procedure will relieve the tension of uncertainty that leadership indecision would create for his listeners.

23. On typology, see Patrick Fairbairn, *The Typology of Scripture,* 2 vols. (reprint, Grand Rapids: Kregel, 1989), one of many reprints of an 1845–47 work. Fairbairn is still highly regarded. See estimates of his strengths and weaknesses and an interaction with recent literature on typology in articles by Roger Nicole, Ronald Youngblood, and S. Lewis Johnson in Earl D. Radmacher and Robert Preus, eds., *Hermeneutics, Inerrancy and the Bible* (Grand Rapids: Zondervan, 1984), 765–99. See also D. L. Baker, *Two Testaments, One Bible* (Downers Grove, Ill.: InterVarsity, 1976).

24. Among helpful books on New Testament use of the Old Testament, see S. Lewis Johnson, Jr., *The Old Testament in the New* (Grand Rapids: Zondervan, 1980); and Walter Kaiser, Jr., *The Uses of the Old Testament in the New Testament* (Chicago: Moody, 1985).

25. For discussions of the "analogy of faith" principle, see Robert L. Thomas, *Evangelical Hermeneutics* (Grand Rapids: Kregel, 2002), 63–80 and Walter C. Kaiser, Jr., "Hermeneutics and the Theological Task," *Trinity Journal* 12NS (1991): 3–14.

26. The best tool for cross-referencing is *The New Treasury of Scripture Knowledge* (Nashville, TN: Thomas Nelson, 1992).

27. Many books on Bible manners and customs are available. Examples are Ralph Gower, *The New Manners and Customs* (Chicago: Moody, 1989) and Fred Wight, *Manners and Customs of Bible Lands* (Chicago: Moody, 1953). Much valuable information is also in J. A. Thompson, *Handbook of Life in Bible Times* (reprint, Downers Grove, Ill.: InterVarsity, 1987) and Wight's work. Lexicons furnish much assistance here, too. More recent examples are Jerry

Hullinger, "The Historical Background of Paul's Athletic Allusions," *Bibliotheca Sacra* 161 (2004): 343–59 and David J. Williams, *Paul's Metaphors* (Peabody, Mass.: Hendrickson, 1999).

28. William Klassen, "Coals of Fire: Sign of Repentance or Revenge?" *New Testament Studies* 9 (1962–63): 337–50; see also Leon Morris, *The Epistle to the Romans* (Grand Rapids: Eerdmans, 1988), 454–55 for the main views and an admission that most scholars favor some kind of consoling view over a harsh one.

29. Isbon T. Beckwith gives six views on the "white stone" in *The Apocalypse of John* (reprint, Grand Rapids: Baker, 1967), 461–63. One of several special works on Revelation 2; 3 that are helpful is Colin J. Hemer, *The Letters to the Seven Churches of Asia in Their Local Setting* (Sheffield, England: JSOT, 1986), 94–102, 105, 237, 242, 244.

30. Yohanan Aharoni and Michael Avi-Yonah, *The Macmillan Bible Atlas,* rev. ed. (New York: Macmillan, 1977); Barry Beitzel, *The Moody Atlas of Bible Lands* (Chicago: Moody, 1985); James Pritchard, *The Harper Atlas of the Bible* (New York: Harper & Row, 1987). Beitzel is most helpful on explanations, and he and Pritchard have fine maps; Aharoni and Avi-Yonah have been most helpful with maps in pinpointing key Bible events. See also Barry Beitzel, *Moody Atlas of Bible Lands Transparencies* (Chicago: Moody, 1990), which includes maps to use in teaching.

31. C. H. Spurgeon, *Lectures to My Students,* original 4 vols. reprinted in 1 (Pasadena, Texas: Pilgrim, 1990), 4:1: "It seems odd, that certain men who talk so much of what the Holy Spirit reveals to themselves, should think so little of what he has revealed to others. My chat . . . is not for those great originals, but for you who are content to learn of holy men, taught of God, and mighty in the Scriptures."

32. The source to use depends on which history is involved. For instance, on the history of a city in Revelation 2; 3, the expositor can look up the city in a regular encyclopedia as well as in a biblical encyclopedia or dictionary. He also can check introductions of the better-researched commentaries and use special works that concentrate on Revelation 2; 3, such as Hemer (see note 29 in this chapter).

33. See note 30 in this chapter.

34. For example, Barber is very helpful; see note 17 in this chapter.

Chapter Eight—Exegesis and Expository Preaching

1. Stott has written, " The great doctrines of creation, revelation, redemption and judgment all imply that man has an inescapable duty both to think and to act upon what he thinks and knows" (John R. W. Stott, *Your Mind Matters* [Downers Grove, Ill.: InterVarsity, 1972], 14). Keiper concurs: "If we fully enter into the power of biblical thinking, we shall become a miracle people, having a healthy mind in Christ, being an example of our heavenly citizenship on earth, and continually and daily cleansed by His Word (see John 15:3)" (Ralph L. Keiper, *The Power of Biblical Thinking* [Old Tappan, N.J.: Revell, 1977], 159). Hull is more specific: " Transformation comes through the commitment of the mind. Without the proper knowledge and thinking we have no basis for

personal change or growth. The mind is the pivotal starting place for change" (Bill Hull, *Right Thinking* [Colorado Springs, Colo.: Navpress, 1985], 8).

2. "Cheater's Greek (or Hebrew)," an expression coined to describe alleged timesaving methods of learning and using the original languages, is not adequate for this purpose. Reputed shortcuts to learning a language have proven themselves time and again to be counterproductive in the study of Scripture. If the expositor has laid the right kind of foundation in his training and has maintained his familiarity with the languages through a disciplined program of a few minutes of review a day, several days a week, he will not need to rely constantly on "crutches" to translate his text in the original languages. Those who pretend to know the languages of Scripture but rely on such crutches are the ones to whom the well-known warning is appropriately applied, "A *little* knowledge of Greek (or Hebrew) is a dangerous thing." The combination of a solid foundation in Greek and Hebrew training and a consistent review program has proven itself to be sufficient for many expositors of the Word. Those for whom circumstances have made this combination an impossible goal to achieve should be *extremely* cautious in their use of the biblical languages and should avail themselves of every opportunity to check and double-check opinions about the text before sharing them with others.

3. William S. LaSor, " The Sensus Plenior and Biblical Interpretation," in *Scripture, Tradition, and Interpretation,* ed. by W. W. Gasque and W. S. LaSor (Grand Rapids: Eerdmans, 1978), 267–68.

4. Larry D. Pettegrew, "Liberation Theology and Hermeneutical Preunderstandings," *Bibliotheca Sacra* 148, no. 591 (July–September 1991): 283.

5. Paul K. Jewett, *Man as Male and Female* (Grand Rapids: Eerdmans, 1975), 133–35, 142.

6. Anthony C. Thiselton, *The Two Horizons* (Grand Rapids: Eerdmans, 1980), 105, 110; see also, " The New Hermeneutic," in *New Testament Interpretation,* ed. by I. Howard Marshall (Grand Rapids: Eerdmans, 1977), 317.

7. Krikor Haleblian, " The Problem of Contextualization," *Missiology: An International Review* 9, no. 1 (January 1983): 97–99, 103.

8. I. Howard Marshall, *The Origins of New Testament Christology,* updated ed. (Downers Grove, Ill.: InterVarsity, 1990), 57, 62 (note 50), 78–79, 82 (note 49), 85, 108 (note 11). For other examples of evangelical scholars who question the accuracy of the Gospels, see Robert L. Thomas and F. David Farnell, eds., *The Jesus Crisis; The Inroads of Historical Criticsm into Evangelical Scholarship* (Grand Rapids: Kregel, 1998, 13–34.

9. The scope of this chapter does not permit a full portrayal of all the hermeneutical pitfalls that are current. A few more examples from other recent sources may help to show what to beware of and avoid:

> 1. Anthropologists Smalley and Kraft say that changes in culture necessitate alterations in the meaning of divine revelation to adapt it to a new cultural situation (William A. Smalley, "Culture and Superculture," *Practical Anthropology* 2 [1955]: 58–71; and Charles H. Kraft, *Christianity in Culture* [Maryknoll, N.Y.: Orbis, 1979], 123). In other words, divine revelation is

non-absolute. In contrast, the grammatical-historical method of interpretation assumes the absolute nature of divine revelation.

2. Missiologist Bonino contends that there is no truth in the Bible apart from its application in a present-day situation (J. M. Bonino, *Doing Theology in a Revolutionary Situation* [Philadelphia: Fortress, 1975], 88–89). This position overemphasizes the role of application and makes it determinative of the historical interpretation. Application should follow interpretation and be based upon it, not vice versa.

3. Feminist writer Russell notes that the biblical text can only be considered as authoritative when it is nonsexist, that is, when it does not violate a feminist liberation perspective (Letty M. Russell, "Introduction: Liberating the Word," in *Feminist Interpretation of the Bible,* ed. by Letty M. Russell [Philadelphia: Westminster, 1985], 16). By her own admission this places her at odds with the grammatical-historical method of interpretation (in *Feminist Interpretation of the Bible,* see also Russell's "Authority and the Challenge of Feminist Interpretation," pp. 55–56, and Elisabeth Sch|ssler Fiorenza's, " The Will to Choose or to Reject: Continuing Our Critical Work," p. 132). To have some parts of Scripture as more authoritative than others flies in the face of a normal hermeneutical approach.

4. Philosopher Thiselton presupposes something in the interpreter's present experience—that is, assumptions made or questions asked by the interpreter—as interpretation's starting point (Thiselton, "New Hermenteutic," p. 316). The grammatical-historical approach says that the text must be the starting point. Thiselton's theory forces the text to deal with an issue that is probably irrelevant to the original intent of the writer.

5. Exegete Carson sides with secular modern linguistic theory in questioning the time-honored practice of distinguishing slight differences in meaning between synonyms used side-by-side in the text (D. A. Carson, *Exegetical Fallacies* [Grand Rapids: Baker, 1984], 48–54). His position is fallacious because it does injustice to the precision of inspired Scripture. Grammatical-historical interpretation has upheld the validity of these distinctions between synonyms, but Carson disagrees.

10. For extensive elaboration on the pervading presence of interpretive confusion within evangelicalism, see Robert L. Thomas, *Evangelical Hermeneutics: The New Versus the Old* (Grand Rapids: Kregel, 2002).

11. As a service to expositors everywhere, an ongoing project of the New Testament faculty and students at The Master's Seminary is the production of "exegetical digests" of various New Testament books and portions of books. These digests consist of all the exegetically relevant material derived from the top eighty to one hundred sources pertaining to the book or section of Scripture covered. They provide instant access to the best of exegetical data that an expositor would spend many hours of preparation to discover. This type of resource has proven to be a great time-saver in sermon preparation for many. The lengthiness of the *Exegetical Digest of I John,* 508 pages, illustrates the magnitude of the exegetical task facing the expositor.

12. See John MacArthur and Wayne Mack, *Counseling: How to Counsel Biblically* (Nashville: Thomas Nelson, 2005) for a thoroughly consistent Scriptural approach to counseling.

13. Robert L. Thomas, *Introduction to Exegesis* (Sun Valley, Calif.: author, 1987), 15–16.

14. Caution needs to be exercised in choosing English words that are analogous to Greek words, however. "Dynamite," for instance, conveys a markedly incorrect impression of what the Greek word *dynamis* connotes.

15. Wonderly refers to this level of what consumers may tolerate as either a "horizon of difficulty" or a "threshold of frustration" (William L. Wonderly, *Bible Translations for Popular Use,* vol. 7 of *Helps for Translators* [London: United Bible Societies, 1968], 37–39); sec Eugene A. Nida, *Toward a Science of Translation* (Leiden: Brill, 1964), 132–44.

16. A preacher who prefaces his sermon with "I don't have anything new to give you today, but . . . ," has, in essence, told his congregation, "We may as well pack up and go home right now." He is confessing that his training for sermon preparation has been inadequate or that he has not been disciplined enough in his schedule to prepare the way he should have.

17. The interest span of a given audience can be increased by patiently and gradually increasing the amount of instructional emphasis from message to message. Listeners will grow progressively in their ability to sustain concentration on a passage under discussion over longer and longer periods. Of course, in other cultures the attention span may vary considerably from what most Americans can tolerate.

18. Guarding against selfish motives and pride and at the same time trying to maintain the interest of listeners for *their* benefit is probably the greatest challenge for the preacher. It entails self-examination to determine whether his motivation is from his "crucified-with-Christ" self for the purpose of self-aggrandizement or his "raised-with-Christ" self for the purpose of edifying others (see Rom. 6:11). The Spirit-controlled expositor will defer only to the latter type of motivation in this decision, as well as in all decisions of his Christian life (see Robert L. Thomas, "Improving Evangelical Ethics: An Analysis of the Problem and a Proposed Solution," *Journal of the Evangelical Theological Society* 34, no. 1 [March 1991]: 17–19).

Chapter Nine—Grammatical Analysis and Expository Preaching

1. It is necessary to qualify word studies with the term "legitimate" because too many preachers engage in illegitimate etymological studies (that is, there is no such thing as an "original meaning" apart from specific contextual settings) and semantical transfers (that is, taking the meaning of a word in one context and inserting that meaning into a different context without contextual reassessment). As profitable as many word books are (e.g., *Theological Dictionary of the Old Testament; Theological Wordbook of the Old Testament; Theological Dictionary of the New Testament; New International Dictionary of New Testament Theology*), their articles and how they are used must be carefully monitored to guard against contextual and other hermeneutical errors. For cautions in this regard, see James Barr, *The Semantics of Biblical Language* (Oxford: Oxford University Press, 1961) and Moses Silva, *Biblical Words and Their Meaning: An Introduction to Lexical Semantics* (Grand Rapids: Zondervan,

1983). Concerning backgrounds of New Testament words, see David Hill, *Greek Words and Hebrew Meanings* (Cambridge: University Press, 1967).

2. The following is a recent reminder of this responsibility: "WE AFFIRM that the only type of preaching which sufficiently conveys the divine revelation and its proper application to life is that which faithfully expounds the text of Scripture as the Word of God. WE DENY that the preacher has any message from God apart from the text of Scripture" (Article XXV, "Articles of Affirmation and Denial, The Chicago Statement on Biblical Hermeneutics," International Council on Biblical Inerrancy [Chicago, 1982]).

3. John R. W. Stott, *Guard the Gospel* (Downers Grove, Ill.: InterVarsity, 1973), 106.

4. Kuiper, "Scriptural Preaching" 242, 250–54.

5. Henry, *God, Revelation,* 4:479.

6. Runia, "What is Preaching?" 32; see Barker, "Jeremiah's Ministry," 229.

7. Such challenges are not made naively to pastor-teachers who labor alone or have minimal assistance in smaller churches. Never enough hours can be found in the day to accomplish what seems necessary. Yet, the ultimate ministerial priority of feeding God's sheep is confirmed throughout His revelation. Failure to place this priority consistently at the top is biblically inexcusable.

8. James S. Stewart, *Heralds of God* (reprint, Grand Rapids: Baker, 1971), 110.

9. Kaiser, *Exegetical Theology,* 19, 48, 22, 50.

10. Ibid., 49, 104, 156, 160.

11. E.g., its contextual setting, conceptual development, structural indications, stylistic vehicles, grammar, syntax, etc.

12. The discussion of methodology in this chapter will illustrate how this is done and offer some practical suggestions.

13. Kaiser, *Exegetical Theology,* 152.

14. On the superiority of propositional preaching, see Ferris D. Whitesell and Lloyd Perry, *Variety in Your Preaching* (Westwood, N.J.: Revell, 1954), 75–94, and Charles W. Koller, *Expository Preaching Without Notes* (Grand Rapids: Baker, 1962), 52–53.

15. The same textual controls apply to all consecutive levels of subpoints.

16. Thomas R. Schreiner, *Interpreting the Pauline Epistles* (Grand Rapids: Baker, 1990), see especially "Tracing the Argument" (chapter 6); Schreiner's summary of the different relationships that units have to one another is especially helpful (pp. 111–12).

17. For English diagramming help, see Donald W. Emery, *Sentence Analysis* (Fort Worth: Holt, Rinehart, and Winston, 1961). For help in the Greek text, see John D. Grassmick, *Principles and Practice of Greek Exegesis* (Dallas: Dallas Theological Seminary, 1974); Schreiner, "Diagramming and Conducting a Grammatical Analysis," chapter 5 of *Pauline Epistles;* Richard P. Belcher, *Diagramming the Greek New Testament* (Columbia, S.C.: Richbarry, 1985); and for examples from both the Hebrew and Greek texts, see Lee L. Kantenwein, *Diagrammatical Analysis* (Winona Lake, Ind.: BMH, 1979).

18. See the examples throughout Kaiser's *Exegetical Theology.*

19. The arguments of most passages reach their conclusions through such syntactical means.

20. Unfortunately, many are not competent in this necessary part of exegesis. Though some basic word-study and grammatical skills are still operative, the skills necessary for analyzing the syntactical skeleton of a passage have too often become rusty. Furthermore, no crash courses are available for rapidly regaining (or possibly, acquiring for the first time) a functional proficiency. Nevertheless, a serious commitment to proficiency will bear fruit through a consistent review of various texts being readied for delivery. Dusting off and using works on Hebrew and Greek grammar and syntax *in conjunction with* message preparation is the place to begin. For some helpful tools, see Francis Brown, S. R. Driver, and Charles Briggs, *A Hebrew-English Lexicon of the Old Testament* (reprint, Oxford: Claredon Press, 1968), 252–55, on options for the conjunction *waw* (see A. Ross, *A Hebrew Handbook* [Dallas: Dallas Theological Seminary, 1976], 37); Lambdin, *Introduction to Biblical Hebrew;* Waltke and O'Connor, *Introduction to Biblical Hebrew Syntax;* Williams, *Hebrew Syntax: An Outline;* Dana and Mantey, *A Manual Grammar of the Greek New Testament,* especially paragraphs 209–23 [with summary chart at end] on conjunctions, paragraphs 224–42 on particles, and paragraphs 243 ff. on clauses; Chamberlain, *An Exegetical Grammar of the Greek New Testament;* Moulton, Howard, and Turner, *A Grammar of New Testament Greek;* etc.

21. Attention should be paid to various genre (e.g., dialogue, lament, covenant structure; see respectively, Job and Habakkuk, Jeremiah and Lamentations, Deuteronomy). On the hermeneutical (and consequently homiletical) significance of literary and genre analysis, see Articles X, XIII, XIV, and XV of "Articles of Affirmation and Denial, The Chicago Statement on Biblical Hermeneutics," International Council on Biblical Inerrancy (Chicago, 1982); also note, e.g., Tremper Longman's *Literary Approaches to Biblical Interpretation* (Grand Rapids: Zondervan, 1987). In addition, recognition of strictly *literary* devices is especially informative and may even disclose organizational clues (e.g., biblical acrostics, strophic units; see respectively, Ps. 119 and Lam. 3; Jer. 17:5–8 and Hab. 2:6–20). An awareness of basic patterns of the conceptual parallelisms in Hebrew poetry is essential (for a brief summary, see F. F. Bruce, "The Poetry of the OT," in *New Bible Commentary Revised*). For other aids in recognizing significant stylistic phenomena in examining a passage, use traditional hermeneutical textbooks and exegetical commentaries committed to theologically orthodox literary analysis.

22. The fruit of Hebrew and Greek word studies needs to be capsulized semantically for purposes of incorporation into a larger homiletical outline. This condensation is sometimes facilitated and made smoother by using an English thesaurus.

23. Function is the key in these domains. Technical jargon of grammar or syntax has no place in the pulpit; however, functional description is essential in incorporating the author's flow of thought and ensuring that it is clear to the congregation.

24. Kaiser, *Exegetical Theology,* 158, 160.

25. This not only guards against wrenching the verse from its contextual setting hermeneutically, but it also supplies valuable data for an introduction when the time comes to preach the sermon. In all the forthcoming examples and in future sermonic analysis, due care in maintaining contextual integrity will be assumed.

26. It would be theologically advantageous to show how frequently this combination of words, along with other very closely related expressions, support this emphasis upon mindset.

27. The occurrences of the preposition ל (lĕ) following the combination of כּוּן (kûn) plus לְכָב (lēbāb) absolutely confirm the verse's focus on mindset.

28. This verse is one among many in the Greek New Testament that employ Hebrew (conceptual) parallelism.

29. This adds to the evidence that these are maxims or universals.

30. This indicates that men do not give birth to themselves physically, and it is not possible for them to regenerate themselves in the metaphysical realm (see John 1:12–13 in this Gospel's introduction).

31. This makes the participial phrases substantive.

32. This is a preposition well suited to denote source or origin.

33. This emphasizes their qualitative nature, especially in comparison with their respective articular occurrences just before.

34. Note the impact of the Hebrew root פּשׁע (pšʿ). It occurs in the first member of the couplet immediately after the participle that speaks about concealment, and it is the implied object after the participles which connote confession and abandonment in the second member of the couplet.

35. The participles in both couplets (one in the first and two in the second), although anarthrous, function as substantives, each depicting the subject about whom an evaluation or judgment is forthcoming. Their anarthrous phrasing combines with the basic emphasis of participles on continuity of action increasing attention toward these as habitual or characteristic activities.

36. Corroboration also comes from the adverbial statements standing under the leading verb τρέχωμεν (trechōmen).

37. Because the advantages and methodology of diagramming have been previously illustrated and because of the complexity of a diagram of Heb. 12:1–2, only the outline of this passage is reproduced here.

38. Needless to say, besides being preached in one bird's-eye sermon, a Bible book also lends itself to an expositional series of sermons. A particularly effective way to preach through a book is to do a "keyhole" sermon at the outset covering the whole book, and then to expand each of its major phases of argument in subsequent messages.

39. The diagram used to produce this outline is not reproduced here, because of its length (involving three chapters of Hebrew text) and because the principles and advantages of diagramming already have been illustrated. The major-point levels and levels immediately under them can be derived just as well from rhetorical and conceptual features discernible through comparing the Hebrew text with a good translation (see the brief comments made under the previous heading, "General Suggestions").

Chapter Ten—Study Tools for Expository Preaching

1. Wilbur M. Smith, *The Minister in His Study* (Chicago: Moody, 1973), 10.
2. Charles H. Spurgeon, *Commenting and Commentaries* (reprint, Edinburgh: Banner of Truth, 1969), 1.
3. Ibid., 1.
4. See Charles H. Spurgeon, *Lectures to My Students* (reprint, Grand Rapids: Zondervan, 1954), 305–20. Spurgeon makes a passionate plea for earnestness with respect to pulpit work.
5. John Fletcher Hurst, *Literature of Theology: A Classified Bibliography of Theological and General Religious Literature* (New York: Hunt and Eaton, 1895), *v*.
6. Warren W. Wiersbe, *A Basic Library for Bible Students* (Grand Rapids: Baker, 1980), 7–8.
7. See Cyril J. Barber, *The Minister's Library* (Chicago: Moody, 1985), I:3–31. The section entitled "How To Set Up Your Library" contains much valuable information.
8. A biblical expositor will find the following periodicals helpful: *Banner of Truth, Biblical Archaeology Review, Bibliotheca Sacra, Grace Theological Journal, Interpretation, Journal of Biblical Literature, Journal of the Evangelical Theological Society, Review and Expositor, Southern Baptist Journal of Theology, The Master's Seminary Journal, Themelios,* and *Westminster Theological Journal.*
9. This would include CD-ROM publications by Nelson, Abingdon, Zondervan, Eerdman, IVP, Baker, Master Christian Library, Galaxie Software, and Oxford University Press.
10. Ibid., 1:*xiv–xv.*
11. Several ways to keep up with new materials as they become available are: reading *Christianity Today* and *Themelios* carefully, especially the issues devoted to new books; subscribing to a major book discount house that publishes catalogs identifying new books as they appear; and reading book reviews in key periodicals.
12. A list of suggested bibliographies is provided later in this chapter.
13. Many major seminaries in the United States have a good inventory of books and are set up to order others, e.g., Westminster Theological Seminary in Philadelphia, Pennsylvania; Southern Baptist Seminary in Louisville, Kentucky; Luther Theological Seminary in St. Paul, Minnesota; and Dallas Theological Seminary in Dallas, Texas.
14. At the time of this writing, excellent discount houses include: Christian Book Distributors, P.O. Box 3687, Peabody, Massachusetts 01961–3687, www.christianbook.com; Scripture Truth Book Co., P.O. Box 339, Fincastle, Virginia 24909, www.scripturetruth.com; Eisenbrauns, P.O. Box 275, Winona Lake, Indiana 46590, www.eisenbrauns.com; and Reformation Heritage Books, 2919 Leonard Street, N.E., Grand Rapids, Michigan 49525, www.heritagebooks.org. Software can be purchased at discount at www.rejoicesoftware.com.
15. Helpful American sources include: Baker Book House-Used Department, 2768 East Paris Ave. S.E., Grand Rapids, Michigan 49546, usedbooks@bakerbookretail.com; Kregel's Book Store, P.O. Box 2607, 525 Eastern Avenue, S.E., Grand

Rapids, Michigan 49501, www.kregel.com; Archive Bookstore, 1387 E. Washington, Pasadena, California 91104, www.archivesbookshop.com. Helpful sources in the United Kingdom include: Christian Book Centre, 1021 Argyle Street, Glasgow G38NA, Scotland; Pendlebury Books, Portland Ave., Stamford Hill, London N16; Geneva Books, 58 Elms Road, Southside, London SW490L. Other such sources can be found in the yearly editions of *Sheppard's Book Dealers in the British Isles* (Surrey, England: Martins Publishers Limited, 1989). A large number of bookstores can be accessed from www.addall.com.

16. Preserved Smith, *Erasmus, a Study of His Life, Ideals and Place in History* (New York: Harper and Brothers, 1923), 194–95.

17. Howard F. Sugden and Warren W. Wiersbe, *When Pastors Wonder How* (Chicago: Moody, 1973), 64.

Chapter Eleven—A Study Method for Expository Preaching

1. Jay E. Adams, "Editorial: Good Preaching is Hard Work," *The Journal of Pastoral Practice* 4, no. 2 (1980): 1 (italics in the original).

2. Peter Lewis, *The Genius of Puritanism* (Haywards Heath, Sussex, England: Carey, 1979), 17 (caption to illustration on opposite page).

3. Helpful books on Bible study include Irving L. Jensen, *Independent Bible Study* (Chicago: Moody, 1981); Walter C. Kaiser, Jr., *Toward an Exegetical Theology* (Grand Rapids: Baker, 1985); John MacArthur, *How to Get the Most from God's Word* (Dallas: Word, 1997); Richard Mayhue, *How to Interpret the Bible for Yourself* (Winona Lake, Ind.: BMH, 1986); and Robert A. Traina, *Methodical Bible Study* (Wilmore, Ky.: by the author, 1952). In the use of these and similar books, however, caution is necessary to detect deviations from time-tested principles of hermeneutics.

4. Traina, *Bible Study,* 31–32 (italics in the original).

5. Ibid., 32–33.

6. Cited in Mayhue, *How to Interpret,* 49.

7. *American Poems,* 3d ed. (Boston: Houghton, Osgood, 1879), 450–54; first published as "In the Laboratory with Agassiz, By a former pupil," in *Every Saturday* 16 (4 April 1874), 369–70.

8. For fuller bibliographic information about works cited, see chapter 10 of this book, "Study Tools for Expository Preaching."

9. Mayhue, *How to Interpret,* 64.

10. Helpful books on meditation include Jim Downing, *Meditation: The Bible Tells You How* (Colorado Springs, Colo.: Navpress, 1979), and Peter Toon, *From Mind to Heart* (Grand Rapids: Baker, 1987). For the most thorough treatment, see John MacArthur, gen. ed., *Think Biblically* (Wheaton: Crossway, 2003), esp. pp. 37–53.

11. For a more detailed discussion of this aspect of preparation, see chapter 12 of this book, "Central Ideas, Outlines, and Titles."

12. For a suggested method of grammatical analysis, see chapter 9 of this book, "Grammatical Analysis and Expository Preaching."

13. More information on diagramming is found in chapter 9 of this book, "Grammatical Analysis and Expository Preaching."

14. More about introductions and conclusions is discussed in chapter 13 of this book, "Introductions, Illustrations, and Conclusions."

Chapter Twelve—Central Ideas, Outlines, and Titles

1. That is, studies of individual words.
2. That is, the discipline that examines how words, phrases, and clauses are joined to each other.
3. See Warren Wiersbe, *The Dynamics of Preaching* (Grand Rapids: Baker, 1999).
4. James Moffatt, *A Critical and Exegetical Commentary on the Epistle to the Hebrews,* International Critical Commentaries (reprint, Edinburgh: T. & T. Clark, 1968), 158; see 156, 192.
5. J. Armitage Robinson, *Commentary on Ephesians* (reprint, Grand Rapids: Kregel, 1979), 19.
6. That is, the noun in the genitive case acts as a subject and performs the action implied in the substantive that it qualifies.

Chapter Thirteen—Introductions, Illustrations, and Conclusions

1. Haddon Robinson, *Biblical Preaching* (Grand Rapids: Baker, 1980), 159.
2. For other helpful discussions of Introductions, see J. Daniel Baumann, *An Introduction to Contemporary Preaching* (Grand Rapids: Baker, 1972), 135–42; John Broadus, *On the Preparation and Delivery of Sermons* (reprint, Grand Rapids: Associated Publishers and Authors, n.d.), 99–103; Robinson, *Biblical Preaching,* 159–67; Warren and David Wiersbe, *The Elements of Preaching* (Wheaton, Ill.: Tyndale, 1986), 75–78.
3. G. Campbell Morgan, *Preaching* (reprint, Grand Rapids: Baker, 1974), 81.
4. Donald R. Sunukjian, "The Credibility of the Preacher," *Bibliotheca Sacra* 139, no. 555 (July–Sept 1982): 255–66.
5. Specific samples of introductions, illustrations, and conclusions can be found in several books I have authored, using material that came primarily from a preaching/teaching ministry: *Divine Healing Today* (Winona Lake, Ind.,: BMH, 1983); *How to Interpret the Bible for Yourself* (Winona Lake, Ind.: BMH, 1986); *A Christian's Survival Guide* (Wheaton, Ill.: Victor, 1987); *Unmasking Satan* (Wheaton, Ill.: Victor, 1988); *Spiritual Intimacy* (Wheaton, Ill.: Victor, 1990).
6. For other helpful discussions of Illustrations see Jack Hughes, *Expository Preaching* (Fearn, Ross-shire, Great Britain: Christian Focus, 2001); Haddon Robinson, ed., *Biblical Sermons* (Grand Rapids: Baker, 1989); William E. Sangster, *The Craft of the Sermon* (London: Epworth, 1954), 201–98; C. H. Spurgeon, *Lectures to My Students,* third series (reprint, Grand Rapids: Baker, 1977), 1–200; Faris Whitesell, *Power in Expository Preaching* (Old Tappan, N.J.: Revell, 1963), 75–89.
7. Spurgeon, *Lectures,* 52.
8. These reasons elaborate on Spurgeon's material in *Lectures,* 31–53.
9. Although most books of illustrations will not be consistently helpful, the following volumes have been the most fruitful sources I have used: Michael P. Green, *Illustrations for Biblical Preaching* (Grand Rapids: Baker, 1989); Charles Little, *10,000 Illustrations from the Bible* (reprint, Grand Rapids: Baker,

1981); Paul Lee Tan, *Encyclopedia of 7700 Illustrations* (Rockville, Md.: Assurance Publishers, 1979); *The Treasury of Scripture Knowledge* (reprint, Old Tappan, N.J.: Revell, n.d.).

10. For other helpful discussions of conclusions see also Baumann, *Introduction,* 142–45; H. C. Brown, H. Gordon Clinard, and Jesse J. Northcutt, *Steps to the Sermon* (Nashville: Broadman, 1963), 121–25; David L. Larsen, *The Anatomy of Preaching* (Grand Rapids: Baker, 1989), 119–30; Sangster, *Craft,* 128–43.

11. Morgan, *Preaching,* 87.

12. For further discussion, read Jack Kuhatschek, *Taking the Guesswork Out of Applying the Bible* (Downers Grove, Ill.: InterVarsity, 1990). Sinclair Ferguson offers a fresh idea on how to use 2 Tim. 3:16–17 as a stimulus for application ideas in Richard Allen Bodey, ed., *Inside the Sermon* (Grand Rapids: Baker, 1990), 80. See also Jay E. Adams, *Truth Applied* (Grand Rapids: Zondervan, 1990).

13. Baumann, *Introduction,* 142.

14. John R. W. Stott, "Christian Preaching in the Contemporary World," *Bibliotheca Sacra* 145, no. 580 (October–December 1988): 370.

Chapter Fourteen—Thematic, Theological, Historical and Biographical Expository Messages

1. David L. Larsen, *The Anatomy of Preaching* (Grand Rapids: Baker, 1989), 31.

2. Dwight E. Stevenson, *In the Biblical Preacher's Workshop* (New York: Abingdon, 1967), 196.

3. Ibid., 13. Using Scripture out of context attributes something to God that He did not say, thus evacuating His power from the message.

4. Ibid., 155–56.

5. John A. Broadus, *On the Preparation and Delivery of Sermons* (reprint, New York: Harper, 1944), 136–37.

6. Charles W. Koller, *Expository Preaching Without Notes* (Grand Rapids: Baker, 1962), 22.

7. Broadus, *Preparation,* 133.

8. That is, a reading of meaning *into* the text rather than obtaining meaning *from* the text.

9. Merrill F. Unger, *Principles of Expository Preaching* (Grand Rapids: Zondervan, 1955), 52.

10. The severity of wrongdoing when proof-texting should not be underestimated. Stevenson (*Preacher's Workshop,* 157) defines it as "using a text to silence opposition and compel consent. . . . This kind of preaching uses the Bible not as 'a searchlight to be thrown upon a shadowed spot,' but as a bludgeon to gain mastery."

11. Haddon Robinson, "The Heresy of Application," *Leadership* 18 (Fall 1997): 23.

12. Robert Law, *The Tests of Life* (reprint, Grand Rapids: Baker, 1982).

13. David E. Aune, *The New Testament in Its Literary Environment* (Philadelphia: Westminster, 1987), 13.

14. Tremper Longman III, *Literary Approaches to Biblical Interpretation* (Grand Rapids: Zondervan, 1987), 83.

15. Leander E. Keck, *The Bible in the Pulpit: The Renewal of Biblical Preaching* (Nashville: Abingdon, 1978), 101.
16. Sidney Greidanus, *The Modern Preacher and the Ancient Text* (Grand Rapids: Eerdmans, 1988), 123.
17. James W. Alexander, *Thoughts on Preaching* (reprint, Carlisle, Penn.: Banner of Truth, 1975), 512.
18. Broadus, *Preparation,* 134.
19. Ibid., 60.
20. Ibid.
21. Ibid., 65–66.
22. Ibid., 61.
23. Unger, *Principles,* 49.
24. Broadus, *Preparation,* 71.
25. This type also allows the preacher to conceal his thesis until the end of the sermon. Although the thesis should be kept in mind throughout the sermon, it would not be revealed until the close, when the case has already been made. This approach is often beneficial for maintaining audience interest (e.g., Peter's sermon in Acts 2). It can be effectively employed with a hostile audience, too.
26. Discussions here are limited to preaching biblical personalities. Extra-biblical stalwarts of the faith furnish some additional excellent instruction and examples. But the history of Christianity outside the Bible is best left for illustration and elucidation. See R. Larry Overstreet, *Biographical Preaching* (Grand Rapids: Kregel, 2001).
27. Ilion T. Jones, *Principles and Practice of Preaching* (New York: Abingdon, 1956), 112.
28. Koller, *Expository Preaching,* 32.

Chapter Fifteen—Expository Preaching from Old Testament Narrative

1. The English word "story" sometimes conveys the notion of a fictional account. In this essay, however, the word is always used to denote what is factual and in accord with actual happenings. The "God-breathed" quality of Scripture guarantees the historical accuracy of narrative portions.
2. Adams argues that stories are the best teachers, particularly where the story appeals to the senses: "It is true that *we learn best what we see, touch or hear* and that, in discursive language, a story comes closest to the very experience of an event" (Jay E. Adams, "Sense Appeal and Storytelling," *The Preacher and Preaching,* ed. by Samuel T. Logan, Jr. [Phillipsburg, N.J.: Presbyterian and Reformed, 1986], 350). A well-known preacher described how he was impacted by the narrative sermons of evangelist Billy Sunday, who captivated thousands: "When he preached on Elijah, he did it so vividly that I thought I was looking at Elijah. When he preached on Naaman going down into the dirty Jordan, I suffered all of the agony that Naaman suffered. For nearly an hour Naaman lived in Billy Sunday" (William Ward Ayer, " The Art of Effective Preaching," *Bibliotheca Sacra* 124 [January–March 1967]: 38).

3. The present discussion will focus on preaching the narrative portions of the Old Testament. It will not deal with either narrative preaching, which turns every passage or topic into a narrative preaching format, or with narrative theology, a theological system in which stories play a major role. Neither will it deal comprehensively with characteristic features or methods of preaching biblical narrative. Much has already been written on this subject. Works dealing specifically with the nature of Old Testament narrative and the method of preaching it are Walter C. Kaiser, Jr., *The Old Testament in Contemporary Preaching* (Grand Rapids: Baker, 1973); *Toward an Exegetical Theology* (Grand Rapids: Baker, 1981); *Toward Rediscovering the Old Testament* (Grand Rapids: Zondervan, 1987); *Preaching and Teaching from the Old Testament* (Grand Rapids: Baker, 2003); Tremper Longman III, *Literary Approaches to Biblical Interpretation* (Grand Rapids: Zondervan, 1987); and Leland Ryken, *How to Read the Bible as Literature* (Grand Rapids: Zondervan, 1984). A comprehensive text which deals with all types of biblical literature and methods of preaching them is Sidney Greidanus, *The Modern Preacher and the Ancient Text* (Grand Rapids: Eerdmans, 1988). Perhaps the three best brief discussions of the nature of biblical narrative are John Goldingay, "Preaching on the Stories in Scripture," *Anvil* 7, no. 2 (1990): 105–14; Tremper Longman III, "Storytellers and Poets in the Bible," *Inerrancy and Hermeneutic: A Tradition, a Challenge, a Debate*, ed. by Harvie M. Conn (Grand Rapids: Baker, 1988); and Leland Ryken, "And It Came to Pass: The Bible as God's Storybook," *Bibliotheca Sacra* 147, no. 586 (April–June 1990): 131–42. A thought-provoking application of Longman's work coauthored by Raymond Dillard addressing the use, and sometimes misuse, of biblical narrative by Christian counseling theorists is Tremper Longman III, and Raymond B. Dillard, "Hermeneutics and Counseling," *The Institute of Biblical Counseling Perspective* 2, no. 1 (1988): 21–30.

4. The "story line" is the plot or general plan of a story.

5. Gabriel Fackre, "Narrative Theology: An Overview," *Interpretation* 37, no. 4 (1983): 341.

6. Henry Grady Davis, *Design for Preaching* (Philadelphia: Fortress, 1958), 157. These characteristics make narrative easier to preach with few or no notes for the simple reason that the message is couched in real-life situations involving people, places, and events. Research has demonstrated that stories are easier than most sermon formats to remember, both for the preacher as he delivers the sermon, and for the congregation as they take the message with them. For an interesting study of how professional storytellers learn the stories they recount for hours at a time, see Albert B. Lord, *The Singer of Tales* (Cambridge, Mass.: Harvard University Press, 1960).

7. In this way narrative behaves like the story, selectively "omitting much that is irrelevant or that in real life may distract, while focusing on and emphasizing the major factors in the event" (Adams, "Sense Appeal," 351).

8. Savran maintains that much of the direct discourse of narratives is artistically patterned: " The phenomenon of quotation describes the intersection of a number of central aspects of the narrative. It is both direct speech of the

present narrative moment and recollection of prior words. It presents the quoting character as the teller of his own story, but also as the subject of the narrator's discourse. Perhaps most important is the way quoted direct speech functions as an exegetical exercise, a rereading or respeaking of the past at a later time and in a new context" (George W. Savran, *Telling and Retelling: Quotation in Biblical Narrative* [Bloomington: Indiana University Press, 1988], *ix*).

9. Regarding the confusion of story line with fiction, Sternberg argues, "With God postulated as double author, the biblical narrator can enjoy the privileges of art without renouncing his historical titles" (Meir Sternberg, *The Poetics of Biblical Narrative: Ideological Literature and the Drama of Reading* [Bloomington: Indiana University Press, 1985], 82).

10. Defining prose continues to present a major challenge to all who attempt to systematize genre. For purposes of this discussion, prose is "the ordinary form of written or spoken language without rhyme or meter" (*Webster's Unabridged Dictionary*, 2d ed. [New York: Simon and Schuster, 1972], 1445). When writers like Polzin speak of biblical Hebrew prose, they intend a broader connotation (Robert Polzin, *Late Biblical Hebrew: Toward an Historical Typology of Biblical Hebrew Prose* [Missoula, Mont.: Scholars, 1976]). The line between prose (narrative) and poetry in biblical Hebrew is fine. James Kugel sees the distinction as western and artificial (James Kugel, *The Idea of Biblical Poetry* [New Haven: Yale University Press, 1981], 69). Cloete challenges Kugal's thesis on the grounds that "the lines or cola . . . are the distinguishing characteristic of verse" (W. T. W. Cloete, "Verse and Prose: Does the Distinction Apply to the Old Testament?" *Journal of Northwest Semitic Languages* 14 [1988]: 13).

11. "Prose tends to suppress ornamentation or figures of speech. A general principle is that, the more the author intends to inform about the real world, the more literariness decreases" (Tremper Longman III, "Storytellers," 138).

12. Normally, the resulting "message" of the narrative cannot be reduced to theological propositions without losing its uniquely persuasive character (Robert C. Tannehill, "Narrative Criticism," *A Dictionary of Biblical Interpretation*, R. J. Coggins and J. L. Houlden, eds. [Philadelphia: Trinity, 1990], 489). Also, didactic biblical literature (letters, commandments, etc.) can be restated concisely in lists of admonitions and prescriptions more easily than narrative.

13. A story is a series of events that can be seen to have a beginning, a middle, and an end. It is important, of course, to recognize the logical relationships among these three parts. The beginning always describes a situation of need that must be addressed through some kind of action. The middle grows out of the beginning by describing what is done about this needed action. The end, in turn, grows out of the middle by showing what happens as a result of the action taken in the middle. At the same time, the end relates to the beginning by resolving its situation of need. The end allows the reader to say, "Yes, this is 'the end,'" either by showing how the need described in the beginning has been met . . . or by describing how all reasonable opportunity for future action has been cut off (Thomas O. Long, *Preaching and the Literary Forms of the Bible* [Philadelphia: Fortress, 1989], 71–72).

14. Donald E. Demaray, *Introduction to Homiletics,* 2d ed. (Grand Rapids: Baker, 1990), 103.

15. David G. Buttrick, *Homiletic: Moves and Structures* (Philadelphia: Fortress, 1987), 335.

16. John Goldingay, " That You May Know that Yahweh Is God: A Study in the Relationship between Theology and Historical Truth in the Old Testament," *Tyndale Bulletin* 23 (1972): 58–93.

17. Longman, "Storytellers," 146.

18. Ryken, *How to Read,* 44. Not all agree that narrative is capable of this universal quality. "An opposing view is skeptical or agnostic about how narrative relates to universal human experience (if, indeed, there is any such reality), and starts with the specific characteristics of Christianity. . . . The first [position] assumes a common basis in human consciousness; the second questions that and stresses specificity and differences" (David F. Ford, "Narrative Theology," *A Dictionary of Biblical Interpretation,* R. J. Coggins and J. L. Houlden, eds. [Philadelphia: Trinity, 1990], 490). The perspective of Martin Noth ("The 'Representation' of the O. T. in Proclamation," *Essays on Old Testament Hermeneutics,* ed. by Claus Westermann, trans. by James Luther Mays, 2d. ed. [Richmond, Va.: John Knox, 1964], 86) that biblical characters cannot function as "ethical models" is unacceptable.

19. Walter C. Kaiser, *Toward an Exegetical Theology* (Grand Rapids: Baker, 1981), 92. " To 'principlize' is to state the author's propositions, arguments, narrations, and illustrations in timeless abiding truths with special focus on the application of those truths to the current needs of the Church" (ibid., 152). See also Richard L. Mayhue, "Rediscovering Expository Preaching," *The Master's Seminary Journal* 1, no. 2 (Fall 1990): 121.

20. Henry H. Mitchell, "Preaching on the Patriarchs," *Biblical Preaching: An Expositor's Treasury,* ed. by James W. Cox (Philadelphia: Westminster, 1983), 37. But to what the narratives are calling their reader has been debated repeatedly. Should the congregation be looking for ethical directives, theological instruction, or both? We cannot deny that the teaching of the narrative will somehow result in some form of ethical response (Carl G. Kromminga, "Remember Lot's Wife: Preaching Old Testament Narrative Texts," *Calvin Theological Journal* 18, no. 1 [1983]: 33). For a historical chronicling of the ethical-vs.-theological debate over the purpose of biblical narrative, see Sidney Greidanus, *Sola Scriptura: Problems and Principles in Preaching Historical Texts* (Toronto: Wedge, 1970). Goldingay combines theology and ethics when he argues that the narratives aim at the following: (1) the *commitments* that faith entails; (2) the *experiences* that the faith may involve; and (3) the *events* on which the faith is based (Goldingay, "Preaching," 106–9).

21. Greidanus, *Modern Preacher,* 225. An added advantage of preaching narrative as story applies to believers with learning disabilities who need a strong plot structure, simple vocabulary, concrete language, and a clear beginning, middle, and end to the lesson. They will comprehend narrative sermons better than the abstract types (Augusta Baker and Ellin Greene, *Storytelling: Art and Technique* [New York: R. R. Bowker, 1977], 77).

22. It is tempting to draw ethical examples from the Joseph story. Some think the author intended Joseph's behavior to be a moral example because they view the text as wisdom literature. Characteristically, wisdom literature is well-suited for exemplary purposes in that it prescribes behavior as an ethical response to the fear of God. In Joseph's words, " You meant evil against me, but God meant it for good" (Gen. 50:20a), Von Rad hears echoes of Prov. 16:9: "The mind of man plans his way, but the LORD directs his steps" (James L. Crenshaw, *Gerhard Von Rad* [Waco, Texas: Word, 1978], 122–26). Crenshaw has persuasively argued against Von Rad's classification of this as wisdom literature, however (James L. Crenshaw, "Method in Determining Wisdom Influence upon 'Historical' Literature," *Journal of Biblical Literature* 88 [1969]: 129–42). Another major problem in determining whether the Joseph story is ethical, theological, or both is that many narratives such as this are part of the larger literary context of redemption history. What, then, constitutes a preaching unit within such large narrative units? Because the Joseph story is introduced with the תּוֹלְדֹת (*tôlĕdōt,* "the generations of") formula (see Gen. 5:1; 6:9; 10:1; 11:10, 27; 25:12, 19 and 36:1, 9), it is safe to take Gen. 37:2 to mark its beginning and the end of Genesis its conclusion. Setting limits for a preaching unit is not always this easy, however.

23. This is not to say that subsections of narratives may not be used to preach or teach topical, biographical, or other conceptual formats originating with the preacher or another writer of the Bible. Smaller units of stories do affirm various truths, but do not do so independently of the total narrative of which they are a part. The function of such lessons as subordinate to the primary message of the whole story must be kept in perspective. This is the only way to assure that one's interpretation of the passage and expositional preaching based on it will capture the intention of both its divine and human authors.

24. For Coats, Joseph's attitude toward his dreams and treatment of his brothers after their arrival in Egypt raise a question of just how exemplary his behavior was (e.g., G. W. Coats, "From Canaan to Egypt: Structural and Theological Context for the Joseph Story," *Catholic Quarterly Monograph Series* 4 [Washington: Catholic Biblical Association of America, 1976]: 82–86).

25. Stuart's advice is wise: "Avoid especially the principle of imitation (the idea that because someone in the Bible does it, we can or ought to do it, too). This is the most dangerous and irreverent of all approaches to application since virtually every sort of behavior, stupid and wise, malicious and saintly is chronicled in the Bible" (Douglas Stuart, *Old Testament Exegesis: A Primer for Students and Pastors,* 2d ed. [Philadelphia: Westminster, 1984], 84).

26. This approach should not be confused with Carmichael's. He argues that the Deuteronomic laws and perhaps some or all of Proverbs were based on earlier narrative portions (Calum M. Carmichael, *The Laws of Deuteronomy* [Ithaca, N.Y.: Cornell University, 1974]). Briefer explanations of Carmichael's theory of narrative and law are found in his articles " Uncovering a Major Source of Mosaic Law: The Evidence of Deut. 21:15–22:5," *Journal of Biblical Literature* 101 (1982): 505–20, and "Forbidden Mixtures," *Vetus Testamentum* 32 (1982): 394–415.

27. Note that this approach to Old Testament narrative would probably ignore Joseph's important statement, "You meant evil against me, but God meant it for good" (Gen. 50:20a). These words capture the major theological lesson of the story.

28. Cautioning the reader against assuming correspondences between narrative traditions in western literature and the Bible, Longman wrote, "In ordinary reading, much of this understanding happens automatically. We passively let the narrator shape our interpretation of the event he or she is reporting to us; we make an unconscious genre identification. But as interpreters of the text, it is important to make these explicit. This is doubly so for the Bible, since it is an ancient text and the conventions employed are often not ones we are used to" (Longman, "Storytellers," 148, alluding to Anthony C. Thiselton, *The Two Horizons: New Testament Hermeneutics and Philosophical Description* [Grand Rapids: Eerdmans, 1980]).

29. V. Philips Long. " Toward a Better Theory and Understanding of Old Testament Narrative," *Presbyterion* 13, no. 2 (Fall 1987): 105.

30. Ryken, *How to Read,* 68. Regarding the real but often unspoken fear that narrative interpretation is an impossibly complex process, Ryken responded, "Such a myth of complexity, however is to be rejected. The literature of the Bible is subtle and artistically crafted but essentially simple. . . . Talking about the Bible's literature does not require intricate tools and theories. It does, however require *literary* tools" (Ryken, "And It Came," 137).

Chapter Sixteen—Moving from Exegesis to Exposition

1. Leith Anderson, "Excellence in Preaching," *Christianity Today* 26 (17 September 1982): 54.

2. Robert A. Traina, *Methodical Bible Study* (Wilmore, Ky.: Author, 1952), 179–80. Also see Robert B. Chisholm, Jr., *From Exegesis to Exposition* (Grand Rapids: Baker, 1998) and Ramesh Richard, *Preparing Expository Sermons* (Grand Rapids: Baker, 2001).

3. Ibid., 180.

4. J. I. Packer, *God Has Spoken* (London: Hodder and Stoughton, 1965), 74.

5. C. H. Spurgeon, *Lectures to My Students: Third Series* (reprint, Grand Rapids: Baker, 1977), 2.

6. Ibid., 3.

7. Ibid., 2.

8. Ibid., 5.

9. "Go therefore and make disciples of all the nations, baptizing them in the name of the Father and the Son and the Holy Spirit, teaching them to observe all that I commanded you; and lo, I am with you always, even to the end of the age."

10. For a discussion of this important point see C. H. Spurgeon, "The Need of Decision for the Truth," *Lectures,* 39–53.

11. See Arturo G. Azurdia, III, *Spirit Empowered Preaching* (Fearn, Ross-shire, Great Britain: Christian Focus, 1998) and Stephen F. Olford, *Anointed Expository Preaching* (Nashville: Broadman & Holman, 1998).

12. Michael Fabarez, *Preaching that Changes Lives* (Nashville: Thomas Nelson, 2002); Keith Willhite, *Preaching with Relevance* (Grand Rapids: Kregel, 2001).

Chapter Seventeen—Bible Translations and Expository Preaching

1. This chapter was originally presented at the Thirty-fifth Annual Meeting of the Evangelical Theological Society in Dallas, Texas, in December 1983 and published in the Spring 1990 issue of *The Master's Seminary Journal* under the title "Bible Translations: The Link between Exegesis and Expository Preaching" (pp. 53–73). A few additions and updates have been made to the original essay.

2. For a discussion of all five areas in which translations may be classified, see Robert L. Thomas, *How to Choose a Bible Version* (Fearn, Ross-shire, Great Britain: Christian Focus, 2000).

3. W. C. Kaiser, Jr., *Toward an Exegetical Theology* (Grand Rapids: Baker, 1981), 18–19.

4. Glassman suggests that "target" is no longer acceptable to designate the language into which a translation is made because it suggests shooting a communication at a target and treats communication as a one-way street instead of expecting a response. He prefers "receptor" to stress the fact that a language has to be decoded by those to whom it is directed (E. H. Glassman, *The Translation Debate: What Makes a Bible Translation Good?* [Downers Grove, Ill.: InterVarsity, 1981], 48).

5. J. P. Lewis, *The English Bible/From KJV to NIV* (Grand Rapids: Baker, 1981), 279; S. Kubo and W. F. Specht, *So Many Versions?* rev. and enlarged ed. (Grand Rapids: Zondervan, 1983), 341–43; F. F. Bruce, *History of the English Bible* (New York: Oxford, 1978), 233. J. P. M. Walsh ("Contemporary English Translations of Scripture," *Theological Studies* 50, no. 2 [June 1989]: 336–38) finds the motivation behind dynamic equivalence laudable: a zeal for souls and a desire to make the riches of Scripture available to all. Yet he notices a troublesome underlying premise, that there is a message that "can be disengaged from the concrete, historically and culturally determined forms in which it was originally expressed, and gotten across to readers in other forms, equally determined by history and culture, which are different from those of the original text. . . . The truth of the Bible exists . . . in a certain embodiment, but that embodiment is of no real importance." He feels that this premise of dynamic equivalence carries almost a "gnostic" aura.

6. J. Van Bruggen, *The Future of the Bible* (Nashville: Nelson, 1978), 69. Some are so avidly committed to the dynamic equivalence approach that they are extravagantly critical of formal equivalence. They deny its ability to communicate anything to the average person. Glassman is typical of this extreme when he writes, "Every example I could give of formal correspondence translation would simply reinforce the point that, for the most part, it does not communicate to the ordinary person today, if indeed it ever did" (Glassman, *Translation Debate*, 50–51). This picture of formal equivalence is grossly misleading. To represent this approach as non-communicative is to erect a "straw man" that does not resemble the actual situation even faintly. Kohlenberger is also guilty

of painting such a distorted picture of literal translation (J. R. Kohlenberger III, *Words about the Word: A Guide to Choosing and Using Your Bible* [Grand Rapids: Zondervan, 1987], 63). Carson joins the others in crass exaggeration, if not outright error, when he writes, "There is widespread recognition of the dismal inadequacy of merely formal equivalence in translation, butressed [sic] by thousands and thousands of examples" (D. A. Carson, "The Limits of Dynamic Equivalence in Bible Translation," *Notes on Translation* 121 [October 1987]: 1, reprinted from *Evangelical Review of Theology* 9, no. 3 [July 1985]).

7. Van Bruggen, *Future,* 81; Robert L. Thomas, "Dynamic Equivalence: A Method of Translation or a System of Hermeneutics?" *The Master's Seminary Journal* 2, no. 2 (Fall 1990):169–72.

8. P. Schaff and H. Wace, *A Select Library of Nicene and Post-Nicene Fathers of the Christian Church* (Grand Rapids: Eerdmans, 1954), *vi,* 113; Lewis, *English Bible,* 233; Harvey Minkoff, "Problems of Translations: Concern for the Text Versus Concern for the Reader," *Bible Review* 4, no. 4 (August 1988): 35–36.

9. Bruce, *History,* 19, 238; D. Ewert, *From Ancient Tablets to Modern Translations* (Grand Rapids: Zondervan, 1983), 185.

10. Bruce, *History,* 153–54.

11. E. Nida, *Toward a Science of Translating* (Leiden: Brill, 1964), 159–60, 166–76.

12. Bruce, *History,* 233.

13. Nida, *Toward a Science,* 159–60, 165–66; W. L. Wonderly, *Bible Translations for Popular Use* (London: United Bible Societies, 1968), 50–51.

14. Bruce, *History,* 14–15.

15. Van Bruggen, *Future,* 27.

16. Lewis, *English Bible,* 153–54.

17. Van Bruggen, *Future,* 149.

18. Kubo and Specht, *So Many,* 230.

19. Lewis, *English Bible,* 222.

20. Kubo and Specht, *So Many,* 92.

21. Nida, *Toward a Science,* 156, 164.

22. Kubo and Specht, *So Many,* 174–75.

23. Van Bruggen, *Future,* 112.

24. Nida, *Toward a Science,* 140; Wonderly, *Bible Translations,* 203–5. Kohlenberger mentions two other tests that have been used to measure readability, one is a battery of language comprehension tests prepared by Dwight Chappell during the 1970s and the other is called the Fog Readability Index (Kohlenberger, *Words,* 60–61).

25. Wonderly, *Bible Translations,* 204–5.

26. Cited by Nida, *Toward a Science,* 184–92.

27. Wonderly's approach has been altered slightly so as to facilitate a more detailed analysis, as will be explained in the fourth step.

28. Wonderly has one category, "structural alterations," in place of the two categories, "lexical alterations" and "syntactical alterations," which are suggested here. It is proposed that this further division encourages a more definitive examination of the differences that are of this nature. Lexical and syntactical matters are somewhat distinct from each other.

29. The above discussion views translations as deviating from the text of the source language in varying degrees. Glassman represents a group who see the two approaches to translation, not from the perspective of relative closeness to the original text, but from the standpoint of being two approaches to translation that are entirely different in kind (Glassman, *Translation Debate,* 47–48). He appears to be saying, in other words, that dynamic equivalence makes no attempt to represent the individual words or syntactical constructions of the original. The dynamic-equivalence translator rather interprets the meaning of the text and proceeds to express that *meaning* in whatever words and constructions may seem appropriate to him.

30. Beekman and Callow refrain from using "paraphrase" to describe the results of their dynamic equivalence translations because of the pejorative connotation it carries in the minds of most Christians (John Beekman and John Callow, *Translating the Word of God* [Grand Rapids: Zondervan, 1974], 21). Because of a more technical connotation of the word found in linguistic circles, however, Glassman uses "paraphrase" without apology to describe legitimate translation technique (Glassman, *Translation Debate,* 27).

31. For further discussion of how to measure differences between free and literal translations, see Thomas, *How to Choose,* 90–101.

32. "Preface," *New International Version* (Grand Rapids: Zondervan, 1978), *viii;* see R. G. Bratcher, " The New International Version," *The Word of God* (Atlanta: John Knox, 1982), 162. Kohlenberger seems to classify the NIV as a "basically F-E" (that is formal equivalence) translation (Kohlenberger, *Words,* 93), while at the same time referring to its "fluid D-E [dynamic equivalence] style" (Kohlenberger, *Words,* 92). His appraisal is puzzling. Probably the NIV should be classed as D-E because its translators sought to convey "the meaning of the writers," which they deem to be more than a "word-for word translation" that retains "thought patterns and syntax" of the original.

33. Kubo and Specht, *So Many,* 80–81.

34. Lewis, *English Bible,* 206.

35. Kubo and Specht, *So Many,* 211.

36. C. H. Dodd, "Introduction to the New Testament," *New English Bible* (New York: Oxford, 1971), *vii.*

37. Lewis, *English Bible,* 321–22.

38. Kubo and Specht, *So Many,* 92, 230.

39. Lewis, *English Bible,* 222.

40. Bruce, *History,* 259.

41. Lewis, *English Bible,* 182–83.

42. Van Bruggen, *Future,* 192.

43. Kubo and Specht, *So Many,* 161.

44. Ewert, *Ancient Tablets,* 259.

45. Kubo and Specht, *So Many,* 163.

46. Ibid., 170.

47. Ewert, *Ancient Tablets,* 259. The step of translation where the interpretation of the translator is incorporated is called "analysis." He is responsible to perform a thorough exegetical examination of the passage to be translated to

discover what it meant to the ones who first read and heard it (Glassman, *Translation Debate*, 59–61). Properly fulfilled, this responsibility entails the implementation of the grammatical-historical method of interpretation. Having accomplished this, he transfers the meaning to the receptor language and restructures it in the form that he conceives will be most palatable to the recipients in the new language.

48. Lewis, *English Bible*, 133. For a closer look at dynamic equivalence or "functional equivalence" as the method has been called more recently, see Thomas, "Dynamic Equivalence," 149–75.

49. Ambiguity is studiously avoided in the dynamic-equivalence approach. The translator's responsibility is viewed as one of giving intelligible meaning to everything he translates, even passages over which the best exegetes have struggled for centuries (Glassman, *Translation Debate*, 101–11; see Carson, "The Limits," 7). The alleged need to do this stems from a low estimation of the English reader's ability or motivation to study the passage for himself. It becomes a sort of spoon-feeding approach to translation where nothing is left to the initiative of the user of the translation.

50. Lewis, *English Bible*, 360.

51. Actually, a further refinement in meaning between the renderings of this group of versions lies in whether they adopt the English rendering of "castrate," "emasculate," or "mutilate." The last of the three is the most severe, involving the whole body, and the first is the least severe, involving only the reproductive capability. A precise interpretation of the text entails a determination of which of these was in Paul's mind as he wrote.

52. E.g. Van Bruggen, *Future*, 105–9. Kohlenberger recognizes the problem of the excessive-commentary element in versions such as the Amplified Bible, the Living Bible, and Wuest's Expanded Translation (Kohlenberger, *Words*, 66–67), but he is apparently oblivious to its presence in the NIV.

53. Robert P. Martin, *Accuracy of Translation and The New International Version* (Edinburgh: Banner of Truth, 1989), 41–62, furnishes additional examples of interpretations presented as translations.

54. Kubo and Specht, *So Many*, 235–36; Lewis, *English Bible*, 133.

55. Bruce, *History*, 169, 233.

56. Kubo and Specht, *So Many*, 82–83.

57. Ibid., 253–54.

58. Communicative effectiveness is especially advantageous when using the Scriptures for evangelistic purposes. No one can debate the conclusion that the interest of non-Christians is gained much more quickly through the use of a free translation or paraphrase. This is the advantage developed by Glassman when he criticizes Christians for the high "fog index" of their terminology when dealing with people who are unfamiliar with theological language (Glassman, *Translation Debate*, 49–50; see H. G. Hendricks, *Say It with Love* [Wheaton, Ill.: Victor, 1972], 32–33).

59. E.g., G. D. Fee, "I Corinthians 7:1 in the NIV," *Journal of the Evangelical Theological Society* 23, no. 4 (1980): 307–14. Fee takes issue with the NIV's

translation of γυναικὸς μὴ ἅπτεσθαι (*gynaikos mē haptesthai*) by the word "marry" rather than by the more literal "touch a woman."

60. Van Bruggen, *Future*, 106. Dodd calls this approach of avoiding interpretation whenever possible "a comfortable ambiguity" (Dodd, "Introduction," *vii*). He acknowledges that free translation is impossible without eliminating this ambiguity. See also Fee, who, in "I Corinthians," p. 307, calls it "the safe route of ambiguity." Dodd and Fee portray the dynamic-equivalence practitioner as a courageous scholar who does not shy away from hard choices.
61. S. T. Byington, " Translator's Preface," *The Bible in Living English* (New York: Watchtower, 1972), 5.
62. Van Bruggen, *Future*, 99.
63. Lewis, English Bible 116, 156, 260, 291; Kubo and Specht, *So Many,* 80, 150, 242, 338; W. LaSor, "Which Bible Is Best for You?" *Eternity* 25 (April 1974): 29.
64. Kubo and Specht, *So Many,* 230, 338; Lewis, *English Bible* 116, 222; Bruce, *History,* 259.

Chapter Eighteen—Delivering the Exposition

1. Charles Edward Jefferson, *The Minister As Prophet* (New York: Crowell, 1905), 17, 23.
2. Alex Montoya, *Preaching with Passion* (Grand Rapids: Kregel, 2000).
3. D. Martyn Lloyd-Jones, *Preaching and Preachers* (Grand Rapids: Zondervan, 1971), 257.
4. G. Campbell Morgan, *Preaching* (reprint, Grand Rapids: Baker, 1974), 36.
5. Ibid., 37.
6. Walter C. Kaiser, *Toward An Exegetical Theology* (Grand Rapids: Baker, 1981), 239.
7. Lloyd-Jones, *Preaching,* 97.
8. C. H. Spurgeon, *An All-Around Ministry* (reprint, Edinburgh: Banner of Truth, 1960), 316–17.
9. Richard L. Mayhue, "The Authority of Scripture," TMSJ 14 (Fall 2004).
10. Bruce Mawhinney, *Preaching with Freshness* (Eugene, Oreg.: Harvest House, 1991), 196.
11. Morgan, *Preaching,* 13.
12. E.g., John A. Broadus, *On the Preparation and Delivery of Sermons,* rev. ed. (reprint, San Francisco: Harper and Row, 1979), 265–73.
13. Haddon Robinson, personal correspondence, 13 May 1991.
14. Ibid.
15. Phillips Brooks, *Lectures on Preaching* (reprint, New York: Dutton, 1907), 8. Brooks's exact words are, "Truth through Personality is our description of real preaching."
16. Lloyd-Jones, *Preaching,* 222.
17. Broadus, *Sermons,* 264–65.
18. C. H. Spurgeon, *C. H. Spurgeon Autobiography Volume 1: The Early Years, 1834–1859,* rev. ed. (reprint, Edinburgh: Banner of Truth, 1962), 234.
19. Lloyd-Jones, *Preaching,* 264.

20. Arthur Bennett, ed., *The Valley of Vision* (reprint, Edinburgh: Banner of Truth, 1975), 186.

Chapter Nineteen—Frequently Asked Questions about Expository Preaching

1. See Haddon W. Robinson, ed., *Biblical Sermons* (Grand Rapids: Baker, 1989) for questions and answers with Robinson and eleven of his former students. See also Richard Allen Bodey, ed., *Inside The Sermon* (Grand Rapids: Baker, 1990), which contains thirteen autobiographical essays on preparing to preach. Compare to "'Faithfully Proclaim the Truth': An Interview with John F. MacArthur," *Preaching* (November–December 1991): 2, 4, 6, 8, 10.
2. See the discussion of this point in chapter 16.
3. See the discussion of illustrations in chapter 13.
4. See the discussion of application in chapter 16 and the epilogue.
5. For a discussion of true worship, see John F. MacArthur, Jr., *The Ultimate Priority* (Chicago: Moody, 1983).
6. Read A. Duane Litfin, "The Perils of Persuasive Preaching," *Christianity Today* 21 (4 February 1977): 14–17, for an expanded discussion of this point.

Epilogue—The Listener's Responsibility

1. Jay E. Adams, *A Consumer's Guide to Preaching* (Wheaton, Ill.: Victor, 1991), 7.
2. Gardiner Spring, *A Plea to Pray for Pastors* (reprint, Amityville, N.Y.: Calvary, 1991), 3.
3. John Angell James, *Church Members' Guide* (reprint, Amityville, N.Y.: Calvary, 1991), 69–70.
4. Adams, *Consumer's Guide,* 24–25.
5. Jeremiah Burroughs, *Gospel Worship* (reprint, Ligonier, Penna.: Sola Deo Gloria, 1990), 195, 197.
6. Adams, *Consumers Guide,* 14–15.
7. John Leith, "Calvin's Doctrine of the Proclamation of the Word and Its Significance for Today in the Light of Recent Research," *Review and Expositor* 86 (1989): 38.
8. Adams, *Consumer's Guide.* 47.
9. Leith, "Calvin's doctrine," 32.

Subject Index

The Master's Seminary Contributors

Irvin A. Busenitz, Th.D.

Vice President of Academic Administration, Professor of Old Testament

David C. Deuel, Th.M.

Former Associate Professor of Old Testament

John F. MacArthur, Jr., D.D., Litt. D.

President, Professor of Pastoral Ministries

Richard L. Mayhue, Th.D.

Senior Vice President and Dean, Professor of Pastoral Ministries and Theology

Donald G. McDougall, Th.M.

Associate Professor of New Testament

James E. Rosscup, Th.D., Ph. D.

Professor of Bible Exposition

James F. Stitzinger, Th.M., M.S.L.S.

Director of Library Services, Associate Professor of Historical Theology

Robert L. Thomas, Th.D.

Professor of New Testament

George J. Zemek, Th.D.

Former Professor of Theology